ALASKA POLITICS AND GOVERNMENT

GERALD A. MCBEATH AND THOMAS A. MOREHOUSE

Alaska

Politics &

Government

JK
9516
.M33
1994
West

UNIVERSITY OF NEBRASKA PRESS

LINCOLN & LONDON

Library of Congress
Cataloging-in-Publication Data
McBeath, Gerald A.
Alaska politics and government /
Gerald A. McBeath and Thomas A. Morehouse.
p. cm.—(Politics and governments
of the American states)
ISBN 0-8032-3120-2 (cl : alk. paper).—
ISBN 0-8032-8149-8 (pb : alk. paper)
1. Alaska—Politics and government—1959-
I. Morehouse, Thomas A., 1937-
II. Title. III. Series.
JK9516.M33   1994
320.9798—dc20
93-5390   CIP

For Jenifer and Dolores

Other volumes in the Politics and Governments of the American States series:

Alabama Government and Politics
By James D. Thomas and William H. Stewart

Arkansas Politics and Government: Do the People Rule?
By Diane D. Blair

Colorado Politics and Government: Governing the Centennial State
By Thomas E. Cronin and Robert D. Loevy

Kentucky Politics and Government: Do We Stand United?
By Penny M. Miller

Maine Politics and Government
By Kenneth T. Palmer, G. Thomas Taylor, and Marcus A. LiBrizzi

Mississippi Government and Politics: Modernizers versus Traditionalists
By Dale Krane and Stephen D. Shaffer

Nebraska Government and Politics
Edited by Robert D. Miewald

New Jersey Politics and Government: Suburban Politics Comes of Age
By Barbara G. Salmore and Stephen A. Salmore

Oklahoma Politics and Policies: Governing the Sooner State
By David R. Morgan, Robert E. England, and George G. Humphreys

CONTENTS

MAPS, TABLES, AND FIGURES

JOHN KINCAID

Series Preface

The purpose of this series is to provide intelligent and interesting books on the politics and governments of the fifty American states, books that are of value not only to the student of government but also to the general citizen who wants greater insight into the past and present civic life of his or her own state and of other states in the federal union. The role of the states in governing America is among the least well known of all the 83,217 governments in the United States. The national media focus attention on the federal government in Washington, D.C., and local media focus attention on local government. Meanwhile, except when there is a scandal or a proposed tax increase, the workings of state government remain something of a mystery to many citizens—out of sight, out of mind.

In many respects, however, the states have been, and continue to be, the most important governments in the American political system. They are the main building blocks and chief organizing governments of the whole system. The states are the constituent governments of the federal union, and it is through the states that citizens gain representation in the national government. The national government is one of limited, delegated powers; all other powers are possessed by the states and their citizens. At the same time, the states are the empowering governments for the nation's 83,166 local governments—counties, municipalities, townships, school districts, and special districts. As such, states provide for one of the most essential and ancient elements of freedom and democracy, the right of local self-government.

Although, for many citizens, the most visible aspects of state government are state universities, some of which are the most prestigious in the world, and state highway patrol officers, with their radar guns and handy ticket books, state governments provide for nearly all domestic public services.

Whether elements of those services are enacted or partly funded by the federal government and actually carried out by local governments, it is state government that has the ultimate responsibility for ensuring that Americans are well served by all their governments. In so doing, all of the American states are more democratic, more prosperous, stronger financially, and better governed than most of the world's nation-states.

This is a particularly timely period in which to publish a series of books on the governments and politics of each of the fifty states. Once viewed as the "fallen arches" of the federal system, states today are increasingly seen as energetic, innovative, and fiscally responsible. Some states, of course, perform better than others, but that is to be expected in a federal system. Each state is unique in its own right. It is our hope that this series will shed light on the public life of each state and that, taken together, the books will contribute to a better, more informed understanding of the states themselves and of their often pivotal roles in the world's first and oldest continental-size federal democracy.

DANIEL J. ELAZAR

Series Introduction

The more than continental stretch of the American domain is given form and character as a federal union of fifty different states whose institutions order the American landscape. The existence of these states made possible the emergence of a continental nation in which liberty, not despotism, reigns, and self-government is the first principle of order. The great American republic was born in its states, as its very name signifies. America's first founding was repeated on thirteen separate occasions over 125 years, from Virginia in 1607 to Georgia in 1732, each giving birth to a colony which became a self-governing commonwealth. America's revolution and second founding was made by those commonwealths, now states, acting in congress, and its constitution was written together and adopted separately. As the American tide rolled westward from the Atlantic coast, it absorbed new territories by organizing thirty-seven more states over the next 169 years.

Most of the American states are larger and better developed than most of the world's nations. Each has its own story; each is a polity with its own uniqueness. The American states exist because they are civil societies. They were first given political form and then acquired their other characteristics. Each has its own constitution, its own political culture, its own relationship to the federal union and to its section. These in turn have given each state its own law and history: the longer that history, the more distinctive the state.

It is in and through the states, no less than the nation, that the great themes of American life are played out. The advancing frontier and the continuing experience of Americans as a frontier people, the drama of American ethnic blending, the dispossession of aboriginal peoples, the tragedy of slavery and racial discrimination, the political struggle for expanding the right to vote— all found, and find, their expression in the states.

The changing character of government, from an all-embracing concern for every aspect of civil and religious behavior, to a limited concern for maintaining law and order and providing the social benefits of the contemporary welfare state, has been felt in the states even more than in the federal government. Some states began as commonwealths devoted to establishing model societies based on religiously informed visions (Massachusetts, Connecticut, and Rhode Island); at the other end of the spectrum, one state, Hawaii, is a transformed pagan monarchy. At least three states were independent for a significant period of time (Hawaii, Texas, and Vermont). Others were created from nothing by little more than a stroke of the pen (the Dakotas, Idaho, and Nevada). Several are permanently bilingual (California, Louisiana, and New Mexico). Each has its own landscape and geographic configuration which time and history transformed into a specific geo-historical location. In short, the diversity of the American people is expressed in no small measure through their states, the politics and government of each of which have their own fascination.

Alaska Politics and Government is the tenth book in the Center for the Study of Federalism and University of Nebraska Press series Politics and Governments of the American States. The aim of the series is to provide books that will appeal to three audiences: political scientists, their students, and the wider public in each state. Each volume in the series examines the specific character of one of the fifty states, looking at the state as a polity—its political culture, traditions and practices, constituencies and interest groups, and constitutional and institutional frameworks.

Each book also reviews the political development of the state to demonstrate how that state's political institutions and characteristics have evolved from the first settlement to the present, presenting the state in the context of the nation and section of which it is a part, and reviewing the roles and relations of the state vis-à-vis its sister states and the federal government. The state's constitutional history, its traditions of constitution making, and its constitutional change are examined and related to the workings of the state's political institutions and processes. State–local relations, local government, and community politics are studied. Finally, each volume reviews the state's policy concerns and their implementation, from the budgetary process to particular substantive policies. Each book concludes by summarizing the principal themes and findings to draw conclusions about the current state of the state, its continuing traditions, and emerging issues. Each also contains a bibliographic survey of the existing literature on the state and a guide to the

use of that literature and state government documents in learning more about
the state and its political system.

Although the books in the series are not expected to be uniform, they do
focus on the common themes of federalism, constitutionalism, political culture, and the continuing American frontier in order to provide a framework
within which to consider the institutions, routines, and processes of state
government and politics.

FEDERALISM

Both the greatest conflicts of American history and the day-to-day operations of American government are closely intertwined with American federalism—the form of American government, in the eighteenth-century sense
of the term, which includes both structure and process. American federalism
has been characterized by two basic tensions. One is between state sovereignty—the view that in a proper federal system, authority and power over
most domestic affairs should be in the hands of the states—and national supremacy—the view that the federal government has a significant role to play
in domestic matters affecting the national interest. The other tension is between dual federalism—the idea that a federal system functions best when
the federal government and the states function as separate entities, each in its
own sphere—and cooperative federalism—the view that federalism works
best when the federal government and the states, while preserving their own
institutions, cooperate closely on the implementation of joint or shared programs.

It hardly needs to be said that Alaska's position in the Union is unique.
Separated from the contiguous forty-eight states by Canada, it is by far the
largest of the fifty states in area and the second smallest in population. Cli-
matically unique, it seems to be a permanent land frontier. Its shared myth
encompasses the self-image of perennial pioneers in a perennially hostile environment. For the first half of the twentieth century Alaskans battled hard to
achieve statehood. Since then they have battled equally hard for less federal
involvement in their lives while reaping the benefits of statehood. Both
struggles have lent a special flavor to Alaska's relationship with the federal
government.

Statehood not only brought Alaska the usual array of twentieth-century-
style federal aids and opportunities to acquire additional federal assistance,
but also 104 million acres of federal land granted under federal land grant
programs dating back to 1803 and not in use since Arizona and New Mexico
were admitted as states in 1912. But even benefits bring conflict. In Alaska's

case, as described in this volume, conflicts developed over federal and state differences of opinion as to how to distribute Alaska's new bounty, as well as perceived discriminatory treatment of Alaska's land and resources by the federal government. Consequently, in the mere twenty years after statehood was finally achieved, Alaska established a statehood commission which went so far as to consider secession from the Union as an option for Alaska's future. Federal–state relations always seem to be in turmoil in Alaska, and the feeling of being something of a distant colony of Washington remains.

CONSTITUTIONALISM

The American constitutional tradition, established by the first founders and reaffirmed by subsequent generations, grew out of the Whig understanding that civil societies are founded by political covenant through which the powers of government are delineated and limited and the rights of the constituting members are clearly proclaimed in such a way as to provide moral and practical restraints on governmental institutions. That constitutional tradition was modified by the federalists, who accepted its fundamental principles but strengthened the institutional framework designed to provide energy in government while maintaining the checks and balances that they saw as needed to preserve liberty and republican government. At the same time, the federalists turned nonbinding declarations of rights into enforceable constitutional articles.

American state constitutions reflect a melding of these two traditions. Under the U.S. Constitution, each state is free to adopt its own constitution, provided that the constitution establishes a republican form of government. Some states have adopted highly succinct constitutions, like the Vermont Constitution of 1793, which has 6,600 words and is still in effect with only fifty-two amendments. Others are just the opposite. For example, Georgia's Ninth Constitution, adopted in 1976, has 583,000 words.

State constitutions are potentially far more comprehensive than the federal constitution, which is one of limited, delegated powers. Because states are plenary governments, they automatically possess all powers not specifically denied them by the U.S. Constitution or their citizens. Consequently, a state constitution must be explicit about limiting and defining the scope of governmental powers, especially on behalf of individual liberty. Thus, state constitutions normally include an explicit declaration of rights, almost invariably broader than the first ten amendments to the U.S. Constitution.

The detailed specificity of state constitutions affects the way they shape each state's governmental system and patterns of political behavior. Unlike the open-endedness and ambiguity of many parts of the U.S. Constitution that allow for considerable interpretation, state organs, including state supreme courts, generally hew closely to the letter of their constitutions because they must. Thus, formal changes in state constitutions occur frequently through constitutional amendment, whether initiated by the legislature, special constitutional commissions, constitutional conventions, or by direct action of the voters, and, in a number of states, the periodic writing of new constitutions. As a result, state constitutions have come to reflect quite explicitly the changing conceptions of government which have developed over the course of American history.

Overall, six different state constitutional patterns have developed. One is the commonwealth pattern, developed in New England, which emphasizes the Whig idea of the constitution as a philosophic document designed first and foremost to set a direction for civil society and to express and institutionalize a theory of republican government. A second pattern is that of the commercial republic. The constitutions fitting this pattern reflect a series of compromises required by the conflict of many strong ethnic groups, religious denominations, and commercial interests generated by the flow of heterogeneous streams of migrants into particular states and the early development of large commercial and industrial cities in those states.

The third type is found in the South and can be described as the southern contractual pattern. Southern state constitutions are used as instruments to set explicit terms governing the relationship between polity and society, such as those which protected slavery or racial segregation, or those which sought to diffuse the formal allocation of authority in order to accommodate the swings between oligarchy and factionalism characteristic of southern state politics. Of all the southern states, only Louisiana stands somewhat outside this pattern and represents a fourth type, since its legal system was founded on the French civil code. Louisiana's constitutions have thus been codes—long, highly explicit documents that form a pattern in and of themselves.

A fifth pattern is frequently found in the less populated states of the Far West, where the state constitution is first and foremost a frame of government explicitly reflecting the republican and democratic principles dominant in the nation in the late nineteenth century, but also emphasizing the structure of state government and the distribution of powers within that structure in a direct, businesslike manner. Finally, the two newest states, Alaska and Hawaii, have adopted constitutions following the managerial pattern developed and promoted by twentieth-century constitutional reform movements in the United States. Those constitutions are characterized by conciseness, broad grants of power to the executive branch, and relatively few structural restrictions on the legislature. They emphasize the conservation of natural resources.

Alaska's constitution was written at the height of the post–World War II effort to introduce managerialism into government. It is the first of the two great managerialist constitutions produced at that time (the other was written for Hawaii when it was admitted into statehood a year later). The trend in that direction began with the writing of a new constitution for New Jersey in 1944 and continued until the end of the postwar wave of constitution writing in the early 1980s. The prevailing constitutional doctrine nationwide was that government should be organized for purposes of greater efficiency. Among other things, the managerial model required that administration be concentrated in the hands of the executive branch with clean lines of hierarchical authority from the governor on down and with no possibilities of interference by the legislature in the administrative hierarchy. State offices are independently elected. The legislative branch is in the hands of a professionalized legislature with proper staffing. The number of local governments is reduced as much as possible, with no overlapping.

When Alaska wrote its constitution, it took its principal advice from nationally known experts on public administration who advocated the managerial approach. With one or two exceptions, and except where the realities of politics absolutely prevented it, the state took their advice. Since 1959, however, one thrust of state government has been to moderate the managerial model to reflect the need and desire for more popular government, as this volume describes. The authors have considerable sympathy for Alaska's original constitutional model as it has been adapted to changing values and needs; the volume itself describes how that model has been modified.

THE CONTINUING AMERICAN FRONTIER

For Americans, the very word *frontier* conjures up the images of the rural-land frontier of yesteryear—of explorers and mountain men, of cowboys and Indians, of brave pioneers pushing their way west in the face of natural obstacles. Later, Americans' picture of the frontier was expanded to include the inventors, the railroad builders, and the captains of industry who created the urban-industrial frontier. Recently television has celebrated the entrepreneurial ventures of the automobile and oil industries, portraying the magnates of those industries and their families in the same larger-than-life frame as was once done for the heroes of that first frontier.

As is so often the case, the media responsible for determining and catering to popular taste tell us a great deal about ourselves. The United States was founded with a rural-land frontier that persisted until World War I, more or less, spreading farms, ranches, mines, and towns across the land. Early in the nineteenth century, the rural-land frontier generated the urban frontier based on industrial development. The creation of new wealth through industrialization transformed cities from mere regional service centers into generators of wealth in their own right. The frontier persisted for more than one hundred years as a major force in American society as a whole, and perhaps another sixty years as a major force in certain parts of the country. The population movements and attendant growth on the urban-industrial frontier brought about the effective settlement of the United States in freestanding cities from coast to coast.

Between the world wars, the urban-industrial frontier gave birth in turn to a third frontier stage, one based on the new technologies of electronic communication, the internal-combustion engine, the airplane, synthetics, and petrochemicals. These new technologies transformed every aspect of life and turned urbanization into metropolitanization. This third frontier stage generated a third settlement of the United States, this time in metropolitan regions from coast to coast, involving a mass migration of tens of millions of Americans in search of opportunity on the suburban frontier.

In the 1970s, the first post–World War II generation came to a close. Many Americans began speaking of the "limits of growth." Yet despite that anti-frontier rhetoric, there was every sign that a fourth frontier stage was beginning in the form of the rurban, or citybelt-cybernetic, frontier generated by the metropolitan-technological frontier.

The rurban-cybernetic frontier first emerged in the Northeast, as did its predecessors, as the Atlantic Coast metropolitan regions merged into one another to form a six-hundred-mile-long megalopolis (the usage is Jean Gottman's)—a matrix of urban and suburban settlements in which the older central cities yielded importance, if not prominence, to smaller ones. It was a sign of the times that the computer was conceived at MIT in Cambridge and developed at IBM in White Plains, two medium-sized cities in the megalopolis that have become special centers in their own right. This event in itself is a reflection of the two primary characteristics of the new frontier: the new locus of settlement is in medium-sized and small cities, and appears in the rural interstices of the megalopolis.

The spreading use of computer technology is the most direct manifestation of the cybernetic tools that make such citybelts possible. In 1979 the newspapers in the Northeast published frequent reports of the revival of small cities of the first industrial revolution, particularly in New England, as the new frontier engulfed them. Countrywide, the media focused on the shifting of population growth into rural areas. Both phenomena are as much a product of direct dialing as they are of the older American longing for small-town or country living. Both reflect the urbanization of the American way of life no matter what lifestyle is practiced, or where.

Although the Northeast was first, the new rurban-cybernetic frontier, like its predecessors, is attaining its true form in the South and West, where citybelt matrices are not being built on the collapse of earlier forms but are developing as original forms. The present sunbelt frontier—strung out along the Gulf Coast, the southwestern desert, and the fringes of the California mountains—is classically megalopolitan in citybelt form, and it is cybernetic with its aerospace-related industries and sunbelt living made possible by air conditioning and the new telecommunications.

The continuing American frontier has all the characteristics of a chain reaction. In a land of great opportunity, each frontier, once opened, has generated its successor and, in turn, has been replaced by it. Each frontier has created a new America with new opportunities, new patterns of settlement, new occupations, new challenges, and new problems. As a result, the central political problem of growth is not simply how to handle the physical changes brought by each frontier, real as they are. It is also how to accommodate newness, population turnover, and transience as a way of life. That is the American frontier situation.

Alaska became a state when the United States was at the height of the metropolitan-technological frontier, but the state itself was still very much in the rural-land frontier stage. The metropolitan frontier made its appearance in the Anchorage area in the 1960s in a very modest way, but Alaska is basically the last great expression of America's rural-land frontier, the major if not only place that the metropolitan frontier and the land frontier exist side by side. At the same time, Alaska is the place where the advancing line of civilization has run squarely into the frontier as a permanent wilderness which, in our fast-moving world, in essence makes the frontier a permanent backwater. Alaska still offers challenges to individuals, but these challenges have little or no impact on the course of civilization. Alaska indeed has less than a frontier character in the first sense than most other states, with little or nothing of the other frontier stages.

Alaska remains a kind of safety valve for Americans who want to find a place for themselves that is less susceptible to the pressures of contemporary life. Its emptiness, geographical remoteness, and harsh climate affect its politics and its relations with the rest of the United States.

THE PERSISTENCE OF SECTIONALISM

Sectionalism—the expression of social, economic, and especially political differences along geographic lines—is part and parcel of the American political ties that link groups of contiguous states together. The original sections were produced by variations in the impact of the rural-land frontier on different geographic segments of the country. They, in turn, were modified by the pressures generated by the first and subsequent frontier stages. Sectionalism is not the same as regionalism. The latter is essentially a phenomenon— often transient—that brings adjacent state, substate, or interstate areas together because of immediate and specific common interests. Nor are sections homogeneous socioeconomic units sharing a common character across state lines: they are complex entities that combine highly diverse states and communities with common political interests that generally complement one another socially and economically.

For example, New England is a section bound by the tightest of social and historical ties, even though the differences between the states of lower and upper New England are quite noticeable even to the casual observer. The six New England states consciously seek to cooperate with one another in numerous ways. Their cooperative efforts have been sufficiently institutionalized to create a veritable confederation within the larger American Union. It is through such acts of political will that sectionalism best manifests itself.

Intrasectional conflicts often exist, but they do not detract from the longterm sectional community of interest. More important for our purposes, certain common sectional bonds give the states of each section a special relationship to national politics. This is particularly true in connection with specific political issues that are of sectional importance, such as the race issue in the South, the problems of the megalopolis in the Northeast, or the problems of agriculture and agribusiness in the Northwest.

The nation's sectional alignments are rooted in the three great historical, cultural, and economic spheres into which the country is divided: the greater Northeast, the greater South, and the greater West. Following state lines, the greater Northeast includes all those states north of the Ohio and Potomac

Rivers and east of Lake Michigan. The greater South includes the states
south of the Northeast area but east of the Mississippi, plus Missouri, Arkansas, Louisiana, Oklahoma, and Texas. The rest of the states compose the
greater West. Within that basic framework there are eight sections: New England, the Middle Atlantic, the Near West, the Upper South, the Lower
South, the Western South, the Northwest, and the Far West.

From the New Deal years through the 1960s, Americans' understanding
of sectionalism was submerged by their concern with urban-oriented socioeconomic categories, such as the struggle between labor and management or
between the haves and have-nots in the big cities. Even the racial issue, once
the hallmark of the greater South, began to be perceived in nonsectional
terms as a result of black immigration northward. This is not to say that sectionalism ceased to exist as a vital force, only that it was little noted in those
years.

Beginning in the 1970s, however, there was a resurgence of sectional
feeling as economic and social cleavages increasingly came to follow sectional lines. The sunbelt-frostbelt contribution is the prime example of this
new sectionalism. "Sunbelt" is the new code word for the Lower South,
Western South, and Far West; "frostbelt" is the code word for the New England, Middle Atlantic, and Great Lakes (or Near Western) states. Sectionalism promises to be a major force in national politics, closely linked to the rurban-cybernetic frontier.

A perennial problem of the states, one that is hardly less important than
direct federal–state relationships, is how to bend sectional and regional demands to fit their own needs for self-maintenance as political systems. One
of the ways in which the states are able to overcome this problem is through
the use of formal political institutions, since no problems can be handled
governmentally without making use of those institutions.

Some would argue that the use of formal political institutions to deflect
sectional patterns on behalf of the states is "artificial" interference with the
"natural" flow of the nation's social and economic system. Partisans of the
states would respond not only by questioning the naturalness of a socioeconomic system that was created by people who migrated freely across the
landscape as individuals in search of opportunity, but also by arguing that the
history of civilization is the record of humanity's efforts to harness the environment by means of inventions, which are all artificial in the literal and real
sense of the term. Political institutions, of course, are among the foremost of
those inventions.

In one sense Alaska is clearly a continuation of the Northwest; most of its settlers either have come up from the Pacific Northwest or have come across from the interior Northwest. In another sense, it is unique in that it does not really have the political sentiments of the Northwest. Alaska is pioneering a new worldwide pattern, as indicated by its increased role as a bridge to Russia and East Asia.

THE VITAL ROLE OF POLITICAL CULTURE

The United States as a whole shares a general political culture that is rooted in two contrasting conceptions of the American political order that can be traced back to the earliest settlement of the country. In the first, the polity is conceived as a marketplace in which the primary public relationships are products of bargaining among individuals and groups acting out of self-interest. In the second, the political order is conceived as a commonwealth—a polity in which the whole people have an undivided interest and in which citizens cooperate in an effort to create and maintain the best government in order to implement certain shared moral principles. These two conceptions have exercised an influence on government and politics throughout American history, sometimes in conflict and sometimes complementing each other.

The national political culture is a synthesis of three major political subcultures. All three are of nationwide proportions, having spread, in the course of time, from coast to coast. At the same time, each subculture is strongly tied to specific sections of the country, reflecting the streams and currents of migration that have carried people of different origins and backgrounds across the continent in more or less orderly patterns. Considering their central characteristics, the three are called *individualistic, moralistic,* and *traditionalistic*. Each subculture reflects its own particular synthesis of the marketplace and the commonwealth.

The *individualistic political culture* emphasizes the democratic order as a marketplace in which government is instituted for strictly utilitarian reasons, to handle those functions demanded by the people it is created to serve. Beyond the commitment to an open market, a government need not have any direct concern with questions of the "good society," except insofar as it may be used to advance some common view formulated outside the political arena, just as it serves other functions. Since the individualistic political culture emphasizes the centrality of private concerns, it places a premium on limiting community intervention—whether governmental or nongovernmental—into private activities to the minimum necessary to keep the marketplace in proper working order.

The character of political participation in the individualistic political culture reflects this outlook. Politics is just another means by which individuals may improve themselves socially and economically. In this sense politics is a business like any other, competing for talent and offering rewards to those who take it up as a career. Individuals who choose political careers may rise by providing the governmental services demanded of them and, in return, may expect to be adequately compensated for their efforts. Interpretations of officeholders' obligations under this arrangement vary. Where the norms are high, such people are expected to provide high-quality public service in return for appropriate rewards. In other cases, an officeholders' primary responsibility is to serve himself and those who have supported him directly, favoring them even at the expense of the public.

Political life within the individualistic political culture is based on a system of mutual obligations rooted in personal relationships. In the United States, political parties serve as the vehicles for maintaining the obligational network. Party regularity is indispensable in the individualistic political culture because it is the means for coordinating individual enterprise in the political arena and is the one way to prevent individualism from running wild. Such a culture encourages the maintenance of a party system that is competitive—but not overly so—in the pursuit of office. Alaska presents the limiting case of individualized politics, in that partisan ties are weak to the point of nonexistence. Only among the political elite do parties provide some direction for political action.

Since the individualistic political culture eschews ideological concerns in its businesslike conception of politics, both politicians and citizens look upon political activity as a specialized activity that is essentially the province of professionals and of minimal concern to the lay public. In sum, it is no place for amateurs to play an active role. Furthermore, there is a strong tendency among the public to believe that politics is a dirty—if necessary—business, one that is better left to those who are willing to soil themselves by engaging in it. In practice, where the individualistic political culture is dominant there is likely to be an easy attitude toward the limits of the professionals' perquisites. Since a fair amount of corruption is expected in the normal course of things, there is relatively little popular excitement when any is found, unless it is of an extraordinary character or magnitude. It is as if the public is willing to pay a surcharge for services rendered, and rebels only when the surcharge becomes too heavy. (Of course the judgments as to what is normal and what is extraordinary are themselves subjective and culturally conditioned.)

Public officials committed to giving the public what it wants normally will initiate new programs only when they perceive an overwhelming public demand for them to act. The individualistic political culture is ambivalent about the place of bureaucracy in the political order. Bureaucratic methods of operation fly in the face of the favor system, yet organizational efficiency can be used by those seeking to master the market.

To the extent that the marketplace provides the model for public relationships in American civil society, all Americans share some of the attitudes that are of first importance in the individualistic political culture. At the same time substantial segments of the American people operate politically within the framework of two political subcultures.

The *moralistic political culture* emphasizes the commonwealth conception as the basis for democratic government. Politics, in the moralistic political culture, is considered one of the great activities of humanity in its search for the good society—a struggle for power, it is true, but also an effort to exercise power for the betterment of the commonwealth. Consequently, both the general public and politicians conceive of politics as a public activity centered on some notion of the public good and properly devoted to the advancement of the public interest.

In the moralistic political culture, there is a general commitment to utilizing communal—preferably nongovernmental, but governmental if necessary —power to intervene in the sphere of private activities when it is considered necessary to do so for the public good or the well-being of the community. Accordingly, issues have an important place in the moralistic style of politics, functioning to set the tone for political concern. Government is considered a positive instrument with a responsibility to promote the public's general welfare, though definitions of that positive role may vary considerably from era to era.

Politics is ideally a matter of concern for every citizen. Government service is public service, placing stronger moral obligations on those who serve in government than on those in the marketplace. Politics is not considered a legitimate realm for private economic enrichment. A politician is not expected to profit from political activity and in fact is held suspect if he or she does.

The concept of serving the commonwealth is at the core of all political relationships, and politicians are expected to adhere to it even at the expense of individual loyalties and political friendships. Political parties are considered useful political devices but are not valued for their own sake. Regular party ties can be abandoned with relative impunity for third parties, special local parties, nonpartisan systems, or the opposition party if such changes are believed to be helpful in achieving larger political goals.

In practice, where the moralistic political culture is dominant today, there is considerably more amateur participation in politics. There is also much less of what Americans consider corruption in government and less tolerance of actions that are considered corrupt, so politics does not have the taint it so often bears in the individualistic environment.

By virtue of its fundamental outlook, the moralistic political culture creates a greater commitment to active government intervention in the economic and social life of the community. At the same time, its strong commitment to communitarianism tends to keep government intervention local wherever possible. Public officials will themselves initiate new government activities in an effort to come to grips with problems that are as yet unperceived by a majority of the citizenry.

The moralistic political culture is alive in Alaska, where, as the authors of this volume point out, "avoiding the mistakes of the older states" is a popular notion as it applies to the moralistic as well as the managerial models of government. New groups, often religiously based, reinforce this notion by focusing on the ethics of government at the state and local levels.

The moralistic political culture's major difficulty with bureaucracy lies in the potential conflict between communitarian principles and large-scale organization. Otherwise, the notion of a politically neutral administrative system is attractive. Where merit systems are instituted, they tend to be rigidly maintained.

The *traditionalistic political culture* is rooted in an ambivalent attitude toward the marketplace coupled with a paternalistic and elitist conception of the commonwealth. It reflects an older, precommercial attitude that accepts a substantially hierarchical society as part of the ordered nature of things, authorizing and expecting those at the top of the social structure to take a special and dominant role in government. Like its moralistic counterpart, the traditionalistic political culture accepts government as an actor with a positive role in the community, but it tries to limit that role to securing the continued maintenance of the existing social order. To do so, it functions to confine real political power to a relatively small and self-perpetuating group drawn from an established elite who often inherit their right to govern through family ties or social position. Social and family ties are even more important in a traditionalistic political culture than are personal ties in the individualistic culture, where, after all is said and done, one's first responsibility is to oneself. At the same time, those who do not have a definite role to play in politics are not expected to be even minimally active as citizens. In many cases, they are not even expected to vote. As in the individualistic political culture, those active in politics are expected to benefit personally from their activity, although not necessarily by direct pecuniary gain.

Political parties are not important in the traditionalistic political culture because they encourage a degree of openness that goes against the grain of an elitist political order. Political competition is expressed through factions, an extension of the "personal politics" characteristic of the system. Thus, political systems within the culture tend to have loose one-party systems if they have political parties at all. Political leaders play conservative and custodial roles rather than initiatory roles unless they are pressed strongly from the outside.

Traditionalistic political cultures tend to be antibureaucratic. Bureaucracy by its very nature interferes with the fine web of social relationships that lie at the root of the political system. Where bureaucracy is introduced, it is generally confined to ministerial functions under the aegis of established powerholders. The traditional political culture of the early American states shares some meaning with Alaska's Native political culture, which emphasizes consensual decision making, respect for traditions as expressed by elders, and communal values.

While Alaska includes settlers from all three political subcultures, the state's political culture is primarily an amalgam of the individualistic and the moralistic. From the days of the Klondike gold rush, the individualistic political culture has been a chief motivating force for coming to Alaska. The general culture is individualistic with a vengeance, almost to the point of ideology. The same individualistic orientation has entered the state's political ideology. There is also a strong moralistic strain. As you will see, *Alaska Politics and Government* discusses all this in greater depth.

CONCLUSION

Alaska, with a land area one-sixth that of the continental United States and a geographic spread that, if superimposed on the map, would reach from northern New England to southern California, is truly the "great land." Alaska's small population, rigorous climate, and permanently wild character make it unique among the states. While its relations with the lower forty-eight states are those of a peripheral neighbor, however massive, on the new global map, it has acquired a certain centrality and is a major source of fish and oil. Companies and individuals that rely on or exploit these resources co-exist uneasily and add tension to the state's politics. They can also come into disastrous conflict, as they did in the case of the *Exxon Valdez* oil spill in 1989.

The Alaska case challenges conventional interpretations of federal–state and state–local relations. Alaska's polity has developed within the confines of U.S. federalism and constitutionalism; yet it represents a degree of independence rare among American states. Alaska is a section of the United States, and is equal in size and diversity to regions such as New England, the South, and the Midwest. Alaska's politics and government show how the American frontier accommodates migration and technology while relentlessly striving to preserve the autonomy of the state and its residents against seemingly overwhelming odds.

Acknowledgments

We are immensely grateful for the support and assistance many gave us in preparing this book. Jennifer Brice, a research assistant in the Department of Political Science (1990–91), University of Alaska Fairbanks (and former reporter for the *Fairbanks Daily News-Miner*), chased down dozens of facts. She copyedited each chapter of the book and contributed immeasurably to the fluency and readability of the manuscript. Jennifer also helped with logistics and production in ways too numerous to mention.

Martha Eliassen Bristow, a research assistant in the Department of Political Science, U A F (and former reporter for the *Anchorage Daily News* and *Fairbanks Daily News-Miner*), provided assistance in a revision of the manuscript in 1991–92. She did research on hundreds of historical records, newspapers, books, and government documents. Martha also edited the manuscript. Her careful attention to style and deft use of language significantly aided the revision process.

Six experts on American state government provided valuable advice and constructive suggestions for improvement of the manuscript: John Kincaid, Executive Director of the U.S. Advisory Commission on Intergovernmental Relations; Thomas Cronin, McHugh Professor of Government, Colorado College; Daniel Elazar, Director of the Center for the Study of Federalism, Temple University; Charles Press, Professor of Political Science, Michigan State University; Claus-M. Naske, Professor of History, University of Alaska Fairbanks; and Neal Gilbertson, Associate Professor of Political Science, Idaho State University.

We thank the following Alaska reviewers who commented insightfully on one or more chapters: Terrence Cole, Associate Professor of History, University of Alaska Fairbanks; Victor Fischer, Director of Russian Relations,

University of Alaska; Gordon Harrison, Director, Alaska Legislative Research Agency; Brian Rogers, Vice-President for Finance, University of Alaska; Linda Leask, Editor, Institute of Social and Economic Research, University of Alaska Anchorage; Matthew Berman, Associate Professor of Economics, Institute of Social and Economic Research, University of Alaska Anchorage; Jay Rabinowitz, Chief Justice, Alaska Supreme Court; and Andrew Kleinfeld, Judge, U.S. Ninth Circuit Court of Appeals. Steve Colt, Assistant Professor of Economics, Institute of Social and Economic Research, contributed essential data on Alaska Native regional corporations.

Twenty graduate students in U A F's Third Taft Seminar for Teachers tested the first version of the manuscript. We are especially grateful for the detailed critiques of Ernest Manewal (Sheldon Jackson College, Sitka), David Kingsland (U A F School of Education), Betty Baker (Howard Luke Junior/ Senior High School, Fairbanks), Sally Young (T O K School) and Sherry Modrow and Rebecca Morse (Adult Learning Programs, Fairbanks).

In Anchorage, Marybeth Holleman provided energetic and accurate research assistance. Teresa Hull also contributed to many important research tasks. In Fairbanks, we thank Linda Barker, History Department, and Linda Ilgenfritz, Political Science Department, U A F, for help in production of the book. Sheri Layral, History Department, and Doris Nichols, Foreign Languages, assisted in preparing intermediate copies of the manuscript. Merillee Waugh, of the Dean's Office, College of Liberal Arts, and Wendy Clayton, Office of Faculty Development, helped produce final copies of the manuscript.

For the assignment of special assistance, we are grateful to three university administrators: Janice M. Reynolds, Vice Chancellor for Academic Affairs, University of Alaska Fairbanks; Anne Shinkwin, former Dean, College of Liberal Arts, University of Alaska Fairbanks; and Lee Gorsuch, Director, Institute of Social and Economic Research, University of Alaska Anchorage.

We owe a huge debt to Alaska. The Alaska people, environment, and ideas brought us to the North. They stimulate our efforts to interpret the ever-changing political community of the state. We hope readers will point out any errors and omissions that remain in the book and will join with us in the continuing dialogue on Alaska politics and government.

ALASKA POLITICS AND GOVERNMENT

Introduction

Many Americans view Alaska's North Slope, the northernmost extension of
the United States, as the nation's last wilderness. In 1980, the eastern portion
of this frigid coastal plain was protected from development by federal legislation. Since then, this expanse of permafrost-laden tundra, calving grounds
for nearly two hundred thousand caribou, has inspired intense national and
state controversy. Geologists now predict that a region within the Arctic National Wildlife Refuge (ANWR) contains the next major oil and gas find in an
energy-hungry North America.

ANWR pits the interests of Alaska economic development against those
of national environmental conservation. It also juxtaposes the consensus of
opinion in the United States, which has favored preserving the refuge,
against the will of a majority of Alaskans, who look to ANWR for future economic security. Governor Walter Hickel embodied this collective Alaska
will when, in his state-of-the-state address in January 1992, he announced
that the state would file suit against the federal government to open ANWR
for oil and gas development. He also used the occasion to press for removal
of other prohibitions—the ban on export of Alaska oil overseas, the requirement that products bound to and from Alaska use American ships—that
limit Alaska's opportunities to benefit from its own resources. "Today we
must draw a line," Hickel said. "Alaska has had enough."[1]

Because ANWR development was part of a national energy strategy endorsed by President George Bush, the issue played in Congress in late 1991.
Responding to intense pressures from national environmental organizations,
the Democratic leadership in the House and Senate deleted ANWR from the
energy bill. Alaska's two Republican senators, Ted Stevens and Frank Murkowski, threatened to filibuster to bring ANWR back into the package. A

90–5 Senate vote to close debate indicated the lengths Alaska would have to go to affect national policy on ANWR. To that end, in early 1992 Governor Hickel launched an $800,000 advertising campaign called "Arctic Storm" to convince residents of the Lower 48 states that developing ANWR would be in the nation's best interest. The Hickel administration planned to spend an additional $1 million on the campaign if needed.

ANWR is a dominant issue in Alaska politics and government of the 1990s; it also serves to illustrate the major themes introduced in this book. ANWR represents the desire of Alaskans to make their own decisions without influence from Outside interests or the federal government; at the same time, the ANWR case shows Alaska's dependence on these external forces and the outrage that dependency inspires in Alaska residents.

ANWR also focuses attention on Alaska's need to support itself financially. Since the 1970s, oil revenues have supplied about 85 percent of the state's budget; thus, the decline in oil production at Prudhoe Bay places the state in a precarious position. Developing a diversified, sustainable revenue base is the state's foremost objective. Development proponents argue that ANWR and other existing resources, including the state's $15 billion Permanent Fund account, could help cushion the transition from an oil-dependent economy to one based on renewable resources.

These themes of independence, dependence, and the search for sustainable economic development configure the treatment of Alaska history, government, and political processes.

SELF-GOVERNMENT: THE DRIVE FOR POWER

The theme of independence, translated into self-government, encompasses the interests of individuals, groups, regions, and the entire state. It also illuminates a large portion of Alaska's history.

Native Alaska was self-governing, as groups formed their own councils and negotiated or fought wars with others over territory and fish and game resources. The period of Russian colonization diminished Native self-government. Russian fur traders, merchants, and other settlers oppressed Natives, and yet they were in turn oppressed by their own government across the Pacific. Complaints of early settlers and transients focused on their lack of authority to govern their own lives. When America purchased Alaska from Russia in 1867, the drive for independence gained momentum.

The statehood movement best represents the struggle for power by territorial residents. Frustrated by decisions taken outside Alaska—political decisions made in Washington, D.C., and economic decisions made by powerful business concerns in Seattle—statehood leaders campaigned for the largest measure of independence granted to any state. Achieving statehood, however, did not reduce the desire for more independence from outside authority. In fact, the statehood experience intensified the pursuit of independence from federal government controls. The tone of intergovernmental relations is tense, producing ammunition for Alaska's political leaders in rhetorical campaigns. As an Associated Press reporter observed after Governor Hickel's state-of-the-state address in January 1992, the speech contained no new initiatives, but it "was heavy with the kind of anti-Washington rhetoric that politicians have long found popular in Alaska."[2]

A second facet to self-government is regional competition. Each of Alaska's five major regions (Southeast, Southcentral, Interior, Western, and Northwest Alaska) is the size of a large state. Geographical divisions, remoteness, and isolation create parochialism. Rural regions seek funding and support for their traditions and values; urban regions equally request assistance to meet the needs of their vastly larger populations. Regional conflict over the distribution of power in the legislature, over the state budget, and over the award of offices is very pronounced in Alaska.

A third aspect of self-government is the manner in which groups and communities work for independence. Local governments under the state constitution seek the powers of "home rule," which enable them to create laws de novo, without legislative authorization. In rural Alaska, the Native sovereignty movement attempts to institute a zone of protection against cultural, ethnic, and political intrusion by non-Natives. The movement is opposed by the state, however, and by groups such as sportsmen's councils, whose members fear restrictions on their pursuit of fish and game in Native regions.

A fourth element of self-government in Alaska stems from Alaskans themselves, who have—or believe they should have—a great deal of individual freedom. An important strain of Alaska individualism, which corresponds to sentiments elsewhere in the United States, is "get government off my back." Many Alaskans wish not only to escape government regulation, however; they want to appropriate common property resources, ranging from public lands for private homesites, to state oil and gas royalty and tax income for individual economic benefit. In March 1992, former Libertarian gubernatorial candidate Dick Randolph called for a "share-the-wealth" amendment to the state constitution, which would directly distribute to state residents a large percentage of the income from Alaska's resource bounty.

These four components of self-government and independence conflict but also may reinforce one another. They contribute dynamic tension to Alaska's government and politics.

DEPENDENCE: QUEST FOR EQUALITY

The experience of Alaska, from the period of Native migration to the present, has been colored by dependency. This lack of equal influence is a major factor explaining the drive for power and independence.

Nature constrains human choice in Alaska to a greater extent than elsewhere in the United States. The environment is harsh, even cruel, in most regions of the state for much of the year. Geographic barriers impede transportation and communication, leaving the regions isolated from one another and from the Outside. Obviously, the state itself is isolated from the contiguous, or Lower 48, states.

Such environmental constraints curb the desire for independence and self-government. It is hard to go it alone during long stretches of inclement weather. The frontier code of individualism and self-reliance runs counter to the need for community support for endeavors such as raising and educating children, providing emergency medical care and relief, and establishing ceremonies that connect lives and create values. Thus, the environment reinforces dependence on others.

Hostile environmental conditions and isolation also place adverse pressures on institutions. Families, churches, schools, firms, and government bureaucracies all are fragile vessels when removed from close contact with parent organizations. The environment raises greatly the costs of operating institutions and increases their dependence on parent organizations financially, which breeds resentment.

The chief manifestation of dependence is Alaska's reliance on the Outside for biological survival. A sparse population and small market make production of food, other basic necessities, and manufactured goods prohibitively expensive. Cost efficiency dictates dependence on external producers and markets. Paying the bill requires, more often than not, subsidies from external governments. The pattern of federal control and the sporadically virulent response to it in Alaska are emblematic of the tensions between the conditions of dependence and the quest for equality.

SUSTAINABLE ECONOMIC DEVELOPMENT: THE PURSUIT OF WEALTH

Alaskans' quests for independence and equality are meaningless without the ability to survive in a market-driven world. Only with internally generated and continuing economic activity will the state be able to accomplish the objectives of independence and equality. Four dimensions define the problems and possibilities of economic growth and wealth.

The first concern is whether the state can develop a pattern of growth based on renewable resources. The history of resource development in Alaska is replete with examples of one-time-only developments, producing the boom-and-bust cycles so familiar to Alaskans. Gold, copper, oil—all are depleted as they produce wealth. Even Alaska's strategic advantage may be nonrenewable, as it is dependent on changing configurations in world politics. Alaska's pursuit of wealth focuses on twin objectives: discovery of the next supergiant energy or mineral resource, and enhancement of resources that over time can supply sufficient revenue to pay for state services.

The disposition of state wealth is a second issue of economic development. Should wealth be saved for the next generation or spent at the current time? Whose claims on state wealth are the most valid? Can wealth be spent in a manner that generates new wealth, or should it be conserved because the risks of investment failure are too great? Given uncertainty regarding "spending to produce," which is always the case in risky economic situations, who should bear the risk and who should make the choice?

A third issue is conservation versus development of Alaska's nonrenewable resources. The resource bounties fueling Alaska's economy are significant on a world scale. In most cases, their value increases as they are depleted, causing one to ponder whether exploitation should be delayed. A related issue is preservation of environmental values threatened by economic development activities. The overriding question is the extent to which claims to preserve economic and environmental resources for the next generation can justify retarding actions that would benefit Alaskans today.

Finally, intrusive federal actions and external circumstances have a major impact on Alaskans' pursuit of wealth. What many Alaskans call a federal "lock-up" of land in the Alaska National Interest Lands Conservation Act (ANILCA) of 1980 frustrated their wishes to continue mineral exploration. The solidification of OPEC as an oil cartel dictating higher global oil prices, and later its disintegration through intracartel wars and conflict, made Alaska's economic development hostage to world events that state leaders could not influence.

Our book presents these themes of Alaska government and politics, while reviewing the state's course over one-third of a century. In chapters 1 and 2, we set the stage by introducing the Alaska character and describing the history of Alaska from colony to state. In chapters 3, 4, and 5, we examine three unique emphases in Alaska politics: a political economy heavily dependent on a single, nonrenewable resource; a relationship with the federal government expressing dependency, which promotes frustration and antagonism; and the "special relationship" between the federal government and Alaska's large Native population, which reflects the most serious social policy issues in the state and another source of tension in state politics.

In chapters 6, 7, 8, and 9, we cover the Alaska Constitution and the three branches of government in Alaska. Alaska's constitution is considered a model among the American states, because it embodies a progressive design of government, with strength in the legislative, executive, and judicial branches. The main question we examine in this volume is how efficiently state leaders have used this institutional strength in coping with the continuing internal and external forces driving Alaska's political economy.

In chapters 10 and 11, we present the processes of politics in Alaska, with a focus on political organizations and political participation. In chapters 12 and 13, we introduce the two different systems of local government, urban and rural. In chapter 14, we conclude this thematic introduction to government and politics in the forty-ninth state, offering general conclusions about the capabilities and prospects of Alaska government in the last decade of the century.

Because the story of Alaska's politics and government is ultimately a story of Alaska's people, we begin with an examination of the Alaska character and the forces that have shaped it.

CHAPTER I

The Alaska Character

Alaska is a state of extremes. Its size, harsh climate, and relative isolation distinguish it physically from the other states. Natural resources make Alaska one of the wealthiest states, and yet its dependence on oil revenues makes it one of the most economically vulnerable. Culturally, Alaska is one of the most diverse states, with the highest percentage of Native Americans among its small population. Most residents, however, moved in from somewhere else. These physical, economic, and social factors shape Alaska's political character. They determine how Alaskans form their governments, how they participate in public affairs, and what public policies they expect from their lawmakers. In this chapter, we launch a discussion of Alaska government and politics by focusing on the character of the "last frontier," setting the stage for later interpretations of unique governmental practices in America's forty-ninth state.

ALASKA AS A PLACE

The name *Alaska* is derived from an Aleut word meaning "the land toward which the action of the sea is directed." Alaskans frequently refer to their state as the "Great Land," a term derived from the Russian, *Bolshava Zemlya*. The state's physical attributes live up to this label in every respect. With its 378 million acres, Alaska is by far the largest state in the Union. Alaska stretches 1,400 miles from its northernmost tip at Point Barrow to its southernmost extension near Ketchikan, and the farthest-west point off the Aleutian isle of Attu is more than 2,400 miles west of Alaska's border with Canada. Alaska's area is one-fifth the size of the contiguous states combined; a map of Alaska superimposed on the Lower 48 stretches from Canada to the Gulf of Mexico, from the Atlantic to the Pacific Ocean.

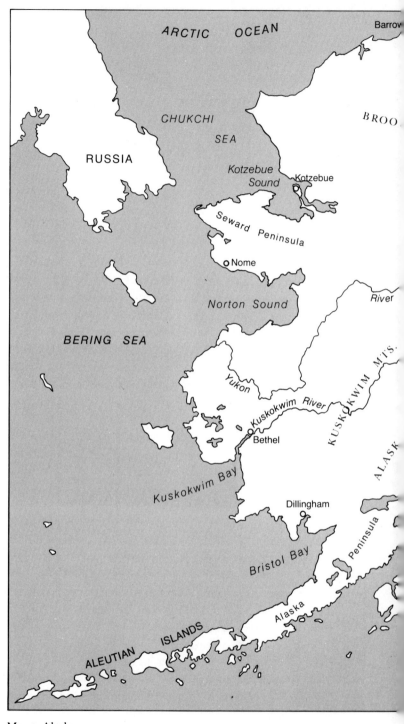

Map 1. Alaska

Alaska boasts 6,640 miles of Pacific and Arctic ocean coastline. North America's third-longest river, the 1,875-mile Yukon, courses 1,400 miles from the Canada border to the Bering Sea. Hundreds of navigable waterways and major rivers, such as the Kuskokwim and Tanana, traverse the state. The retreat of the last ice age left behind about three million lakes and ponds. Still, Alaskans allow Minnesota, with ten thousand lakes, to seek distinction as the "Land of Lakes."

Departing glaciers and the movement of massive tectonic plates also created the highest North American mountain, 20,320-foot Mount McKinley, in the Alaska Range. Other significant ranges include the Brooks Range, which is the northwestern spur of the Rocky Mountains and cuts off the North Slope from the rest of Alaska; the Wrangell and Chugach mountains in southcentral Alaska; the Kuskokwim Mountains, which divide west from southwest Alaska; and the Saint Elias Mountains, which separate southeast Alaska from the rest of the state. These ranges provide dramatic scenery, yet they also impede transportation and physically isolate entire regions.

Episcopal Archdeacon Hudson Stuck described the geographical carving up of Alaska in the preface to his 1914 memoir, *10,000 Miles with a Dog Sled:* "Alaska is not one country but many, with different climates, different resources, different problems, different populations, different interests; and what is true of one part of it is often grotesquely untrue of other parts. . . . Not only do these various parts of Alaska differ radically from one another, but they are separated from one another by almost insuperable natural obstacles, so that they are in reality different countries."[1]

Although Stuck's perspective was from a dog sled, modern travelers can see the dramatic variations among regions from an airplane. The north features treeless tundra whose mosses, lichens, and flowers blossom in a crazy quilt of color during the Arctic spring, providing a welcome, albeit brief, respite from the unrelieved whiteness of winter. Below the Arctic Circle, scraggly spruce trees dot the tundra landscape; rivers and lakes in the Interior and western Alaska provide shimmering landmarks. At the opposite end of the state, in the Southeast, towering Sitka spruce and lush shrubs and mosses inhabit misty rain forests; along the Aleutian Chain, rough waters encroach on windblown, rocky islands whose very appearance discourages human habitation.

Geologically, Alaska is a "new" land, with rocks and soils formed during the Jurassic and Cretaceous ages, between 195 and 65 million years ago. Areas of permanently frozen soil called permafrost underlie the ground in continuous and discontinuous patches. Such ground conditions can complicate even the relatively simple business of building a home or other structure in the far North. Alaska also is a dynamic land. Earthquakes are common and potentially destructive. The 1964 Good Friday earthquake, which measured 9.2 on the Richter scale, caused extensive damage in Anchorage and stirred tidal waves that wreaked havoc in other southcentral communities. More than eighty potentially active volcanoes simmer in Alaska, a greater number than in any other part of North or South America.[2] About half of them have erupted at least once in the past two centuries.

Topology, geology, and seismology have complicated settlement in Alaska, and so has meteorology. In the Arctic and interior regions especially, temperatures and weather fluctuate widely throughout the year. In the far North, winter temperatures plummet to 120 degrees below zero, if one accounts for the chill from the wind off the Arctic ice pack. Conditions moderate little in the Interior. Summers are warmer, but winters are colder on average than those on the Arctic coast. The highest recorded temperature in Alaska was 100 degrees Fahrenheit at Fort Yukon on June 27, 1915; the lowest temperature was 80 degrees below zero at Prospect Creek on January 23, 1971.[3] Both communities are in the Interior. Although other regions of the state lack such dramatic extremes, they have distinctive climatic phenomena, too. Gale-force winds typically hit the coastal areas and islands of the Aleutians and western Alaska, where the handful of trees that survive are hunched and twisted. In the rain-forest climate of the Southeast, the sun is shut out for all but a few days every year and, in Ketchikan, the annual average precipitation is 155 inches.

The challenges provided by climate and geography were reflected in the pattern of early human settlement in Alaska. The first inhabitants, Natives, followed abundant species of game and established communities along the coasts, along rivers, or in protected valleys. They were nomadic peoples who migrated with the seasons and the species they hunted.

Although Westerners who came later to Alaska also were affected by nature, they were less responsive to seasonal and regional variation. They congregated in places that were congenial to resource exploitation, such as the Aleutians for furs, the Southeast for fisheries, and Juneau, Nome, and Fairbanks for gold. Later, during construction of the Alaska Railroad, Anchorage attracted settlers who wanted jobs. As these early settlers developed first a marine navigation system and then a road network to connect populated regions of the territory, their communities gained permanence. Four-fifths of the present population live in a handful of cities, while the remaining fifth, primarily Alaska Natives, disperse themselves over hundreds of thousands of miles of land. The 1990 census found only 550,043 people, making Alaska America's least populous state after Wyoming, and far and away the most sparsely settled.

ALASKA'S RESOURCES

Different resources attracted different settlers to Alaska. Anthropologists believe aboriginal people crossed the Bering land bridge in pursuit of migratory mammal herds twenty thousand to thirty thousand years ago. Mammoth remains discovered in interior Alaska indicate how far inland early settlers followed game. Eskimoid peoples inhabited the Aleutians and western and northern coasts. They harvested seals, walrus, fish, and, to a lesser extent, land animals such as caribou, moose, bears, sheep, and birds. Because the wildlife resources were finite, they limited the populations of the Native groups that pursued them. None of the Alaska species has been domesticated. Today Alaska Natives rely on fish, land mammals, marine mammals, and other wild resources for a significant portion of their table fare. In a 1987 study, rural residents in ninety-eight communities reported a median per capita harvest of 252 pounds of wild foods each year.[4] These foods also provide a dietary supplement for Caucasian hunters.

As Athabaskans and Southeast Indians settled in Alaska, they became more dependent on fish, which explains why their villages grew up along rivers with productive runs of fish (particularly salmon) and along sections of the southeast coast with abundant sea resources. The economies of these regions, including the Interior, the Southeast, and along western rivers and coastline, still revolve around commercial fish harvests. With a value of more than $1 billion annually, commercial fishing is second only to oil in the state's natural resource economy. Fisheries remain the largest private-sector employer. Before statehood, they drew more residents than any other resource.

In the twentieth century, subsurface mineral resources have attracted and sustained many migrants directly or indirectly. Gold stimulated development in several regions of the state. Miners Joe Juneau and Richard Harris discovered the precious metal in the Southeast in 1880; the former lent the capital city his name. A turn-of-the-century gold rush temporarily made Nome (a corruption of "no name," as it was listed on early maps) Alaska's largest city, with a population of 12,488 in 1900. Felix Pedro, an Italian immigrant, discovered gold by the Chatanika River in 1902; the ensuing boom crowned Fairbanks the jewel of the territory in the 1920s and 1930s.

Copper and silver have long been mined in Alaska, with large operations

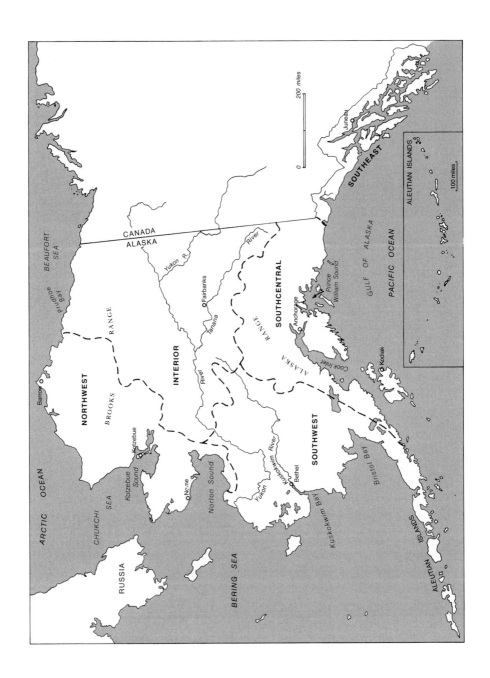

Map 2. Major Regions of Alaska

under way in the Interior and a silver mine at Green's Creek in the Southeast. Recently, the Canadian firm Cominco has begun to exploit zinc deposits at the Red Dog Mine in the northwest Arctic; a world-class molybdenum mine is being established in Ketchikan at Misty Fjords. Platinum, titanium, chromium, and other strategic minerals hold out hope for future mining in the state.

Alaska also harbors the largest coal deposits in the United States. Promoters say the reserves in interior Alaska, on the North Slope, and at the Beluga fields near Anchorage are sufficient to supply America's coal needs for five hundred years. Most of Alaska's accessible coal is soft and wet, two drawbacks balanced by its low sulfur content and environmental desirability. Commercial exploitation occurs only on a modest scale at the Usibelli Mine in Healy, which exports most of its coal to South Korea.

Richfield Oil Company discovered marketable quantities of oil in the 1950s on the Kenai Peninsula, where its Swanson River fields continue to produce oil and gas. The state's largest oil patch, however, is Prudhoe Bay on the North Slope. Discovered in 1968, this supergiant field has an estimated recoverable volume of 12 billion barrels. During the 1990s, it produced about three-fourths of the 1.8 million barrels flowing through the trans-Alaska pipeline daily.[5] At this production level, Alaska was meeting over a fifth of America's oil needs.

Geologists suspect that vast reserves of oil and natural gas still underlie the North Slope. Oil companies have drilled exploratory wells with the goal of offsetting the predicted serious decline in Prudhoe Bay production in the 1990s. The domestic oil industry has pinned its hopes on the coastal plain of the Arctic National Wildlife Refuge, which stretches from Prudhoe Bay to the Canada border. Exploration and possible development hinge on stable world oil prices and less environmental scrutiny of the sort triggered by the spill of 11 million gallons of crude oil into Prince William Sound in March 1989.

Forests abound in southeast Alaska and, to a lesser extent, in the south-central and interior regions of the state. Forest products, a treasured commodity in Japan and East Asia, are a valuable export for Alaska. Their trade also attracts foreign investment to pulp mills in Sitka and Ketchikan.

Conditions for agriculture are not auspicious. Soils are uneven; the climate is harsh, though it does offer long sunlight hours that produce colossal seventy-pound cabbages and other gargantuan vegetables. Transporting products to market is difficult and costly because of the limited network of roads, rail lines, and harbors. Markets, within the state and without, are poorly developed. Nevertheless, farming communities continue to survive. Two examples are the Matanuska-Susitna Valley, settled during the depression, and the Delta-Clearwater area, where the state recently poured millions of dollars into a barley project that has, by most accounts, failed.

A final natural resource of note is Alaska's pristine beauty, which has made tourism a vibrant and politically powerful industry and the second-largest primary employer in the state.[6] Cruise ships and planes transport more than half a million visitors to Alaska annually. The average tourist spends a few days basking in the midnight sun, viewing wildlife at Denali National Park, and snapping pictures of everything from pioneer settlements to the pipeline.

The state's geographic proximity to the Russian Federation is a resource of a different sort that the U.S. government has exploited since the onset of the cold war. The Bering Strait, a two-mile-wide ribbon of turbulent water closed by ice for most of the year, is all that separates Alaska's Little Diomede Island from Siberia's Big Diomede Island. The distance between the two mainlands is fifty-six miles at the closest point. On three occasions in the 1980s, "wanderers" from California illustrated just how narrow the gap is by attempting the icy trek between the superpowers. U.S. authorities intercepted each in turn and sent them back to U.S. soil.[7]

The U.S. Department of Defense established large military reservations in the state. In the wake of the cold war, the fate of these reservations is uncertain. The installations include army posts at Fort Richardson near Anchorage, Fort Greely near Delta, and Fort Wainwright, which features a new light infantry division, near Fairbanks. Eielson Air Force Base is also located south of Fairbanks; Elmendorf AFB borders downtown Anchorage, and the village of Galena hosts a third air base. Adak and Kodiak islands have naval installations, and a radar installation exists on Shemya in the Aleutians. Salaries of military personnel contribute a hefty sum to the state economy, as do military construction and renovation dollars. The military presence in Alaska is a continuing reminder of the federal role in Alaska government.

THE ALASKA PEOPLE

The distribution and dynamics of the Alaska population are unique among the states. Alaska has the only Native American population living at or near sites of original settlement. Over the years, it has had the largest percentage of transients, whether they were adventurers, traders, soldiers, missionaries, or temporary workers. It also features the most recently established community of non-Native settlers. The nature of this configuration, a pot with continually changing elements, adds much volatility to Alaska politics.

Alaska Natives

Eskimos, Aleuts, and Indians comprise the indigenous population of Alaska; collectively, they are called Alaska Natives. Alaska Eskimos, the largest Native group in Alaska, include the Inupiat people of the North Slope and Northwest and the Yupiks of western Alaska and some areas of the Interior. Initially, they migrated from inner Asia to Alaska in pursuit of land and sea mammals. Although Eskimos now live in coastal and interior villages, the rites and objects of hunting still define their cultures. For example, whale hunting is the central activity in Inupiat Eskimo life today; informal leadership in the community is accorded to whaling captains (*umialik*) who meet with success.

Northern Inupiat differ from western Yupik Eskimos, who diverge into the Pacific Ocean and Bering Sea communities. Yupik Eskimos outnumber the Inupiat and comprise the largest ethnic group in the Alaska Native population. Because Western contact came late to the Yupik people, they have held onto their traditional culture more tenaciously than any other Alaska Native group. In many Yupik villages, even the youngest generation speaks the traditional language, which remains in regular community use.

The Aleuts are an Eskimoid population, although they are considered distinct. Russian arms and diseases nearly destroyed them during the eighteenth and nineteenth centuries. Through intermarriage with Russians, a creole group arose and acculturated to Western ways. Today Aleuts are scattered among villages in west, southwest, and southcentral Alaska, in addition to their ancestral home on the Aleutian Chain.

Indians living in southeastern Alaska, including the Tlingit, Haida, and Tsimshian, represent a complex Pacific Northwest coastal culture that developed around relatively permanent villages. Composed of families and clans, the village was a spatial, social, and political unit. Areas outside the boundaries, customarily used for fish camps, hunting, and berry picking, fell within a broader sphere belonging to the village. Villages formed alliances usually based on kinship ties. Hostile alliances fought territorial wars. Defeat in war often meant enslavement to the conquering tribe.

Southeast Indians shared a language and identity; Tlingits believed in a common ancestry. Lineage forged the strongest ties connecting Tlingit villages. When Russian explorers and traders intruded on Tlingit areas, they met armed resistance from organized communities. In fact, the political unity of Tlingit communities impeded European penetration.

Aboriginal Indians of the Pacific Rim differed from those elsewhere on the Alaska land mass because they were more populous and lived in settled communities. Southeast and southcentral Indian tribes include the Eyak, Tlingit, Haida, Chugach, Kenai, and Tanaina. The largest communities today are the Tlingit and Haida, known throughout the southeast region and state for their clan-based societies, colorful dress, and handsome totem artifacts. Southeast Indians have acculturated to a high degree; only traces of the indigenous language appear in community speech. The Tsimshian (originally from Canada) now reside on Annette Island, the only congressionally created Indian reservation in Alaska.

Native peoples in most other regions of Alaska lacked the extremely rich resource base of the Southeast groups. Except for some areas on the eastern Aleutians and at the mouth of the Yukon and Kuskokwim rivers, game and fish populations in a given locale rarely sufficed to sustain a large community over time. Limited subsistence resources strongly influenced social and political organization. In small and impermanent communities, little structure developed to shape life. Individual action was more pronounced. Groups of interrelated families did, however, join together for economy's sake in the hunt for large mammals such as whales or migratory herds of caribou. These other Natives had a broader territorial scope that was less focused on structured communities than that of Southeast Natives.

Athabaskan Indians, who are linguistically related to the Navajo Indians of the American Southwest, originally populated interior Alaska. They were the most nomadic of all Alaska Native groups, traveling along the rivers and lakes and through the forests of the Interior in pursuit of fish and game. Little of their aboriginal language survives today, for Athabaskans have been in contact with Western civilization for nearly one hundred years. Some customs, however, such as sharing ceremonies, or "potlatches," remain an important part of life in Interior villages. Most Athabaskans now live close to the state's road system, reducing the isolation that best protects the Native lifestyle.

The Eskimo, Aleut, and Athabaskan languages provided a sense of identity and distinguished distant kin from aliens. Extensive trading networks crisscrossed the interior and Arctic regions, although trading was sporadic. Trade routes also linked Alaska's Eskimos with Inuit throughout the circumpolar North. At the time of European contact, Eskimo, Aleut, and Athabaskan bands often were powerless to defend their communities and unite against outsiders. In fact, Eskimos and Athabaskans had warred against each other for nearly one thousand years.

Although Alaska's Native population is not homogeneous, the Native population as a whole has common experiences and rights, which have increased in value since statehood. The foremost experience is "immemorial use and occupancy of Alaska lands, based on residence from the beginning." The foremost right is sovereignty, defined as the "political" relationship between the tribes and the federal government. Although their sovereignty is qualified as "dependent" and is subject to much legal dispute, Natives are constitutionally distinct from transients and non-Native residents of the state because of their trust relationship with the federal government, which protects their rights as Native Americans.[8]

Transients

The 1990 census, along with surveys performed in the 1980s, indicates that most Alaskans are newcomers who have lived in the state less than ten years. The population has surged and declined ever since Westerners first weighed anchor off the territory in the eighteenth century. The periods during and after the gold rushes and pipeline construction were especially volatile. Throughout Alaska history, transients have included explorers, traders, missionaries, teachers, miners, fishermen, oil-field and support-sector workers, and soldiers.

Explorers were the first Westerners to reach Alaska. Arriving by sea along the Aleutians and the western, northern, and southeastern coasts, they "discovered" Alaska on behalf of their governments and trading companies, then returned home. A small number put down roots and intermarried with indigenous people. American whalers Charles Brower and Albert Hopson, who founded powerful dynasties at Point Barrow in the late nineteenth century, are notable examples.

The first Westerners encountered by Natives were Russians who plied furs and other wares along the inland waterways and coasts. Communities such as Fort Yukon in the Interior grew up along points of frequent contact between Natives, traders, and merchants. Some traders even joined the settlers. Most, however, extracted their profit from the Alaska fur trade and then departed.

Missionaries, whose objective was to convert the Natives to Christianity, followed the traders. First came the representatives of the Russian Orthodox Church, who brought the Aleuts and some of the Yupik Eskimos over to their faith. Mission societies of American churches followed; initially, there were Catholics and traditional Protestants such as Moravians, Episcopalians, and Presbyterians. Fundamentalist churches such as the Pentecostal, Assembly of God, and Baptist sects arrived in the twentieth century. Like the fur traders before them, the missionaries were short-term residents. Most considered their work in Alaska a calling of limited duration. After purchasing Alaska in 1867, the U.S. government treated the district as a colonial outpost, staffing it with roving military detachments. This pattern continues today. Teachers and civil service administrators in most rural areas of the state serve a short tenure, rarely staying for more than two or three years.

Alaska's natural resources also attracted transients. The extraction of most of Alaska's resources does not require long-term, year-round work. Miners exhausted the lodes of gold, silver, and copper, then departed for other mines or retired to warmer climes. Traditionally, the majority of people who fished Alaska waters commercially were nonresidents who returned at the end of the season to Seattle or California. The U.S. military buildup resulting from the onset of the cold war attracted another surge of transients. Some soldiers choose to retire in Alaska; others regard it strictly as a foreign posting.

Energy development in Alaska similarly employed many nonresident workers. Alaska lacked a skilled labor force sufficient to drill wells and design, construct, and operate an eight-hundred-mile pipeline, a situation that led to out-of-state hiring by the oil companies. State lawmakers responded by enacting local-hire legislation, which the U.S. Supreme Court declared unconstitutional in 1978. Animus against new out-of-state workers is one of the most potent political forces in Alaska.

Immigration rises and falls with opportunities for economic and social development. Transient immigrants have always made up a sizable portion of the state population; they also heat up political conflict by competing with settlers for jobs, incomes, and other benefits.

Settlers

Twentieth-century "pioneers," beckoned by the North's opportunities and challenged by its climate and isolation, created modern Alaska. Some adventurers made it their home in the eighteenth and nineteenth centuries. They established the state's oldest settler communities in Kodiak and Sitka. Not until the turn of the twentieth century did a critical mass of Caucasian immigrants descend on the gold deposits and fisheries.

For the early settlers, Alaska was indeed the "last frontier" of North America. As their communities grew, pioneers developed into a powerful force in state politics. Today the term *pioneers* generally refers to non-Natives who made their home in Alaska before statehood.

Institutions and benefits mark this status. The Pioneers of Alaska, a private fraternal organization open to those who have lived in Alaska at least thirty years, have active "igloos" in communities throughout the state. From the state government, pioneers receive such perks as longevity bonuses for people over sixty-five, and inexpensive housing and nursing home care in Pioneer Homes, located in the larger communities. The state also grants special opportunities for land selection and ownership to long-time residents. In the case of some benefits, such as the longevity bonus, the courts have ruled it unconstitutional to exclude elderly people who are not "pioneers."

Today few non-Natives can lay claim to pioneer status; aesthetic distinctions based on length of residency continue to be made, however. For instance, people who migrated to Alaska before the 1968 Prudhoe Bay oil discovery pride themselves because they suffered adversity before Alaska became a rich state. People who arrived after 1968 claim to have created the oil boom that still benefits most Alaskans. The definition of a "sourdough" changes with time. For the greenest newcomers, known as "cheechakos," anyone who has endured an Alaska winter is a sourdough. Long-term residents tend to look on grizzled old men, veterans of blizzards and bear encounters, as true sourdoughs.

Most political leaders in Alaska support giving benefits to citizens based on the length of their stay (durational residency). In their view, everyone does not deserve an equal slice of the citizenship pie. Instead, they believe, benefits should be commensurate with costs; the longer the residence, the greater the reward. The equal protection clause of the Fourteenth Amendment to the U.S. Constitution conflicts with this view.

Nevertheless, it was exactly this perspective that prompted legislators to decide in 1979 to distribute oil wealth in the form of Permanent Fund dividends proportionally, based on length of residence. Anchorage attorneys Ron and Patricia Zobel challenged the decision in court. They became pariahs, receiving hate mail and death threats, but the U.S. Supreme Court, in *Zobel v. Alaska* (1980), sided with them. Many Alaskans regard the decision overturning the initial distribution scheme as yet another in a series of punitive actions against their state on the part of the federal government.

The largest single category of Alaska settlers are non-Natives who moved in after statehood. Their long-term settlement in Alaska distinguishes them from transients who exploit resources without paying the bill. No other state or territory extracts such a high price in isolation and discomfort from its residents, a circumstance that fosters a superior attitude among some old-timers. The feeling fuels countless attempts to discriminate against "outsiders" with no tenable commitment to the state. The institutions of state and local government, therefore, respond to residents with vested interests. Irony is inherent in the views of some settlers: as non-Natives, they are reluctant to extend the logic of durational residency to Native rights and benefits.

ALASKA IDEAS

Alaskans form their ideas about government and politics in response to their distinct environment. The diversity of weather and geographic conditions across the state, as well as differing degrees of isolation, suggests that residents' responses may not be uniform. If Alaska is not one country but many, then its people belong to many nationalities, too. One thing they have in common, however, is change; it is their catalyst. Over the thousands of years that Native bands ranged across the Alaska landscape, their concepts of community and the environment evolved. Through contact with settlers, Native people learned about Western governmental institutions and political processes. Non-Native settlers and transients brought with them preformed notions of how politics should work. Their ideas bumped up against the Alaska environment and changed in response to its challenges. In some cases, the discrepancies between preconceptions and reality blurred; in others, they became exaggerated.

Roots of the Settler Political Culture in Alaska

Political scientist Daniel Elazar is the foremost advocate of the political-culture interpretation of the formation of public policies in American regions, states, and communities. His ideas suggest a framework for the ways in which frontier regions developed historically. Elazar believes that the United States shares a political culture based on two differing conceptions of political order. Each conception is rooted in the behavior of the earliest colonial settlers of North America: "In the first, the political order is conceived as a marketplace in which the primary public relationships are products of bargaining among individuals and groups acting out of self-interest. In the second, the political order is conceived to be a commonwealth—a state in which the whole people have an undivided interest—in which the citizen co-operates in an effort to create and maintain the best government in order to implement certain shared moral principles."[9]

From this contradiction of values, Elazar proceeds to construct three ideal types of political culture, and he links each type with the historical evolution of regions of the United States, acknowledging that the westward migration of peoples admixes types. His objective is to show the influence of political ideas and values on practical forms of government and public policies. Two of the types—individualist and moralist—adhere to the central conceptions of political order. He notes that the individualist political culture "emphasizes the conception of the democratic order as a marketplace. In its view, a government is instituted for strictly utilitarian reasons, to handle those functions demanded by the people it is created to serve. A government need not have any direct concern with questions of the 'good society' except insofar as it may be used to advance some common conception of the good society formulated outside the political arena just as it serves other functions."[10] Elazar finds that behavior of Americans in the mid-Atlantic states conforms roughly with the individualist ideal. These states had a thriving capitalist ethos. Religious diversity flourished, breeding tolerance for different points of view. The view of the state was that it should serve individual ends.

The moralistic political culture, in contrast, "emphasizes the commonwealth conception as the basis for democratic government. Politics, to the moralistic political culture, is considered one of the great activities of man in his search for the good society—a struggle for power, it is true, but also an effort to exercise power for the betterment of the commonwealth. Consequently, in the moralistic political culture, both the general public and the politicians conceive of politics as a public activity centered on some notion of the public good and properly devoted to the advancement of public interest."[11] The Puritan colonies of New England corresponded most closely to this value scheme. They fostered a communitarian spirit that sought to use politics to create the perfect commonwealth and that designated those who had lost the faith.

The final type Elazar advances is traditionalism: "The traditionalistic political culture is rooted in an ambivalent attitude toward the marketplace coupled with a paternalistic and elitist conception of the commonwealth. It reflects an older, pre-commercial attitude that accepts a substantially hierarchical society as part of the ordered nature of things, authorizing and expecting those at the top of the social structure to take a special and dominant role in government."[12] Elazar applies the traditionalist rubric to the Old South. This region was a distinct socioeconomic and political section of colonial America, and it contrasted with the values of the mid-Atlantic and New England regions. It was a quasi-feudal, precapitalist order that emphasized the institution of slavery. The elite who ruled southern politics espoused the necessity of status and hierarchy in society.

The Elazar model of the development of political cultures takes a peculiar form in Alaska. Alaskans came from a hodgepodge of backgrounds, and they settled in different types of communities. Some settlers uprooted themselves from the American South or other parts of the country where the traditionalistic culture flourished. The majority came from the northern tier states of Minnesota, North Dakota, Montana, Washington, and Oregon. When these settlers arrived, they were most familiar with the individualistic and moralistic cultures. The environment they encountered in Alaska reinforced these traditions in some respects and altered them in others. Conditions encountered by settlers before and after statehood have shaped Alaska's unique political culture.

The harsh environment demanded a high degree of self-reliance. "Frontier" individualism developed early and continues to modify Elazar's model of market-type individualism. Far from kin and living in isolated settings devoid of infrastructure, Alaska's settlers were forced to plumb their own resources. The novels of Jack London, a favorite author of many Alaskans, overflow with images of the daily struggle to survive against an unimaginably cruel environment. Beating the odds instilled in settlers a strong sense of independence.

It also made them feel superior to "outsiders." The term is tinged with a pejorative connotation, as though non-Alaskans could not possibly understand or meet the challenges of life in the state. Regular combat against a hostile environment fosters egoism and chauvinism. Alaskans tend to be fiercely loyal to the state and its traditions; they boost it more strongly than Texans praise Texas. Governor Walter Hickel captured the sentiment in his inaugural address when he called Alaskans "one country, one people."

Living the independent life in Alaska can give rise to unique pathologies. One of the most well known is "cabin fever," which in its extreme form is called seasonal affective disorder. In residents of both polar regions, a shortage of daylight hours in winter may bring on serious depression; sufferers are lethargic, irritable, and withdrawn. They lose concentration and initiative, and they may crave carbohydrates and gain weight.[13] In addition to cabin fever, child and spouse abuse are more prevalent in Alaska than in other states, and Alaskans consume more alcohol per capita than other Americans. Violent crime indices for assault, rape, and murder exceed the national average;

suicide rates are high, too. The social ills of frontier life are epidemic in some villages, where Natives must walk a tightrope between traditional values and Western demands.

Few Alaskans lead lives of complete independence. In practical terms, survival requires dependence on others. Friends and neighbors replace family members far away. In small towns and large, community affairs are imbued with an intensity and personalism fast disappearing in most parts of the United States. Localist values have produced, in part, Alaska's political regionalism. Leaning on others extends to dependence on institutions, a condition that adds tension and ambivalence to Alaskans' peculiar brand of individualism.

Alaskans often compare their institutional dependency to that of Third World states. Alaska's colonial experience resembled that of non-Western states before and after independence. Alaska was exploited by outside interests before statehood and, some would argue, after it as well. Alaskans lacked the means to influence policies affecting them.

Dependency defines three aspects of Alaskans' attitudes toward government and politics. First, there is the dependence on friends and neighbors and a view of the community as composed of quasi-kin, which grants a communitarian ethic to political relationships. The second element is egalitarian. During the colonial era, Alaska lacked established elites; people in power were either federal agents or representatives of absentee landlords who controlled the state's resources. Settlers united against these superior powers. The third and related component of dependency is populism, expressed by opposition to the eastern or "Outside" establishment and the federal government and by support of equal distribution of benefits.

Because of the premium placed on individualism and independence in Alaska, dependency promotes dynamic conflict. The state's experiences as a colony and as a state reinforce a sense of inferiority to and discrimination by outside forces. Such feelings are used to justify opposition to these outside forces in the form of rhetoric and deed. From opposing fish traps in territorial Alaska to demonstrating against federal land policies, non-Native settlers have united in their anger toward external control. On the extreme end is the Alaskan Independence Party, which has advocated secession from the United States.

Conditions in Alaska have also shaped a moralist attitude toward government and politics. The tiny settler population brought a personal flavor to politics. Because ordinary people knew the government and civic leaders, they could hold them accountable. The simplicity of life in Alaska led to a correspondingly simple, easy-to-control pattern of politics. Close-knit communities and the small state population drove home the importance of each citizen and each vote, contributing to feelings of efficacy, involvement, and moral responsibility.

Religion, in part, forms a basis for moralistic attitudes. Alaska has a large fundamentalist Christian community, which nearly equals the traditional denominations in membership and definitely exceeds them in vigor. On contemporary moral issues such as abortion, the death penalty, sex education, school textbook selection, alternative lifestyles, gambling, alcohol, and substance abuse, the fundamentalist community is unified and powerful. Fundamentalists are intent on imposing their values on the rest of the community through political action and public policy.

Public expectations run high on broader issues of public morality such as corruption in government, conflicts of interest, and influence peddling. These expectations, however, are cushioned by some tolerance of corruption and sleaze and by public as well as private greed. Religious orientation and personal politics join hands to monitor official behavior. Relative to other states, Alaska experiences few gross breaches of the public trust. The contradictory individualistic strains in Alaska political culture tend to rationalize exploitation of public resources for individual, group, or especially regional advantage.

Frontier individualism, dependency, and moralism are rooted in the experiences of settlers during colonial days and after statehood. Developed in response to Alaska's environment, all three ideologies figure in people's relationship to the land.

Transients and settlers have regarded Alaska as a frontier to be explored and, ultimately, conquered. Its resources appeared to be infinite; to achieve its prizes required strong, individual labor against the vagaries of nature. Even in the 1990s, most non-Native Alaskans believe the land can support continued, intensive resource exploitation for the benefit of all citizens. Because Alaska is the only remaining frontier in the United States, the people's attitudes toward it have national as well as statewide implications.

In Alaska, discussions about the land and the environment often focus on access issues. Historically, settlers complained that the federal government restricted their opportunities to develop natural resources. Because the land mass appeared so vast and so untouched by humans, Alaskans resented efforts to cut off certain areas to development. Debate over the Arctic National Wildlife Refuge recrystallized this issue in the early 1990s. The majority of residents favor oil exploration and development in ANWR; they object to federal controls limiting access to what they perceive as the state's next motherlode.

One might think the beauty of the land would unite Alaskans in support of preservationist values. It does not. A majority of the population values development and believes it can proceed without much harm to the environment. Only a minority are "environmentalists" in the sense commonly used in American politics. In coalition with national environmental groups, this minority has been able to stall an onslaught on Alaska's remaining wilderness. Native political culture also figures in this drama.

Native Political Culture

The traditional cultures of Native Alaskans are unlike the traditionalistic cultures rooted in the colonial American experience. Formal institutions of government are Western creations. Alaska Natives' experience was with traditional governments based on the kin structures that dominated tribal affairs. The need to react as one body to environmental pressures, such as the changing migration routes of wildlife and competition among groups for resources, as well as the need to handle quarrels within and among families, created the conditions for politics and conflict resolution. The attitudes of Native Alaskans today toward government and politics bear traces of their experiences with traditional governments. It is possible to isolate two types of Native traditionalism, one associated with migratory hunting societies and one originating in relatively permanent societies.

The aboriginal peoples who followed land and sea mammals evolved a quasi-governmental system based on knowledge of the hunt. In Eskimo whaling communities, leadership was divided between an *umialik* (whaling captain), who led the hunt, and a shaman, who interpreted the cosmos to the community. Although the community had leaders, it operated by consensus. The fact that any individual or family was welcome to leave the community for another or to live alone operated as a strong constraint on power.

In Yupik Eskimo communities, associations of older men resembling councils existed at the time of European contact. The elders' councils advised leaders and commented on their actions. In all Native societies, elders played important political roles based on their knowledge of the hunt and their ability to train the younger generations. Deference to elders was a vital cultural trait. Northern Athabaskan communities had chiefs and shamans too, though they were usually younger members of the tribe. As in the Yupik and Inupiat bands, sharing resources through traditions such as potlatches was a way of preserving life. In none of these aboriginal communities was leadership "institutionalized" in an office filled by orderly succession through heredity, rotation, or election. Attitudes toward power revolved around skills and knowledge helpful to subsistence.

In contrast, the Indians of southeast Alaska lived in settled communities with strict social and political codes. Tlingit and Haida societies, for instance, were divided into two portions, termed *moieties* by anthropologists. Generally, there was the Raven moiety and the Eagle moiety; marriages were arranged between individuals of opposite moieties. Among the Tlingits, moieties were further divided into broad family groups, or clans. Several families lived together in large households. Westerners used the familiar terms *tribe* and *chief* in early descriptions of the Tlingits, but these concepts did not apply to the old Tlingit culture:

> There was no "chief" or head man of one side, one clan or even of a whole lineage. The highest ranking person was the spokesman of the house or "hit-saati." In some places, the spokesman of the oldest house of a particular lineage was more influential than others, but he could only speak directly for his house. To become a spokesman, one had to be born into the proper family and then be selected or approved as a spokesman. . . . The household and local lineage were the individual's source of security and prestige. A Tlingit was born, raised, lived and died as a member of a lineage.[14]

Although males were in positions of control in the society, lineage was matrilineal. A person inherited from his or her mother's brothers and sisters.

Survey research of late twentieth-century Native communities reveals a continued preference for traditional means of conflict resolution and decision making. Natives favor taking the opinions of everyone into account instead of allowing the majority to prevail. Leaders are obliged to provide for the wants of the entire community and to heed the voice of the past: the elders.

Individualism is also a factor in Native cultures. Defined within each community, it is expressed in many different ways: as sensitivity toward individuals' identity and pride, through care not to push or embarrass, and by a nonconfrontational, indirect style of communication and problem solving. Although they prize individual strength and resilience, Natives rank the needs of the individual below the needs of the community.

CONCLUSION

The environment, resources, people, and ideas of Alaska set it apart from other states and countries. The Great Land's physical characteristics match its name. Mountain ranges crisscross it, long rivers traverse it, vast oceans border it. Alaska's land is dynamic. It experiences the abrupt, cataclysmic changes of earthquakes, floods, and volcanoes as well as the barely perceptible transitions of retreating glaciers. Alaska's weather and climate are diverse in the extreme, ranging from the barren, wind-pummeled sub-Arctic plains to the lush, fertile rain forests of the Southeast.

A land so rich in natural resources has attracted waves of migrants. Animal and fish populations have supported aboriginal subsistence lifestyles for thousands of years. Alaska's stock of gold, copper, silver, and other hard-rock minerals have yielded world-class finds, spurring development rushes. The latest and largest mineral discovery, "black gold," transformed the Alaska economy. Rich commercial fisheries off the coasts draw foreign and domestic fleets to Alaska's waters. Hardy forests support a wood products industry. The beauty of Alaska inspires poets, artists, and writers; it also draws hundreds of thousands of tourists. Alaska's strategic location makes it a geopolitical prize of the United States, qualifying it for many military installations and their millions of dollars in federal support.

These diverse resources have enticed an increasingly diverse population. Alaska Natives formed many nations before the arrival of Europeans in the eighteenth century. Westerners came as explorers, missionaries, traders, miners, teachers, and soldiers to exploit the land and its people. Gradually, non-Natives settled in Alaska. The environment acted in different ways on these three categories of Alaska people: Natives, transients, and settlers. The ideas they formed reflected their experiences. Native Alaskans revered traditions enabling their cultures to survive, traditions emphasizing community with strains of individualism. Non-Natives developed a sense of frontier individualism and self-reliance, laced with an attitude of moral superiority toward outsiders. But their susceptibility to environmental change made them dependent on the distant federal government as well as on local communities for survival. This dependence bred ambivalence toward governments and populist responses to external demands.

Alaskans' ideas greatly influenced their government and politics. The strength of the three branches of their government mirrors their desire to make the state self-reliant and to reduce political (but not economic) dependence on the federal government and other external powers. The pluralistic nature of the state's political process, with weak parties, strong interest groups, energetic media, and the highest rate of nonpartisan identification of any state, denotes a drive toward personal independence rare in twentieth-century America.

CHAPTER 2

From Colony to State

The story of Alaska's transformation from colony to state is actually two stories, told from two different perspectives. The first, from traditionalist historiographers, is a tale of struggle against oppression and focuses mainly on the settlers who created modern Alaska. Traditionalists consider Native and early colonial contributions to Alaska's history not as significant as those made by "pioneers." Revisionists, on the other hand, focus on the Alaska environment and how various groups have responded to it over time. They approach each era in Alaska history, from Native settlement through modern times, by recording events and their contribution to Alaska's development.

Traditionalists are represented most authoritatively in *The State of Alaska,* by former territorial governor Ernest Gruening, and in *Alaska,* by Jeannette Nichols. These books are chronicles of neglect by the federal government and of abuse by powerful Outside economic interests that "held Alaska in fief, plundering its natural resources, stifling competition, retarding the development of territorial government and using its political influence at the national capital in generally pernicious ways."[1]

The revisionist interpretation of Alaska history is a generation younger than the traditional view. It is represented in the works of Terrence Cole, Claus-M. Naske, and William Wilson. These writers question whether any particular devil theory can explain Alaska's problems, past or present. They take a more neutral approach in their treatment of the trials and tribulations of the statehood struggle.

The traditionalist and revisionist approaches are quite distinct, yet they overlap in a discussion of the themes of this book. Both traditionalists and revisionists note the tension between independence and dependence, and both chronicle the quest for wealth in a resource-rich land. Traditionalists speak in a moral voice when they say that Alaska should be able to construct its future without the baggage of the other states or the federal government; revisionists emphasize choices individuals make as they continually adapt to and change the northern environment. It is this environment that has set the agenda since the first humans migrated to Alaska from Asia thousands of years ago.

In this chapter, we summarize the growth of the state through four historical periods: precontact Native history dating back twenty thousand to thirty thousand years, European discovery and Russian rule (1741–1867), U.S. colonial rule (1867–1912), and the territorial era (1912–58).

NATIVE HISTORY

Anthropologists cannot yet pinpoint the origins of North and South America's aboriginal population. One hypothesis proposes that ancestors of today's Native peoples reached the continents by sea. The most widely held theory suggests that migrants traveling by land first settled the New World. The probable route of entry was the Bering land bridge, a swatch of land nearly one thousand miles wide stretching from Siberia to Alaska. The land bridge formed when Pleistocene ice sheets locked up much of the earth's water supply and lowered sea levels. Between one and two millennia ago, the seas rose up and divided Alaska and Siberia once more.[2]

Ancestors of American aboriginals traveled from northern Asia over the land bridge in several waves. The first migrants probably arrived well over twelve thousand years ago. They and their successors were the progenitors of Indian races scattered all the way from interior Alaska and northern Canada to the tip of the South American continent. More than ten thousand years ago, ancestors of the Aleuts and Eskimos began their journey from northern Asia. They migrated to the Arctic and sub-Arctic regions of what are today Alaska, Canada, and Greenland.

Archaeologists and biologists have yet to answer this intriguing question: What relationship exists between northern Asians and Alaska Eskimos, Aleuts, and Indians? Blood-type studies of the modern populations reveal no similarities; nevertheless, the possibility remains that their ancestors were related.[3]

None of the indigenous groups in Alaska developed a writing system. In all groups, however, rich oral histories linked the present to the past. Explorers and early traders pieced together these accounts, which anthropologists study to derive a sense of Native social and political organization before Western influence.[4]

When Europeans arrived in Alaska in the middle of the eighteenth century, they encountered a variety of aboriginal groups. They marveled at the richness of the material traditions: the colorful clothing made of animal skins and adorned with bird feathers and beadwork, the stately sculptures such as the totem poles in the Southeast, and the whalebone cemeteries in the Northwest. They saw tools and weapons that had not evolved beyond the Stone Age yet were well adapted to the northern subsistence lifestyle. Food was sufficient. The visitors recognized widely varying Native life ways attuned to land and sea. Anthropologist Ernest S. Burch, Jr., describes the precontact population of Alaska as divided into nations or countries:

> These nations were tiny ones in terms of population, but they were nonetheless just as distinct from one another as Israel and Syria, or as Germany and Austria, are today. Each of these nations had dominion over a clearly delimited territory, and each of them was comprised of a clearly defined citizenry. . . .
>
> The tiny nations of Native Alaska had their great leaders and their villains, and their triumphs and tragedies, just as the great nations of Europe and Asia had theirs. The citizens of these tiny nations could and did engage in international intrigue and in war. . . . Most of the countries that are known to us endured for at least several generations, and probably much longer, which is a reasonably respectable span of time even by twentieth-century standards of national longevity. Technically, one should speak in the plural—of Alaska Native histories, not of Alaska Native history—for each of these nations had its own.[5]

The Alaska Native heritage has, in many respects, been transformed into a collective memory of a golden age. Wars between tribes and bands, slavery and death for the defeated, starvation, disease, and pestilence are deemphasized in the retelling of precontact Native history. The positive recollection of the past helped Natives survive two centuries of contact with Western civilization, which decimated populations and destroyed communal livelihoods. Today Alaska Native traditions survive as much more than costumes and weapons preserved in glass museum cases. Unlike many other Native American groups in the United States, Alaska Natives enjoy an enduring heritage. It lives on in the languages, the village communities, the artwork, the subsistence economies, and the views of nature and society so unlike those of the non-Native majority.

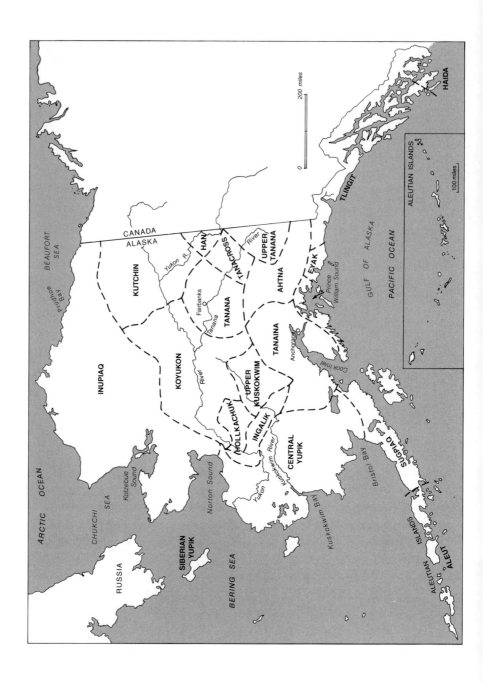

Map 3. Native Peoples and Languages of Alaska

RUSSIAN COLONIZATION

Most Native North and South Americans first glimpsed Europeans in the sixteenth and seventeenth centuries, during the age of exploration and empire building led first by Spain and Portugal, then by England and France. It was also an era of mercantilism in international economic relations. The dominant principle of exploration was to enrich the mother country by exploiting all sources of wealth, especially precious metals, within the colony.

For obvious reasons of distance and climate, the globe's polar regions were among the last to attract Europeans. Also, the eighteenth-century development of free-trade principles temporarily reduced the competition of nation-states for colonial real estate. The resources of non-Western areas appeared likely to be made equally available to all trading nations.

Thus Alaska Natives lived undisturbed until imperial Russia's interest in North American expansion was piqued. While European states busily established domains in the Americas and Asia, the Russian giant underwent domestic reforms in Tsar Peter the Great's modernization program, fought wars with neighboring nations, and populated the Siberian land mass. Not until late in Peter's reign (1682–1725) did interest coincide with opportunity for expansion to North America.

The person who deserves the most credit for "discovering" Alaska is Vitus Bering, a Danish seafarer in Russian service. Shortly before Tsar Peter died, he commissioned Bering to go to Kamchatka, a peninsula in eastern Siberia, and from there to sail to America.[6] Bering's orders were to determine if the continents were joined and if European settlements existed in northwestern North America. He was also to claim the land for Russia. Bering's first voyage on the *Gabriel* in 1728 carried him through the strait that now bears his name and brought him within sight of Saint Lawrence Island. Poor weather forced him to return to Russia. During a second, larger expedition of two ships, Bering sighted most of the Aleutian islands and sailed as far as Kayak island. The commander of the other ship, Aleksei Chirikov, reached what is thought to have been Prince of Wales Island in the Alexander Archipelago on July 15, 1741.[7] On the way back to Kamchatka, Bering's ship was wrecked. Bering and many of his crew died of scurvy, a painful and debilitating tissue disease caused by lack of fresh fruits and vegetables.[8] The spot of land east of Kamchatka where the daring explorer died and where surviving members of his crew spent the winter is now known as Bering Island.

Some survivors of Bering's expedition brought back sea otter pelts collected on the island. The furs found a ready market in China and were bartered for Chinese goods. Russia began to lay claim to Alaska as a seemingly inexhaustible source of valuable furs.

Within four decades, explorers of other nations reached Alaska. Spaniards made four expeditions north to Alaska from Mexico and California and named the port towns of Cordova and Valdez. British Captain James Çook sailed northward in 1776 and mapped the Alaska coast. Meanwhile, the British established a market in Canton, China, for Alaska otter pelts. In the late 1780s, one French and several American ships explored Alaska waters.[9] It was imperial Russia, however, that founded the first European settlements in Alaska and created the Russian-American Company for exploiting Alaska's fur resources.

During the early years of Russian activity in Alaska (1743–90), small companies of traders claimed harbors in the Aleutian islands of Unalaska and the Pribilofs and in the islands of southcentral Alaska. The fur merchant Grigory Ivanovich Shelikhov established the first permanent settlement at Three Saints Bay on Kodiak Island in 1784. By all accounts, he was a flamboyant character. A self-made capitalist and consummate storyteller, he claimed not only to have discovered Kodiak Island, but to have converted every Native there to the Russian Orthodox faith.[10]

While pursuing the fur trade, Russian merchants smoothed the way for colonization of Alaska. They charted the waters, built settlements in rough wilderness, and established relations of a sort with Natives in the area. The fur hunters, called *promyshlenniki* in Russian, were unregulated. Descended from the Cossacks, they were a restless, free-roaming people who had conquered Siberia for the Russians. In Alaska, they conquered the Aleuts. The early fur hunters were particularly rapacious: "Each vessel would locate an island, winter on it, kill off all the animals, and return in spring. As for what they did to the people on the islands, 'God was high in His heaven and the tzar far away.'"[11] The hunters forced Aleut men to hunt sea otters and build dwellings. After a time, the women were willing to sleep with the Russians through the winter in exchange for a few pieces of iron, which Aleuts considered a most precious metal.[12] Liaisons that were formed for the sake of convenience and pleasure became a foundation for the settlement of Russian America. "The hunters took mates because the women were as essential to domestic economy as they were pleasant for creature comforts. No male fingers were capable of doing the intricate sewing necessary to make waterproof mukluks, seagoing kamleikas, or the extraordinary feather parkas."[13]

From the Russian-Aleut pairings issued a growing creole population, and it was these children and resulting family relationships that kept many a restless Russian in Alaska. Shelikhov had decreed that no mixed-blood children could be taken to Russia. According to Aleut law, a child belonged to its mother, not its father, and taking a child by force to Russia would cause great anger among the Natives.[14] Despite the love of many Russians for their half-Aleut offspring, however, the opportunistic behavior of the traders and hunters in general, coupled with European ailments such as smallpox, measles, and venereal disease, may have reduced the Aleut population by as much as 80 percent.[15]

In the 1790s, the first Russian Orthodox priests traveled to Alaska to convert the Natives. They quickly "saved" the ones who lived in the Aleutian Islands; later they collected the souls of many along the Yukon River. One distinguished and highly regarded priest was Father Ivan Veniaminov. He arrived on the Aleutians in 1824 and immediately set about learning the Aleut language. He devised an alphabet, wrote a grammar, and translated several Orthodox religious texts into Aleut. Veniaminov also founded a school to teach Aleuts practical skills such as carpentry and metalwork. For the benefit of posterity, he left behind astute observations of volcanoes, meteorology, and the Aleut culture.[16]

Although the first trading companies were small, by the 1780s a few large partnerships dominated the trade. They experienced serious difficulties with food supply, disease, and management of restive traders and Native populations. After 1785, British and American competition depleted the supply of furs, prompting Shelikhov to seek the intervention of Empress Catherine II in 1788. Catherine, a free trader and fearful of drawing European attention to Russia's northern North American activities, declined to charter the monopoly Shelikhov requested.[17] A decade later, Shelikhov's son-in-law and successor, Count Nikolai Rezanov, obtained a trading monopoly from the new tsar, Paul I.

The Russian-American Company modeled itself on the successful British East India Company. Chartered in 1799, it held a royal monopoly on all fur trade within areas explored by Russians in North America. The company was both a business corporation and a government. Its mission was to increase profit from the fur trade for the benefit of shareholders, who were primarily officials of the regime. As the agent of the Russian state, it also bore responsibility for the security of the trade. The company was empowered to assume authority over all Russian settlements north of 55 degrees latitude. It was also obliged to expand colonization, further trade with adjoining states, and make Natives loyal subjects of the tsar and faithful members of the Orthodox Church.[18]

The third manager of the Russian-American Company and the most significant actor in the Russian colonization of Alaska was Alexander Baranov. In 1790, Baranov was persuaded by Shelikhov to manage his company in Alaska; when Shelikhov's firm became one of the bases for the Russian-American Company, Baranov stayed on. For more than a generation, Baranov stabilized the trade and brought home profits for his employers. He maintained secure fortifications and made New Archangel (Sitka) the capital of Russian America. He negotiated with British and American suppliers to provision settlements. Diverging from the policies of his predecessors, Baranov treated the Aleuts in a comparatively enlightened manner, curbing the most egregious depredations of the Russian traders and diverting some money to Native health and welfare. He conducted limited warfare with the Tlingits, who resisted Russian settlement.

Baranov abolished gambling, forbade prostitution, and encouraged baptism of the offspring of Russian-Aleut unions. He did not allow anyone to distill alcohol but kept a vat of crabapples, rye meal, and cranberries fermenting with yeast. Off-duty men could help themselves to as much as they wanted. He valued discipline and hard work, but he also encouraged merrymaking and dancing.[19] Not universally loved, Baranov survived several assassination plots, some hatched by his own men and priests.

After more than two decades of service, Baranov was named colonial governor of Alaska and granted stock in the Russian-American Company. When his wife died in Russia after twenty-five years of separation, Baranov was relieved, for now he could take his chiidren by his Native "wife," Anna Grigoryevna, to Russia. He asked an official of the Russian-American Company to secure from the tsar a special decree legitimizing the children, Antipatr and Irina. The document also bestowed on Anna the title "Princess of Kenai."[20]

Baranov was stubborn and a hard taskmaster but roughly democratic in dealing with company employees. His age and declining vigor, deficits in the company's accounts, and criticism of his management style led to his forced retirement in 1818.[21] At the time Baranov left, the Russian-America Company's worth was estimated at 7 million gold rubles, up 5.8 million in twenty-one years. Net profit for the year 1816–17 alone was close to 1.25 million rubles.[22] Baranov himself was motivated neither by money nor power; he had given most of his earnings away over the years. He died an impoverished and broken man on the Indonesian island of Java while trying to return to Russia.

The fact that Baranov's successors were naval officers reflected a major change in company policy. The wanton hunting of sea otters had depleted the species, making company operations less profitable. The navy wanted to pay more attention to protecting Russian interests in the Pacific than to challenges from other powers.

The French Revolution and the Napoleonic Wars temporarily interrupted Russian and European interest in the North Pacific. Cessation of hostilities brought a spurt of British and American ships and traders who increasingly profited from the Alaska fur market. On land, the British-chartered Hudson's Bay Company, with its network of forts and sophisticated agents, arrived at the southern boundaries of Russian America by 1833. The Russian-American Company reached an accommodation with the Hudson's Bay Company in 1839. It acknowledged the trading rights of the latter in territory claimed by Russia in exchange for nominal payments and supplies of food and manufactured goods.[23]

Russian naval officers instituted several operating changes during their stewardship of the company. Fur depletion prompted an interest in exploration, so they established posts as far north as Unalakleet and at Nulato in the Interior. Several governors, notably Baron Ferdinand von Wrangell, supported expeditions to conduct scientific studies. Increasingly, creoles comprised the bulk of the labor force; by 1860, they outnumbered Russians three to one. The Aleuts acculturated partially and received less arbitrary treatment. Relations with the Tlingits improved. Social changes such as new housing, clinics, and schools, including church schools for Natives, eased the hardships of life in New Archangel, Kodiak, and Unalaska.[24] Yet the fur trade continued to decline; the company neared bankruptcy as the tsar signed its third charter in 1844. Other enterprises, namely coal mining and some gold and mica mining, failed to reduce the government subsidies needed to support Russia's American possessions. Grand Duke Constantine, brother of Tsar Alexander II, spoke for many imperial advisers when he said that Alaska was "a luxury that Russia could not afford."[25]

Three midcentury events led Russia to sell its American possession. First, the country lost the Crimean War, a grueling conflict that drained the imperial treasury and shifted the European balance of power against the tsarist state. Russia needed a major modernization program to regain its strength. Second, conflict within China occurred in concert with changing fashions and the decline of the furbearing animal population, destroying the fur market while simultaneously creating new opportunities for Russian expansion into Asia. Third, heeding the trumpet call of "manifest destiny," the new American republic moved west. The Civil War delayed the march somewhat; after it ended, the idea of expanding into Alaska began to take root.

These movements within Russia and America, as well as changes in the international configuration of power, culminated in the sale of Alaska to the United States in 1867 for $7.2 million, roughly two cents an acre. The tsar and his officials were eager to rid themselves of their costly North American possession, which they could not defend and from which they believed they would gain few benefits. U.S. Secretary of State William Henry Seward was a visionary who sought a strong role for his country in the Pacific and Asia.[26] He and other American expansionists saw an opportunity to gain a large strategic territory at a reasonable cost and, at the same time, to solidify good relations with Russia.

U.S. COLONIAL RULE: 1867–1912

A company of U.S. soldiers accepted Russia's cession of Alaska to the United States on October 18, 1867. As the Stars and Stripes unfurled over the Sitka fort, the Russian governor's wife swooned, a fitting touch of melodrama in a largely symbolic event.[27]

For more than a year, Congress dithered over the Treaty of Cession and over paying the $7.2 million bill. Partly, lawmakers remained ignorant of Alaska's land and resources, and they lacked interest in a possession so remote and cold. Their attitude explains the sloganeering of the time against "Seward's icebox" and "Seward's folly." Much was actually known about Alaska, however, and most newspapers supported acquisition. Congress delayed paying Russia for the land primarily because of far more pressing concerns: southern Reconstruction after the Civil War and impeachment proceedings against President Andrew Johnson.

Few settlements existed for the United States to occupy in Alaska. Russia left only five inhabited towns, with fewer than seven hundred non-Native inhabitants, most of whom departed quickly following the sale. In the first fifteen years of American rule, fewer than three thousand Americans migrated to Alaska. As far as the rest of the country was concerned, no compelling reason arose to defend the area and provide it with law. A few hundred soldiers guarded the colony for the first ten years. When the army left to fight the Nez Perce Indians in the Pacific Northwest, a customs collector was left in charge. The only U.S. laws extended to Alaska concerned commerce, navigation, and prohibition of liquor sales and imports.[28]

Residents of Sitka in 1879 called on the United States for help because

they feared another massacre such as the uprising seventy-seven years earlier, when Tlingit warriors killed almost fifty Russian and Aleut men, captured the women, and tossed their babies into the sea.[29] When the navy dal-
lied over sending assistance, Sitka residents appealed to the British for
protection. The U.S. Navy vessel arrived several months after a British war-
ship.

In the 1860s and 1870s, few resources attracted migrants to Alaska. The
sea otter trade had crashed; the Alaska Commercial Company was taking
only a modest number of seals from the Pribilofs, where it occupied former
Hudson's Bay Company posts. Commercial salmon fishing was a localized
enterprise in Sitka and Klawock. The timber industry produced only enough
for local needs. Placer mining was also conducted on a small scale.[30]

Two developments soon changed this picture. First, during the 1860s and
1870s, Alaska became more accessible. Steam-powered ships made navigation significantly more rapid and reliable. Improvements in communication,
particularly telegraph lines and the first transoceanic cables, narrowed the
gap between Alaska and populated areas of the country.

Second, and most important, a series of large mineral finds inaugurated
the first Alaska gold rush. Russians had discovered gold but had kept its
small-scale mining a secret. When miners Joe Juneau and Richard Harris
found surface gold deposits near the Gastineau Channel in 1880, American
newspapers spread the news nationwide and precipitated a stampede. The
new town of Juneau had 1,250 inhabitants by 1890. Within six years of the
Juneau discovery, miners found large gold deposits on the Forty Mile River,
a Yukon tributary in Alaska. Then, in 1893, a large discovery was made in
the Birch Creek area of the Yukon Territory.

From fewer than seven hundred settlers in 1867, the population boomed
more than tenfold to eight thousand in 1890. The explosion of the settler population without a corresponding network of government services created
tension and conflict. Settlers resorted to "miners' law" to protect claim stak-
ing and mete out rough frontier justice. Miners petitioned Congress, sending
a delegate in 1881. Media hype about the gold rush vented complaints about
lawless conditions. Congress responded by passing the Organic Act of 1884,
a temporary, simple, and cheap way to end military rule and institute civil
government.[31] The legislation made Alaska a federal "district," a limbo between colonial and territorial status; it provided for the presidential appointment of a governor, a district court judge, and a tiny law-enforcement staff;
and it extended the laws of Oregon, then the closest state to Alaska (Washington was still a territory), to the district. Like the Treaty of Cession, the

First Organic Act recognized Native rights to land they occupied "from time immemorial" but left the disposition of these rights to a future Congress.

The great Klondike and Nome gold strikes tested the effectiveness of the Organic Act. In 1896, gold was discovered in the Klondike of Canada's Yukon Territory. Skagway boomed, escalating into Alaska's largest city as miners from around the world sailed to the head of the Lynn Canal and then hauled their gear over the Chilkoot Pass to the gold fields.

Alaska's gold-rush towns were communities of chaos in which the strongest force prevailed. The Soapy Smith gang ran Skagway in the 1890s. In the absence of government authority, the gang assessed its own "taxes" on residents and visitors, expropriating all the wealth it could uncover. One scam was to urge newcomers to send telegrams to relatives on arrival and then bill them five dollars in advance for return messages sent collect (Skagway had no telegraph line).[32] Although Jefferson Randolph "Soapy" Smith played the role of paterfamilias and dispensed patronage liberally, he was more crook than custodian. The gang leader died in an Old West–style shootout in 1898. A member of a vigilante task force whose goal was to "clean up" Skagway shot Soapy through the heart at the same instant the outlaw's gun fired. Smith died instantly; his nemesis, Frank Reid, lingered for an agonizing few days.[33]

The discovery of gold on Nome's beaches drew nearly twenty thousand miners to the Seward Peninsula gold rush of 1898–99. Within a year, the town filled up with con men, gamblers, pimps, and prostitutes. Several instances of claim jumping occurred, no doubt encouraged by the general atmosphere of lawlessness. Both the judge of the Second Judicial District, Arthur Noyes, and the administrator of mines, Alexander McKenzie, president of the Alaska Gold Company, were corrupt. They falsified mining deeds and switched claims; then they hired men to work the mines, saving most of the profits for themselves. Two U.S. senators and President William McKinley supported Noyes and McKenzie, a situation that impeded their eventual removal and reduced their penalties to slaps on the wrist.[34]

The Dawson and Nome gold strikes made front-page news across the nation, airing the adversities of mining as well as Alaska's political problems. Congress responded with legislation modifying the First Organic Act. Lawmakers extended the Homestead Act to Alaska in 1898. The following year, they revised the Oregon code on criminal procedures to better fit Alaska conditions. In addition, they levied taxes on businesses, including canneries. Then, in 1900, Congress adopted a civil code, added two judicial districts to accommodate the doubling in population that resulted from the gold rush, and moved the capital from Sitka to Juneau. Finally, it provided for the incorporation of towns and permitted property taxes, limiting the rate to 1 percent and prohibiting borrowing.[35] Five years later, the Nelson Act established schools for Native Alaskans while directing license fees outside towns to road building, care of the insane, and education. Then, in direct response to pressures from Alaskans who demanded representation along with their taxation, Congress in 1906 granted Alaska the right to send a nonvoting delegate to Congress.

Creation of a delegate's post was critical to the development of home rule for Alaska. The first two delegates were forgettable; the third was the charismatic James Wickersham, former Alaska district court judge.

Wickersham first gained notice by his campaigns against the Alaska Syndicate. In 1906, the international banking house of J. P. Morgan & Co., with the Guggenheim brothers, formed the partnership. It owned rich copper mines in the Chitina Valley and controlled the Northwestern Commercial Company, which owned the Alaska Steamship Company and Northwest Fisheries, an association of twelve of the largest salmon canneries in Alaska. In describing Wickersham's attack on this "corporate octopus," Evangeline Atwood comments: "Alaska became a *cause célèbre* in the national controversy between those who were convinced that corporate greed would gobble up the natural resources which rightfully belonged to all Americans and those who believed that the American economy was based on private enterprise and that outlawing private investors was tantamount to socialism."[36]

Upon his election, Wickersham lobbied for Alaska interests; he fought tirelessly for an elected territorial legislature and mine inspection laws. Wickersham eventually won a measure of home rule for Alaska in the passage of the Organic Act of 1912, known as the Second Organic Act.

Along with a record of integrity and diligence on Alaska's behalf, Wickersham left behind a legacy of colorful anecdotes about his life and career. In his early years in Alaska, dispensing justice on the frontier often required resourcefulness. Once, when he was on his way to hold court in Rampart and Circle City, his riverboat grounded on a sandbar. Wickersham secured another ride for himself and his family but left several old men who had been called for jury duty aboard the stranded boat. Wickersham asked a deputy marshal to take a basket of food to the men and at the last minute suggested including a bottle of whiskey to ward off the chill. When filling out the paperwork sometime later, the deputy marshal asked how he should itemize the whiskey in the account book. The judge suggested listing it under "subsistence." The deputy's receipt to the Justice Department therefore read, "Basket of food, $10; one bottle of subsistence, $5." The marshal's office communicated with the Justice Department for more than two years and was never reimbursed for that item.[37]

Not all the stories about Wickersham make such light reading. When he was thirty-one and still a judge in Tacoma, he had an affair with a nineteen-year-old woman while his wife was out of town. The woman, Sadie Brantner, later accused him of seducing her. A lurid trial ensued; the jury returned a guilty verdict, but the case was dismissed because Brantner kept changing her story. The furor never completely died down. Wickersham's enemies revived it during each political campaign, even in his last one in 1930 when the judge was seventy-three years old.[38]

THE TERRITORIAL ERA: 1912–1958

Alaskans looked to the establishment of territorial government to give them the means to govern themselves independently and proceed with the fast, orderly development of resources. They gained some rights of citizenship but could not vote in federal elections. Alaskans could elect their own legislators, who met in biennial sessions in the new capital of Juneau, but the body lacked independent fiscal authority.

In a flurry of activity at the first session in 1913, the territorial legislature proclaimed its autonomy. It gave women the right to vote; developed labor legislation, such as the eight-hour day and regulation of mining conditions; granted aid to schools and set up a territorial board of education; and expanded the self-government rights of some Native villages.

In the opinion of critics, however, territorial status did not significantly enhance the self-governing abilities of Alaskans. They were correct in that the federal government had a history of treating territories shabbily. Like other former colonies, Alaska's lawmaking powers were circumscribed by Congress, which could veto any legislative act. America's formation of new states and its expanded involvement in world affairs after the Spanish-American War of 1898 limited federal scrutiny of Alaska.

The critics proved doubly right in their assessment of the unique obstacles erected to self-rule in Alaska. The people lacked the right to elect their territorial governor. Alaska had no judiciary of its own to handle conflict in the territory or its localities. All courts were federal. The congressional "Alaska lobby" of mining and fishing interests added a clause to legislation forbidding the territorial legislature any jurisdiction over fish and game and over settlement and management of Alaska lands. The territory was also denied the power to set up county governments, borrow money, or raise taxes on property.

The first three decades of territorial government did bring some federal actions to aid the development of Alaska's resources and infrastructure. Nevertheless, Alaskans felt frustrated about the lack of assistance for meeting their basic needs. Local and territorial governments showed signs of both initiative and foot-dragging.

Resource development issues illustrate the vacillations in policy. Commercial fishing boomed during the early decades of the twentieth century. Operated by nonresidents and owned by Outside investors, canneries and fishing fleets failed to manage the fisheries prudently, however. The resource began to fall off by the 1930s; the salmon pack peaked in 1936.[39] Absentee fishing interests strongly opposed government regulation of fish traps. These huge log-pole and net constructions trapped large numbers of fish near the mouths of salmon-spawning streams and threatened to deplete the runs. Congress sidestepped the controversy by developing a hatchery program and providing authority to limit fishing in territorial waters.[40]

Federal mining laws directly aided gold and silver mining, as well as copper mining; by the 1920s, copper production rivaled the output of gold. When the gold rushes ended, mining declined, leaving only a few small-scale placer operations and a handful of large dredging operations. President Franklin D. Roosevelt's decision to devalue the dollar in 1934 raised the price of gold and increased its production.

Historically, Alaskans have complained about the high price of goods and the lack of locally grown cereals and vegetables. Local and territorial initiative, however, yielded little agricultural development. It was the federal government that, in a twist of New Deal Works Progress Administration programs, founded the Matanuska Valley farming colony near Anchorage in the mid-1930s. The government recruited 201 welfare recipients and their families from northern states and provided them with cheap land, loans to purchase equipment and supplies, and a new community infrastructure.[41] Some failed and departed, but the colony emerged as a qualified success. Fifteen years later, one-third of the original colonists remained in the area; many who left found jobs in other parts of Alaska.

Development of an economic and social infrastructure came just as haltingly during the first three decades of quasi–home rule. The territorial government constructed fewer than twenty-five hundred miles of road and only one that went any distance: a dirt and gravel track from Fairbanks to Valdez, now a paved highway named after Major Wilds P. Richardson, the first head of the Alaska Road Commission. The federal government made the territorial era's first change in transportation when Congress authorized construction of the Alaska Railroad.

The Alaska Railroad represented the last gasp of the transcontinental railroad-building movement. Progressive reactions to railroad barons made government construction and operation of an Alaska line less controversial by the second decade of the twentieth century. A reformist president, Woodrow Wilson, first called for construction of the railroad from interior Alaska to Seward to foster development of Alaska's resources.

Work on the railroad began in 1915, but construction difficulties and funding delays from Congress postponed completion until 1923. Railroad construction brought an economic boom to the state, employing forty-five hundred workers at the peak of activity. Anchorage, the territory's largest city by World War II, was only a construction site when work began.[42] It became the headquarters of the Alaska Engineering Commission, which built a complete town, including utility services and schools. The first president of the United States to visit Alaska was Warren G. Harding, who traveled from Anchorage to Fairbanks by train in 1923; he also hammered in the last spike on the line. Harding became ill on the return trip and died soon afterward. In the long run, building the railroad did not spur development.

The air age brought greater improvements in transportation because airplane travel was better adapted to Alaska conditions. In the 1920s and 1930s, places once isolated for most of the year became linked to the outside world. The territorial legislature funded construction of nearly one hundred airfields; the federal government, through airmail contracts, heavily subsidized air transportation to Alaska locations. By World War II, Alaska had "116 times as many planes, which flew 70 times as many miles, carried 23 times as many passengers, carried 1,034 times as much freight and express, and 48 times as much mail as the United States on a per capita basis."[43]

In the area of social services, however, the territorial government remained stingy and behind the times. It provided no health benefits, few welfare supplements, and only minimal education facilities and programs for urban youth. The federal government held responsibility for educating Alaska Natives and providing for their health needs. Federal initiatives during the New Deal brought a blanket of social services, such as relief payments and work programs, including public facility construction employing hundreds of people and the innovative Civilian Conservation Corps program.

Overall, during the three decades of territorial rule leading up to World War II, Alaskans' expectations for economic development and government services were not met. Critics attributed this failure to neglect on the part of the federal government. The charge contains some truth. On balance, however, the federal government did much more for Alaska than its small population warranted.[44]

Territorial and local governments, such as they were, also neglected economic development opportunities. Constrained in their abilities to raise revenues, local governments were not culprits. The fault lay with lawmakers for refusing to take advantage of the territory's tax capacity, a situation that territorial governor Ernest Gruening ended by cajoling and threatening the legislative body into action in 1949. It can be argued that the expectations of Alaskans for the territory's economic development were unrealistically high.[45] The federal role, however, was to increase dramatically during and after World War II.

Alaska's strategic significance was a factor lurking in the background of discussion at the time of purchase. Its geography became key with the onset of the air age and Japan's increasingly aggressive behavior in Asia. These developments made Alaska the geopolitical prize of the United States, prompting air-power advocate Brigadier General William "Billy" Mitchell to say, "[He] who holds Alaska will hold the world."[46] The Japanese invasion of Pearl Harbor on December 7, 1941, suggested that his words were true.

By the early 1940s, military planners for America's Pacific campaign had sketched a large role for Alaska. The army built new air bases near Fairbanks and Anchorage. Naval bases and air stations were constructed in Kodiak, Sitka, and Dutch Harbor in the eastern Aleutians.

To supply the military and create a logistical chain of defense for landing fields, the U.S. Army built the Alaska-Canada Highway. Known informally as the "Alcan," the Alaska Highway was the first road connecting the territory to the contiguous forty-eight states. During a nine-month period in 1942, thousands of soldiers and civilian employees carved fourteen hundred miles of road from the brush and tundra. Cursed for its potholes and praised for its beauty, the highway—now modern and paved—remains the only direct land route to Alaska.

Military commanders used Alaska's bases principally as staging areas for the Pacific campaign. Alaska was the delivery route for aircraft and destroyers that the United States sent to the Soviet Union under lend-lease programs. Its role became defensive in 1942 when Japanese planes attacked Dutch Harbor and troops occupied Attu and Kiska, two small islands in the western Aleutians. Although a sideshow to the main battles of Midway and the Marshall Islands, the invasion represented the first hostile landing in the

United States since the War of 1812. Roughly five hundred thousand men—American, Canadian, Russian, and Japanese—took part in the fifteen-month Aleutian campaign. Historians estimate that close to ten thousand were killed in land, sea, and air battles. The campaign, described by one author as "one of the toughest of World War II," provided the United States with its first theater-wide victory.[47]

After an expensive battle in 1943, U.S. forces retook Attu; the Japanese evacuated Kiska before American soldiers arrived. The U.S. military forcibly evacuated Aleuts from the western Aleutians for the duration of the war, an action for which the Aleuts have only recently received government compensation.

Through wartime planning, mobilization, and action, Alaska's military population peaked at 152,000 in 1943 and then declined to 60,000 at the conclusion of hostilities in 1945. The territory's civilian population increased by 50 percent, reaching 112,000 in 1950. From 1941 through 1945, the federal government spent over $1 billion in Alaska. Benefits to the territory included modernization of the Alaska Railroad as well as expansions of roads, airfields, and harbors.[48]

Japan's defeat did not curtail federal military spending in Alaska. The state of the cold war in 1947 brought new growth in the military presence. The federal government constructed a huge air force base at Eielson, south of Fairbanks, for long-range bombers. It expanded other defense facilities: Fort Richardson Army Base and Elmendorf Air Force Base near Anchorage, Fort Greely near Delta, and outposts on the islands of Kodiak, Adak, and Shemya. In 1952, construction began on the distant early warning (DEW-line) system along the northern Canada and Alaska coasts to detect hostile strategic bombers. By the late 1950s, work was completed on a Ballistic Missile Early Warning (BMEW) site at Clear, developed in response to the threat of intercontinental ballistic missiles. Not until the mid-1950 did military spending begin to decline from its peak of $513 million in 1953. By then, the statehood campaign was well under way, with strong national allies helping to ease Alaska's entry into the Union.

Historians point to several dates as the beginning of the Alaska statehood movement. As early as 1914, territorial legislators campaigned for changes in the Organic Act and for statehood. In 1916, delegate Wickersham submitted the first bill to Congress on statehood. On his visit to Alaska in 1923, President Harding said that Alaska was destined for ultimate statehood. But for two decades, the call met with indifference from federal bureaucrats and members of Congress.

World War II shattered the passivity of America's political elite regarding Alaska; its strategic importance was by then universally recognized. By the end of the war, the population had risen to 138,000 and the economy had been diversified somewhat. Consequently, a reasonable case could be made for statehood. In the 1940s, the statehood campaign began in earnest.

Anthony J. Dimond, Alaska's delegate to Congress from 1933 to 1944, introduced the first serious statehood bill in 1943. His successor one year later, E. L. "Bob" Bartlett, advocated it even more strongly. First, however, support had to be solidified within Alaska. Territorial governor Ernest Gruening proposed an information campaign and territorial referendum. A private group commissioned journalist George Sundborg to write a pamphlet entitled "Statehood for Alaska," which presented a persuasive case. In 1946, by a three-to-two vote in a territorial referendum, Alaskans supported the concept.[49] From 1946 until the attainment of statehood in 1959, the territorial legislature consistently called on Congress to grant Alaska first-class status.

The relevant federal department, Interior, expressed support for statehood in 1945. Public opinion nationwide advocated it as well, as a 1946 Gallup poll indicated. Favorable hearings took place in the U.S. House in 1948. A year later, the territorial legislature reformed Alaska's tax laws; it instituted an income tax that later proved influential to the campaign.[50]

Also in 1949, the legislature formed the Alaska Statehood Committee. Its objective was to ignite both territorial and national support for the idea of Alaska statehood and to gather assistance for the transition. The chairman of the committee was Robert Atwood, publisher of the territory's largest newspaper, the *Anchorage Times*. In March 1950, the U.S. House of Representatives passed an Alaska statehood bill, but movement stalled at that point. The Korean War pushed the statehood campaign to a back burner.

Three unresolved issues remained. First was the statehood land grant. Bills in Congress specified that grants limited to 20 to 45 million acres be accomplished by the traditional method of selecting specific townships. This scheme would have scattered state holdings throughout Alaska in a patchwork pattern. Second came the institutional question of the U.S. Senate. With Democrats and Republicans nearly evenly divided, the prospect of admitting any new state was alarming. Because Alaska had voted Democratic since the 1932 presidential election, Republicans and conservative Democrats, who correctly saw the 1950s as pivotal years for civil rights legislation, felt threatened. Any change in the partisan lineup could affect cloture votes on civil rights bills. The third issue, which encompassed the first two, was preparedness. No territory had been admitted to statehood since 1912, and Congress had raised the ante by requiring more stringent justification for membership in the Union.

At this time, leaders of the statehood campaign struck a new strategy: they would write a state constitution and hold an election both to ratify the document and to elect two senators and a representative to Congress. Called the Tennessee Plan, this scheme was the means Tennessee and several other territories had used to gain statehood.

The territorial legislature appropriated funds for a constitutional convention, designed voting rules to select delegates, and chose the University of Alaska in Fairbanks as the site for the seventy-five-day session from November 1955 through February 1956. With assistance from the Public Administration Service and advice from several consultants familiar with progressive state constitutions, the fifty-five delegates drafted a short, simple, fundamental document. It rectified the problems of the territorial era (described at length in chapter 4), and experts have praised it as a model constitution in its own right.

The newly drafted constitution went on the ballot in October 1956, along with a measure proposing that fish traps be banned. The constitution passed with a vote of 17,447 to 8,180; opponents of fish traps won 21,285 votes, while supporters garnered only 4,004.[51]

In the same election, voters selected Ernest Gruening and William A. Egan as designees to the U.S. Senate and Ralph Rivers as designee to the House of Representatives. The three Democrats immediately went to Washington, D.C., and lobbied Congress for statehood.

By 1954, the size and nature of the Alaska statehood land grant had been resolved. A new formula was to be applied to Alaska, recognizing its need for state land to spur development without a rigid observance of section lines. Hawaii's statehood campaign suggested that the issue of party balance would become moot because that territory had voted Republican in previous elections. The issue of political maturity was completely resolved. By the time the House voted again in 1958, the margin of support for Alaska statehood had increased. Within a month, the Senate assented. Editorials in the *New York Times, Washington Post, Chicago Sun-Times,* and other papers endorsed statehood, as did many groups, such as the Federation of Women's Clubs, the Jaycees, Kiwanis, and the Veterans of Foreign Wars.[52]

Ultimately, few interests opposed statehood. Mining and fishing groups feared that state government would increase regulation and taxation of economic development activity, but their arguments failed to sway either the

Senate or President Dwight D. Eisenhower. Initially, Eisenhower saw no reason to create a state from a vast and largely unpopulated area whose greatest value, it seemed, was in national defense. Reservations aside, Eisenhower signed the statehood bill in July 1958. Statehood took effect on January 3, 1959.

CONCLUSION

In this chapter, we have summarized the mainstream rendition of Alaska's political history in chronological segments, stressing the highlights of each period. Many historiographers see overarching themes in the history of the land. Some Alaska historians interpret the state's course as having been charted by external helmsmen and point with passion to the years of dependence on the federal government. Others argue that the state's growth depends on external markets for Alaska's resources. A third interpretation pictures Alaska's history as a relentless struggle of individuals to create a new life under adverse conditions. A balanced view of Alaska's past, however, must synthesize elements from each of these approaches, for each helps to explain the present. This conclusion results from a lengthy review of generalizations concerning the role of history in contemporary Alaska.

First, consciousness of the state's past and its effect on the present is segmented. For example, few non-Native Alaskans possess keen awareness of the rich historical traditions of Alaska Natives. Few know the significance of costumes worn by Tlingits, of dance music played by Eskimo drummers, or of potlatches held by Athabaskans. Significantly, few appreciate the value of these traditions to the Alaska Native population. Similarly, although most Alaskans know that Alaska was once a Russian colony and that Alaska Day marks the cession of Alaska to America, few understand the ramifications of the past for modern life. The fact that villagers on the mid-Kuskokwim and western coast celebrate "slavick" (Russian Orthodox Christmas) comes as a surprise to many Alaskans. More recent episodes from the territorial era, such as the Nome gold rush or the Soapy Smith gang in Skagway, stand as matters of local but not statewide interest.

Second, unlike Marylanders, who celebrate more than three hundred fifty years of history as a colony and state, Alaskans emphasize the recency of their state's political development. Indeed, Alaska's history as a U.S. possession, territory, and state spans fewer than one hundred twenty-five years; buildings under seventy-five years old are declared historical monuments. This recency deprives the political process of the restraint found in most other states, where the historical record is replete with failed experiments and incremental successes. History does little to constrain development in Alaska.

Third, although Alaska has been endowed with a natural resource economy, the products of which depend on regional and world market conditions, contemporary Alaskans and their leaders believe the future does not necessarily depend on natural-resource exports. For example, although most economists wax pessimistic about the possibilities of manufacturing in the state, several major efforts have been made to develop value-added processing industries, such as petrochemicals. What most Alaskans wish for—a self-sustaining economic base—has no historical root.

Fourth, notwithstanding massive contributions by the federal government to the state, the popular perception prevails that Alaska has been exploited and discriminated against by the feds. Awareness of the states' traditional role in the federal system is limited. Citizens tend to focus on the drawbacks at the expense of the benefits (discussed in chapter 4).

Fifth, a belief exists that individual Alaskans brought about the achievements in Alaska history while governments (federal, state, and local) were incidental factors or obstacles to progress. This widely held view acts as a powerful constraint on government at both local and state levels. These five generalizations are expressions of the individualist and moralist political cultures, as well as of Alaskans' perception of dependency.

CHAPTER 3

Political Economy: Myths and Realities

Shortly after the wreck of the *Exxon Valdez* spilled eleven million gallons of oil into Prince William Sound, the now-defunct *Anchorage Times* commented editorially on the economic benefits of the clean-up: "Forget for the moment all the reasons behind the big economic surge the state is experiencing these days, and think only about the positive side of the ledger. From a laundry that washes oily protective uniforms worn by beach cleaners to helicopter rentals to booming business in restaurants, hotels, motels and boarding houses, Alaskans are reaping a golden harvest."[1]

Like other places, Alaska achieves economic prosperity at a price. It seems clear that the paychecks and profits that came from cleaning up the spill were not worth the costs of hundreds of miles of oiled shorelines, thousands of dead animals and birds, closures of million-dollar fisheries, and disruption of communities. Much of the clean-up income, moreover, went to out-of-state workers and businesses. Understandably, many Alaskans find talk of the "benefits" of the spill more than a little offensive. Others, however, consider the event yet another instance of fortuitous economic opportunity in the North.

Alaska's political economy is in many respects as accidental and unpredictable as the oil spill. It is built on unusual concentrations of natural resources and on uncertain movements in world commodity markets. It is characterized by conflict between development and environmental values and between resident and nonresident interests. Disparity between political and economic components is another feature of Alaska's political economy: the state has an elaborate system of government and politics but a shallow and tenuous economic base. Finally, because so much of Alaska's land and resources are publicly owned, government policies can wield great influence over economic decision making.

It is difficult for any group of people to conduct political and economic affairs on foundations as shifting and unstable as Alaska's without some kind of reinforcement. To help them deal with the situation, Alaskans have adopted a set of myths about their resources and the forces that affect development. However inaccurate and whatever their distorting effects, myths help Alaskans understand their political and economic condition and suggest some things they might do about it. In this chapter, we discuss the characteristics of Alaska's political economy and the ways that Alaskans have attempted to shape it to their ends, including their use of myths. These myths reflect overarching themes of Alaska's government and politics: the tension between the desire for independence and the reality of dependence, and the search for a stable economy amid unstable conditions.

THE UNCERTAIN ECONOMY

The discovery of North America's largest petroleum reservoir at Prudhoe Bay is the outstanding illustration of Alaska's uncertain economy. Not only was the discovery an improbable event, but its timing was the most bountiful accident that ever happened in Alaska.[2] Atlantic-Richfield Company announced the discovery in 1968, just five years before the energy crisis, the explosion of world oil prices caused by the Arab-Israeli war, and the oil embargo imposed by Arab members of the Organization of Petroleum Exporting Countries (OPEC). Just after the trans-Alaska oil pipeline was completed in 1977, the Iranian revolution, the Iran-Iraq war, and OPEC collaboration again panicked world oil markets, tripling oil prices that were already four to five times higher than their pre-1973 levels.

The stalling for more than five years of trans-Alaska pipeline construction, brought about by Native land claims and environmental obstacles,[3] put an important twist on the confluence of events. At the time, many Alaskans considered the delay to be another conspiracy by outsiders against Alaska's development. Actually, it pushed the peak oil flow into the brief hiatus from 1979 to 1983 when world oil prices skyrocketed, reaching forty dollars per barrel. Consequently, the oil that flowed from Alaska's pipeline in the late 1970s and early 1980s was worth ten to twelve times as much as it would have been before these world upheavals.

The state counted its petroleum revenues in billions rather than millions of dollars during the early 1980s. Oil money spurred huge increases in state spending and, in turn, rapid expansions in the population and economy. Both the economy and politics of Alaska boomed as never before. Another sharp but short-lived increase in oil prices occurred in the fall of 1990, after Iraq invaded Kuwait. Contrary to expert predictions, however, the Persian Gulf War pushed oil prices lower rather than higher, as world markets adjusted quickly to events in the Middle East.

People naturally want to maintain the incomes, public services, and private amenities that an economic boom brings, and they want to increase them if they can. One result of the Prudhoe Bay oil boom was the exacerbation of traditional divisions between the interests of long- and short-term residents. By 1985, when the great Alaska oil boom crested, about half the residents were recent arrivals who had come to the state since the start of pipeline construction in 1974. They were drawn to Alaska because it represented economic opportunity and a chance for a new start in a dynamic frontier region. Most were young; some brought families; many came alone. They were interested first of all in earning as good a living as possible. It was in their short-term interest, therefore, to maintain the economic momentum through continued state spending at the highest possible levels.

This interest was not confined to newcomers. There was widespread popular support for the oil industry in Alaska. Prodevelopment attitudes were, and still are, common.[4] Everyone benefited to some extent from state spending of petroleum wealth. As Governor Bill Sheffield said in his 1983 budget address to the legislature, "Ladies and gentlemen . . . we have enough money to make Alaska a better place for everyone." The legislature felt very much in tune with the governor's sentiments: billions of dollars flowed to municipal governments, school districts, contractors, small and large businesses, state employees, home buyers, students, and others.

Alaska enacted the greatest single distribution of state revenues per capita by any state in the nation's history, a massive transfer of public wealth to a staggering array of public and private purposes. The unprecedented generosity of Alaska's state government astonished Americans throughout the country when the state sent oil-dividend checks of one thousand dollars each to every Alaska resident in 1982.[5]

This large-scale distribution of wealth made state government the focal point of the politics and the economy of Alaska. Lobbyists from all quarters converged on the state capital, overwhelming the government with demands for larger shares of the windfall. When petroleum revenues began to decline in the mid-1980s because of the downturn in world prices, the demands for state action did not abate but grew even more insistent.

State government expanded the size of its budgets and the diversity of its programs. The government lobby of municipalities, school districts, and state and local government employees adopted perhaps a higher profile than the private-sector lobby of oil, construction, banking, business, and labor.

The growth of interest group pressures in the petroleum era unbalanced Alaska's political economy even more than usual.[6] The precariousness of the political structure became increasingly evident in the late 1980s as the reality of falling oil prices cut state petroleum revenues in half, from their 1982 peak of more than $4 billion (see table 1). Dependent on state government spending, nearly half the population was directly threatened by the instability of the base on which the whole economic structure rested.

Despite the near universal participation of Alaskans in the political economy of oil, some people abstained or dissented. Former state legislator Eric Sutcliffe expressed his concerns in an open letter he circulated widely throughout the state at the height of the oil boom: "It would be a lot easier to tolerate the negative aspects of an increasing population base if it was attributable to the actual growth of the economy. For the most part, however, the manner in which the State has spent its billions has had virtually no influence on whether or not a company extracted one more ounce of minerals or one more barrel of oil. True, Alaska has grown, but only in numbers and not in substance."[7]

Earlier many residents of Fairbanks had complained about the effects of the pipeline construction boom in their community. A survey in 1976 reported: "Long-term residents and residents oriented toward a self-reliant, wilderness lifestyle feel that they share a disproportionate amount of the costs of pipeline impact."[8] Many long-term Alaskans made similar observations during the 1980s when they saw another wave of tens of thousands of newcomers. Like those who came during the pipeline boom of the 1970s, the new immigrants sought economic opportunity, only now the boom was powered by state spending instead of construction of a $9-billion pipeline. There was also the incentive of the thousand-dollar checks, which the national media had commented on widely.

TRADITIONAL ECONOMY AND PERSISTENT MYTHS

Alaska's oil boom economy of the 1970s and 1980s played against a backdrop of traditional components: a vacillating and selective national interest in Alaska's resources, unevenness and instability in the pattern of economic growth, and local expectations and fortunes tied to a boom-bust cycle. First

Table 1: State General Fund Revenue Sources in Alaska, Selected Fiscal Years

	1973		1979		1982		1986		1988		1990	
	1990 Dollars	% of Total	1990 Dollars	% of Total	1990 Dollars	% of Total	1990 Dollars	% of Total	1990 Dollars	% of Total	1990 Dollars	% of Total
State												
Petroleum	126	14	1,236	60	4,315	83	2,923	77	2,129	69	2,097	68
Investment Earnings	179	19	89	4	391	8	215	6	145	5	118	4
Federal Grants	330	36	330	16	227	4	326	9	485	16	511	17
Other	287	31	396	19	265	5	319	8	332	11	362	12
Total, General Fund	922	100	2,049	100	5,198	100	3,783	100	3,091	100	3,088	100

Sources: Alaska Department of Revenue, "Revenue Sources"; Alaska Department of Administration, Division of Finance, "Alaska Annual Financial Report."

one, then another, resource attracted attention and was intensively exploited. So rich were the sources of furs, gold, copper, salmon, and finally oil, that developers could profit despite Alaska's high production and transport costs.

Alaska's economy is shaped and limited by the state's distance from markets, extreme climate, and sparse population. Traditionally, however, Alaskans have tended to deny the significance of such natural and structural factors. They have preferred to attribute their economic limitations, frustrations, and misfortunes to conspiratorial forces. Human nature finds it easier to blame one's ills on enemies and call for quick fixes than to understand the complex structures and uncontrollable natural conditions really at work. Alaska's development mythology reflects these realities and illusions.

There are many variations on the mythology, which is a mixture of fact and fantasy. Its persisting features can be described as follows. First, Alaska is a natural resource storehouse. Billions of tons of coal, trillions of cubic feet of gas, and huge deposits of hardrock minerals await exploitation. Second, the best way to ensure the development of these resources is to build "infrastructure," including roads, railroads, ports and harbors, cheap energy sources, and other industrial support. The absence of adequate infrastructure holds back resource development in Alaska. Third, the mythology insists that Alaska's economy can and must be diversified. The economy is overdependent on one or two natural resource exports. It will be diversified when Alaska exports a broader array of its abundant resources and when more processing and manufacturing takes place in the state.

Fourth, says the mythology, government is primarily responsible for opening up the resource storehouse, building infrastructure, and promoting diversification. In the past, only the federal government had the necessary authority and financial resources to accomplish these tasks. Now state government is Alaskans' principal vehicle for economic development because it has the power and the money; what it often lacks is simply the will. Fifth, the mythology holds that while state government is mostly ineffective, it is the federal government that continues to pose the major obstacle to the state's development. Moreover, federal officials often have environmentalist allies who want to stop development. Finally, the development mythology holds that if all else fails, "the big strike" might yet occur. Around the turn of the century, there were strikes in the gold fields of Juneau, Nome, and near Fairbanks. Just before statehood there were strikes in the oil fields of Cook Inlet and the Kenai Peninsula. By far the biggest strike was at Prudhoe Bay in 1968.

The fantasy elements of the development mythology are associated with significant events; they correspond to the real experiences of Alaskans. For this reason, the mythology is a formidable part of Alaska's political culture. The mythology can also be harmful because it diverts attention from economic realities. It substitutes slogans for thought and pins Alaskans' hopes on big strikes or, for some, even on the benefits of otherwise disastrous events, such as the 1964 earthquake and 1989 oil spill, which brought large amounts of public and private money to the state.

THE POLITICAL ECONOMY OF OIL

At the height of the oil boom in 1984, a prominent Anchorage economist and banker, Robert Richards, wrote about "the horrible mess in Juneau." State spending was "out of control" and had "absolutely no rhyme or reason." He pointed out that the spending spree was an especially critical matter "because of the known certain end to the joyride that will occur when Prudhoe Bay revenues subside" around 1990. He predicted that state government would face "a massive fiscal crisis in the early 1990s if a sensible spending, saving, and investment policy is not adopted now." He found, however, that "the legislature, and to a somewhat lesser extent the governor, have ignored this. They are enthusiastically committed to a course of action that not only ignores the future fiscal problem, but indeed exacerbates it. They are behaving like drunken sailors guzzling ever greater quantities of the capital spending elixir, totally ignoring the agonizing hangover which they are creating."[9] Despite Richards's highly charged prose and his unsuccessful race for governor in 1986, most observers of the Alaska economy agreed with him. What Richards and others failed to forecast was the sharp drop in the world market price of oil in the mid-1980s. Thus the crisis arrived earlier and in a milder form than had been predicted.

A Fiscal Trap

A fiscal trap was laid when world oil prices quadrupled between 1979 and 1982 in the wake of the Iranian revolution and OPEC's production restrictions. As noted earlier, these events occurred just as Prudhoe Bay oil reached peak production levels, bringing huge revenues to the state. Between 1978 and 1982, Alaska's petroleum revenues increased by 600 percent, from about $700 million to more than $4 billion.

State government walked into a trap when it followed a policy of unsustainable spending: it was spending nonrecurring revenues from a nonrenewable resource with an unstable price, and it spent most of the revenues available. The largest increases in spending occurred in new and expanded programs of subsidized loans for housing and business, grants and subsidized loans for hydroelectric construction, and capital and operating grants for municipalities and school districts.

The fiscal trap was sprung when the oil shortage turned into an oil glut and prices fell to half their top levels. By the mid-1980s, the state suddenly found itself facing large shortfalls between current spending and projected revenues. At first, lawmakers found it relatively easy to cut capital spending and reduce the new loan programs and generous operating budgets. As the budget required deeper cuts, however, widespread losses of jobs, incomes, businesses, and property occurred. Alaska suffered an economic collapse, as did the other major oil-producing states at about the same time.

Forty thousand more people left Alaska than came to the state during the recession of the late 1980s. The transiency accompanying the 1980s boom was more extensive and more volatile than that of the pipeline boom of the 1970s. During the first half of the decade, the population grew by more than seventy-three thousand, nearly a fifth of Alaska's 1980 population (table 2). More than half these newcomers left the state in the late 1980s.

State government mostly muddled through the budget crisis. As indicated, much nonessential spending could readily be cut. In addition, oil revenues often came in above conservative state projections, and various surplus funds were available to patch up annual budgets. But another crisis loomed on the horizon, and it was one the state could not count on muddling through: a further drop in revenues during the 1990s caused by a fall in oil production as the huge reservoir at Prudhoe Bay approached depletion. According to state projections, oil production will decline by 5 to 8 percent a year during the 1990s until total production is cut in half by the year 2000. State petroleum revenues, already halved by oil price deflation in the 1980s, face another 50 percent cut due to the production decline in the 1990s.[10]

The ultimate impact on Alaska's economy could be devastating. In 1988, petroleum revenues made up 85 percent of state government general funds, and state spending accounted directly and indirectly for about one-third of all public and private jobs and personal income in Alaska. In the southeast region, where state government jobs are concentrated in Juneau, and in the rural Interior, where a market economy scarcely exists, more than 40 percent of economic activity relied on state spending. Many Native villages are much more heavily dependent than that. Even in the railbelt, which comprises the state's richest private economy, state spending supports almost a

Table 2: Migration to and from Alaska, 1980–89

Year (7/1 to 7/1)	Migrants In	Migrants Out	Net Migration
1980–81	46,678	40,884	5,794
1981–82	59,617	39,043	20,574
1982–83	64,087	39,748	24,339
1983–84	57,492	43,466	14,026
1984–85	54,386	45,780	8,606
1985–86	52,951	57,097	–4,146
1986–87	37,685	57,330	–19,645
1987–88	33,909	50,103	–16,194
1988–89	40,716	46,665	–5,949
			39,303

Source: Alaska Department of Labor, Research and Analysis, Demographic Unit, 1990.

third of all economic activity.[11] Removing up to half of petroleum revenues from the Alaska economy could translate into employment and income losses of 10 to 20 percent and more across the state's regions by the end of the 1990s.

The extent of the overall decline depends on several factors: the price of oil, new resource discoveries and developments, and state revenue and expenditure policies. Price increases in response to another possible round of oil shortages in the 1990s will not likely compensate for lost revenues due to the production decline at Prudhoe Bay. Consequently, Alaskans need to look primarily to new resource development as well as fiscal policy responses.

Resource Development

Little or no prospect exists that any resource reservoir equivalent to Prudhoe Bay will be found and developed in Alaska for the next decade or more.[12] In the first place, the Prudhoe Bay field is a "supergiant" field. Its twelve billion recoverable barrels of oil rank it among the rarest of geological occurrences, virtually a one-in-a-million find. There is very little chance that another such discovery will be made in Alaska. There is even less of a chance of finding such a field on state lands, which yield by far the most substantial revenues in the form of bonuses, royalties, and taxes to state government. Discovery of even a "giant" field, with at least one billion recoverable barrels, on state land might only delay the fiscal reckoning by a year or two. That, moreover, requires the further assumption that such a field could be brought into production much faster than the five to ten years normally required to develop remote Arctic oil fields.

The most promising oil field prospect in the 1990s underlies the coastal plain of the Arctic National Wildlife Refuge (ANWR) east of Prudhoe Bay. Geologists estimate that it might hold as much as three to four billion barrels of oil, making it roughly one-third the size of Prudhoe Bay. Because ANWR belongs to the federal government, the state would not receive bonus money or full royalties from oil. Alaska would, however, collect a share of the royalties, severance taxes, and some economic benefits from construction activities. Even optimistic assumptions about ANWR's possibilities, if they came true, would delay the state's fiscal reckoning by only one or two years. In 1992, there was still substantial opposition in Congress to opening ANWR to drilling because of environmental risks and other disagreements about the Bush administration's national energy strategy. At the end of the year, additional obstacles blocked ANWR. In October, Congress passed and President Bush signed a national energy bill from which both ANWR exploration and automobile efficiency standards had been removed. Eliminating these provisions neutralized environmentalist and industry opposition to the bill, clearing the way for passage. In November, Arkansas governor Bill Clinton's election as president cast an additional layer of doubt on prospects for opening ANWR, since Clinton had opposed such a move in his campaign.

More realistic than ANWR or other major developments is the opening of smaller-scale oil fields on the North Slope and in the adjacent Beaufort Sea. Additional oil may be recovered from existing fields by applying advanced technology. Such developments would buy state policy makers some time, but none of this activity is likely to make up for Prudhoe Bay losses.

If not another big strike in oil, what about the rest of Alaska's resource "storehouse," the abundant nonfuel minerals, coal, fish, and timber? What about the growth of tourism as a renewable resource? Unfortunately, Alaskans have been living at a supergiant, Prudhoe Bay level; none of these resources, or any plausible combination of them, can replace Prudhoe Bay oil in Alaska's economy in the 1990s.

Minerals such as the zinc and silver extracted at major world-class mines, including Red Dog in northwest Alaska and Green's Creek in the Southeast, have economic significance on a merely regional or local level. Red Dog and Green's Creek contain unusually large and rich deposits, necessary to develop minerals economically in remote, high-cost Alaska. The mines can generate two hundred to four hundred long-term jobs and can pay annual taxes and royalties of $10 million to $20 million, but this activity is not on the scale of Prudhoe Bay. Many Red Dogs and Green's Creeks would have to be discovered and developed quickly to replace Prudhoe Bay in the state's economy. Moreover, the profitability of these mines depends on mineral prices set in world markets. Mainly because of low silver prices, the Green's Creek mine shut down indefinitely in early 1993, and Red Dog operated at or near break-even because of low zinc and lead prices.

Alaska has billions of tons of low-sulfur coal, but its high water content and remoteness from transport facilities increase production costs. Most of the sub-bituminous coal mined in Alaska is too expensive to compete effectively in export markets with Australian and Pacific Rim products. A small amount, about 1.5 million tons, of the better coal is consumed inside the state and exported every year, a figure that could double in the 1990s. In terms of jobs, incomes, and state revenues, however, coal mining contributes little to the statewide economy. For coal to replace Prudhoe Bay oil in the economy, the current rate of production would have to be stepped up by two thousand to three thousand times.

Alaska is home to some of the world's richest and most productive offshore fisheries, particularly the salmon fisheries of Bristol Bay. Most are already being harvested at or near their sustainable biological yields, but some potential remains for increased onshore processing. Forest products, mainly pulp and unprocessed logs, provide income to small communities in the rain forests of the Southeast but are not of statewide significance.

Tourism is an important Alaska renewable resource industry, and it is growing. This industry brings hundreds of thousands of visitors to the state each year, people who spend money and create jobs. Tourism-related jobs are generally low-wage and seasonal, however, accounting for only about 3 percent of the state's total employment and wages in the late 1980s. In terms of its contribution to the economy as a whole, tourism accounted for less than 1 percent of gross state product (total value of goods and services produced in Alaska).

In general, Alaska's renewable resources can augment only modestly the resident economy in the 1990s.[13] In light of this economic reality, one option left to Alaskans is to make the most of the oil revenues still in their hands. The recent record on this score, however, is not encouraging.[14]

Political Choices: Saving versus Spending

In the spring of 1981, near the end of a rancorous legislative session, the Democratic leadership of the Alaska House of Representatives was overthrown in a late-night coup by a Republican-led coalition (see chapter 7). With the state awash in oil revenues, a legislative coalition of "spenders" replaced the coalition of "savers," and the already high rate of spending shifted into higher gear.

In retrospect, referring to any group of Alaska legislators in the early 1980s as savers may be misleading. As soon as revenues from Prudhoe Bay began to flow into the state treasury, most state legislators, responding to insistent demands from their districts, stood more than ready to appropriate money. All were spenders; some were just bigger spenders than others. In normal times, every legislator wants to bring home the bacon. During the oil boom in Alaska, fattening up their districts was not merely a major objective of legislators, but an obsession.[15]

Throughout the 1970s, the annual capital budget averaged about $130 million (table 3). In 1981, it soared to $1.4 billion, and one year later it peaked at more than $1.8 billion. In just two years, the legislature had committed $7,000 in capital projects for every person in Alaska. Just as suddenly, when oil prices dropped after 1982, capital spending fell sharply. Operating budgets grew at a more even pace, doubling from $1.3 billion in the late 1970s to $2.5 billion in the mid-1980s. As the capital budget took the brunt of the oil price decline of the 1980s, the operating budget leveled off at about $2.3 billion at the end of the decade.

Still, even this moderated level of general expenditures made Alaska by far the highest per capita spender among the states in the late 1980s, according to the Advisory Commission on Intergovernmental Relations (ACIR). Taking into account relative population size, levels of service demand, and labor costs, ACIR calculated that Alaska spent over three times more than its allotted "representative" national share of state expenditures in 1987. (Washington, D.C., ranked a distant second, spending at less than twice its representative level, with Wyoming and New York ranked third and fourth, spending about one-and-a-half times their representative shares.)[16]

Even if the Permanent Fund dividend were removed from ACIR's calculations, Alaska would still rank first among the states in its relative level of spending. That is in part because of other high costs of doing business in the remote North. These expenses include unusually high transportation, construction, and maintenance costs as well as diseconomies of small scale, such as in the delivery of public education to sparsely settled regions. Nevertheless, it is also likely that Alaska state government has ranked particularly high on state spending tables because the money has been there to spend.

The 1981 house coup came about primarily because of the capital budget,

Table 3: State General Fund Appropriations in Alaska, 1971–91
(In Millions of 1990 Dollars)

Fiscal Year	Total Appropriations	Operating Budget	Capital Budget
1971	843.0	733.6	109.4
1972	862.3	780.5	81.8
1973	966.9	817.8	149.1
1974	903.1	876.7	26.5
1975	1114.8	962.1	152.7
1976	1226.6	1116.0	110.6
1977	1345.7	1230.2	115.4
1978	1421.5	1279.6	141.9
1979	1642.5	1365.4	277.1
1980	1591.9	1419.7	172.2
1981	3295.7	1862.1	1433.6
1982	4151.9	2179.5	1972.4
1983	3408.8	2442.9	965.8
1984	3553.3	2459.4	1093.9
1985	4332.2	2551.0	1781.1
1986	3112.9	2506.3	606.6
1987	2631.3	2193.8	437.4
1988	2465.6	2251.3	214.3
1989	2458.5	2314.8	143.7
1990	2352.0	2209.2	142.8
1991	2273.6	2165.3	108.3

Sources: 1971–78, from Oliver Scott Goldsmith, "Sustainable Spending Levels from Alaska State Revenue," Alaska Review of Social and Economic Conditions 20 (February 1983): 21; 1979–89, from State of Alaska, FY 90 Executive Budget; 1990–91, from Alaska Executive Budget Book, FY 1991.

which was where the "free money"—discretionary funds over which legislators exerted the most control—was concentrated. Shortly before the coup, as oil revenues began to mount, legislative leaders initiated what developed into an ingenious scheme for dealing with capital appropriations. The capital budget was split into thirds, with one portion going to the house, one to the senate, and one to the executive. Within the two houses, members received specified amounts of cash to spend in their districts as they saw fit. The legislature dropped even the pretense of systematic budgeting when it eliminated program budget formats because they posed an obstacle to line-item spending decisions.[17] This straightforward pork-barrel approach remained in effect until the mid-1980s, when big capital budgets became unaffordable.

The most constructive fiscal innovation since statehood is the Alaska Permanent Fund. It was created before the state spending boom began, a fact that helps to explain the fund's existence. At the urging of the governor and legislative leaders, voters in 1976 adopted an amendment to the state constitution requiring that 25 percent of petroleum lease bonuses, royalties, and rentals be deposited in the fund and used only for "income-producing investments." Exclusion of severance taxes from the fund meant that only about 10 percent of oil revenues had to be deposited. Fund management policy was left up to the legislature, which established a Permanent Fund Corporation. Subsequent legislation determined that the fund should be conservatively managed as a savings account and that only the earnings, not the principal, could be spent.

By 1993, sound investments by the Permanent Fund Corporation had propelled the principal to more than $15 billion. Savings required by law account for 40 percent of the total, and "inflation proofing," or redeposited earnings, accounts for 25 percent. Surprisingly, 35 percent of the savings stems from special deposits of surplus funds by the legislature during the boom years. Whether lawmakers made the extra deposits because money poured in faster than they could spend it or because the deposits helped to ease their consciences over free spending is unclear. A few legislators, at least, believed in the soundness of saving some of the surplus. In this case, good policy was also good politics, as the Permanent Fund yielded increasing dividend payments to voters.

As of 1992, Permanent Fund earnings have primarily gone toward the annual distribution of dividends ($2.7 billion) and inflation proofing ($2.1 billion). Only a small amount ($236 million) has been transferred to the general fund for use in state government.[18] By now, any proposal to use fund earnings for anything other than dividends and inflation proofing attracts controversy. Politicians who suggest that earnings be used to support state government as oil revenues decline risk being labeled "fund raiders."

The legislature enacted the dividend program in 1980, based on two supporting arguments. First, dividends were considered the most efficient way to deliver the benefits of petroleum development equally to all state citizens. Many advocates of the program also believed that it would provide a way to curb government inefficiency and bureaucratic growth. Second, they argued that dividends would create a popular constituency with a vested interest in protecting the fund from raids on its principal. As indicated, this argument has since been extended to protection of earnings as well.

A third objective of the program was to reward long-term residents over newcomers by linking the size of the dividend to the length of residence.

This goal did not survive a court challenge. Between 1982 and 1989, every Alaska citizen who had lived in the state for at least six months was eligible to receive a dividend. In 1989, the legislature passed a law requiring two years' residence for eligibility, but the courts found this requirement too restrictive, so it was reduced to one year.

State law requires the dedication of half the fund earnings to dividends. In recent years, dividend payments have totaled about a half billion dollars annually, an amount equal to a quarter of the state's annual budget. Individual payments have ranged from eight hundred to one thousand dollars. Dividends often add significantly to individual and especially to family incomes. They have generated a strong sense of "loyalty" to the fund and support for existing policies governing the fund's use.

The same year the legislature enacted the dividend program, it abolished the state individual income tax, making Alaskans the least-taxed citizens in the nation. Local property and sales taxes also were reduced as state government increased revenue sharing and other aid to local governments (see chapter 12). A recent *U.S. News & World Report* article ranked Alaska's tax burden fifty-first, behind all the other states and the District of Columbia. Moreover, the article noted that the gap between Alaska and the fiftieth state greatly exceeded the gap between the fiftieth and first states.[19]

In an effort to keep the state spending machine from overheating, the legislature in a 1981 special session approved a "spending limit," which voters adopted one year later as an amendment to the state constitution. Governor Jay Hammond pushed the legislature hard for the spending limit law. In exchange for lawmakers' approval of the limit, he agreed to the legislature's $1.8 billion capital budget that year. In the 1982 election, he told voters that the limit "may be our last chance to control the juggernaut which otherwise will likely crush us into bankruptcy."[20]

As many had anticipated, the spending limit ended up limiting virtually nothing. Its drafters in the legislature and governor's office set a ceiling of $2.5 billion on appropriations. They also provided for raising the ceiling in response to population growth and inflation, and they allowed for various exceptions to the ceiling. By the time the limit was to go into effect in 1984, however, revenues had already fallen nearly to the level of the ceiling; soon they dropped below it.

To deal with the state's growing fiscal and economic problems, some Alaskans wanted to save more money in the Permanent Fund while others wanted to spend more on infrastructure to diversify the economy. The savers argued that as oil ran out, so would the state's money, and "things were only going to get worse." It would be most prudent, they said, to cut spending, especially for capital projects, and invest more of the oil revenues in a portfolio of securities through the Permanent Fund. By increasing the future earnings of the fund, they asserted, the state would be able to rely on recurring revenues to support state government in the long haul, thereby softening the blow of Prudhoe Bay's inevitable depletion.[21] This approach echoed the main argument behind creation of the Alaska Permanent Fund.

The savers also pointed out that few development projects existed on which the state could usefully spend money. They believed it more sensible to invest in safe securities outside Alaska than in risky ventures within the state. They predicted that the latter "investments" would end up merely being subsidies.[22]

Spenders took the opposite position. They argued that the state should spend money on development inside Alaska, which was the best way to expand Alaska's economic base, provide immediate jobs and incomes, and ensure a viable economy in the future. They pleaded for investments in highways, railroads, dams, ports, harbors, and whatever else might stimulate resource development and production in Alaska. They believed such investments, combined with positive attitudes from business and government leaders, represented the key to Alaska's resource storehouse. Although they did not contest cutbacks in operating budgets, they promoted increased capital spending for industrial infrastructure. They did not necessarily disagree with increasing savings; they simply believed that savings should not come at the expense of necessary capital projects.[23]

Support continues for both these positions inside and outside state government. Generally, the main proponents of the savings approach have been university researchers, consultants, and other advisers to the executive branch and to managers of the Permanent Fund. The chief advocates of the "spending to diversify" approach have been business and civic leaders concentrated in Anchorage. The leading advocacy organization is Commonwealth North, an elite group of businesspeople and civic activists. One of Commonwealth North's founders is Walter Hickel, who, as governor, incorporates the group's aspirations for capital projects as part of his vision of Alaska as an "owner state."

State politicians generally have tried to accommodate as many interests as possible. Consequently, spending has taken precedence over saving. From 1977, the year that Prudhoe Bay oil began to flow through the trans-Alaska pipeline, through 1990, the state took in $33.2 billion in oil revenues. Of this amount, 80 percent, or $26.7 billion, was spent, and 20 percent, or

$6.5 billion, was saved.[24] As oil revenues decline, opportunities for saving also diminish.

Spending has gone toward an extremely diverse array of programs and projects. No consistent attention has been given to the kinds of projects that might generally be recognized as essential to industrial development. During the period of growing capital budgets, the diversifiers scored highest with large-scale hydropower projects and a batch of subsidized business and other loans. Nevertheless, they were unable to win the commitment of funds they desired, and still seek, in an "Alaska development fund," "Alaska investment fund," or similarly named capital spending vehicle.

Diversification strategies have been tried. In the early years of the oil boom, the state attempted to launch new industries and to expand existing ones through a costly combination of efforts, almost all of which failed. By offering its royalty oil under favorable terms, for example, the state endeavored to promote petroleum refining and petrochemical export industries in Alaska. The offer was insufficient to overcome the high construction, operations, and transport costs of doing business. After pouring $150 million into a program to create an agricultural products export industry, the state retreated in the face of mounting financial, climatic, logistical, and even insect infestation problems. Another program, the Alaska Renewable Resources Corporation, undertook to expand the fishing, timber, and other renewable resource industries into new kinds of production and processing through subsidized loans. Bankrupt enterprises and loan defaults soon overwhelmed the program, and the legislature abolished it.

Neither the savers nor the spenders got exactly what they wanted, primarily because the effective political majority encompassed a large and disparate range of interests, each of which desired money for its particular cause. Pressure from many directions led to the apparent lack of rhyme or reason in state spending that Robert Richards, the banker and candidate, and others criticized. There was, however, a pattern to the spending: the oil money was treated as a common property resource. A common property resource is one that everyone has access to and can use but that no one person has the responsibility or incentive to protect or conserve. An example is a forest full of trees available to everyone in a region where timber is a valued resource. Under normal conditions, the wood will be cut and hauled away as fast as users can get to it. Unless some external check is imposed, what one person leaves behind another will take. Acting individually, no one has the incentive to plant seedlings or to leave behind stands of young or mature trees for the enjoyment or use of others. Everyone wants to cut and run.

Something similar happened to the state's oil money. For individual law-makers and lobbyists, the price of restraint appeared too great. External checks on their spending were absent. If an individual legislator remained aloof from the scramble, there was no doubt that others would quickly take up the budgetary slack. Under the circumstances, a fiscal conservative ran a high risk of being labeled a fool or an obstructionist.

During the 1982 election campaign, Lieutenant Governor Terry Miller, a former senate president running for governor, commented on the inability of individual members of the legislature to resist the pressure to spend: "Many well-meaning legislators . . . know if they don't participate in the system, then others will participate in it for them, and if they don't get aggressive and active, their constituency will suffer. And so it's one of the circumstances where the legislature desperately needs help, and it can only come from the governor's office."[25] Miller wanted to occupy the one office that he thought could impose an external check on the legislative propensity to spend all available revenues. He had just seen the governor make a deal with the legislature for a dubious spending limit in exchange for the largest capital budget of the oil boom years. Miller did not survive the Republican pri-mary election.

The new governor, Democrat Bill Sheffield, led the call for a "major projects fund," a source for high-level spending on industrial infrastructure. He did not obtain it, mainly because the legislature saw the proposal as the governor's bid to control capital spending decisions at the expense of indi-vidual legislators.

It is doubtful that Miller or any other candidate could have used the gover-nor's office or any other position to resist the juggernaut. Spending the state's oil wealth provided an unprecedented opportunity for legislators to demonstrate their regional and local loyalties in ways their constituents would appreciate and understand: through a vast array of projects and pro-grams, grants, contracts, loans, and dividend and longevity checks. Legisla-tors continued to ignore or flout the governor's periodic, ineffectual efforts to lead or resist the tide of spending. They were able to do that with political impunity because the governor, too, was swept along with the tide.

The legislature was the most prominent institution in Alaska state govern-ment during the 1980s oil boom. In the absence of direction and leadership, lawmakers responded to the dominant forces in the political system: local-ism, regionalism, and special interests. Apart from the "outsider" oil indus-try, which fueled state revenues by more than 80 percent, Alaskans felt liber-ated from the constraint of having to pay for what they got. The elimination of the individual income tax, the lowering of property and sales taxes, and the relatively light taxation of businesses outside the oil industry severed the ties between taxes and expenditures and between payers and beneficiaries.

In the free-for-all environment that prevailed in Alaska in the 1980s, neither the savers nor the industrial diversifiers realized their goals. Both groups advocated courses that required more planning, consistency, and discipline than were possible. Instead of one major interest getting all or most of what it wanted, everybody got something. The result was a fair amount of saving under the circumstances, a lot of capital spending, and new and expanded government programs of many kinds.

Oil Industry Influence

All this was made possible by state petroleum revenues: primarily production or severance taxes, royalties, corporate income taxes, and property taxes, with severance taxes and royalties accounting for about three-fourths of total petroleum revenues. Because the royalty rate (a one-eighth state share) is set before oil leases are sold to companies, state and industry officials focus mainly on severance tax rates. These rates have been relatively stable—fluctuating between 12 and 15 percent—since 1977, when North Slope oil began to flow and the state legislature established the groundwork of the oil tax structure. (North Slope production is primarily from the Prudhoe Bay field and nearby Kuparuk reservoir, which account for 90 percent of Alaska oil production. Smaller producing fields are taxed at much lower rates.)

The oil tax policy structure was put in place by the legislature in the 1970s, before the industry settled into the state on completion of the trans-Alaska pipeline. Subsequently, the legislature enacted more specific tax policies some of which were highly advantageous to the industry.[26] One changed a corporate income tax accounting procedure (from "separate accounting" to "modified apportionment"), which resulted in sheltering substantial industry profits during the early 1980s, when oil prices and profits were at their peak.

Another measure favorable to the industry, the Economic Limit Factor (ELF), was intended to reduce taxes on marginally producing fields as an incentive to continued production. The incentive would also apply to the Prudhoe Bay and Kuparuk fields, however, despite their continuing overall high productivity and profitability; state policy makers were aware that the ELF formula would need to be changed in order to remove the unneeded incentive for the continued development of these fields.[27] Supported by a bare senate majority, the industry was able to block change in the E L F for two years after it was applied to Prudhoe Bay and Kuparuk.

It was only after the Prince William Sound oil spill and the widespread public reaction to it that the state senate finally agreed in 1989 to legislation modifying the E L F formula to eliminate the tax breaks for the giant North Slope fields. Substantial state revenues—$185 million, according to the state—were lost during the two years that the old E L F formula was applied to these fields.[28]

A third significant instance of oil industry influence on policy making occurred three years after the oil spill, in 1992. The legislature was considering measures to ensure that the Alyeska Pipeline Service Company, the oil companies' pipeline and terminal management consortium, would fully respond to future tanker spills. Strong industry opposition to this bill was centered this time in the state house of representatives, and only last-minute legislative maneuvering resulted in its passage. At the time, oil continued to seep from Prince William Sound shores and the damage from the three-year-old spill was still being assessed.

The main political target of the industry has been the state senate, consisting of twenty members. The industry and its allies need the votes of only eleven members to block unfavorable legislation. During the 1980s and early 1990s, campaign contributions from the industry flowed most generously to industry-friendly Republican candidates. Former state senator Ed Dankworth, one of the industry's chief lobbyists in Juneau, not only helped make sure that industry money reached potential supporters, but also played an influential role in organizing Republican-led coalitions for control of the senate. In 1992, the oil industry was the largest single source of campaign funds for state legislative candidates, contributing $422,000. Labor unions were second, at $354,000.[29]

Industry influence in state policy making is not unbounded, however. The E L F ultimately was modified, and the Alyeska oil-spill-response bill was passed. Further, in terms of overall state taxes, oil companies pay about the same proportion of their Alaska value-added production in state taxes as they do elsewhere in the United States.[30] Finally, state government, as well as the oil industry and the federal government, has received a major share of the economic returns from North Slope production over the years.[31]

In this rough accounting, it appears that the oil industry has significantly influenced but not consistently dominated oil-tax and regulatory policy in Alaska. But even if heavily qualified, this conclusion may well meet with skepticism, given the overwhelming economic role of the industry in Alaska and the high stakes involved. We do not know the extent to which the industry has succeeded in blocking other tax increases and regulatory measures that might otherwise have been enacted. We do know that there is little sentiment among state policy makers for increasing industry taxes. Most of them are fearful of killing the goose that lays the golden eggs, or discouraging further investment in Alaska, which is a favorite theme of the industry.

Although it is true that higher taxes *could* discourage oil production and investment in Alaska, it does not mean that *any* increase in industry taxes would have such an effect. A particularly attractive target for increased tax rates is the income earned from the companies' extremely profitable North Slope fields. These are, after all, the richest and most prolific fields in North America. State policy makers lack adequate independent information about the economic costs of production and transport, however, in part because these costs involve inaccessible industry data. That undoubtedly reinforces the more fundamental political obstacles to raising taxes on an industry that already provides most of the state's general revenues.

Our own judgment is that the oil industry's political reach in Alaska is extensive, that it has clearly been effective in important instances, but that its influence on policy making is also limited. A basic condition of industry's political limits is that the state of Alaska owns and controls the lands producing almost all the oil wealth. Thus the industry must deal primarily with a small number of highly visible state officials. The latter, in turn, are not confronted with thousands of private owners of oil lands. In other oil-producing states, such as Texas and Oklahoma, these landowners comprise the core local constituency of the industry, and they are reinforced by large numbers of investors, suppliers, service businesses, and other direct stakeholders. These support groups also exist in Alaska, but in Alaska's small-scale economy a large proportion of the industry supplies and services is imported.

The limited extent of the industry's constituency in Alaska is one of the reasons why the oil companies do not play a consistently dominating role in state policy making. Other reasons are suggested elsewhere in this book: the relative openness and accessibility of the state's politics; the configuration of interest groups in which local governments, school organizations, and other public authorities dependent on oil revenues are prominent; and populist values and attitudes, which in this case tend to balance Alaskans' prodevelopment interests.

Industry "institutional" advertisements, which are apparently intended to soften up public attitudes toward the oil companies, are familiar television fare to most Alaskans. These commercials, through a variety of sentimental photogenic images, may suggest to many Alaskans that there is no incompatibility between oil development and the preservation of all that is good about Alaska's communities, landscapes, and animal life. Along with the industry's well-publicized charitable donations and other gestures of good citizenship, perhaps these advertisements pay off politically while the industry does some genuine good. Nevertheless, despite the television soft sell and the campaign finance hard sell, and all the efforts in between, the oil industry does not appear to have fully captured the hearts and minds of Alaskans or their political leaders. This is not necessarily to suggest that oil-generated revenues and incomes have not commanded Alaskans' full attention and interest, however.

Future Prospects

Alaska still has an oil economy. The question is how long it will last. Maybe, despite the objective indicators, Alaska's economic optimists will influence the public psychology, buoying expectations and helping to keep the economy afloat through the 1990s. Optimists might pin their hopes on several possibilities. First, the world price of oil could increase significantly. Second, additional small-scale oil discoveries might occur near existing fields, allowing them to be brought into production quickly. Third, enhanced recovery could significantly extend the life of the North Slope fields. Fourth, settlement of outstanding legal claims against oil companies for unpaid taxes and royalties could bring in a billion or more dollars. Fifth, if Congress and the Clinton administration relent, a major oil discovery might be made on the coastal plain of ANWR. Finally, if the high costs of developing Prudhoe Bay and other North Slope gas reserves can be overcome, a trans-Alaska gas pipeline might be built, bringing short-term construction jobs and longer-term royalty and tax income to the state.

Alaska's policy makers may be able to muddle through for several years, given good luck and judicious use of various reserve funds, but the aforementioned possibilities are not a secure basis for fiscal and economic planning. More likely, filling the fiscal gap left by the depletion of Prudhoe Bay will require further budget cutting combined with additional sources of recurring revenue. There is no question that Alaska has unused fiscal capacity. In the late 1980s, the Advisory Commission on Intergovernmental Relations ranked Alaska first among the states in its per capita revenue-raising capacity and third in terms of its tax effort in tapping that capacity. This apparently favorable standing, however, is built almost entirely on taxation of oil, in which Alaska ranked first in both capacity and effort. In other common areas of taxation among the states, there were major discrepancies between Alaska's tax capacity (high) and effort (low). These areas included personal income taxes, sales taxes, and corporate income taxes.[32]

The two most fiscally promising sources of new state revenue are a restored personal income tax and earnings of the Alaska Permanent Fund. Together they could fill about two-thirds of the projected $1-billion hole in the year 2000.[33] Once eliminated, however, an income tax is hard to restore. It may be one of the last solutions the legislature turns to in dealing with the state's fiscal problem. Equally controversial, and competing with the income tax for last place on the agenda, is the diversion of Permanent Fund earnings from dividends to support of state government operations.

Governor Steve Cowper suggested in 1987 that the state had two choices: to bring back the income tax or to redirect dividends. He left the decision up to the legislature. Rejection of both alternatives was virtually universal, so nothing was done. The governor had pointed merely to a projected crisis, not a clear and present danger. In any case, the price of oil skipped upward just in time to balance the budget that year; it did so again during the Persian Gulf crisis of 1990–91.

The Alaska Permanent Fund may represent the state's most important source of resource wealth in the 1990s. One critical policy issue facing Alaskans during this decade is reconsideration of the fund's purpose. They must decide whether it should continue to be used primarily as a source of dividend payments to individual citizens, or whether it should also or alternatively be turned to its original purpose: a renewable source of funding for state government when the nonrenewable resource of Prudhoe Bay is gone.

CONCLUSION

Alaska's political economy is out of balance. Political interests, organizations, and activity are extensive and elaborate, but the economy remains relatively undeveloped and vulnerable. These conditions result from Alaska's dependence on natural resource exports, the prominence of state and federal governments in the economy, and the state's remoteness from national commercial and governmental centers.

Before oil, Alaskans looked to the state and federal governments for jobs, income, programs, and projects. They also desired access under favorable terms to the minerals, forests, and fisheries controlled almost exclusively by the government. After oil was discovered, they wanted state government to distribute oil wealth quickly and generously; the legislature responded to their demands with enthusiasm. Alaska became the model of a "rent-seeking" state: a place where an unusually large number of political activists and entrepreneurs converge on government for all the benefits it can possibly bestow and where the clients of government programs include virtually the entire population.

These developments occurred in a fragmented governmental and political system. Party loyalty meant little or nothing. Legislators often outmaneuvered or simply ignored the governor; they tended to resist any leadership that might frustrate their individual interests in delivering benefits to their constituents. In this political environment, interest groups and lobbyists thrived. The Alaska electorate was split into groups divided by region, length of residence, and race, among other characteristics. None of these features of Alaska political life was new, but all were greatly intensified with the coming of oil.

The Alaska development mythology reflects and responds to real political and economic conditions: a tenuous and volatile economy subject to uncontrollable and dimly understood external forces. The mythology also mirrors the fact that government is the main owner as well as regulator of resources in the state. People need to believe that Alaska is a resource storehouse where government holds the key, that "owner state" spending on infrastructure will result in diversification, and that the federal government and Outside environmentalists impede development.

The development mythology offers what any good belief system should: explanations for real and imagined ills as well as palliatives for curing them. The myths make a complex and confusing situation understandable; they further suggest that policy makers could bring about development if they only had the wit and the will. Successive generations of Alaskans cling to their development mythology; variations of it have been around for a long time. Not even the economic upheavals of the Prudhoe Bay oil boom have altered its basic features.

CHAPTER 4

Alaska and the Federal Union

Three years after the big oil discovery at Prudhoe Bay in 1968, construction still had not begun on a pipeline to transport the oil to a port at Valdez. Native land claims, the National Environmental Policy Act, and right-of-way restrictions in the federal Mineral Leasing Act blocked the project. To remove any one of these obstacles required decisions by federal policy makers. Many Alaskans felt frustrated and angry with far-off politicians who, they believed, delayed profits, jobs, and public revenues. An editorial in the *Nome Nugget* voiced these emotions in the early 1970s: "Alaskans are a proud people. We should not be treated as we are. We should be allowed to go ahead and do things the way we want them. The resources are ours, not those of the U.S. government. . . . The way we see it, Alaska is getting a shellacking from the people in Washington. We should thumb our collective noses at those birds, tell them to go to hell, and then go our own way."[1] The *Nome Nugget* never had more than a small, regional circulation, and its feisty, sourdough editor, Albro Gregory, was not a representative Alaskan in a rapidly changing post-statehood Alaska. Nevertheless, Gregory's strong sense of independence and his grievances against the federal government represented the sentiments of many Alaskans at the time.

By the end of the 1970s, oil was flowing through the pipeline, and money and jobs abounded. Yet many Alaskans still resented the federal government. In 1980, voters created an Alaska Statehood Commission to review "the status of the people of Alaska within the United States, and to make recommendations on that relationship." It was, as the commission later stated, "the first time since the Civil War that citizens of a state have by their vote indicated unease with the federal union."[2] The vote came in reaction to several years of intense conflict over control of federal lands in Alaska. At about the same time, a new threat arose: members of Congress from the Northeast and Midwest wanted to place limits on the state's revenues from the bonanza strike at Prudhoe Bay.

After more than two years of study, the statehood commission completed its business in relative obscurity. The commission concluded that, whatever the benefits of any alternative status for Alaska, such as territory, commonwealth, or independent nation, "none is preferable to statehood."[3] It called for a lifting of various federal restrictions, as well as for continued vigilance against forces that favored congressional limitations or federal taxes on state resource revenues. (No federal restrictions were subsequently lifted, nor did Congress limit or tax the state's oil revenues.) Few people inside or outside Alaska paid much attention to the commission's final report, which was issued just as the oil boom reached a crescendo.

The commission was not an isolated episode in Alaska's statehood history. "Unease with the federal union" is part of Alaska's political culture. Without the federal government to blame for their ills, some Alaskans might even lose hope for the future. Many Alaskans find it difficult to face the real problems confronting Alaska's development because these problems are too elusive and complex, too persistent and intractable, to confront head-on. In the fall of 1989, state senate leader Jan Faiks addressed an Anchorage resource development group; the title of her talk was "Alaska's Story: Striving for Economic Survival in Spite of the 'Feds.'" In his 1992 state-of-the-state address, Governor Walter Hickel complained that "what the United States has done to Alaska is a scandal," and he vowed to sue the federal government for reneging on the promises of statehood and blocking the state's development.

An episode at the close of 1992 showed that tensions about state-federal relations were widespread. Because the cities of Anchorage and Fairbanks did not meet air quality standards under the Clean Air Act, the Environmental Protection Agency required that gas stations sell only oxygenated fuel during winter months. The new fuel cost consumers fifteen cents more per gallon and produced nauseous fumes, which many Fairbanks residents claimed brought on respiratory difficulties. After a week of spontaneous protests, radio station owner Frank Delong organized the Citizens for Reformed Gasoline, which launched a petition drive. One activist proceeded to set up a tent in the November chill outside the state office building, where he collected signatures for the petition and delivered harangues against federal, state, and local governments. Within two weeks, nearly twenty thousand interior residents had signed petitions, and Governor Hickel declared that Fairbanks would be exempt from the E P A edict—an action with which the E P A quickly and quietly concurred. Even the smell of federal government activity is bothersome to Alaskans.

By several measures, the federal presence in Alaska exceeds that of any other state. The federal government owns over 60 percent of Alaska's lands, controls the harvesting of fish and marine mammals from its oceans, exercises a special trust responsibility for Alaska Natives, and exploits the state's strategic military location in the North Pacific and Arctic oceans. To maintain its vast operations in the state, the federal government pays the salaries of thousands of civilian and military personnel. It grants aid to Alaska Natives and supports state and local programs. On a yearly basis, the federal government spends as much or more than the state government in Alaska.

Many Alaskans are ambivalent about their relationship with the United States. In general, they realize that the state benefits greatly from belonging to a rich and powerful nation. The federal government has bestowed resources, rights, and authority on the government and people of Alaska. Yet, critics point out, Alaska has never achieved the full promise of statehood because of the controls Congress and federal agencies continue to exert over its land, resources, and people. A succession of Alaska political leaders has considered two types of controls especially objectionable. The first type restricts Alaskans' access to fish, wildlife, mineral, and timber resources. The second prohibits them from discriminating against "outsiders" and newcomers in the distribution of public benefits.

Three themes emerge from the story of federal-state relations in Alaska. The first involves Alaska's hundred-year colonial relationship with America, Alaskans' quest for independence, and the recent transition to statehood. The second theme pertains to Outside versus Alaska control of the region's resource wealth, a major conflict underlying the statehood drive. The third deals with residents' demands for rights and entitlements from both the state and federal governments—demands that sometimes pit the governments against each other.

FROM COLONIAL TERRITORY TO SOVEREIGN STATE

Before it became a state, Alaska was essentially a colony. Like traditional colonies, it was controlled and exploited by outsiders. Little power, and a very limited local basis for building power, rested in the territory itself. The immigrant white population was too small and transient, the land too remote, and the environment too hostile to warrant much federal concern about the shortcomings of the territorial government. Powerful vested interests worked to maintain the status quo.[4] Alaska officially attained the status of a federal territory in 1912. As such, it gained the authority to elect a legislature whose form, powers, and responsibilities Congress could prescribe. The territory lacked control over its fisheries and wildlife, it could assume no debts without the permission of Congress, it could not enact land legislation, and its taxing powers were strictly limited.

The territorial system limited local power and served as a vehicle for external control of Alaska's natural resources. Virtually up until statehood, Alaska resource development policy came about through a series of accommodations between federal officials and absentee private interests in Washington, D.C., Seattle, and other power centers. The colonial nature of the natural resource export economy emerged clearly: capital, labor, and virtually all goods and equipment were imported; unprocessed products and profits were exported. Conservation practices, particularly in the declining salmon fisheries, were ignored or inadequate. Finally, little or no development of local economies occurred beyond the levels needed to support extractive and export enterprises.[5]

Colonial Alaska was catapulted into the twentieth century primarily by global events and technology, only secondarily by the political movement for statehood. World War II was the most important factor. It placed Alaska on the map strategically, flooding the territory first with soldiers and then, when the war ended, with returning veterans and other immigrants from the Lower 48 states. The cold war supplied further momentum when the Defense Department staked an Arctic defense line across Alaska and the Canadian north. Postwar immigrants to the territory brought along their families as well as their expectations for the political rights and public amenities to which they were accustomed in the states. Major technological advancements in air travel and electronic communications during the 1950s effectively linked Alaska with the rest of the country socially and economically. These conditions set the scene for statehood.

Benefits and Constraints of Statehood

Statehood benefited the majority of Alaskans in the form of resources, authority, and rights. On the down side, it introduced new federal constraints and extended old ones, primarily concerning federal laws and landownership. Many Alaskans tend to take the benefits of statehood for granted and to rebel at the unfairness of the constraints. Actually, they gained a great deal in their statehood transaction with the federal government.

The statehood land grant of 103.4 million acres, combined with the transfer of control over most fish and wildlife, brought a resource windfall. Back in 1959, the commercial potential of Alaska's fisheries and oil provinces was not as clear as it is today. Within the first decade of statehood, oil was discovered at Prudhoe Bay and the salmon fisheries greatly increased their productivity. Together with the government and defense industries, these resources formed the foundation of Alaska's economy and the sources of most employment and income in the state. In the late 1950s, statehood proponents gambled that the land and resource grants would eventually yield much of the money to support state government. Their bet paid off hugely in the 1980s.

Statehood did more than convey land and resources to Alaska's people. It gave them the government institutions and legal tools they needed to capture and redistribute benefits from resource exploitation. In territorial days, outsiders, or non-Alaskans, received most of the benefits, including jobs, incomes, and profits. Reacting largely to this colonial experience, the writers of the Alaska Constitution drafted a natural resources article proclaiming that the new state's goals were to settle land and develop resources for the maximum benefit of residents.

In 1959, Alaskans received the right to form a state government to help them pursue such objectives. Alaska had the regulatory power to control resource development and the tax power to extract a share of the profits. The state also possessed the power, and soon the revenues, to establish multiple programs for distributing wealth among its citizens. The new state looked to the federal government for a great deal of assistance during the first decade, including special transition grants and massive reconstruction aid after the 1964 earthquake. Twenty years later, the windfall of tens of billions of dollars from the North Slope oil fields had enriched the state beyond its citizens' wildest expectations.

Statehood also conferred on Alaskans the political opportunities available to citizens of all states through representation in Congress. Alaska realized a great advantage from the Connecticut Compromise crafted by the nation's founding fathers: one of the least populous states, Alaska nonetheless elects two U.S senators, as does every other state. Alaska's senators serve a population less than one-fiftieth the size of that represented by California's two senators. On the other hand, like five other low-population states (Delaware, Montana, North Dakota, Vermont, and Wyoming), Alaska has only one member in the U.S. House of Representatives.

As liaisons between the forty-ninth state and Washington, D.C., Alaska's congressional delegates face challenging jobs. Many Alaskans mistrust the federal government and believe that it presents the main stumbling block to the state's progress. They phrase their complaints and demands in multitudinous ways. What their messages boil down to is that they want their resources, institutions, and rights, but they do not want federal officials telling them what they can and cannot do with them. Desire to have their statehood cake and eat it too is ingrained in Alaska's political culture.

What exactly are the federal constraints that Alaskans complain so much about? There are two sets of them: one derives from federal constitutional and statutory powers; the other is based on federal land and resource ownership.

The interstate commerce clause of Article I of the federal Constitution underlies one persisting conflict. Because the clause restricts state legislation in the field of interstate commerce, Congress can and does prohibit the export of North Slope crude oil to Japan. This ban was part of the deal struck in Congress authorizing construction of the trans-Alaska oil pipeline in 1973. Alaska political leaders nonetheless persist in demanding that the ban be lifted. That would lower the cost of transporting the oil to market, thereby increasing the state's profit margin from oil taxes and royalties. Under the "Jones Act" (Merchant Marine Act of 1920), U.S. maritime regulations mandating the use of expensive American vessels and crews in American waters push up transportation costs for everything, not just oil, that travels by sea to Alaska. Congress enacted this limitation as a means of building up the U.S. merchant marine industry, including the port of Seattle, which was ably represented by Senator Wesley Jones of Washington.[6]

Other provisions of the federal Constitution that have thwarted objectives of Alaska political leaders over the years are the equal protection and privileges and immunities clauses of the Fourteenth Amendment. The courts cite the clauses when preventing Alaska policy makers from imposing durational residency requirements on citizens who wish to partake of the petroleum wealth. Direct benefits whose durational residency requirements the courts struck down include the annual Permanent Fund dividends of up to one thousand dollars to every resident and the monthly "old folks" or longevity bonus of two hundred fifty dollars for every resident sixty-five years old and older. Schemes to pay individual Alaskans according to how long they have lived in the state have all proven unconstitutional. Now the benefits are distributed equally to every resident with enough longevity to vote.[7] The courts have also looked askance at "local hire" laws that favored long-term residents over newcomers and transients. Yet state politicians continue to come up with bills aimed at discriminating against short-timers, and the courts predictably strike them down.

Even if they have lived in the state for only a few years, many residents favor restricting the access of other, more recent arrivals to the benefits and opportunities of living in Alaska. Politicians often respond eagerly to this anti-outsider sentiment. They appeal to the voters by boasting about how long they have lived in the state and by using "Alaska first" rhetoric. Disregarding the courts, they call persistently for local-hire legislation.

Congress's power to pass laws affecting Native Americans acts as another controversial constraint on state government.[8] Alaska Indians, Eskimos, and Aleuts have a "special relationship" with the federal government, which retains ultimate responsibility for policy decisions affecting their welfare. The federal relationship underlies the "sovereignty" movement in which Natives assert inherent powers of self-government. The state government and most of Alaska's non-Native population strongly oppose such political claims (see chapter 5).

Many Alaskans regard federal landownership as the most onerous Outside constraint on their personal freedoms. With ownership comes the power to write the rules determining what may or may not be done on the land. Federal rules, particularly those applying in wilderness areas, parks, and wildlife refuges, can be quite restrictive. They affect mining claims, timber harvest, hunting, and road construction. Many residents of Alaska consider these restrictions particularly burdensome in a place that is supposed to be the last frontier.

The federal government's proprietary authority extends not only to Alaska's land but to its waters between three and two hundred miles offshore. This authority further limits the state's ability to regulate fisheries for the benefit of its residents. Citizens of other states and nations receive the same rights and derive the same benefits from Alaska fisheries as Alaskans. The state of Alaska cannot unilaterally prohibit the harvesting of certain offshore resources, such as high-seas salmon, by outsiders. Nor can it control the harvesting by Alaska Natives of marine mammals or birds regulated under federal laws and international treaties. In 1989, when the U.S. State Department wanted to reward Poland's new democratic government with a share of the bottomfish harvest off Alaska shores, Alaska fishermen could only protest ineffectually.

Rhetoric of Independence

Alaska has other characteristics that magnify many of its citizens' feelings of alienation from federal institutions, even from the rest of the country. The state's physical separation and remoteness, sparse settlement and small population reinforce the notion that Alaskans not only are different, but that larger states discriminate against them in national councils of government. Further, the state's natural resource export economy, like that of Third World colonies, makes it susceptible to exploitation by outsiders and their allies in big government. Finally, many long-term Alaskans harbor memories or feelings about federal mistreatment and neglect of Alaska during the territorial period.[9]

The founders and faithful followers of the Alaskan Independence Party are one small but vocal minority that refuses to forget Alaska's territorial history. They see evidence of continuing federal usurpation all around them. In the state's official election pamphlet in 1990, the Independence Party proclaimed the main plank in its platform: "We seek the vote we were entitled to in [the] 1958 [vote on statehood]—three choices, to remain a state, commonwealth status, or to become a separate and independent nation. This was due us as a non-self-governing territory of the United States." In early 1990, when Lithuania's defiance of the Soviet Union attracted worldwide attention, the Alaskan Independence Party ran a full-page advertisement in the state's newspapers comparing Alaska to Lithuania and asking for a hearing before the United Nations.

The cofounder and state chairman of the Alaskan Independence Party is Joe Vogler, an octagenarian miner, land developer, and resident of Fairbanks since 1943. A newspaper story in the early 1980s described Vogler as the "quick-witted, sharp-tongued elder statesman of Alaska's political fringe." It also quoted his view of the federal government: "They have no authority here. Tell them to get the hell out. I still think Alaska has the total right to sovereignty over its own resources—onshore, offshore. I don't think the federal government should get one thin dime."[10] In Vogler's estimation, environmentalists who support federal restrictions on use of lands and resources are "wilderness worshippers" whose beliefs violate his freedom of religion as a Christian.

Vogler ran for governor on the Alaskan Independence Party ticket three times, winning 5 percent of the vote in 1974, less than 2 percent in 1982, and a high of 5.5 percent in 1986. He played the same antifederal government theme in all his campaigns. In 1986, for example, he pledged to free Alaska from federal controls and from "bureaucrats run amuck." In a highly controversial political maneuver during the 1990 election campaign, the Alaskan Independence Party candidates for governor and lieutenant governor stepped aside to allow Walter Hickel and his running mate to take their places (see chapters 8 and 11).

Hickel, a prominent Republican, former governor, and former secretary of the interior, won a plurality vote in a three-way race. In his campaign, Hickel ignored the antifederal and antistatehood language of the Independence Party platform. After assuming office, he distanced himself from party chairman Vogler, who had put him on the ticket, but he also stepped up the antifederal rhetoric, as indicated in his 1992 state-of-the-state address to the legislature. Hickel's first year in office was a string of frustrations and embarrassments, and the legislature ignored or rejected his most publicized initiatives, including a major budget rollback, a water pipeline to California, and a deepwater port at Anchorage. In the tradition of Alaska political leaders, Hickel found it expedient to divert attention from his troubles to a malfeasant federal government.

Few Alaskans would dream of surrendering the benefits that accrue to them as citizens of a state and nation so richly endowed with resources and opportunities. Yet, much as they reap the benefits, their leaders complain regularly about the constraints of statehood.

THE FEDERAL PRESENCE

Because of the state's large federal landholdings, strategic military location, Native population, and remote communities, federal agencies possess unusually high profiles. Figure 1 lists the most important federal agencies in Alaska and summarizes their responsibilities. By far the largest in terms of employment and expenditures is the Department of Defense. Since World War II, Alaska has hosted a large and relatively stable U.S. military presence.

The federal government owns more than 60 percent of Alaska, even after transferring 44 million acres to Native corporations under the Alaska Native Claims Settlement Act of 1971; this percentage excludes the 103 million acres it is still conveying to the state under the Alaska Statehood Act. The Department of the Interior, which manages 52 percent of Alaska's land, is the second-largest federal agency in the state. Interior's land and resource management agencies are the Bureau of Land Management, Fish and Wildlife Service, and National Park Service. The Forest Service in the Department of Agriculture administers most of the rest of the federal landholdings.

Figure 1. Missions of Major Federal Agencies in Alaska

Department of Agriculture: Includes agencies working in rural economic development, management of national forests, prevention of hunger and malnutrition, protection of public health, and promotion of agriculture.
— The Forest Service manages the 23.2 million acres of national forest lands of the Tongass and Chugach national forests, which include two national monuments and fourteen wilderness areas.

Department of Commerce:
— The National Oceanic and Atmospheric Administration, the largest commerce agency operating in Alaska, is responsible for weather forecasting, coastal zone management, and the Sea Grant Program. Also part of NOAA is the National Marine Fisheries Service, which studies and manages marine resources, including offshore fisheries and marine mammals.

Department of Defense: The largest federal department in Alaska in both total expenditures and employment. Most military personnel are in Anchorage and Fairbanks; army, navy, and air force military installations are scattered throughout the state on 2.5 million acres of land. There were 25,000 military personnel and 23,000 military dependents in Alaska in 1990, over 10 percent of the state's population.

Department of Health and Human Services: Administers a broad range of social programs and services for the elderly, children of low-income families, people with mental and physical handicaps, and Native Alaskans.
— The Public Health Service is responsible for physical and mental health programs. In Alaska, the Health Research and Services Administration operates emergency medical services, maternal and child health services, and community health services. The Indian Health Service works through the Alaska Area Native Health Service. Native programs include the community health aide program in more than 150 rural communities, medical centers in each of seven service areas, and the Alaska Native Medical Center in Anchorage.

Department of the Interior: Manages 192 million acres of public lands and natural resources of those lands in Alaska.
— The Bureau of Indian Affairs administers educational, training, and social assistance programs for Alaska Natives.
— The Bureau of Land Management manages 65 million acres of public lands and their resources.
— The Fish and Wildlife Service is responsible for wild birds, mammals, inland sports fisheries, and research activities. It manages 76 million acres of national wildlife refuges in Alaska.
— The National Park Service administers fifteen national parks, monuments, historic sites, and recreation areas in Alaska, which cover approximately 51 million acres.
— The Geological Survey explores and classifies lands for mineral potential, surveys and maps public lands, and collects royalties from resource leases.

Department of Transportation: Provides a mix of transportation activities and planning and construction funds for Alaska's transportation system.
— The Federal Highway Administration, the largest federal grant program in Alaska, administers grants to the state for highway planning and construction.
— The Federal Aviation Administration operates traffic control and navigation systems, manages air space, and regulates air commerce.
— The Coast Guard is responsible for maritime law enforcement, commercial vessel safety, marine environmental protection, port safety and security, and marine search and rescue.

Department of Veterans Affairs: Operates programs for veterans and their families through the Alaska Regional Office of the Veterans Health Service and Research Administration and the Veterans Benefits Administration. National cemeteries are located in Anchorage and Sitka.

The Interior Department also handles social service and development programs for Alaska Natives through its Bureau of Indian Affairs. Other federal agencies administering important Native programs include the Department of Education, the Public Health Service in the Health and Human Services Department, and the Department of Housing and Urban Development. Together, federal agencies contributed $280 million annually in entitlement funds exclusively for Alaska Natives in the late 1980s. That adds up to nearly $4,000 in health, housing, education, and other special services for every Native in the state.

Other federal programs, such as Aid to Families with Dependent Children, Medicaid, and Food Stamps, are available to all citizens, not just Natives. Although they represented only 16 percent of the state's population in 1990, Natives accounted for roughly 40 percent of enrollment in core public assistance programs. The programs provided between $2,500 and $7,500 a year to each eligible individual or family in the mid-1980s.[11]

On a per capita basis, federal highway spending in Alaska greatly exceeds that in other states. Even though Alaska has only about as many miles of road as Vermont, building and maintaining them is much more costly because of the harsh climate and wilderness conditions. Also, because the federal government owns so much of Alaska, the state contributes lower matching funds for construction than do other states. In 1990, Alaska received about six dollars in federal highway funds for each dollar of state funds committed to federally subsidized roads, a ratio surpassed only by Hawaii.

The Federal Aviation Administration enters the picture because, without air transportation, many small communities in rural Alaska would be cut off from the rest of the world. According to FAA figures, one out of every fifty-eight Alaskans, about eight times the national average, is a licensed pilot; one out of every fifty-eight, roughly fifteen times the national average, owns an airplane.[12]

The state's remote communities also depend heavily on federal assistance for health programs. The Alaska Area Native Health Service, part of the Indian Health Service of the U.S. Public Health Service, spent more than $150 million annually in Alaska in the late 1980s. Village health clinics and many volunteer emergency medical technicians also receive aid through the U.S. Department of Health and Human Services.

Federal Impacts and Alaska Ambivalence

There is no question that the federal government delivers substantial or even disproportionate benefits to Alaska. Yet many Alaskans are extremely ambivalent about the federal presence. The impacts of land claims and oil, the biggest forces of change since statehood, show just how problematical the federal presence can be. Native land claims resulted in a federally imposed freeze on virtually all major land transactions in Alaska in the late 1960s, thereby blocking construction of the trans-Alaska oil pipeline after the Prudhoe Bay discovery. Federal environmental standards under the National Environmental Policy Act (NEPA), which Congress passed in 1969, posed a second obstacle. Responding to pressure to move the oil to lucrative markets, Congress passed the Alaska Native Claims Settlement Act in 1971. The act granted Alaska Natives $962.5 million and title to forty-four million acres; it also set up twelve in-state regional corporations to administer the land and money. Two years later, caught between the NEPA environmental barrier and the Arab oil embargo, Congress passed the Trans-Alaska Pipeline Authorization Act.[13] Delivering on one of the promises it made in the Native claims act, Congress passed the Alaska National Interest Lands Conservation Act (ANILCA) in 1980. It dedicated more than one hundred million acres of Alaska land to federal conservation systems such as national parks and preserves, wildlife refuges, national forests, wilderness areas, and wild and scenic rivers.

These events illustrate sources of the dependent, love-hate relationship between Alaska and the federal government. Alaskans opposed the pipeline delay and blamed the federal government for it. They were delighted when Congress resolved Native land claims, which many had opposed, and lifted the NEPA restrictions. Then many were outraged by the Alaska lands act, which they perceived as yet another threat to their autonomy.

One man protested the Alaska lands bill by camping on a cot in front of the Fairbanks post office for eleven days in January, resulting in frostbitten fingers. Other demonstrators in Fairbanks, the center of resistance, carried signs with slogans such as "Free Our Land" and "We Don't Need the Lower 48 Running Us!" President Jimmy Carter was even burned in effigy. In the "Great Denali Trespass," more than one thousand people with snowmachines and guns converged on a new national monument for a day of hunting, which was outlawed in the area. Thus, many Alaskans considered the 1980 Alaska lands act a bitter defeat. Reviewing five years under the act in 1985, the *Fairbanks Daily News-Miner* editorialized: "Like no other state, Alaska lives under the federal mantle. Though some Alaskans prefer to snuggle under the warmth of the federal interest in protecting our land and allocating our resources, many Alaskans feel smothered beneath the weight of the blanket."[14]

As the editorial writer suggests, the conflict surrounding the Alaska lands act is part of a larger political question about the legitimacy of the federal role in Alaska. Of course, many other Alaskans cheer these federal actions, believing that the wilderness, wildlife, and scenic values of their state need more, not less, federal protection. Still, majority sentiment typically favors development, or the opportunity to develop, with minimum interference. Political leaders often tap and mobilize this sentiment not only at election time but in state-of-the-state addresses, other political rituals, and the day-to-day competition for popular attention and support (see chapter 11).

The dedication of over a quarter of Alaska lands to federal conservation systems struck many residents as yet another in a long history of "lock-ups" intended, among other things, to thwart the settlement of Alaska and the development of its resources. The way that the ANILCA settled ownership rights forced Alaskans to contend with federal rather than state agencies over specific uses of the land such as hunting, mining, and access.

Resentment over ANILCA flared up in the "Tundra Rebellion," Alaska's version of the western states' "Sagebrush Rebellion." Starting in Nevada in the late 1970s, the leaders of the Sagebrush Rebellion called for the transfer of large blocks of federal lands to the states. By almost a three-to-one margin, Alaska voters in 1982 approved an initiative that claimed state ownership of all remaining federal lands in Alaska, with the exception of Denali National Park, certain national monuments, and other special federal reserves. Because constitutional and legal barriers clearly invalidated the claim, it was little more than an expression of sentiment. Nonetheless, it demonstrated Alaskans' continuing opposition to federal land controls, as well as their persistent belief that federal action or inaction has inhibited economic development.

In reality, Alaska's development hinges primarily on global economic and political forces, not on the whims of federal policy makers. With its natural resource export economy, the state has always been vulnerable to the volatility of world fur, mineral, fish, and timber markets. Its exposure increased when the economy turned to oil. Events in the Middle East, which have caused wild fluctuations in world oil prices since the 1970s, directly affect Alaska's economy and politics (see chapter 3). In this unstable environment, Alaskans look to the federal government to enact supportive policies affecting the development, transport, and pricing of petroleum. At the same time, they consider the federal government one of the principal threats to their stability.

Although Alaskans often view Washington-based decisions regarding

Table 4: Employment in Alaska, 1970–89 (In Thousands)

Sector	1970	1975	1980	1985	1989
Military	31.4	25.3	22.0	23.1	24.6
Federal civilian	17.1	18.3	17.7	17.6	18.2
State/Local government	18.5	28.8	36.3	49.2	48.8
Private	80.7	148.0	158.5	223.5	226.5
Total Employment	147.7	220.4	234.5	313.4	318.1
Percentage Federal	32.8%	19.8%	16.9%	13.0%	13.5%

Sources: Alaska Department of Labor, Statistical Quarterly; U.S. Department of Commerce, Bureau of Economic Analysis (Annual printouts).

their resources as problematic, they cannot deny the social and economic benefits of the federal fiscal impact. Federal funding through government grants and paychecks has remained relatively constant over the years, alleviating some effects of the oil boom and bust.

The military presence, for example, has stayed fairly stable since World War II. In 1990, more than fifty-seven thousand military personnel and dependents resided in Alaska, accounting for over 10 percent of the state's population. The military spent over $1 billion in Alaska in 1988. Federal money spent inside the state boosts employment, which, in turn, increases the spendable income of Alaskans. The multiplier effect of federal spending in Alaska is approximately 1.8, raising the economic impact of the military's 1988 budget to nearly $2 billion.

The end of the cold war and planned reductions in U.S. military forces are likely to diminish Alaska's military establishment in the 1990s. The federal Defense Base Closure Commission alarmed many Alaskans in 1991 when it considered closing Anchorage's Fort Richardson Army Base. By military standards, Fort Richardson is a small base, but its six thousand soldiers and civilian employees collect an annual payroll of over $170 million. With multiplier spinoffs, the base accounts for about 5 percent of Anchorage's jobs. Alaska's U.S. senator Ted Stevens, ranking Republican on the Senate's defense appropriations subcommittee, protested the proposed closure, prompting the commission to postpone considering Richardson until its next round of base closings in 1995. Because the army ranks Fort Richardson near the bottom of its list of "fighting installations" for military value, it probably will be a prime candidate for closure at that time.

Federal civilian and military employment constituted 13.5 percent of total employment in the state in 1989 (table 4). This figure represented a decrease

Table 5: Federal Funding Per Capita for Selected States

| | 1985 | | 1990 | |
	Rank	Total $	Rank	Total $
U.S. Average		3,253		3,974
Alaska	1	4,859	2	5,867
Virginia	3	4,728	1	5,874
New Mexico	4	4,532	3	5,703
Maryland	2	4,737	4	5,671
Hawaii	6	4,334	6	4,927
North Carolina	50	2,399	50	3,043
Wisconsin	49	2,399	48	3,052
Indiana	44	2,614	49	3,051
Michigan	48	2,445	47	3,142

Source: U.S. Department of Commerce, Bureau of the Census, "Federal Expenditures by State for Fiscal Year 1985," "Federal Expenditures by State for Fiscal Year 1990."

from earlier years not because federal employment declined, but because state and local government and private-sector employment grew dramatically during the oil boom. In 1970, federal employment accounted for one-third of all Alaska employment. Its share of the public-sector employment pie shrank during the early 1980s, reviving again as the oil-based economy declined later in the decade.

Annual federal spending of more than $2.5 billion attributable to Alaska military and civilian operations surpassed the total of the state's annual general fund budget at the end of the 1980s. Per capita federal spending in Alaska is perennially among the highest of all the states (table 5). Alaska ranked second in 1990 at more than $5,800 per capita, primarily because of wages paid to federal civilian and military personnel (table 6). Alaska ranked last in direct federal payments to individuals per capita, mainly because the state's young population does not draw on Social Security and Medicare benefits, in contrast to the older populations of other states, such as first-ranked Florida. In terms of total federal funds received by a state, Alaska ranked a low forty-fourth in 1990.

Before the pipeline construction and oil boom, federal revenues as a percentage of combined state and local revenues far exceeded the national average (table 7). As oil money flowed into state coffers and was passed through to local governments, the federal aid percentage dropped from 34 percent in

Table 6: Federal Expenditures in Alaska (In Millions of Dollars)

	1981	% of Total	1990	% of Total
Grants to state and local governments	448	21.6	717	22.2
Salaries and wages	794	38.3	1237	38.3
Direct payments for individuals	257	12.4	612	19
Procurement	563	27.1	529	16.4
Other programs	12	0.6	132	4.1
Total	2074	100	3227	100

Source: U.S. Department of Commerce, Bureau of the Census, ''Federal Expenditures by State for Fiscal Year 1990.''

1974 to 7 percent in 1982, well below the national average. Federal aid followed the same pattern as federal employment, growing to a greater proportion of state revenues when oil dollars began to dry up. In 1989, federal aid rose to 12 percent of the combined revenue, a figure still below the national average.

THE CONTINUING STRUGGLE

A strain of self-reliant individualism runs through many of the state's residents. These Alaskans resent having to depend on the far-off federal government for anything. The state's political leaders play to this sentiment by pointing regularly to existing and potential federal threats, keeping them at the center of Alaska's political life.

Alaska newspapers, radio, and television constantly include federal-state issues in their news coverage. Controversies over federal policies affecting natural resource rights enter people's living rooms on a daily basis through the media. Specific issues include land use and ownership, Native subsistence rights, fisheries enforcement on the high seas, export of North Slope oil, and mining regulation. In recent years, specific federal-state battles have been fought over the questions of opening the Arctic National Wildlife Refuge east of Prudhoe Bay to oil exploration, limiting the timber harvest from the Tongass National Forest in southeast Alaska, and federal leasing of petroleum exploration and development rights in Bristol Bay, one of the world's most productive salmon fisheries.

Table 7: Revenue Sources for State and Local Governments, Alaska and the U.S. Average (Selected Fiscal Years, 1962–89; in Percent)

Combined state and local government revenues	1962		1967		1974		1977		1980		1982		1986		1989	
	U.S. Avg.	Alaska	U.S. Avg.	Alaska	U.S. Avg.	Alaska	U.S. Avg.	Alaska	U.S. Avg.	Alaska	U.S. Avg.	Alaska	U.S. Avg.	Alaska	U.S. Avg.	Alaska
State sources	41	47	41	33	43	44	42	62	44	74	45	82	46	76	47	67
Local sources	46	19	42	15	37	22	36	17	34	14	36	11	36	17	37	21
Federal sources	13	34	17	52	20	34	22	21	22	12	19	7	18	7	16	12
All sources	100	100	100	100	100	100	100	100	100	100	100	100	100	100	100	100

Sources: U.S. Department of Commerce, Bureau of the Census, "Census of Governments," 1962, 1967, and 1977; and "Governmental Finances," 1973–74, 1979–80, 1981–82, 1985–86, and 1988–89.

Note: Includes all revenues except utility, liquor-store, and insurance-trust revenues.

Of these three cases, the state has identified with the "antidevelopment" side in only one, the Bristol Bay fisheries dispute. It took this position mainly because of the economic importance of the fisheries and the political strength of organized fishermen, not because the state is more sensitive to environmental issues than federal agencies. Further, the federal government, not the state, would realize most of the economic benefits of petroleum development on the submerged lands of the outer continental shelf; the fishing communities of Bristol Bay would likely bear the brunt of the costs. In the case of the Arctic National Wildlife Refuge, on the other hand, oil exploration and development would require substantial onshore construction activity, creating jobs and royalties not forthcoming from federal offshore leasing.

Federal and state governments tend to conflict over resource development policies in Alaska when their economic interests differ or, more precisely, when powerful state and national interest groups take opposite sides. Despite the prominent role of the state and federal governments in the cleanup of the Prince William Sound oil spill in 1989, historically neither party has put a premium on environmental values when substantial economic values were at stake.

Political Culture and the Colonial Heritage

For many non-Native Alaskans, statehood meant freedom from the federal controls they blamed for retarding Alaska's development for the better part of a century. State government's mission, as they saw it, was to lead the way toward growth and progress based on natural resource exploitation and to ensure that the benefits flowed to Alaska residents. Their hopes and expectations, however, were balanced and even contradicted by their desire to preserve the "Alaska lifestyle," a frontier way of life stemming from the state's remoteness, extreme climate, scenic wilderness, small population, and relative underdevelopment.

Alaska's political culture before the petroleum boom of the 1970s and 1980s could be called small-town, populist, and parochial. Newcomers during that period, while cultivating the Alaska lifestyle, also brought north the values they had acquired in the south. They warmed to Alaska's frontier character, but they also wanted to make money, improve their standard of living, and rise as high as possible on the economic ladder. Alaska's mostly new, young, and ambitious population widely shared the objective of economic development; they, too, looked to the state to lead the way.

The interwoven threads of Alaska's political tapestry—development versus preservation, hostility toward the federal government, and a vision of the state as a vehicle for economic development—have remained remarkably constant over the tumultuous years. Although Alaska has changed in many ways since statehood, it remains remote, sparsely populated, and mostly undeveloped. Its residents are still relatively young and economically ambitious. For many, Alaska continues to represent the land of opportunity, if the state will only prepare the way and the federal government will not create obstacles.

Alaskans tend to exaggerate both their fears and hopes about federal activity affecting their state.[15] This tendency is one political cultural element with origins in Alaska's colonial heritage. Territory residents popularly believed the federal government deliberately promoted Alaska's exploitation by powerful outside interests. Fish traps were the most hated example. At the same time, residents felt that federal officials neglected or dismissed Alaskans when they wanted federal support for activities to benefit them, not outsiders. Increasingly, they looked to statehood to solve their problems, most of which they could trace to unfair, undeserved, and unwanted federal controls.[16]

Statehood neither solved Alaska's development problems nor removed the federal government's dominating presence. It did, however, enable Alaskans to structure their own state institutions, capture resource rents for their own uses, design their own policies for development, and elect their own representatives to Washington. Since statehood, Alaskans have reacted against their colonial past but they have not escaped it. This fact is apparent in the development strategies they pursue and the role their representatives play in Washington.

Representation in Washington

The main function of Alaska's congressional delegation is to minimize or overcome federal obstacles and to advocate federal policies that actively promote development. Apart from constituent casework, little else that Alaska's senators and representatives did during the first two decades of statehood mattered as long as they could deliver federal funds and projects while visibly fighting federal restrictions and promoting prodevelopment policies. Their duties have evolved as Alaska's population has grown and diversified. Now that the communications media have permeated the state, people pay attention to national and international issues as well as ones close to home. Still, the state's development, or lack of it, remains a chief concern.

In 1992, Alaska's three-man, Republican congressional team was made up of a former attorney, a former banker, and a former schoolteacher. Senator Ted Stevens, now the senior member of the delegation, was, at the time of his appointment, an attorney with a strong background in public and private practice in Alaska. Governor Walter Hickel appointed him to the U.S. Senate in 1968 on the death of Democrat E. L. "Bob" Bartlett. Stevens had run unsuccessfully for the Senate seat in 1962 and 1968. In the 1968 Republican primary, he lost to Elmer E. Rasmuson, president of National Bank of Alaska and one of the wealthiest men in the state. Over the decades, Stevens has been a tireless, albeit occasionally acerbic, advocate for resource development and a strong military presence in the state. A 1972 report by Ralph Nader's research group called him "short-tempered, not short-sighted," a description that still fits today.[17] Stevens's long tenure in the Senate has made him a force to reckon with on national as well as Alaska issues.

Alaska's open primary system helped elect Senator Frank Murkowski in 1980. Republican and conservative crossover votes probably contributed to the defeat of the long-time incumbent, Democrat Mike Gravel, in the primary. In the general election, Murkowski handily defeated his Democratic challenger, Clark Gruening, the grandson of former territorial governor and U.S senator Ernest Gruening, whom Gravel had ousted in the 1968 Democratic primary. In the 1986 general election, Murkowski beat Republican-turned-Democrat Glenn Olds by a five-to-four margin. Olds, now a member of Governor Hickel's cabinet, has compiled an extensive political résumé, including a stint as ambassador to the United Nations during President Nixon's first term. In 1992, Murkowski defeated Anchorage lawyer Tony Smith by a two-to-one margin. Murkowski's continuing electoral appeal may be attributed largely to the funding and communications advantages of incumbency, his care not to alienate any substantial Alaska interest group, and his conscientious attention to constituency casework. A former banker, Murkowski is the wealthiest member of the congressional delegation.

Representative Don Young, like Senator Stevens, attained his post by appointment and has retained it through election. Young ran against Democrat Nick Begich, a one-term member of the U.S. House, in 1972. Begich defeated Young in the election, which took place just over two weeks from the night Begich's light plane disappeared on a campaign flight between Anchorage and Juneau. (Representative Hale Boggs of Louisiana, majority leader of the U.S. House, accompanied Begich on that fateful trip.) A coroner's jury eventually declared Begich dead, but no one has ever found the wreckage of the plane. Both Begich and Young were formerly school-teachers.

Young has compiled an impressive twenty-year run of electoral victories to the U.S. House. Most of his wins have been by ample margins. In the 1990 and 1992 general elections, former Valdez mayor John Devens came closer than most of Young's Democratic challengers but failed to upset the entrenched incumbent. Young heavily outspent Devens both times, and in 1992 he made an unusual and effective television commercial apologizing for his "abrasive" personal style. Many Alaskans believe that Young's sometimes crude antics unnecessarily alienate potential allies in Washington. At one House committee hearing dealing with animal rights issues, Young defended the use of an animal trap by placing his hand between its tightly closed steel jaws for the course of his testimony. At another House hearing shortly before the 1992 election, he threatened to punch one of his Democratic colleagues, who vigorously opposed him on an Alaska-related development issue.

Young's string of reelections suggests that many Alaskans approve of his combative behavior, particularly when it is directed at federal officials and national environmentalists, who are perceived as opponents of Alaska's development. Personal style may have less to do with Young's success, however, than some basic political factors: incumbency advantages, generally weak Democratic opponents, and strong backing in rural Alaska, or the "Bush," which typically supports Democrats in both statewide and local elections. Young's Alaska residence is in Fort Yukon, an Athabaskan Indian village in the Interior, and his wife, Lu, is an Alaska Native. Young served successively as Fort Yukon council member and mayor and as state representative and senator for the interior region before winning his first election to Congress in 1973.

The state of Alaska, like other states, retains an office in Washington, D.C. An extension of the governor's office, it is headed by a director of state-federal relations with the assistance of a small professional and clerical staff. The office lobbies Congress and administrative agencies, cultivates Washington contacts for the governor and other state officials, and performs casework.

Although they deal with a wide range of issues, staff members devote most of their energy to matters of resource development.[18] Whether the objective is to stop petroleum exploration in Bristol Bay or to promote it in the Arctic National Wildlife Refuge, whether it is to increase the timber harvest in the Tongass National Forest or to impose stricter safety standards on oil

tanker traffic, the state of Alaska continually petitions the federal government to act on issues affecting its natural resource environment and economy.

In addition to its long-standing Washington, D.C., office, the state recently opened trade outposts in Taiwan, Japan, and Denmark. Representatives there work to enhance trade and tourism between Alaska and foreign
countries. Alaska exports millions of board feet of timber, tons of coal, and
large amounts of fish to Asia every year. Its largest export trade is with Japan. Information disseminated by the trade office attracts ever-growing
numbers of foreign tourists to the state. Japanese travelers, in particular, are
fascinated by the aurora borealis, or northern lights. Their presence helps
prop up the tourist industry during winter months, when tourism slows to a
trickle.

CONCLUSION

Alaska's explorers and immigrants have sought to exploit the region's natural resource wealth and to reap the rewards ever since the first Russians came
ashore in the mid-eighteenth century. In the early days, the tsar's administrators demanded furs and other resources from officials stationed in the Russian-American colony; the officials obeyed, largely at the expense of the Native peoples of the region. After the Alaska Purchase, immigrants to the
territory struggled against an outside alliance of big government and big
business for control of fisheries, minerals, and timber; again, the region's indigenous peoples paid most dearly. Statehood and subsequent political development changed the legal statuses and relative powers of the players.
Still, the federal-state struggle for control of Alaska's resources, especially
the terms of their exploitation and the distribution of benefits and costs, can
be viewed as an extension of past conflicts.

Because of the large size of the federal presence, many Alaskans tend to
exaggerate the federal government's real and potential roles in the state's
development. These Alaskans, either cued or reinforced by their political
leaders, underestimate Alaska's economic and geographic handicaps. They
operate on the premise that, in addition to federal opposition, it is primarily
lack of capital and will—not remoteness, climate, or high costs—that holds
back sustained development. Alaskans have shaped their government institutions as instruments of resident-oriented development, often ignoring inef-
ficiencies and failures. A majority of Alaskans expect their representatives
in Washington to carry on a constant struggle against shadowy figures. It appears that politicians who make a good show of doing so impress Alaskans
the most, because that is typically what it takes to get elected.

CHAPTER 5

Federal Indian Policy in Alaska

Alaska is the last of the states in which the federal government confronted the claims of the nation's dispossessed aboriginal peoples. Unlike Indian tribes in the Lower 48 states, Alaska's Eskimos, Indians, and Aleuts were not conquered, forced off their lands and onto reservations, or subjected to oppressive treaties. Alaska Natives were mostly left alone because, as far as most other Americans were concerned, their lands and resources were not worth taking until recently. Given these unique circumstances, federal policy toward Alaska Natives is less developed and more ambiguous than it is toward Native Americans elsewhere.

The absence of developed federal policy has left Alaska state government adrift and somewhat confused in its dealings with the Native population. State leaders have usually made it clear, however, that they strongly oppose Native claims to special status and rights. At the same time, the federal government has asserted its trusteeship responsibilities for the welfare of Alaska Natives, as it has for Native Americans generally. In addition, federal courts have supported the position that Alaska Natives have tribal status similar to that of Indians in the other states. The result is that federal and state policies affecting Alaska Natives often clash, adding intergovernmental conflict to the unusual legal and political complexities of federal Indian policy in Alaska.

In this chapter, we address the complex, dual political status of Alaska Natives. More than any other group or constituency in the state, Natives are caught between the struggle for independence and the quagmire of dependence. We explore why Alaska Natives can claim both special status under federal Indian law and policy as well as equal status with all other citizens under federal and state laws. We also examine why, in the competition for resource use and development, Natives' special interest is so intensely disputed, particularly by Alaska state government and some non-Native interests it represents. This conflict presents serious implications for the social and economic welfare of Alaska Natives.

EVOLUTION OF U.S. INDIAN POLICY

Native Americans were originally independent, self-sufficient tribal peoples. European colonial and then U.S. government authorities recognized many tribes as politically independent nations. Based on their different territorial interests and relationships with the major combatants, Indian tribes took different sides in the wars between the colonial powers and in the war for American independence. Tribes were also strong defenders of their territories, especially during the early years of European settlement.[1] In part because tribes for a time had the physical power to resist invading settlers (in the West, well into the nineteenth century), colonial and U.S. authorities dealt with them "government-to-government." Another rationale for attributing sovereign governmental status to the Indian tribes was provided in early American legal doctrine.

The Marshall Trilogy

At the foundation of American Indian law lies the Marshall trilogy.[2] Chief Justice John Marshall wrote three decisions for the U.S. Supreme Court in the 1820s and 1830s which established the principles of aboriginal land title, federal trust responsibility, and inherent governmental powers of Indian tribes. These rulings continue to shape American Indian law and policy today.

The first decision was *Johnson v. McIntosh* in 1823. In this case, Marshall held that although tribes might sell or otherwise transfer Indian lands to non-Indians, the courts would recognize only those transfers made to the federal government. In the absence of such recognized conveyances, the occupying tribes retained "aboriginal title" to their lands. Such title was subject to disposition only by the federal government.

Marshall based his argument for aboriginal title on the "rule of discovery," an international legal principle derived from the historical practices of European "discovering nations." In order to control competition among themselves, those nations agreed to recognize one anothers' "first discovery" claims on various parts of the Western Hemisphere. Although the Indian tribes, of course, were not parties to the Europeans' agreements, the legal theory was that the tribes held rights of first possession and that these rights could be transferred, changed, or extinguished only by the affected discovering nation. This interpretation remains the basic limitation distinguishing "aboriginal" title from conventional forms of landownership today.

The second decision of the Marshall court was *Cherokee Nation v. Georgia* in 1831. This case arose because the state of Georgia asserted jurisdiction over the Cherokees and seized lands reserved to the tribe by treaties with the United States. Marshall's decision focused on the nature of the relationship of Indians to the U.S. government. He wrote that although Indian tribes could not properly be considered foreign nations, they should be deemed: "domestic dependent nations. . . . Their relation to the United States resembles that of a ward to his guardian. . . . They look to our government for protection; rely upon its kindness and power; appeal to it for relief to their wants; and address the president as their great father." Again drawing on international law and practice, Marshall laid down the principle of the trust relationship: the legal and moral responsibility of the federal government to protect the vital interests of "dependent sovereign" tribes.

The chief justice made his third and most comprehensive statement about the political status of Indian tribes in the case of *Worcester v. Georgia* in 1832. This decision recognized inherent powers of Indian self-government. Samuel Worcester was a politically active missionary on the side of the Cherokees in their struggle with the state of Georgia over control of their lands. Desiring to put a stop to Worcester's activities, state officials arrested him, found him guilty of residing on Cherokee land without a permit or an oath of loyalty to the state, and sentenced him to four years at hard labor. The Marshall court ruled that Georgia's law was "repugnant to the constitution, treaties, and laws of the United States" because it interfered with the federal government's exclusive relationship with the Cherokee tribe, a relationship guaranteed by the supremacy and commerce clauses of the U.S. Constitution.

The *Worcester* opinion reviewed the discovery rule and aboriginal title, the history of contact with the Indian tribes, and the trust relationship between the tribes and the U.S. government. Marshall noted that the Constitution gave Congress exclusive power to make treaties and to regulate commerce with the Indian tribes and that constitutional treaties and acts were the supreme law of the land. Having established the principle of federal supremacy in Indian affairs, he addressed the question of tribal sovereignty: "The settled doctrine of the law of nations is that a weaker power does not surrender its independence—its right to self-government—by associating with a stronger, and taking its protection."

The tribes, in other words, retained "dependent" sovereignty—their original powers as separate nations—except as these powers were limited by the tribes' association with the United States. "Sovereignty," therefore, is not an absolute. It is rather a dynamic and relative condition of self-government, and it is subject to redefinition and adjustment as relationships between tribes and the U.S. government change.

The Marshall court laid down the principles, but the real political status of the Indian tribes would be more directly determined by the overwhelming force of superior power. On hearing of the *Worcester* decision, President Andrew Jackson, who had risen in national politics partly on his reputation as an Indian fighter, reportedly said, "John Marshall has made his judgment, now let him enforce it." This statement, whether or not Jackson actually said it, accurately shows where he stood on the issues of Indian sovereignty and the federal trust responsibility.[3] The state of Georgia in fact rejected Marshall's decision in the *Worcester* case, and Worcester served out his sentence. Moreover, backed by the federal military under presidents Jackson and Van Buren, Georgia succeeded in forcing the Cherokees to evacuate their land and to march the "Trail of Tears" to western Indian country by the end of the decade.[4]

From Dependency to Self-Determination

In nineteenth-century America, the combined ideologies of capitalism, Christianity, racial and cultural superiority, and manifest destiny provided justifications for the guile and the force used to suppress and often destroy the Indian tribes. After the Civil War, the last of the western tribes were conquered, subdued, and forced onto ever-smaller reservations. Now all the tribes were under federal control. Because of the defenseless condition to which most of them had been reduced, they were dependent on federal protection as well. Although still termed "government-to-government," the relationship between federal authorities and tribes had degenerated to that of a superior power attending to dependent, defeated, and demoralized subjects. Federal troops put down the last of the organized Indian resistance by the end of the century.[5]

Around this time, many tribes lost most of what was left of their reservation lands under the notorious allotment policy authorized by the Dawes Act of 1887. This act was finally to solve the "Indian problem" by breaking up the reservations and distributing tribal lands to individual Indians who, as private landowners, were expected eventually to enter the mainstream society and economy. Between 1887 and 1934, when the Indian Reorganization Act ended the discredited allotment program, Indian reservation landholdings fell from 131 million to 43 million acres, a loss of 88 million acres, or two-thirds of all reservation lands.[6]

By the end of the nineteenth century, assimilation policy had replaced physical force as the principal means of controlling the tribes. Bureau of Indian Affairs boarding schools were the main assimilative institutions, and BIA superintendents were the reigning powers on the reservations. "Industrial education" was to provide young Indians with skills needed to enter the bottom ranks of a rapidly industrializing society, and Native languages and religions were to be eradicated. Like the waves of European immigrants flowing into the country at about the same time, Indians were to be "Americanized." It was not until the Indian Citizenship Act of 1924, however, that Indians (including Alaska Natives) who had not previously been made citizens under specific treaties and statutes were granted United States citizenship.

Franklin Roosevelt's New Deal in the 1930s included a new deal for Indians. Social and economic conditions on the reservations, which had continued to deteriorate, were documented by the Brookings Institution in the Meriam Report of 1928. John Collier, the new head of the Bureau of Indian Affairs, was determined to change all that, and he had the president's support. At the urging of the Roosevelt administration, Congress passed the Indian Reorganization Act (IRA) of 1934 (which was fully extended to Alaska in 1936). The act ended the breakup of reservations and allotment of lands, which Collier had previously suspended by administrative order. It also provided new protections for trust lands, encouraged tribes to adopt constitutions for self-government, and authorized federally chartered corporations and funds to support tribal economic development.[7]

Some tribes, understandably distrustful of federal authorities, rejected the IRA as a continuation of BIA paternalism and assimilation in a new form, but most accepted the new program. Overall, the IRA probably did more to reinforce the idea of Indian self-government through formal recognition of tribal powers than it did to improve the social and economic conditions on the reservations.[8]

Another reversal of federal Indian policy occurred after World War II. In 1953, those in Congress who opposed the reservation system, the trust relationship, and special status for Indians argued that Indians should be "freed" from all federal supports and controls. This faction won passage of House Concurrent Resolution 108, which called for an end to the trust relationship and the "termination" of tribes. Under the new termination policy, tribal lands once again were to be broken up and transferred to private groups and individuals. All special federal programs for tribes and individual Indians were to be eliminated. State government powers were to be imposed on all Indians and their reservations. Also in 1953, Public Law 280 extended state criminal and civil jurisdiction over "Indian country"—generally, Indian reservations—in specified states.[9] In 1958, Congress extended this law to Alaska.

P.L. 280, not federal termination of tribes, may be the most important legacy of the termination policy of the 1950s. Congress passed legislation terminating more than one hundred tribes or tribal groups, but many of them have since been restored to tribal status and the trust relationship. Congress abandoned HCR 108 (though the resolution was never officially rescinded), and yet another new federal policy, "self-determination," emerged in the late 1960s and the 1970s.[10]

The self-determination era of federal Indian policy has emphasized powers of tribal self-government in congressional acts, presidential pronouncements, and judicial decisions. In 1968, Congress passed the Indian Civil Rights Act, requiring tribal governments to observe the principles of the Bill of Rights. This legislation also amended P.L. 280, prohibiting further extensions of state jurisdiction in Indian country without tribal consent.

The legislative centerpiece of the new policy was the Indian Self-Determination and Education Assistance Act of 1975 (P.L. 93-638), Congress's clearest rejection of the termination policy. This act reaffirms the trust relationship and special federal programs for Indians. These programs generally were expanded during the 1970s. Most important, the Self-Determination Act also encourages tribes to take over the planning and administration of Indian programs under contracts with federal agencies.

Other legislation in the 1970s, when Indian self-determination policy reached its high point, included measures to support Indian economic development, health care, and educational programs. In 1978, Congress passed the Indian Child Welfare Act, which strengthens tribal control over adoption and guardianship of Indian children.

All this legislation explicitly included Alaska Native villages as "tribes"—for the specific purposes of these legislative acts. This qualification is important because it implies that Congress, which is the ultimate authority in Indian affairs, has not spoken unequivocally or unconditionally about the tribal status and powers of Alaska Natives. More generally, it is also a reminder that federal Indian policy—a cumulative product of changing times and different legislative, executive, and judicial arenas—has never pointed clearly in any one direction in Alaska or elsewhere.

Because many inconsistent statutes have been enacted over the years, court decisions, too, give conflicting answers to questions about tribal status and powers. These questions concern changes in aboriginal land title, the extent of Indian hunting and fishing rights, the relative jurisdictions of tribal and state courts, the limits of tribal and state tax powers, and many other issues.

The current policy of self-determination says that tribes are to some extent sovereign as well as dependent. It says that all Native Americans, including Alaska Natives, are equal citizens under the law and, at the same time, that they are a distinct group of Americans with special political status under a unique set of laws. The law says that Native Americans can have collective, aboriginal title to tribal land and special rights to hunt and fish but, like other Americans, they also can have individual and corporate ownership of private land and resources. The law says further that, like Americans generally, Native Americans have access to federal programs, but they also have additional, exclusive rights to programs enacted especially for Indians.

The contemporary record of Indian policy is one of ambiguity and contradiction. Yet this record also indicates that federal courts have preserved the special political status of Indian tribes, or what University of Colorado law professor Charles Wilkinson refers to as a "measured separatism." He attributes this record ultimately to the commitment judges have to the rule of law and their belief that real promises were made in old treaties that the U.S. Senate approved and made into real laws.[11]

It is a remarkable fact of American political and legal history that, despite Andrew Jackson and all the opposition and contradiction, John Marshall's Indian law principles have survived. Originally derived from the legal doctrines of the eighteenth century, the principles of aboriginal title, the trust relationship, and inherent governmental powers continue to be redefined and applied by the Congress, courts, and executive today, distinguishing the special status of Native Americans from the formally equal status they share with all other Americans. There is no question, however, that these two statuses are in tension with each other and that they continue to be a matter of sharp legal and political conflict. Nowhere is this more apparent than in Alaska.

INDIA N POLICY IN ALASK A

The case of the Alaska Natives is both similar to and different from that of Native Americans elsewhere. It is similar in that Alaska Natives, as the original inhabitants of the region, could claim aboriginal rights, a trust relationship, and inherent governmental powers.[12] It is different primarily in that, until recent times in most of Alaska, there was little pressure on Natives to surrender their lands, including their traditional hunting and fishing grounds. Consequently, Alaska Natives' "dependent sovereignty," or inherent governmental power, was not documented in treaties or institutionalized on reservations (although many special-purpose reservations were created in Alaska; see discussion below). Ironically, the absence in Alaska of these traditional instruments of Indian subordination and control has tended to undermine rather than reinforce the tribal status and powers of Alaska Natives.

Status and Powers of Tribes

The relationship of Native populations to the state of Alaska has two interrelated but analytically distinct parts: tribal status and tribal powers. As a practical matter, there may be less at stake in the question of whether Alaska Native communities are formally recognized as "tribes" than in the question of what tribal powers they may have. Congress has referred to Alaska Natives as "tribes" in Indian legislation beginning in the early years after the Alaska Purchase. Alaska Natives' status as tribes, though often qualified, has many times been affirmed in executive and judicial actions.[13]

The more significant issue is what specific tribal powers Alaska Native communities possess. The extent of their powers depends on such questions as their individual histories and capabilities, the significance of the power to their tribal existence and well-being, the state's interest in the matter, and what federal laws may or may not say about the power in question.[14] Such tribal powers are likely to be determined on a case-by-case basis. It is as if the exercise of powers establishes tribal status rather than the other way around.

If Alaska Native tribal communities were within reservation Indian country, their governmental powers would presumably be greatest.[15] Even in the absence of reservations in Alaska, however, Native communities may still claim independent governmental powers: federal courts have held that Native allotments and "dependent Indian communities" may also be Indian country. The problem lies in determining the extent and applicability of these more elusive (dependent Indian communities) or limited (allotments) forms of Indian country in Alaska and elsewhere.[16]

With one exception, the Alaska Native Claims Settlement Act of 1971 abolished all the reservations and reserves previously existing in Alaska. The exception is the Metlakatla reservation, on Annette Island at the southeast tip of the state, which was established under unique circumstances by an act of Congress in 1891.[17] Its tribal status has been recognized by state as well as federal courts as being the same as that of reservation tribes in the Lower 48 states.

Although Metlakatla is a congressionally recognized reservation tribe, its powers are neither completely clear nor fully settled. Whether based in reservations or not, the powers of tribes are always subject to challenge. States and tribes continually dispute their relative powers in such areas as access to fish and game, control of water rights, extent of sovereign immunity, limits of taxation, and regulation of tribal gambling enterprises. Such powers are constantly questioned, redefined, and adjusted.

In Alaska, the political conflict extends beyond definitions of specific powers to the fundamental issue of whether Native communities have any special powers or rights at all. This more basic issue underlies the conflict over "subsistence" hunting and fishing—Native claims to special rights and priority access to fish and wildlife resources. Many Alaskans see the subsistence issue as a fundamental ideological conflict between equality and special privilege, and they assert that, whatever the law may say, Natives' rights to fish and game should be no different from those of anyone else. This issue is discussed later in this chapter.

Alaska Natives under U.S. Rule

The question of the status and powers of Alaska Natives ultimately needs to be viewed in historical perspective. One of the salient facts in modern Alaska Native history is that Natives came under U.S. rule during the post–Civil War assimilation era of federal Indian policy, when American Indian tribes had been reduced to a condition of almost complete dependency. Federal authorities and popular opinion held that any remaining Indian resistance had to be suppressed. Having defeated the Confederacy, the federal army could now shift its full attention to this task. Then Indians had to be trained, educated, and morally uplifted—they had to be "civilized"—so that they might eventually be assimilated into mainstream society.[18] These attitudes carried over into the federal government's relationships with its new Native wards in Alaska.

The first agents of the U.S. government in Alaska were not teachers and missionaries, but military officers. After the Civil War, their mission was to control and pacify Indians on what was left of the American frontier. On the far edges of that frontier, in Alaska, the military could try to ensure relative peace and order, but they were equipped to do little else to "civilize" the Natives. Whatever its attitudes toward Natives (some individuals were quite hostile), the military's responsibility was to enforce federal customs and Indian liquor laws, preserve order, and protect non-Native traders and settlers.[19]

From the Alaska Purchase until the early 1900s, many statutes, court decisions, and administrative rulings stated directly or indirectly that Alaska Natives were subject to the same federal and territorial laws that applied to non-Natives. At the same time, Congress, courts, and administrators recognized the unique interests and needs of Natives and made many special provisions for them. These special provisions culminated in 1936 amendments to the Indian Reorganization Act which, according to Alaska Indian law expert David Case, "were apparently intended to place Alaska Native land ownership and governmental authority on the same footing as that of other Native American reservations."[20]

Alaska Natives had experienced devastating problems by the end of the nineteenth century: cultural disruption that came with Western occupation, trade, religion, and schools; degradation and collapse of subsistence economies following importation of new technologies and commercial harvests; and the spread of demoralization, hunger, and disease. Presbyterian missionary Sheldon Jackson introduced reindeer herding to Alaska in the 1890s in part as a means of warding off starvation among Natives.[21] By then, large numbers of Natives had died from new diseases, primarily smallpox and influenza, brought by outsiders.

At the time of contact with the Russians in the 1740s, the estimated population of Alaska's aboriginal peoples was seventy-five thousand. By the end of the nineteenth century, their numbers had been reduced to about twenty-five thousand.[22] The largest declines occurred among the Aleuts and Eskimos of the coastal regions. Only in recent years has the size of the Native population returned to the level it was at the time of Russian contact two and a half centuries ago.

Sheldon Jackson also established missionary schools, which later came under the control of the U.S. commissioner of education. These schools were open to both Native and non-Native children. In 1905, however, the Nelson Act established separate systems of public schools, one for "white children and children of mixed blood who lead a civilized life," and the other for "uncivilized Alaska Natives." The Native schools were patterned after the Indian reservation and boarding schools established in other states.[23]

Other special "Indian" measures were extended to Alaska Natives during a period in which the overall objective of federal policy was assimilation. The Alaska Organic Acts of 1884 and 1912 contained provisions protecting Native land rights (though legal dispute continues even today about whether these provisions were intended to protect "aboriginal title"). As early as 1870, Congress exempted Natives from a general prohibition on harvesting fur seals. Several other exemptions from fish and game laws and international treaties followed. In 1902, Congress exempted Native subsistence hunting from regulation under the Alaska Game Act. Later Congress enacted special Native hunting provisions in the Migratory Bird Treaty Act of 1916.[24]

Native land reserves were another area in which Congress and the executive made special provisions for Alaska Natives.[25] Congress made reindeer herding an exclusively Native activity with the Alaska Reindeer Act of 1937. Through such special measures, Congress and the executive were treating Alaska Natives in much the same way that they dealt with Indian tribes elsewhere.

Officially, federal assimilation and allotment policies ended with the coming of Indian reorganization in the 1930s. In Alaska, allotments allowed individual Natives to own land, but the policy was not based on the breaking up of reservations as it was in the Lower 48 states. Many Native villages, about seventy as of recent years, adopted IRA (Indian Reorganization Act) constitutions. Some of the most intense controversies of the pre-statehood years centered on the creation of IRA reservations, which could potentially provide the territorial bases for Indian country and assertions of Native sovereignty.[26]

Before the IRA, more than one hundred fifty special Native reserves had been created in Alaska by executive order. Their main purpose was to support reindeer herding, schools, and vocational education. Some of the reserves encompassed extensive areas for subsistence activities. Only six reserves were established under the IRA in Alaska, and they helped to secure Native hunting and fishing rights in such villages as Venetie in the northern Interior, Hydaburg in the Southeast, and Karluk on Kodiak Island.[27]

IRA reserves provoked fierce battles between territorial leaders and the secretary of the interior over control of Alaska lands and resources. Ernest Gruening, governor of the territory from 1939 to 1953, viewed reservations as barriers to the development of Alaska and the progress of its people. Writing for the statehood cause in the early 1950s, Gruening vehemently opposed Secretary of the Interior Harold Ickes's "arbitrary and disingenuous efforts to impose his reactionary concepts [i.e., IRA and other reservations] on the people of Alaska." Gruening believed that the "people of Alaska" eventually would prevail.[28]

Alaska leaders' opposition, which was reinforced by federal termination policy, blocked all but a few IRA reservations. Also under the termination policy, Congress extended P.L. 280 to Alaska, giving the state broad powers over criminal matters and more limited powers in civil matters in Native communities that might qualify as Indian country.

The ambivalent historical record of American Indian policy had already been extended to Alaska by the end of the territorial period. Thus, in his dispute with Secretary Ickes, Governor Gruening was able to cite court decisions to support his condemnation of reservations and related claims of aboriginal title. One federal court, for instance, had held that the 1867 Treaty of Cession had extinguished aboriginal title, which was a legal basis for reservations (*Miller v. U.S.*, 1947). Later, the U.S. Supreme Court disapproved this decision (*Tee-Hit-Ton v. U.S.*, 1955). Subsequently, in a major decision in 1959, the Court of Claims awarded the Tlingits and Haidas a monetary settlement for the loss of their aboriginal lands.[29]

Gruening and other Alaska political leaders achieved the goal of statehood, but aboriginal land claims, which they disputed, were not disposed of as they had hoped. In fact, statehood added substantial momentum to the Native land claims movement.

Alaska Native Claims Settlement Act

In the early 1960s, the state began selecting lands from the public domain in fulfillment of its land entitlement under the Alaska Statehood Act. This action and related threats to aboriginal land rights caused Native leaders throughout the state to organize regional associations to protest state selections and to intensify their pursuit of a congressional settlement.[30] Both the statehood act and the Alaska Constitution included provisions (similar to those in the Treaty of Cession and the Alaska organic acts) disclaiming state rights to Native lands and looking to Congress to resolve aboriginal claims.

State land selections as well as all other major land transactions in Alaska were stopped by Secretary of the Interior Stewart Udall's "land freeze," beginning in 1966, pending settlement of Native claims. The final impetus to the settlement was the discovery of vast petroleum deposits at Prudhoe Bay in 1968. Transport of the oil required construction of a pipeline across lands claimed by Natives, and the economic stakes were much too great to permit a long delay of the project. This development supplied the incentive to the state, the oil companies, and Congress for agreement with Native leaders on the terms of a settlement act compensating Alaska Natives for extinguishment of aboriginal title.[31]

In some respects, the Alaska Native Claims Settlement Act (ANCSA) of 1971 was an Alaska Native treaty with the U.S. government. Like traditional Indian treaties, in return for grants of limited, designated lands and other benefits to Natives, ANCSA extinguished aboriginal title to much more extensive lands traditionally used and occupied by them. In other respects, ANCSA clearly is not like a traditional treaty. Congress deliberately wrote the act to exclude the traditional features of treaties: reservations and BIA trust responsibility for the land and monetary benefits of the settlement.

ANCSA granted forty-four million acres of land and nearly $1 billion to twelve regional corporations, two hundred village corporations, and nearly seventy-five thousand individual Natives. (A thirteenth regional corporation, based in Seattle for nonresident Alaska Natives, received cash but no land.) The act and subsequent negotiations provided regional corporations with millions of acres of surface and subsurface estate (most surface estate went to village corporations). In some cases, these grants have included valuable petroleum and timber rights.

The regional corporations also received about half the cash from the settlement act and, later, a cash windfall from special provisions of the federal tax code. The tax provisions permitted them to sell "net operating loss" credits (NOLS) to major U.S. corporations that, in turn, were allowed to deduct the losses from their federal tax bills. Pending final Internal Revenue Service approval, these credits are worth hundreds of millions of dollars to the regional corporations and may bring them about two-thirds as much cash (accounting for inflation) as the original land claims settlement.[32]

Congress declared that, among other objectives, the settlement was to be accomplished "in conformity with the real economic and social needs of Natives" (section 2 [b]). In two decades after the act, however, success has eluded most of the Native corporations. The many problems confronting the corporations include delays in land and resource conveyances, lack of economic development opportunities in rural Alaska, and financial and managerial deficiencies. Most of the corporations' ventures into such businesses as seafood processing, banking, and hotels have lost money. Businesses providing services to the oil industry, on the other hand, have been among the more profitable. A few corporations have profited from their petroleum and timber resources, but most have depended heavily on sales of NOLS. A special provision of ANCSA, known as "7(i)," required corporations profiting from resource development to share 70 percent of their net resource returns with all other corporations. This provision has been an especially important source of funds for regional and village corporations in resource-poor regions.[33]

Operating through the statewide Alaska Federation of Natives, the regional corporations have been important political vehicles for the representation of Native interests. With some exceptions, however, most of them have not had significant direct impacts on the economic well-being of their Native shareholders. In 1991, two regional corporations (Arctic Slope Regional Corporation and NANA Regional Corporation, both Inupiat corporations in northern Alaska), stood out by employing some 20 percent of their shareholders in corporate, subsidiary, or joint venture jobs. Most of the corporations, however, employed only between 1 and 5 percent of their members.[34]

Between 1974 and 1990, only one regional corporation paid cumulative dividends totaling more than a few thousand dollars per shareholder. In terms of cumulative net income (the difference between total revenues and total expenses), four of the regional corporations registered losses, and only four showed returns of more than ten thousand dollars per capita during almost two decades of operation (see table 8). Few village corporations could show any profits at all. Counting the initial direct payments from ANCSA as well as dividends from corporations, individual Natives had received as of 1990 an average of only about four thousand dollars in total ANCSA income.[35]

For most Alaska Natives, then, ANCSA has not generated sufficient income to make a difference in their living standards. Improvements in these standards during the 1970s and 1980s can be attributed primarily to the distribution of state oil wealth in the form of services and entitlements available to Alaska citizens generally.[36] Given the limits of rural village economies, Natives are disproportionately dependent on state programs.

State funding for Alaska communities and individuals has followed a pattern similar to that of Native program funding at the federal level, where

Table 8: Alaska Native Regional Corporations

Corporation	No. of Share- holders	ANCSA[a] Land (millions of acres)	ANCSA[a] Cash (current millions)	NOL[b] Proceeds (current millions)	1974–90 Net Income Per Capita (1990 $)	1974–90 Dividends Per Capita (1990 $)
Ahtna, Inc.	1,100	1.7	$ 6.4	$ 4.9	$9,461	$2,402
Aleut Corp.	3,250	1.3	19.5	3.1	–3,046	501
Arctic Slope Regional Corp.	3,740	5.1	22.5	2.5	10,141	1,857
Bering Strait Native Corp	6,200	2.1	38.1	34.8	–6,987	102
Bristol Bay Native Corp.	5,200	2.9	32.5	19.2	4,425	1,606
Calista Corp.	13,310	6.2	80.1	17.9	–7,038	59
Chugach Natives, Inc.	2,110	0.9	11.5	53.0	12,620	761
Cook Inlet Region, Inc.	6,550	2.2	34.4	87.0	44,409	10,456
Doyon, Ltd.	9,060	12.1	53.4	76.6	10,194	1,062
Koniag, Inc.	3,730	1.0	20.0	16.8	–2,131	00
NANA Regional Corp.	5,000	2.2	28.6	2.7	4,689	2,489
Sealaska Corp.	15,700	0.3	93.2	107.7	4,675	1,348
Total	74,950	38.0	$440.2	$426.1	$5,649	$1,792

Source: Steve Colt, "Financial Performance of Native Regional Corporations," *Alaska Review of Social and Economic Conditions* 28 (December 1991): 14, 18–19.

[a] Alaska Native Claims Settlement Act of 1971.

[b] Net operating loss.

budgets tightened in the 1980s. Together federal and state programs for Native and non-Native communities in rural Alaska sustain a major share of the local economies. Government employment, cash payments, and services accounted for as much as half the personal income and two-thirds the economic base of village economies in the mid-1980s. That is why economists refer to the "transfer economies" of Native villages. In many villages, state and federal government transfers play a vital role in filling the gaps left by the erosion of the subsistence economy and the absence of a market economy. Although subsistence can account for as much as half or more of their food, Native villagers depend heavily on cash and service transfers and on government employment.[37]

Through the combined effects of increased state programs, federal aids, and, in some cases, ANCSA-related income, village economies improved in the 1980s. Yet symptoms of social and economic stress remain widespread. While costs of living in rural Alaska are generally twice as high as in the cities, per capita incomes of Native villagers are about half those of urban residents. Village unemployment is typically two to three times greater than urban unemployment. Rural poverty is a persistent problem, with rates two to four times those of the state as a whole. Finally, indicators of social disorganization in rural Alaska are grim: Native suicides and homicides occur at four times the national rate, the accidental death rate is five times higher, and rates of fetal alcohol and sudden infant death syndromes are more than twice as high.[38]

Overall, despite its early promise, the Alaska Native Claims Settlement Act has done little to ameliorate Native social and economic problems. It has also had ambivalent political effects. ANCSA is an equivocal product of overlapping termination and self-determination eras of federal Indian policy. It speaks the language of self-determination, but it does so with a distinct accent of termination and assimilation.

Although the act granted Alaska Natives control of money and land, it assigned this control not to tribal governments but to state-chartered Native corporations. Further, ANCSA extinguished aboriginal hunting and fishing rights as well as aboriginal land title, putting Native subsistence at great risk. Recognizing this threat, the congressional conference committee responsible for the act "expect[ed] both the Secretary [of the Interior] and the State to take any action necessary to protect the subsistence needs of the Natives."[39] Such action could include withdrawing lands for subsistence uses and closing them to nonresidents when resources were scarce.

Finding that Native subsistence was not adequately protected and that neither the state nor the secretary had responded effectively, Congress later included provisions for subsistence hunting and fishing preference rights in the Alaska National Interest Lands Conservation Act of 1980 (ANILCA). These rights were to be assigned to all eligible rural residents, however, and not exclusively to Natives. Congress thus avoided the issue of special privileges for Natives, to which the state strongly objected, and struck a political compromise. At the same time, Congress made clear that its primary concern was to protect the subsistence activities of Alaska Natives, invoking "its constitutional authority over Native affairs and its constitutional authority under the property clause and the commerce clause" (ANILCA, section 801 [4]).

The state of Alaska enacted a rural subsistence preference law as part of the bargain in order to maintain control of hunting and fishing regulation on federal as well as state lands. In response to a suit by urban sport hunters, however, the Alaska Supreme Court in 1989 ruled that the subsistence preference violated the state constitution because it discriminated against urban residents (*McDowell v. State of Alaska*). This decision triggered a federal takeover of hunting and fishing regulation on federal lands (which include over 60 percent of the state) and efforts to amend the state constitution to restore the rural preference.

Strongly opposed by urban sport hunting and fishing interest groups, a proposal to place an amendment before the voters failed by one vote in a special session of the Alaska legislature called by Governor Steve Cowper in 1990. In 1992, Governor Walter Hickel called another special session on the subsistence issue, this time deliberately excluding a constitutional amendment from the session agenda. Instead, he proposed changes in the state's subsistence law that would assign subsistence privileges based on a combination of individual and residence-based criteria. Critics argued that the governor's proposal was likely to be found unconstitutional in state courts and that it would not meet the requirements of ANILCA. The Alaska Federation of Natives (AFN) also opposed the governor's bill because it would not restore a rural preference consistent with the federal law.

Faced with a continuing stalemate among the conflicting interests, the legislature rejected the governor's bill and authorized the state's fish and game boards to bar subsistence from "urbanized" areas, such as the Kenai Peninsula. This measure would reduce harvesting pressures in such areas and reserve them for sport hunting and commercial and sport fishing. An AFN spokesman promptly labeled the new measure a "nonsubsistence bill." The bill did nothing to resolve the conflict between federal and state laws. Federal management of fish and game continues on federal lands.[40]

Law and Politics

The federal courts generally support the special status and rights of Native Americans, including Alaska Natives. This does not mean, however, that complexity, ambiguity, and contradiction have been eliminated from Indian law and policy, as the Alaska case continues to demonstrate. Even where policies appear settled and consistent, there are disputes about their meaning and application. That is because policy contexts are always changing, thus giving rise to further political questions and conflicts. Moreover, the sheer diversity of Alaska Native village conditions, like the diversity of Indian reservations and communities in the Lower 48 states, compounds the problem of devising comprehensive statutory, judicial, or administrative solutions.

Despite their historical failure and disrepute, treaties and reservations elsewhere have provided the basis for clearer answers to questions about the status and powers of Indian tribes. Their absence from Alaska has meant that the political status of Alaska Natives is more ambiguous than is the status of reservation Indians elsewhere. That is not to argue that Alaska Natives should have had Lower 48–style treaties and reservations or that ANCSA should not have been enacted. Depending on timing and circumstance, Alaska Natives could have done much worse than they have under ANCSA. There is simply no way of knowing what might have been; the political uncertainties involved in such speculation are much too great.

From the Marshall trilogy on down, American Indian policy at its best has been shaped by assumptions about what is the right thing to do as well as by what is considered legally sound and politically possible. Like people generally, legislators, executives, and judges often disagree about such matters. This lack of consensus suggests that there is no single, simple, "correct" solution to the issue of Alaska Natives' dual status under American Indian laws.

CONCLUSION

Charles Wilkinson remarks that "the Founding Fathers almost certainly assumed that tribes would simply die out under the combined weight of capitalism, Christianity, and military power."[41] This belief in the withering away of the tribes persisted through the nineteenth century and into the twentieth. It is held by many people even now.

Although often with great reluctance, American politics and law accommodated the existence of the tribes, inventing and applying the doctrines of aboriginal rights, the trust relationship, and inherent powers. In most of the country, these doctrines were institutionalized in treaties and reservations that did as much to mark successive reductions in tribal power as to protect what was left of it. Nonetheless, the Indian tribes had a foothold in the American political system, and they refused to withdraw. Particularly during the late twentieth century, there has been a resurgence of political consciousness and action among the American Indian tribes.

Alaska Natives were the last of the Native Americans to feel the weight of capitalism, Christianity, and superior power on their cultures. They did not, for the most part, need to be conquered because there was plenty of land in Alaska and relatively few takers. After the early Russian occupation, Natives' contact with outsiders was mostly peaceful, and they made room for missionaries, traders, miners, fishermen, government agents, adventurers, and settlers. If Alaska Natives were conquered, it was by this process and by an invasion of politics and bureaucracy. The rules governing landownership and claims on resources changed virtually beneath their feet, often without their knowledge or their understanding of the implications. In Alaska, too, most non-Natives probably shared a widespread belief that the Native peoples would (and should) gradually wither away through assimilation.

By the time of statehood, it was clear that Alaska Natives would lose their lands, resources, and cultures by default if something was not done. What followed was the land claims movement and Alaska Native Claims Settlement Act, which provided Natives with limited tools for their political and economic advancement. In return for land and money, the act extinguished Natives' aboriginal land and subsistence rights and assigned ownership of lands to business corporations. Politically, ANCSA emphasized Natives' formal equality with all citizens, not their special status.

The challenge confronting Alaska Natives is to use these limited political and economic resources to increase control over their communities and to improve their social welfare. Such an effort requires, somewhat paradoxically, that Natives participate effectively in mainstream politics as equal citizens in order to enhance their special status as aboriginal Americans.

CHAPTER 6

A Model Constitution

At the thirty-fifth reunion of delegates to the Alaska Constitutional Convention (held in Juneau in 1991), George Sundborg rhetorically asked his fellow delegates and their guests, "Is everything perfect in state government?" His answer was, "Certainly not, but whatever ills are present in the system, the remedies exist in the Constitution. Alaskans are in charge of their own destiny now."

Although many Alaskans might disagree with the assessment that they are in charge of their own governmental destiny, they would probably share the perception that their constitution is a good one. From its inception, Alaska's constitution has been widely regarded as a model for state constitutional reformers. It created a unified and streamlined state government, included a strong declaration of rights, and set forth a simple set of progressive guidelines for government operations and resource development.

A recent study of the 1955–56 convention recalls, "Political scientists and major newspapers and other periodicals saw the 14,000-word constitution as a concise, flexible plan, a distillation of the best from America's 180 years of experience in self-government."[1] Shortly after the convention ended, the *New York Times* editorialized, somewhat romantically: "The deliberations of this convention and its results speak well for the common sense and civic devotion of the delegates. Its atmosphere was that of a pioneer America. These men and a few women spoke the authentic American language."[2]

Gathering during a thirty-below-zero cold snap in Fairbanks, the convention delegates agreed on their mission: to advance the cause of Alaska statehood. They wanted to convince Congress and the Eisenhower administration that Alaska stood ready for first-class membership in the Union. They had to prove the territory's residents not only ready but willing to achieve statehood. Knowing that a nationwide audience would judge their performance, the delegates' goal was to produce a document that would be viewed inside and outside Alaska as prudent and responsible. If they succeeded, Alaskans would rally behind their new constitution and the cause of statehood.

STATE GOVERNMENT REFORM IN THE 1950S

The 1950s found the United States enjoying a postwar economic and population boom. Depression and war had greatly expanded the role of the federal government in the economic and political life of the nation. The doctrine of dual federalism, a division of federal and state authority into separate spheres of limited government activity, had yielded to a more complex and dynamic pattern of intergovernmental relations. By the early 1950s, the states appeared to be drifting in the wake of an expanding flow of powers and functions to the federal government.

To assess the new intergovernmental system with regard to the states' role, President Eisenhower established the Commission on Intergovernmental Relations, also known as the Kestnbaum Commission for its chairman. The president charged the commission with identifying federal functions that could be "returned" to the states. This mission reflected, in part, a conservative reaction to the growth of federal power and unease with the increasing complexity and confusion of federal grant-in-aid programs.[3]

The commission reported to the president in 1955 that the states needed strengthening. In many cases, state constitutions imposed governmental restrictions that were often "the underlying cause of state and municipal pleas for federal assistance," the commission found. It proposed "fundamental revision" of state constitutions as a remedy.[4]

Members of the Kestnbaum Commission were not the only ones to suggest that deficient constitutions were crippling state governments. Political scientist James W. Fesler issued the following indictment:

Unfortunately, most of the constitutions reflect 19th-century distrust of state governments generally and distrust of each branch particularly. The result was an excess of democracy, expressed in a withholding of powers from the legislature, mincemeating of the executive and politicization of the judiciary. Hogtied, drawn and quartered, many a state government was no government at all. The kingdom was but the sum of its numerous petty and often unpretty principalities. With such a heritage, state governments today find it hard to do the kind of job that will restore public confidence. Even where there's a will, there may be no way.[5]

Alaska's territorial leaders rode a powerful wave of sentiment favoring state government reform when they gathered in 1955. National organizations calling for the reworking of state governments and constitutions included the National Governors' Conference, the Council of State Governments, the League of Women Voters, the National Municipal League, and the Public Administration Service (PAS) of Chicago.[6] (PAS was to serve as the Alaska Constitutional Convention's principal consultant.) The clamor for reform began on the eve of President Lyndon B. Johnson's Great Society, with its massive expansion of federal grant-in-aid programs to states and cities. The U.S. Supreme Court added impetus with its "one-man, one-vote" decisions in the early 1960s. The decisions broke the monopoly of conservative, rural-based political power in many state legislatures; urban representation increased dramatically.

The timing of Alaska's constitutional convention explains some of the national publicity received by the far-off territory.[7] The politics of civil rights influenced public opinion on statehood for Alaska and Hawaii and, consequently, affected the statehood movement and constitution writing in Alaska. In Congress, the issue of statehood for both territories was caught up in the larger North-South conflict over civil rights. Two U.S. senators elected from Alaska or Hawaii, particularly if they were Democrats, which, in Alaska's case, was likely, could tip the balance toward the northern liberals. The civil rights stalemate in Congress blocked both territories' bids for statehood.

Despite Congress's inaction, newspapers and civic organizations nationwide expressed strong support for bringing Alaska and Hawaii into the Union. National Gallup polls showed roughly a three-to-one margin in favor of statehood for both territories in the mid-1950s.[8] The public support probably stemmed primarily from traditional appeals to democratic values of self-government and representation. Many national organizations may also have based their support on the close voting margin in the U.S. Senate on civil rights issues. Although the civil rights question may, in the short run, have delayed a congressional vote on Alaska statehood, the movement generated new forces in Congress that focused attention on the relatively less urgent matters of statehood for Alaska and Hawaii.

WRITING AN ALASKA CONSTITUTION

Important forces were at work in Alaska's corner of the world as well. The territory experienced its own economic and population boom in the aftermath of World War II. Old-time residents were still frustrated with their federal overseers, but new immigrants to the territory brought with them a high degree of political idealism. They had great expectations for economic opportunities on the last American frontier. After the 1954 general election, Alaska's Democratic party stood poised to respond to the sentiments of newer residents. Democrats, who controlled both houses of the territorial legislature, decided the time was ripe to call a constitutional convention. They passed an act authorizing a seventy-five-day session at the University of Alaska campus near Fairbanks. The act called on the convention "to take all measures necessary and proper in preparation for the admission of Alaska as a State of the Union."[9]

Convention organizers wanted Alaska to make a good impression on Congress and the nation. As signals that the convention was not to be "politics as usual," they organized a nonpartisan delegate election and selected the university as a meeting site. The convention act specified the election of fifty-five delegates representing every region. The apportionment scheme ensured that the convention would better represent the territory's diverse and far-flung population than the legislature ever had. Lawmakers selected the number fifty-five to evoke the revered memory of the fifty-five founding fathers at the U.S. Constitutional Convention in Philadelphia in 1787.

Among the delegates elected were thirteen lawyers and nine storekeepers. The rest were miners, fishermen, pharmacists, housewives, ministers, pilots, and newspapermen. Many currently or formerly held office in territorial and local government. Six of the delegates were women; only one was an Alaska Native: Frank Peratrovich, a Tlingit Indian leader from southeast Alaska.[10] All were long-time Alaskans. George Sundborg reminded the delegates who attended the 1991 reunion that, in 1955, they had spent an average of twenty-seven years each in Alaska, for a cumulative total of almost fifteen hundred years.

The delegates organized into committees corresponding to proposed constitutional articles. The committees drew on the expertise of Outside consultants on state constitutions. The leading technical adviser was the PAS of Chicago, represented by Emil Sady. PAS prepared a series of constitutional studies and served as a hiring agent for other expert consultants. These consultants included John Bebout, then assistant director of the National Municipal League, headquartered in New York, and political science professors from various universities around the country.

The helpful resources the experts brought to the convention included the municipal league's "Model State Constitution," New Jersey's recently modernized constitution, and the Hawaii Constitution of 1950. Delegates also paid particular attention to state constitutions that, in Bebout's words, served as "horrible examples of what the convention wished to avoid."[11]

Alaskans proudly perceived that "politics" had no place in the convention. They were correct in the sense that current partisan and interest group politics were mostly implicit, reflected in the preoccupations of individual delegates, rather than explicit in the form of lobbyists seeking a hearing at the convention. As the convention got under way in November 1955, the *Fairbanks Daily News-Miner* observed that "usual political considerations . . . are entirely absent, so far as we can see." Convention president William Egan commented, "It's wonderful and maybe a miracle to see how these fifty-five people have left politics out of this convention."[12] Later Victor Fischer, a delegate who authored a major study of the convention, wrote, "The convention had little to do with current affairs; it didn't affect jobs, business, or any present allocation of power. With few exceptions, the pressures from lobbyists and special interest groups . . . were absent at the convention."[13]

For the time being, the constitution writers concerned themselves less with what specific actions their government would take than with enabling it to act authoritatively in the interests of Alaskans. Their first objective was to obtain statehood; after that they could turn their attention to the uses of statehood powers. The delegates and, indeed, the majority of Alaskans may have assumed that the consensus of opinion aroused by the statehood movement would carry over into the daily operations of state government. Many people believed, for example, that their new government would allow them to "do things right and avoid the mistakes of the older states." In fact, this particular belief has been repeated so often by so many that it has become something of an unofficial state slogan.

CONSTITUTIONAL PROVISIONS

The Alaska Constitution has retained much of its original content. A few significant amendments, discussed below, have affected the purposes as well as the instruments of government. The constitution's relative simplicity, conciseness, and "good government" character are still apparent.[14]

Government Structures

The constitution's articles on the legislature, executive, judiciary, and local government reflect modern reformist values of progressive action and coherence in government. Convention delegates knew well the shortcomings of their territorial government: its legislature was weak, its executive fragmented, and its judiciary a strictly federal body. Local governments were few, far between, and undeveloped. The constitution writers wanted to replace territorial institutions with up-to-date state and local structures.

The Legislature. Article II of the constitution established a bicameral legislature to meet in annual sessions of unlimited length. At 60 members (20 elected to four-year terms in the senate and 40 elected to two-year terms in the house), Alaska's legislative body is smaller than any state's except Nebraska, which has a 49-member unicameral legislature. In 1984, voters approved a constitutional amendment limiting annual sessions to 120 days. They were frustrated by the amount of time legislators were taking to divvy up oil revenues.

Legislative pay and unicameralism were the most contentious issues concerning Article II during the convention. Some delegates felt strongly that an attractive salary would run counter to the public-service, "citizen legislator" purpose of legislative office. Some feared also that per diem pay would provide an incentive to prolong legislative business. In the end, the delegates decided to let legislators set their own level and forms of pay. To this day, the issue of legislative salary remains controversial. Through a referendum, voters rolled back one legislative pay raise in 1976; facing a similar move in 1986, lawmakers rescinded a pay hike they had given themselves three years earlier.

A handful of convention delegates wanted a unicameral legislature, but their proposal was decisively defeated. Shortly after the convention, John Bebout commented that the vote "was influenced by the feeling that Congress might view a unicameral legislature with some misgivings."[15] Concerned about how the nation as a whole and Congress in particular would assess their political maturity, the majority of delegates shied away from the boldness of a unicameral legislature. They did adopt elements of unicameralism, however. As the constitution stands, the two houses meet in joint sessions and vote as one body on veto overrides. Joint sessions are also the vehicle for voting on gubernatorial appointments. A popular advisory vote in 1976 indicated that a majority of Alaska voters supported changing to unicameralism, but no legislature has seen fit to place a constitutional amendment on the ballot.

The Executive. The constitution writers probably departed most clearly from territorial institutions in their concept of the executive. In contrast to the fragmented and scattered territorial executive, the new one established under Article III features a highly unified executive branch under a governor with broad powers of appointment. Alaska is one of only three states in which the governor is the only independently elected statewide official. (The other two are New Jersey and Maine.) The lieutenant governor runs on the same ticket as the governor, and the attorney generalship is an appointed, not elected, office. Candidates for lieutenant governor, called secretary of state until 1970, run by themselves in the primary. Winners of the primary election run with their parties' gubernatorial nominees in the general election. The system of pairing has not always produced politically or personally compatible teams, but it has avoided messy partisan splits between the offices of the governor and lieutenant governor.

The lieutenant governor's only constitutional responsibility is to succeed the governor if the governor dies, resigns, or for some other reason is unable to occupy the office. (This succession has happened only once, in 1969, when President Nixon appointed then-governor Walter Hickel secretary of the interior and Lieutenant Governor Keith Miller moved into the top slot.) Beyond that, the lieutenant governor's duties are prescribed by law or delegated by the governor. The lieutenant governor's only statutory responsibility is to supervise state elections.

Article III limits the number of executive departments to twenty and authorizes the governor to reorganize the bureaucracy by executive order, subject to legislative veto. In general, the governor has direct authority over the departments; he appoints department heads who serve at his pleasure. The governor can also hire or fire the second- and third-ranking employees in each department. Section 26 of Article III also authorizes deviations from this scheme. In the case of the Department of Education, the governor appoints a state board, which selects a department head subject to the governor's approval. A similar arrangement applies to the Department of Fish and Game. Although a few such exceptions exist to the governor's unified authority, on the whole the chief executive wields substantial control over the top leaders of all departments.

The question of whether the attorney general should be appointed by the governor or elected by the people aroused heated debate at the convention. The delegates opted for gubernatorial appointment, but the idea of an elected attorney general, politically independent of the governor, has surfaced in nearly every legislature since statehood. Supporters of the idea have yet to obtain the two-thirds vote in each house needed to place a constitutional amendment on the election ballot. Thus, Alaska remains one of only seven states without an elected attorney general.

The Judiciary. A constitutionally unified judiciary parallels the unified executive. In drafting Article IV on the judiciary, convention delegates looked to New Jersey's recently remodeled judicial system. All Alaska courts come under the rule-making jurisdiction of the supreme court, whose chief justice stands as the administrative head of the state court system. The constitution established a supreme court and superior courts; the legislature later created district courts and a court of criminal appeals.

The authors of the Alaska Constitution also sought to balance political accountability with professionalism in the selection of judges. They settled on the innovative Missouri Plan, under which a judicial council appointed by the governor nominates judges. To retain accountability, the judges are periodically subject to nonpartisan retention elections (see chapter 9).

After compromising nicely on the issue of an appointed versus an elected judiciary, convention deliberations took a somewhat regressive turn when delegates debated residency requirements for judges. Some wished to require judicial nominees to have practiced law in Alaska for at least five years. A few delegates even felt that time served as a federal government lawyer should not count toward meeting the requirement. Given the prevailing antifederal sentiment in the territory, such restrictions probably would have had broad popular appeal. Mindful of their national audience, however, the delegates stuck to the statehood agenda and left definition of judicial qualifications to future legislatures.[16]

Local Government. When it came to Article X, on local government, the convention was quite free to innovate. To protect fishing and mining industries from local taxation and regulation, Congress had prohibited the creation of counties in the territory. Few local governments existed. At the time of the convention, urban reformers nationwide argued for the modernization of American counties, which, for the most part, they said, were institutional relics. Convention consultants also pointed to Alaska's opportunity to establish unified local governments for entire natural regions, "a goal that local government reformers . . . have been striving to attain . . . [for] several generations."[17]

Alaska's boroughs, then, were born as urban areawide and regional structures to unify local government just as the new legislative, executive, and judicial institutions were to unify government statewide. The constitution gave boroughs authority to provide all necessary services and regulations; existing cities and special districts were somehow to become parts of the borough system. The boroughs were to cover the entire state, enveloping urban as well as rural areas. To accommodate vast differences in local needs and conditions, boroughs in developed areas were to be "organized"; in undeveloped areas they were to be "unorganized." The state legislature was to govern unorganized boroughs with assistance from newly formed state agencies.

Article X left much to the imagination. It briefly outlined an innovative, abstract scheme that deliberately bore little resemblance to existing structures either in Alaska or in any of the forty-eight states. In the absence of real-world models, delegate James Hurley stated, the article was "extremely vague, pardon the expression, as to how these things are going to be carried out." He urged the convention to add a "liberal construction" clause to the article in order to encourage future legislatures and courts to support strong local government powers.[18] Although the convention adopted such a clause, it did not prevent confusion and conflict when the borough system was implemented (see chapter 12).

Anticipating differences between boroughs and cities, the delegates included a provision in Article X that actually aggravated the situation. Although cities were to continue to exist within boroughs, the article's framers believed the cities should form "part of" boroughs. To cement this reciprocal relationship, they required city council members to hold a certain number of seats on borough assemblies. In practice, this arrangement institutionalized and intensified conflicts between the two local governments. It was abandoned after voters approved a constitutional amendment in 1972.

Government Functions

Alaska's constitution characteristically says little about state functions and their execution. What it does say, however, reflects a mixture of territorial experience, frontier aspirations, and Outside expertise, much as was noted in the provisions on government structure. The most important constitutional statement about government functions is Article VIII, on natural resources, a unique subject for state constitutional treatment at the time.

Natural Resources. The Alaska statehood movement was largely about control of natural resources. Many residents of the territory believed that the underdevelopment and Outside exploitation of Alaska's resources could be traced to sins of omission and commission by the federal government. They thought the only escape from the trap was for Alaska to become a state so its residents could assume control of fish and wildlife, minerals, forests, and other resources. Accordingly, the convention incorporated these basic objectives of the statehood movement into the natural resources article. The first two sections of the article state that Alaska's lands should be settled and its resources developed for the benefit of the people of the state.

Alaskans focused their hostility toward Outside control and exploitation on the fish trap. Strategically placed at river mouths and island channels, the mechanical devices were hugely efficient at harvesting salmon. More than four hundred traps operated in Alaska waters in the 1950s, most of them owned by Seattle-based canners. The traps were seen as a hated symbol of absentee control and colonial status because they deprived Alaskans of fisheries income.[19]

Convention delegate W. O. Smith, a fisherman from Ketchikan, said, "This one issue [fish traps] is the thing which gave the greatest impetus to the statehood movement, which resulted in the calling of this convention."[20] The constitution did not explicitly outlaw the traps; one delegate argued that mentioning them "would detract from the dignity of the document."[21] Instead, an "ordinance" calling for the abolition of traps on statehood was attached to the constitution; voters approved it overwhelmingly, by a greater margin than the constitution itself, in the 1956 ratification election. Two provisions of the natural resources article dealt with the issue in general terms. Section 3 declares that fish and wildlife "are reserved to the people for common use," and section 15 prohibits any "exclusive right or special privilege of fishery."

In 1972, the "no exclusive right or special privilege of fishery" clause was amended to allow the state to limit the number of fishermen in the salmon and other fisheries and to determine who would receive valuable "limited-entry" permits. As stated in the amendment, its purposes were "resource conservation, to prevent economic distress among fishermen . . . and to promote the efficient development of aquaculture in the state." It is noteworthy that fish traps, by controlling escapement of fish, could represent the ultimate management tool for achieving the conservation and efficiency objectives of limited entry. Essentially the same conservation and efficiency rationale put forward to support limited entry was used to justify abolishing the traps.

Why would Alaskans use similar justifications for apparently contradictory resource policies? Apart from the fact that there is nothing unusual about inconsistencies in public policy, the purpose of both measures—the fish-trap ordinance and the limited-entry amendment—was primarily to strengthen resident control of Alaska fishery resources. Both measures fell within the "Alaskans first" resource objectives expressed in Article VIII. One perverse result of limited entry, however, has been the creation of a valuable private asset, the limited-entry permit, which can be sold to non-resident fishermen. Because the legislature placed minimal restrictions on the transfer of permits, the number of resident permit holders, particularly in rural Alaska, has slowly declined.[22]

At the 1991 reunion of convention delegates, Eldor Lee condemned the limited-entry permit system, calling it an "abomination." Lee, a fisherman from Petersburg in southeast Alaska, said his family had been fishing in Alaska waters for eighty-nine years; now it is allowed only one hand-trolling permit in the southeastern salmon fishery. "The only way to get a permit now is to be rich," he said. Many Alaskans agree with him. Others, particularly the owners of the valuable permits, priced as high as $300,000 or more, vigorously defend the system. An estimated $1 billion in Alaska fisheries value has been transferred to limited-entry permit holders, whose low taxes and fees do not even cover the cost of managing the fisheries. This is privatization of public resources on a grand scale, in apparent conflict with the original purpose of Article VIII.

Another contradiction in the natural resources article relates to its conservation goals. On the one hand, the article subscribes to the well-established progressive conservationist principles of multiple use and sustained yield; it clearly implies that Alaska's land and resources should be managed as a long-term public trust. On the other hand, the article authorizes the sale and grant of state lands, protects private rights in public lands and resources, and, most important, promotes "first-come, first-served" grants of water and mineral rights to private interests. The latter provisions are comparable to some of the more environmentally and economically regressive practices found in the western states.

At the time of the constitutional convention, objectives widely shared among Alaskans transcended their conflicting interests in the territory's resources. They single-mindedly desired statehood and the creation of a state government to control Alaska's resources and ensure that the benefits of development accrued to residents, not outsiders. For the time being, they set aside their conflicting political, conservation, and development interests to work together toward the overriding objective of statehood for Alaska.

Finance and Taxation. Compared to the finance and taxation provisions of most other state constitutions, Article IX of Alaska's constitution remains a model of brevity. Reformist arguments that public accountability can be ensured without hamstringing legislative and executive authorities strongly influenced it, too.[23] Reflecting on their frustrations with territorial government, convention delegates generally agreed with expert consultants who advised giving legislatures broad latitude in determining how public money should be raised and spent; the less said about it in the constitution, the better, they concluded.

Article IX includes several relatively simple provisions concerning standards and processes for property taxation, budgeting, appropriations, and audits. The most notable provisions the convention adopted are one prohibiting the dedication of public revenues to specific purposes and another requiring voter approval of state or local debt for capital projects. Delegates also provided for exceptions to the limits on contracting debt, such as disasters, invasions, or insurrections, as well as to permit use of revenue bonds and special assessments.

Amendments to this article now appear more significant than its original provisions. In 1976, anticipating large increases in state revenues from oil production at Prudhoe Bay, voters approved an amendment establishing the Alaska Permanent Fund and requiring that a designated proportion of oil revenues be dedicated to it. The amendment also dictated that the principal of the fund be used only for income-producing investments, while fund earnings could be used for any purpose determined by law.

By 1993, the principal of the Permanent Fund stood at $15 billion and its earnings at more than $1 billion annually. Alaskans understood at the time they adopted the Permanent Fund amendment that lawmakers would use the earnings to prop up state government when oil revenues declined. But despite a substantial slump in state revenues beginning with the oil-price crash in the mid-1980s, fund earnings have not gone toward paying for state government. Instead, half the earnings have been dispersed to state residents in the form of annual dividend checks. Most of the other half has been redeposited in the fund to offset the annual reduction in real value of the principal due to inflation. The remainder has been retained and managed as an "unencumbered balance" (see chapter 3 for detailed discussion of the fund and the uses of its earnings).

The Permanent Fund may represent the most profound constitutional alteration in Alaska since statehood. In addition to its established roles as proprietor of land and resources and as sovereign government, the state of Alaska has assumed the part of an investment banker with a direct financial trust relationship with its shareholder-citizens. The state government may increasingly be forced to choose among conflicting values and priorities associated with its distinct proprietary, sovereign, and trust responsibilities.

In the early 1990s, Governor Walter Hickel referred frequently to the responsibilities of the "owner state," as if its status as proprietor of resources meant it would need to relax its sovereign regulatory and tax powers in order to promote development. Another major question for the 1990s is whether the "trustee state" will be able to distribute ever-larger dividends to individuals at the same time the "sovereign state" meets more traditional, collectively determined public goals despite the handicap of decreasing oil revenues and tighter state budgets.

Voters amended the finance article of the constitution again in 1982 when they approved an appropriations limit that lawmakers had placed on the ballot. The idea behind the amendment was to cap state spending while excess oil revenues flowed so that money would be left over when the revenues slowed. As it turned out, the legislature set too high a ceiling to limit anything: oil revenues had already begun to slide at the time the voters approved the amendment; the revenues were at or under the limit by the time it went into effect (see chapter 3). In 1990, voters approved another amendment establishing a Budget Reserve Fund. This fund would receive money the state expected to win in litigation over oil taxes and royalties, and it could be used only in case of significant decreases in state revenues.

Health, Education, and Welfare. Apart from the natural resources and finance articles, the constitution says little about state functions. Article VII, on health, education, and welfare, is the shortest article in the document. It briefly states that lawmakers must provide for public schools, public health, and public welfare, and it recognizes the University of Alaska as a corporate institution of the state. The only controversy about this article during the convention centered on a provision adopted by the delegates that prohibits spending public funds for the direct benefit of religious or other private schools. It became controversial again in 1991 when Governor Hickel proposed a voucher system for education. The proposal would allow public funds to be spent in private school education. Because it would require an amendment of this section of the constitution, for which there was little support, the governor dropped it from the list of reforms to Alaska education considered in 1992.

Citizens' Rights and Popular Controls

For a document presumably encoding the values of an individualistic, frontier society, Alaska's constitution contains mostly familiar provisions on the rights of citizens and their controls over government. The constitution says virtually nothing about distinctive rights for Native peoples. The federal government acknowledged Alaska Natives' aboriginal land and resource rights after the 1867 purchase of Russian America but left these rights undefined and largely unprotected for the next century.

Declaration of Rights. Article I of the constitution is Alaska's version of the U.S. Constitution's Bill of Rights with the additional stipulations found in most state constitutions. It guarantees freedom of speech, freedom of religion, the right to petition and assembly, the right to due process, and, of course, the right to bear arms, in much the same language as the federal Constitution. Also familiar are protections of civil rights, prohibitions against unreasonable searches and seizures, restraints against excessive punishment, and basic standards governing criminal procedures.

Alaska's constitution writers could not have found a better model than the Bill of Rights, but they might have been expected to add some Alaska flavor to the state's declaration of rights. A proposal was made to forbid discrimination based on sex, a somewhat avant-garde move for the mid-1950s, but the measure was soundly defeated after a woman delegate argued that the territory had a very good record as far as women's rights were concerned, "and we have nothing at all to complain about."[24] By 1972, Alaskans were prepared to make the commitment to women's rights; they approved an amendment adding "sex" alongside race, color, creed, and national origin as categories with special protections of civil and political rights. The amendment passed by a four-to-one margin. Of the five constitutional amendments on the ballot that year, only the "right-to-privacy" language received a more favorable vote, at six to one.

The right-to-privacy amendment states, "The right of the people to privacy is recognized and shall not be infringed," and adds that the legislature must implement the provision. The state supreme court, not lawmakers, did most to implement the provision when it held in 1975 that individuals were allowed to possess small amounts of marijuana for personal use in their homes.[25] Legislators reacting to the antidrug climate of the late 1980s and the accompanying national "war on drugs" sought to roll back the privacy right to marijuana in the home. They apparently accomplished their goal in 1990, when voters by a six-to-five margin approved an initiative "recriminalizing" the possession of any amount of marijuana. In 1991, however, on the day the law was scheduled to go into effect, Alaskans for Privacy, a group opposed to recriminalization, filed a lawsuit to block its implementation. The group claimed that the law violates the right-to-privacy clause of the state constitution, and the issue was making its way back to the Alaska Supreme Court in 1993.

Voters added a characteristically Alaskan element to Article I in 1988 when they approved a "resident preference" amendment. The principal objective was to increase the chances of a "local hire" law passing a constitutional test in the courts. Because federal and state courts have overturned several previous laws discriminating against nonresidents seeking employment in Alaska, little prospect exists that the broadly worded amendment will significantly change the situation.

Alaska Native Rights. There was some sentiment at the convention to grant constitutional land rights to Natives. But it was the majority sense that Native land rights were too complex to settle hurriedly and were primarily a federal problem (see chapter 5). One delegate argued that pursuing the issue further could "upset the entire possibility of Alaska having any public domain and would be setting up one group of our citizens . . . against the rest."[26]

Delegates instead agreed to include language in the constitution's general provisions (Article XII) disclaiming rights to lands "held by or for" Natives and recognizing that Congress ultimately held the power to dispose of these lands. Similar disclaimers commonly appeared in statehood acts dating to the early nineteenth century to avoid land disputes between new states and the federal government. Essentially the same disclaimer showed up in the 1884 act establishing the territory of Alaska and in the Alaska Statehood Act of 1958.[27]

Delegates did express some sympathy for Native interests. The committee writing the suffrage and elections article proposed that a person be required only to read or speak English in order to vote, a liberalization of a territorial requirement that voters be able to write the language. One delegate thought the change went too far and that all voters should be able to read, speak, and write English. He told the convention that "every citizen who comes over from some foreign land and is naturalized must be able to read and write. Is it so much to ask that Native-born American citizens should not be able to do the same thing?"[28]

Frank Peratrovich, the sole Native delegate, responded that some of the older Native people from his region "can write their name and perhaps write a sentence in English, but they cannot sit down and write letters." He also observed that a 1924 congressional act recognized Native people as citizens. They had voted in elections under provisions of the act, he argued, and therefore the future state should not deny them a right they already possessed. The convention adopted the "read or speak" requirement proposed by the committee.[29] In 1970, voters approved a constitutional amendment lifting the English-language requirement altogether.

Initiative, Referendum, and Recall. The constitution writers tried to balance the authority of representative government with the right of the people to make or repeal laws in the absence of legislative responsiveness. In general, the framers tipped the balance in favor of representative government. Article XI prohibits the use of initiatives and referenda affecting the uses of state revenues, the distribution of state resources, or the creation, jurisdiction, and rules of state courts. In the case of recall, the framers left the definition of grounds and procedures in the hands of lawmakers.

Voters have employed neither initiatives nor referenda frequently since statehood. By 1990, of the fourteen initiatives placed on the ballot, only six had met with approval from a majority of voters. Only one formal referendum had reached a vote: repeal of a legislative salary increase in 1976. The legislature has submitted other laws for voter ratification, but not under the referendum provision of the constitution. The governor, lieutenant governor, and legislators are subject to recall by a majority of voters, although none of these officials has lost a job under this provision. In 1993, petitions for the recall of Governor Hickel were being widely circulated, but few observers expected the effort to succeed. Many more attempts have been made to recall municipal officials, and some have succeeded. For example, in December 1992, Anchorage voters recalled three of the seven members of the school board.

RATIFICATION AND REVISION

The convention completed its work in February 1956, and a ratification election was held the following April. Voters approved the constitution by a two-to-one margin. Only in the Southeast, where communities depended heavily on canneries and other Seattle-based businesses, was the vote relatively close, with a five-to-four approval margin. In the same election, voters in every region overwhelmingly supported the ordinance abolishing fish traps, which passed by a five-to-one margin.

Voters also approved the Alaska-Tennessee Plan, under which they would subsequently elect two U.S. senators and a representative to go to Washington, D.C., to lobby for statehood. George H. Lehleitner, a New Orleans wholesaler of floor coverings and home appliances, had urged the plan on the convention. He believed that a tactic used by the territory of Tennessee in 1796 could work for Alaska 160 years later. Lehleitner's experience in the armed forces in Hawaii during World War II had made him a strong supporter of that territory's bid for statehood. Hawaii statehood leaders had rejected his plan, so he turned his attention to Alaska. After his proposal received the endorsement of Bob Bartlett, Alaska's territorial delegate to Congress, the convention unanimously agreed to put the ordinance on the constitution ballot.[30]

Two years later, the statehood campaign reached a successful conclusion. In the summer of 1958, Congress passed the Alaska Statehood Act; in January 1959, President Eisenhower signed the proclamation admitting Alaska as the forty-ninth state of the Union.

There are several ways of amending the constitution. The legislature can initiate amendments by a two-thirds vote of each house, it can call a constitutional convention, and Alaskans can call a convention once every ten years. It may also be possible for voters to call a convention by passing an initiative, although there is legal uncertainty about this method. None of the latter three options had been exercised by the legislature or the voters as of 1993. Only a few other states regularly offer voters an automatic option to call a convention. In Alaska, as in virtually every other state, all constitutional amendments require voter approval.

As of 1993, the constitution the people approved thirty-six years earlier had been amended only twenty times (in twenty-two places) out of twenty-eight attempts. About half the changes, reviewed in the discussion above of specific articles, were relatively significant. As state constitutions go, Alaska's has undergone comparatively little change. During the 1970s, each of the fifty states adopted an average of thirty-three constitutional amendments while Alaska adopted only twelve, the highest total by far for any decade since statehood.[31] Because Alaska's constitution is a relatively new document, one would expect less need or demand to arise to amend it. Also, other states allow amendment by popular initiative, whereas Alaska's process must originate through either the legislature or a constitutional convention.

There is continuing debate over the question of allowing voters to amend the constitution directly by initiative. In recent times this issue has received more attention because of popular interest in imposing term limits on legislators. There are other potential constitutional changes, too, that legislatures are typically loath to act on, such as reapportionment and redistricting provisions and unicameralism. Although a majority of Alaska voters could call a decennial convention, that is not an attractive option to most opinion leaders because a convention would expose the entire constitution to change. Moreover, many believe that the founders were wise to insulate the constitution from popular initiatives. In 1992, despite popular support particularly for term limits, voters turned down the ten-year call by a resounding two-to-one margin. The reformers had not made their case in the face of apparent voter skepticism about convention politics, costs, and highly uncertain outcomes.

CONCLUSION

Alaskans wrote their constitution primarily to use as a tool in their quest for statehood. Wanting to make a good impression on Congress and the nation, the founders strove to produce a model document reflecting the reformists' standards of the time. The resulting constitution helped, or at least did not hurt, the statehood drive. To further assess Alaska's constitution, we attempt here to explain in what sense it is a model, to what extent it still works, and what difference it has made for state government.

The Advisory Commission on Intergovernmental Relations in the mid-1980s summarized criteria for "effective constitutions" as follows: "In general, state constitutions are best when they are brief and written in simple, clear language, when they include provisions of lasting duration rather than those transitory in nature, and when they are unencumbered by restraints on the state government that are unlikely to be needed. Each, also, should provide for adjustment to emerging conditions by orderly change through amendment and revision."[32] Measured by these criteria, Alaska's constitution was clearly an advanced model in the mid-1950s. In the 1990s, it stands as one of the more "effective" state constitutions. It remains relatively brief, concise, unencumbered, and open to change. These, of course, are merely formal criteria. A more significant test is whether it still "works." Does it, at a minimum, continue to authorize necessary state action, facilitate government operations, and protect the people from undue government interference? In a broad, subjective sense, Alaska's constitution appears to accomplish all these things. It provides a general and reasonably flexible framework for government, leaving the critical details to legislatures, executives, and the courts.

Alaska was a different place in the 1950s when the constitution was written. It had a much smaller population and a much simpler society. Dominated by the consensus issue of statehood, Alaska's politics were more harmonious. Alaskans conflicted with outsiders, the federal government, and absentee corporate owners instead of with one another. Outsiders proved to be easy targets for residents of the territory, who used their frustration as a springboard for the statehood movement. Cultural and political differences within Alaska, particularly those between urban immigrants and rural Natives, were mostly latent or submerged. Clearly, Alaska is a more complex and conflict-ridden political society in the 1990s, but this fact seems not to have detracted from the constitution's workability.

Have the specific form and content of Alaska's constitution affected the way the state has been governed? Would government perform less satisfactorily were it not based on a technically well crafted document? Although no one can know for sure, a reasonable answer to both questions is "yes, but probably not much." A case could be made, for example, that the judiciary article's Missouri Plan facilitates the appointment of professionally qualified judges. Yet the decisions of the judicial council and the governor, among other factors, probably play a more decisive role. Perhaps the local government article, promoting areawide institutions, helps to avoid some of the inequities and conflicts that exist between separate local governments in larger and more fragmented urban systems. Yet, compared to metropolitan areas elsewhere, Alaska cities are small towns with small problems; it would be a mistake to attribute too much to the constitutional scheme for local government.

It can be said with more confidence that the constitution has not seriously hampered change in Alaska government and politics. When state officials and resident fishermen found that the natural resources article prevented imposition of limited entry in the fisheries, they led a successful drive to amend it, creating an exception to the "no exclusive right or special privilege of fishery" and related clauses. Similarly, when the finance article's prohibition of dedicated funds stood in the way of creating the Alaska Permanent Fund, voters agreed to a constitutional exception advocated by state leaders. These amendments and the legislation they authorized signal important shifts in the values and purposes served by Alaska state government. The statehood movement was born largely of popular revulsion against private appropriation of public resources, a sentiment directed mainly against outsiders. Now limited entry in the fisheries and Permanent Fund dividends not only privatize public resources; they facilitate the appropriation of these resources by nonresidents and newcomers.

If a model state constitution is one that incorporates basic principles of the U.S. Constitution, draws an effective framework for government, and accommodates significant political and social change, then Alaska's document appears to have met the test.

CHAPTER 7

Legislative Government

In June 1981, Democrat Russ Meekins, a dissident member of the state house of representatives, took the speaker's chair to reorganize the body. Meekins called for a vote on a new Speaker, house officers, committee chairs, and members of the powerful Finance Committee. Displaced majority members protested on grounds of illegality and unconstitutionality, but the rump caucus prevailed. The new leadership installed itself and proceeded to rewrite the state budget, then in conference committee, from scratch.

Republicans and some Democrats, including more southcentral and rural interests than sat in the previous organization, joined Meekins. The dissidents felt bitter about the way the state was allocating its oil wealth. They were also extremely dissatisfied with the method of distributing capital construction dollars, which left the Republican minority outside the loop.

Ousted majority members cried foul to the press and filed a lawsuit in the supreme court asking the justices to nullify the reorganization. The high court declined to enter the fracas, leaving the new majority in power through the remainder of the legislative term. The coup influenced house organization in the next legislative session as well.

THE LEGISLATURE AS A MICROCOSM OF ALASKA POLITICS

The 1981 coup was a twentieth-century first in American state politics. No other legislature had dismantled its leadership without changing its membership. Characteristically, this first occurred in Alaska, where individualism finds many expressions politically. The state's voter registration laws do not require enrollment in a party; in 1993, about 54 percent of the electorate was not aligned with any political organization. Partisan politics, therefore, wield little power over elected officials in comparison to interest groups or regional interests. Party discipline is virtually absent. Alaska's vast territory, isolated stretches, and widely separated cities guarantee that regional cultures play strong roles in the competition for stakes in state policy making.

The small population increases political opportunities for citizens while it reduces the distance between elected officials and constituents. The "people" are not an abstraction to legislators: they are friends and neighbors. The state legislature reflects populism in Alaska. The chief instigator of the 1981 coup initiated a populistic distribution of capital construction dollars when, as chair of the House Finance Committee in 1979, he gave each member of the house $750,000 to spend in his or her district, as he or she wished. Two years later, Meekins was a member of the minority that decried discrimination in capital construction dollars and demanded an equal share. Rural interests, citing hardship, insisted on an even bigger share.

The framers of the state constitution objected to the weak and constrained legislature of Alaska's territorial era. Consequently, they crafted a strong state legislature. They avoided circumscribing its powers by any of the usual routes, such as special dedication of revenues, restrictions on taxation authority, or limitations on legislative sessions, staff, or salaries.

In this chapter, we discuss the ways the Alaska legislature reflects the state's political cultures and environment. We evaluate the process of legislative government and look at the record over a period of thirty years. The story begins and ends with representation.

REPRESENTATION

Alaska's size, sparse population, and finite transportation infrastructure complicate the business of speaking for the public. A population density of less than one person per square mile, a small (sixty-member) legislature, and a capital remote from most residents present challenges unlike those facing lawmakers in other states.

The Concept of Representation

The term *representation* is neutral with respect to *what* is being represented. Framers of the Alaska Constitution, like those in many states, tried to balance representation of geographic regions with representation of people. The territorial legislature had assigned seats based on population in the area's four judicial districts: Northwest, Interior, Southcentral, and Southeast.[1] As urban populations grew during the territorial period, southcentral residents became increasingly underrepresented, while rural residents became over-represented.

Framers of the constitution sought to give every Alaskan a maximum of representation without drowning out the voice of rural residents.[2] Article VI of the constitution created house districts in rough approximation to population and allocated senate seats mainly on the basis of geographic area. On statehood, senators from sparsely settled northern and western Alaska represented far fewer citizens than senators from urban areas.

U.S. Supreme Court reapportionment decisions in *Baker v. Carr* (1962) and *Wesbury v. Saunders* (1964) invalidated Alaska's constitutional provisions. The one-person, one-vote stricture required a redesign of Alaska's voting districts.

Districting

In 1965, Alaska reconfigured its electoral districts to conform to the Supreme Court decisions. Like the lawmaking bodies of other states, Alaska's legislature is now redistricted after each decennial census.

The governor possesses sweeping redistricting powers in Alaska, powers he shares with an advisory redistricting board. Voters may petition the superior court to correct perceived redistricting errors. The superior and supreme courts have intervened so far in these challenges, which have arisen with every redistricting since 1962. The 1981–82 cycle was notable because Governor Jay Hammond's predominantly Republican commission performed a modest amount of gerrymandering. One of its creations was an icicle-shaped district nicknamed "Iceworm," extending from Southeast up to Yakutat. It captured precincts that had narrowly supported Republican candidates in the past and advanced the number of safe seats in the legislature. This and related actions prompted the courts to step in and make minor adjustments to district lines. For instance, the iceworm district gave way to the "donut" district, which included Cordova, Valdez, Seward, Wasilla, and Palmer, the smaller communities encircling Anchorage.

The redistricting squabbles of the 1980s were tame, however, when compared to the drama of the 1990–91 (and 1992) redistricting. Troubles began with a change in the governor's office. Outgoing governor Steve Cowper had appointed a reapportionment board with a Democratic tilt in 1989, but incoming governor Walter Hickel replaced it with one of his own in 1990. Cowper's board had presented a plan that left most districts intact and favored incumbents; Hickel's board, with a four-to-one ratio of Republicans to

Democrats, fashioned a plan that proposed single-member districts state-wide and altered district lines in most regions. Also, it would have pitted incumbents against each other in thirteen districts, benefiting Republicans.

The Hickel plan drew objections from the Alaska Democratic Party, Native groups, and some local governments, who filed suit in superior court. In May 1992, after a two-week trial, Superior Court Judge Larry Weeks declared Hickel's reapportionment plan unconstitutional. Weeks said the plan ignored constitutional requirements that the board create "contiguous and compact" election districts. Moreover, the constitution directs that the board try to "maintain the social and economic integrity of communities and ethnic groups, while taking into account local government boundaries and major geographic features—such as rivers and mountain ranges."[3] Weeks objected to several of the new districts, including the proposed House District 35, an area the size of Texas whose boundaries straddled the Brooks Range. The district would have combined Inupiat Eskimos of the North Slope and Athabaskan Indians of the Interior, a prospect that distressed both groups. Although Weeks did not accuse the board of gerrymandering or self-dealing, he noted that several members of the board with political ambitions appeared to benefit from new "open" house districts—those districts without incumbents. Weeks also agreed with the Alaska Democratic Party that the board had violated state open meetings and records laws, conducting much of its business behind closed doors.

The state objected to Weeks's ruling, but the Alaska Supreme Court upheld it in late May, directing Weeks to come up with a new, interim redistricting plan by June 18. To that end, Weeks named three independent "masters" to make recommendations: Fairbanks assemblyman Harold Gillam, former state attorney general Wilson Condon of Anchorage, and Brian Rogers, a former state legislator and vice-president of finance for the University of Alaska system, based in Fairbanks.

The Hickel administration stewed publicly over the court's decision. Hickel had called his redistricting proposal among the fairest ever put forward for the state. Also, the U.S. Justice Department approved it for compliance with the federal Voting Rights Act. Alaska attorney general Charles Cole criticized the court for abusing its power and said that the court has been "envious" of the governor's redistricting authority for decades, noting that it has struck down every reapportionment plan since statehood.[4] In 1993, the Reapportionment Board tinkered with the court's plan; a dissatisfied court required a new draft for the 1994 elections.

Generally speaking, Alaska's weaker partisan forces provoke less heated reapportionment battles than those pitched in other states. The allocation of redistricting powers to the executive branch, which is limited by federal and state constitutional constraints, appears to have reduced somewhat the partisan nature of the process and the amount of gerrymandering. Correspondingly, it has increased the role of the courts as mediating actors.[5] Still, given the right circumstances and people, Alaska's legislative reapportionment process can provide a few fireworks.

Alaska's Political Geography

Where Alaskans live conditions their view of state government and politics. Alaska has four well-defined political regions: Southeast, rural Alaska, Southcentral, and the Interior.

Southeast Alaska includes Ketchikan, Sitka, Juneau, and several smaller towns, which usually coalesce into a southeastern group in the legislature. The unity of this group and its proximity to the state capital in Juneau give it bargaining advantages. Its interests in commercial fishing and state government make it unique statewide. Southeast legislators experience the lowest turnover rate, at least partly because they live closest to Juneau and thus their personal lives and careers are least disrupted by the session. The president of the senate in the seventeenth legislature, Dick Eliason (R), has represented Sitka since 1968. House Speaker Ben Grussendorf (D) was elected Sitka's representative to the house in 1980.

Although more than three-fourths of the state is considered rural, only 20 percent of the overall population (and the membership of the legislature) is rural. In the legislature, rural areas form a tightly knit "Bush" caucus that sometimes includes urban members. (Bush originally was used to describe large expanses of wilderness beyond the fringes of civilization, but the term has come to stand for any part of Alaska not accessible by road. This area is home for many of Alaska's Native people and for homesteaders, miners, guides, pilots, trappers, and fishermen.)[6] Rural seats go uncontested more often than urban seats in part because Native constituencies see the advantage of returning to office legislators who bring home benefits to the district. For this reason, rural legislators tend to have more seniority, which they use to position themselves advantageously in the pecking order in Juneau. A good example is John Sackett, an Athabaskan who represented Interior villages in the house and later the senate for nearly twenty years; during his tenure, he chaired both houses' finance committees.

Urban areas now hold the overwhelming majority of legislative seats.

Most urban areas lie along the railbelt, the course of the Alaska Railroad from Fairbanks through Anchorage to Seward. Railbelt delegations frequently sponsor legislative coalitions. Underlying this coalition are commonalities that come from living in cities and sharing economic development objectives. Large fissures in the railbelt coalition, when they occur, result partly from political and ideological differences, but largely from rivalries between Anchorage and other cities, particularly Fairbanks.

By 1992, the population of the southcentral region amounted to nearly 50 percent of the state as a whole. Redistrictings have given this region almost half the seats in the house and senate. The southcentral delegation, however, is sharply fragmented. Anchorage legislators are most numerous, but they divide between downtown and suburban areas, between Republicans and Democrats. No Anchorage legislator has served twenty years; most have been in the legislature for fewer than three terms. The interests of Anchorage, a unified city-borough, diverge from those of the Matanuska-Susitna and the Kenai Peninsula boroughs. These regional boroughs are the fastest growing areas of the state, represented by such veteran lawmakers as Jalmar Kerttula *(D),* who was first elected by Palmer residents in 1960.

Fairbanks is made up of a curious mix of interests because of its strong mining past, large military installations, university population, and fringe politics. Despite local political clashes and value conflicts, Fairbanks's representatives generally speak with one voice in Juneau. The Interior's delegation numbers enough legislators to form a bargaining group; on some issues it has forged successful alliances with southeast and rural legislators against southcentral interests. Former senate president Don Bennett *(R),* who served in the legislature from the 1970s until his death from a heart attack in 1984, drew support from Republicans and Democrats, blue collar workers and university professors because of his ability to bring home capital projects to the Fairbanks area.

In short, the Alaska legislature faithfully reproduces the state's regionalism. Frequently, regionalism is a major factor explaining state legislative outcomes.

Access to the Legislature

Alaska's capital city, Juneau, is accessible only by boat or plane, not by road, from other regions of the state or country. Its isolated setting on the richly forested panhandle that forms southeast Alaska distances it from more than three-fourths of the population. Popular demands for easier access to

lawmakers have fueled six attempts to relocate the capital to the more populous southcentral region. The last effort failed at the polls in 1982.

Alaskans not only want their legislators close by during the session; they
want them home eight months of the year. A constitutional amendment
passed in 1984 limited the length of legislative sessions so lawmakers could
return in a timely manner to their home districts. Voters supported the
amendment because they were frustrated by the legislatures of the early
1980s, which took more than 160 days to do the state's business. During such
marathon sessions, legislators squabbled over division of oil revenues without passing a state budget by July 1, the start of the new fiscal year. Knowing
the value of close contact with voters, most legislators expend a portion of
their office expense account to retain at least one staff member in the local
community during the session. During intersessions and recesses in the legislative term, legislators often conduct hearings on matters of topical interest
in their home communities. During the session, many sponsor weekly call-
in programs on the state's advanced teleconference and audioconference network. Legislative information offices in seventeen communities around the
state handle the network of twenty-four call-in conference sites. Each office
has a permanent, year-round staff, which retains copies of bills and statutes,
determines the status of bills in committees, and allows voters to send legislators public opinion messages (POMs) on any subject, free of charge. Until
1991, the legislature also paid to have itself televised in session; the tapes
aired nightly on the state's public television stations. Through these means,
Alaska citizens can achieve quicker, more direct access to their lawmakers
than residents of other states, despite Juneau's inaccessibility.

REPRESENTATIVES

Forty representatives and twenty senators sit near the summit of state leadership, in the legislature. Their background, experience, and action speak volumes about the state's field for the politically ambitious.

Getting Elected in Alaska

Legislative campaigns in Alaska differ in urban and rural areas. In all parts of
the state, however, the electoral process begins with the candidate. Almost
all are self-starters who aspire to sit in the legislature for a combination of
reasons, including the desire to influence state policy, to gain personal pres-

tige, to reward friends, or to achieve the personal satisfaction that comes from public service.

The process of getting elected in Alaska increasingly resembles that in other states.[7] Candidate organizations raise money to fight competitive, media-centered races. Two factors categorize most of Alaska's urban races as unique, however: the nature of the preliminaries and the effect of friends-and-neighbors' politics.

Alaska encourages citizens to run for legislative office. Filing fees are modest, and state regulations impose few restrictions or constraints. Two rules supply strong incentives for individual initiative: the blanket primary law and voter registration regulations. To register to vote in Alaska does not require identifying with a political party. The party preference segment of the form is clearly marked "optional." Citizens registering to vote can categorize themselves as Republicans, Democrats, Alaskan Independence Party members, Green Party members, nonpartisans, undeclared, or "others." As a result, only 46 percent of voters elect to register with one of the parties, lending a strong flavor of independence to the electoral process.

The open primary law, in existence from territorial days to 1992,[8] permitted voters to select any candidate in a legislative primary race, regardless of party. Political party organizations dispense no major influence in the nomination process. Alaska parties have not given up attempts to influence primary outcomes through preprimary endorsements, however (see chapters 10 and 11).

In a noteworthy incident, Fairbanks Republicans in 1988 tried to nominate Dick Randolph, a flamboyant insurance agent and former Libertarian legislator and gubernatorial candidate, as the party's standard bearer for an open senate seat.[9] Republicans in three out of four committees comprising the senate district endorsed Randolph in the primary and gave him sizable party funds for his race. He ran against Representative Steve Frank, a low-key, middle-of-the-road Republican whose pragmatic approach appealed to moderate Republicans and Democrats alike. Frank defeated Randolph in the primary, probably because independents and Democrats voted in the Republican race. He went on to win the general election by a landslide.

In general election campaigns between candidates of opposing parties, partisan influence waxes a bit stronger. There a more potent force is at work: incumbency. Only four incumbents out of 51 races, 43 of which were contested, lost their seats in the 1988 election. In 1990, only three lost their seats out of 45 contested races. After redistricting in 1992, only three incumbents out of 60 races, 53 of which were contested, lost their seats (one race pitted two incumbents against each other).

The media age caught up with Alaska election campaigns in the 1970s, upping the ante for house and senate seats. The average house race in 1986 cost $46,000, while senate victors paid an average of $112,000.[10] On a cost-per-vote basis, these figures ranked near the top nationally for state legislative races. Money in elections goes for television and radio spots as well as newspaper advertisements, direct mail costs, office expenses, and campaign paraphernalia, in roughly that order.

Friends-and-neighbors' politics influence campaigns from start to finish in urban areas outside Anchorage. When the candidate assembles the group that steers the campaign, it usually includes family members, old friends, neighbors, and business associates. "Hired guns" play important roles, too, as media consultants, direct mail advisers, and opinion analysts. Increasingly, liaisons to political action committees (PACs) form part of candidate organizations, but they sit at the periphery of most steering committees. Alaska campaign spending laws, which facilitate PAC contributions, have strongly influenced the financing of legislative campaigns. Today labor unions, corporations, and other business PACs contribute more than half the dollars in competitive races. Candidates' contributions to their own campaigns and individual donations from friends, neighbors, and associates make up the rest. In addition, friends and neighbors volunteer precious time for get-out-the-vote efforts and late campaign canvassing. Often their last-minute telephone calls to constituents or sign-waving on street corners create the critical margin for victory at the polls.

In rural Alaska, the business of getting elected is simpler. Only regional centers such as Barrow, Kotzebue, Bethel, and Dillingham have television stations. In their cases, the stations are public, not privately owned, so campaign spots are out of the question. Media dollars flow instead toward radio and newspaper advertisements. Above all, the candidate's network of kin, friends, and associates forms the heart of the rural campaign for the legislature. Organizations such as for-profit corporations and nonprofit associations established under the Native claims act also influence campaigns. Their participation tends to enhance kin-based, factional divisions across regions.

Overall, legislative races in Alaska strike hometown themes such as length of residence in the community and activity in local associations. Like candidates everywhere, Alaskans running for office tout their energy, integrity, and fiscal responsibility. Policy-driven campaigns with clear organizational overtones emerge only in the most competitive urban races. An example of a policy-driven race was Democrat Mark Boyer's first run for the house against long-time Fairbanks representative John Ringstad. Boyer accused Ringstad of blocking local-hire legislation because he was in the oil industry's pocket. Although Ringstad argued (correctly) that the courts had struck down every local hire-law to date, his protests rang hollow to voters in the anti-oil climate of the mid-1980s. Boyer nearly lost the 1988 election when his Republican opponent, perennial candidate Urban Rahoi, accused him of being "soft on pot." Ironically, Boyer dusted off the same argument against recriminalizing marijuana that Ringstad had used against local hire: unconstitutionality.

Who They Are

The typical legislator in Alaska is a white Anglo-Saxon Protestant (WASP) male, middle-aged, with a college education and a business or professional occupation. In these respects, Alaska legislators differ little from their colleagues in other states. Today's legislators diverge from their predecessors twenty years ago mostly with respect to gender (see table 9).

The number of women serving in the legislature grew from one in 1967 to fourteen in 1993. The myth of rugged individualism poses more barriers to women than to men. Successful women candidates usually capitalize on experience linking them with the traditional resource economics of their region. The late Senator Bettye Fahrenkamp of Fairbanks, for example, worked as a miner. In her campaigns, she projected a down-home, one-of-the-guys image. Georgianna Lincoln *(R),* elected to the house by interior villages in 1990 and to the Senate in 1992, has fished commercially and worked as an administrator for Tanana Chiefs Conference, the region's nonprofit Native association. Naknek resident Adelheid Herrmann *(D)* also fished commercially before winning a house race in 1986. Even in Anchorage, the state's most cosmopolitan area, women candidates seek to use the frontier mystique to their advantage. Drue Pearce's first campaign for the house in 1984 capitalized on her flying experience; her leading television spot pictured her in the cockpit of a small plane. Women candidates in other states often emphasize issues perceived as "feminine," such as parental leave, universal health care, and improved child care. A female candidate who campaigned solely on such issues in Alaska would likely not survive beyond the primary stage.

Members of the house are a few years younger than members of the senate.[11] The five legislators in the 1991–92 term in their sixties all sought to em-

Table 9: Composition of Alaska State Legislature, 1967–87

| | 1967 | | | 1987 | | |
	House	Senate	Legislature	House	Senate	Legislature
Mean age	43.8	48.8	45.4	42.7	49.9	45.1
Male/Female	39/1	20/0	59/1	31/9	17/3	48/12
White/non-white	35/5	19/1	54/6	36/4	18/2	54/6

Source: Alaska State Legislature, House Research Agency, September 17, 1987.

phasize youth and vigor in their campaigns. The senior citizen population in the state is small, and candidates get little mileage out of issues geared toward the elderly. They do sprinkle their rhetoric liberally with allusions to the "pioneers" and their "sacrifices," though. Alaska has an unusually high proportion of public jobs in the workforce and thus a rich pool of experienced, eligible candidates with time to campaign. The number of retired teachers and government administrators in the Alaska legislature exceeds the national average.

Native Americans make up 16 percent of the Alaska population, the highest figure for any state; eight Natives serve in the eighteenth legislature, beginning in 1993. Rural areas with largely Native populations usually elect Natives to the legislature, but race is not the only criterion. For example, a Yupik Eskimo named Tony Vaska ran for a western senate seat in 1986 against Johne Binkley, a Caucasian. Both men already held house seats. Binkley, who operated a barge along the Kuskokwim River, won with only one hundred votes to spare. Bettye Davis, an African American lawmaker from Anchorage, rounds out minority representation in the legislature.

Most legislators have graduated from college; seventeen in 1993 held advanced degrees in law, public or business administration, or education. Interestingly, candidates tend not to stress their educational background during election campaigns, even though Alaska's voters, on average, are better educated than their counterparts in other states.[12] Legislative campaigns instead play up candidates' self-reliance and independence from formal institutions such as universities. Candidates who portray themselves as self-made individuals often parlay their all-Alaskan image into success at the polls.

Alaska has the lowest percentage of lawyers among its lawmakers of any state legislature. Only four members of the 1993–94 session identified themselves as attorneys, while twenty-six listed their occupation as a form of business, including sales, marketing, financial services, and management consulting. Nationwide, the percentage of lawyers in state legislatures has decreased over the past twenty-five years. In 1967, one-fourth of all legislators were lawyers; by 1979, only one-fifth were lawyers.[13] In addition to the attorneys, the 1993–94 session included eight former schoolteachers and seven commercial fishermen. A smaller number had backgrounds in government, other professions, and blue collar work. Few Alaska legislators list their occupation as "legislator," even though, for many, public service commands more time and provides more income than any other job.

Three years' residence is required to run for state office in Alaska; long-term residence in one's senate or house district always helps a candidate. Although the majority of Alaskans have lived in the state for less than ten years, campaigns often focus on experience gained over the long term. The fact that candidates regard their years of residence as a qualification for public office indicates, again, the power of friends-and-neighbors' politics as well as the appeal of the image of the rugged individualist and hardy pioneer.

Previous political experience is another asset. Eighteen members of the 1991–92 legislature and seventeen members of the 1993–94 body served as aides to senators or representatives before launching their own campaigns. The most recent roster of legislators also included three former mayors, seven former borough assembly members, and five former school board members.

Most lawmakers find that politics is a full-time proposition. Some do not seek reelection because legislative service consumes an inordinate amount of time and energy; it can also fracture family life and career opportunities outside the legislature, especially for those who live beyond the Juneau region. Alaska's lawmakers vacate their seats sooner than lawmakers from other states. From statehood to 1992, the turnover rate has been 43 percent in the house and 28 percent in the senate.[14] In the 1992 election, after redistricting, 50 percent of the house seats and 55 percent of the senate seats turned over. Nationally, about one-third of all state legislators are newcomers during any legislative session.[15]

If the legislature is a political ladder, then the house is the bottom rung. Half the house members in the 1993–94 term had not held previous statewide office. Eventually, though, representatives who want to climb politically set their sights on a senate seat. During the 1993–94 session, fifteen senators, or three-quarters of the body, had served previously in the house.

The next rung on the ladder is the governorship or perhaps a congressional office. The crowded field of eight candidates for the Republican gubernatorial nomination in 1986 included six former or current legislators. Steve Cowper, the candidate who unseated incumbent Democratic governor Sheffield in the primary and who went on to win the general election, had been a two-term house member. Congressman Don Young and U.S. Senator Ted Stevens were state legislators before gaining their congressional seats. A legislative background is not essential to win a statewide election, however, as governors Hickel and Sheffield and U.S. Senator Frank Murkowski have shown. All three men were highly successful in business before entering politics.

Previous service in the legislature gives candidates an advantage in re-election campaigns. The name recognition gained through running for and holding public office translates into support at the polls. This "incumbent effect" permeates every area of American electoral politics. Seniority does not, however, guarantee a position of leadership in the Alaska legislature, as is demonstrated in an examination of legislative organization.

LEGISLATIVE ORGANIZATION

Each legislature has a life of two years. It is not bound by the intentions and wishes of previous bodies, nor can it bind its successors. The short time frame, unlike the governor's four-year term and judges' unlimited terms, lends an atmosphere of frenzy to the legislative session, limited by the constitution to 120 days. Time constraints dictate how each legislature organizes.

The Two Houses

Because house members serve two-year terms, their perspective is shaped by the necessity of returning often to the voters. Senate members are elected to four-year terms, with half the body elected in each statewide race. Senators' outlooks are correspondingly longer-term, except in 1992 when all senate seats were up for election because of reapportionment.

Few constitutional differences divide the two houses. Neither has proprietorship over the state budget. In an unusual twist, the Alaska Constitution requires that the two houses meet in joint session to overturn line-item appropriation vetoes by the governor. Impeachment action begins in the senate, with the house acting as trial court because its members, who face biennial election, are theoretically closer to the people. This reversal of American legislative custom caught the fancy of journalists covering the impeachment hearings of Governor Bill Sheffield in 1985.

The constitution requires both houses to adopt uniform rules of procedure, lending a degree of similarity to their daily operations. Although members of the two houses receive the same salary and benefits, senators have more perquisites because they divide roughly the same resources as the house among fewer members.

Organizing the Legislature

Organization of the two houses governs the outcome of every piece of legislation, especially the state budget. The task of organizing is to find majority support for a particular distribution of offices and power. A simple majority, eleven in the senate and twenty-one in the house, is necessary but rarely sufficient to hold a coalition together. That is because members of the majority may disagree about some issues and may want to bolt from the coalition. Coalition makers generally search for a "working" majority, one that supplies several votes to spare.

The bargaining chips in the game of organizing the legislature are the "spoils": the offices and positions that determine the course of legislation and the shape of the state budget. Specifically, they include the presiding officers and majority leaders of each house, committee chairs, and members of the finance committees. The spoils may be enlarged by dividing committee leadership into cochairs and creating ad hoc committees. The first coalition builder who reaches a working majority with these resources wins.

The Speaker of the house and the president of the senate speak for the two bodies, head the leadership committee or committee on committees, exert major influence over committee assignments, refer bills to committees, and control some perquisites. Majority leaders direct the flow of legislation. The real power lies with committee chairs and in the finance committees. Like feudal chiefs, chairpersons can lock up legislation for the duration of the session or speed it along for quick resolution. The finance committees direct the operating and capital budgets, which determine the pattern of economic activity in the state. A coveted finance committee seat can enable a legislator to protect the home district and aid friends and supporters.

In most years, the legislature begins to organize even before the general election; candidates vie for voter favor by claiming powerful roles in the new organization. Immediately after election results become final, formal organization work begins. It usually concludes within two months, by the start of the session in January. In some years, however, one or the other body has not reached an agreement on organization until nearly a month into the session.

In 1981, the house Democratic organization collapsed near the end of the first session. The Meekins coup enhanced the value of a working majority and, in some cases, lent considerable leverage to dissidents within the majority.

Political parties usually organize state legislatures, but they exercise less power in Alaska than in any other state. In thirty-three years of statehood, the same party has organized both houses only six times. Coalitions organized the house and senate in eight sessions (see table 10).

When political party officials try to wield their clout over lawmakers, their attempts are likely to fizzle or backfire. Two cases illustrate this generalization. In 1983, the Republican party's statewide central committee approved a loyalty pledge. The party asked all candidates seeking support in the general election to swear an oath not to join house or senate coalitions.[16] Few candidates complied. The plan had little effect on Republican legislators, many of whom joined coalitions in the next legislature.

In 1988, Democrats won a majority of twenty-three seats in the house. (They later won a twenty-fourth seat when Mark Boyer was declared the winner of a close contest in Fairbanks.) They formed a party caucus that allocated all committee chairmanships, finance seats, and leadership posts. Although Republicans attempted to form a minority organization, they divided into two groups when some took preferred seats on the Finance Committee. The senate began with a twelve-seat Republican majority but formed a bipartisan coalition of nineteen members, leaving Republican senator Jack Coghill as the sole member of the minority. Coghill objected to the lack of party discipline; at a statewide committee meeting he brought a motion of censure against the Republican coalition leaders, senate president Tim Kelly and majority leader Rick Halford. Neither Kelly nor Halford attended the meeting. Both leaders informed the press that they did not believe the motion would affect them in future campaigns. Kelly ran unsuccessfully for the Republican nomination for lieutenant governor in 1990, a race that Coghill won. Halford placed third in the Republican gubernatorial primary. When the dust settled from the organization of the seventeenth legislature, in 1991, Halford was senate majority leader and there was no minority. For the first time in the history of the state, all twenty senators formed a super, bipartisan coalition. Regional politics and relations with the governor influenced the senate's operation; the lack of partisan organization and a minority had little discernible impact on budget politics.

It would be incorrect to say that parties play no role in legislative organization, but they must compete with interest groups and district demands also seeking to influence legislators. Parties have substantial potential leverage

Table 10: Organization of the Alaska State Legislature

	House of Representatives				Senate			
Year	Republicans	Democrats	Other[a]	Organization	Republicans	Democrats	Other	Organization
1959–60	5	34	1 (I)	Democrats	2	18	0	Democrats
1961–62	20	19	1 (I)	Coalition (R)	7	13	0	Democrats
1963–64	20	20	0	Coalition (R)	5	15	0	Democrats
1965–66	10	30	0	Democrats	3	17	0	Democrats
1967–68	25	15	0	Republicans	14	6	0	Republicans
1969–70	18	22	0	Democrats	11	9	0	Republicans
1971–72	9	31	0	Democrats	10	10	0	Coalition (R)
1973–74	19	20	1 (NP)	Coalition (R)	11	9	0	Republicans
1975–76	9	31	0	Democrats	7	13	0	Democrats
1977–78	15	25	0	Democrats	8	12	0	Democrats
1979–80	14	25	1 (L)	Democrats	11	9	0	Coalition (R)
1981–82	16	22	2 (L)	Democrats until 6/16 / Coalition (R)	10	10	0	Coalition (R)
1983–84	21	19	0	Coalition (R)	11	9	0	Coalition (R)
1985–86	18	21	1 (L)	Coalition (R)	11	9	0	Coalition (R)
1987–88	16	24	0	Democrats	12	8	0	Coalition (R)
1989–90	16	24	0	Democrats	12	8	0	Coalition (R)
1991–92	17	23	0	Coalition (D)	10	10	0	Coalition (R)

Source: Adapted from Stephen F. Johnson, "The Alaska Legislature," in Gerald A. McBeath and Thomas A. Morehouse, eds., *Alaska State Government and Politics* (Fairbanks: University of Alaska Press, 1987), p. 256.

[a] I = Independent; NP = Nonpartisan; L = Libertarian.

because campaign spending laws favor them: they can receive unlimited donations from contributors, and they can give as much money as they wish to candidates. Alaska's parties have not delivered on threats to deny campaign funding to errant members who join coalitions, however. Sporadic attempts to build party discipline within the legislature in the 1980s largely failed.

The PAC arms of Alaska's robust interest groups finance campaigns by as much as 50 percent. Interest groups seek candidates' preelection support for their legislative agendas. They also try to swing legislative organization in their favor or, barring that, to block a configuration antithetical to their purposes. Before the fifteenth legislature, some Prudhoe Bay oil companies supported the reelection and senate organization of Jan Faiks, an Anchorage Republican and committed champion of the oil industry who became senate president. (Former senator Ed Dankworth, known as an oil industry supporter and deal maker in the legislature, had a major hand in the organization.) Faiks's close reelection race in 1986 cost more than $210,000, making it the most expensive in state history. The oil industry raised $42,000 toward the total. Faiks stalled legislative action to rescind the Economic Limit Factor (ELF), which provided oil companies with a two-year tax break of $185 million on fields regardless of whether they were marginal producers.[17]

The state's most influential lobby in the public sector, the National Education Association (NEA-Alaska), enters into campaigns but has never meddled in the organization of either house. It prefers to approach legislators individually for support of its issues, the most important of which has been establishing finality in the negotiation process (which the legislature enacted in the 1991 right-to-strike act for teachers).

Regions exert the strongest pull in legislative organization. Direct pressure from districts drives lawmakers less than their own instinct for self-preservation. As they well know, reelection requires "bringing home the bacon." They lobby their colleagues for organizations that will best benefit their interests.

The state's political geography exhibits fault lines between cities and between urban and rural interests. Coalitions tend to be dominated by two or at the most three regions of the state and to include members from all regions. The most common patterns since statehood have been a railbelt coalition in which leadership and finance committee positions are shared by Anchorage, Fairbanks, and Kenai or Mat-Su legislators, with a few scraps thrown to rural Alaska and the Southeast; an Anchorage-dominated coalition with rural support, leaving the Interior and Southeast outside; and a rural-southeast axis with limited Fairbanks participation, in which Anchorage is largely excluded. The organization of the 1989–90 senate into a large coalition of nineteen members (seventeen by session's end) and the organization of the 1991–92 body into a supercoalition, however, show that consensus-building skills may often be more useful than the ability to forge a working majority from the minimum number of legislators.

A final factor to consider in legislative organization is personality. Through their style, rhetoric, or behavior, some lawmakers make themselves pariahs; therefore, their colleagues exclude them from the body's organization. Others find widespread favor and tend to be invited to join coalitions regardless of their party or region. A good example of one such legislator is Republican Steve Frank from Fairbanks. He has participated in coalitions led by Democrats as well as Republicans and dominated by varying regional interests.

Legislative Staff

The first state legislature employed only a handful of staff members; most legislators performed their own casework, research, and analysis. By the seventeenth legislature, in 1991, the staff had grown to 350. It included personal aides for each legislator, committee personnel, permanent staff agencies, and support workers such as pages, secretaries, accountants, and custodians.

The staff agencies are specialized by function and operate in a bipartisan fashion. Legislative budget and audit staff analyze the appropriations requests of each state agency, assess state revenue requirements, and prepare fiscal notes for bills, most of which affect the budget. The auditors make it possible to monitor the implementation of legislative programs. The Legislative Affairs Agency does legal research and drafting for legislators. In 1990, the House Research Agency and Senate Advisory Council were merged to form one research agency for legislators. Permanent staff support the Administrative Regulations Review Committee and the Code Revision Committee. The last staff agency on the list is the ombudsman's office, created to investigate grievances against state agencies, but not the legislature.

Committee aides help prepare for committee hearings, perform some research related to committee legislation, and conduct casework pertaining to the committee functions of legislators. The most numerous staff members, however, are personal legislative aides. Their prime function is casework, that is, handling inquiries on pending legislation, researching and solving problems for constituents, and finding other ways to make legislators look good in the eyes of the voters.

Legislative staff receive good pay; some make as much as legislators during the 120-day session. As noted earlier, some Alaskans have used their legislative staff experience as a stepping-stone to legislative office. Lawmakers distribute the highly valued jobs like plums for the politically ambitious. Loyalty to one's boss stands as the chief requirement of service.

LEGISLATIVE PROCESS: MAKING POLICY IN THE ALASKA SETTING

Once the legislature organizes, the rough outline for state policy making falls into place. The policy-making process itself seems chaotic and unruly; description and analysis often lose the rhythm of what elsewhere has been called the dance of legislation.[18] As a product of the legislature, the budget provides the best example of how policy making works. After considering the legislative process, we analyze its influences on Alaska's legislators.

The Process

Most of the two hundred to three hundred bills the legislature passes yearly are housekeeping matters: changing the way state agencies operate and clarifying statutory and regulatory authorities. Requests originate with agency personnel, who also make recommendations to legislators on broader aspects of state policy. Interest groups generate the second-largest number of ideas for legislation. For example, insurance companies request that the state's tort laws be rewritten to make it harder for people to collect damages. Constituents are a third source of legislative ideas; separating them from interest groups is often difficult, however. Legislators who promise in their campaigns to change certain state practices usually seek to implement the modifications when they attain office.

Whatever the source of ideas for legislation, their implementation follows a similar path: introduction, movement through substantive and rules committees, floor action, and resolution of differences between the two houses.[19] Introducing legislation is simple; it is accomplished by having the title read into the record by the house clerk or senate secretary. This introduction also constitutes the first of three required "readings" of the bill. Some legislators "pre-file" bills, or enter them before the session starts. All bills must meet a filing deadline that falls on the thirty-fifth day of the second session. After filing and introduction, the next step is referral to one or more committees, a prerogative of the presiding officer.

Usually, committee referral is routine. In two cases, however, it attains special significance. In the first instance, the ruling coalition may refer controversial legislation it opposes to a hostile committee. In the fourteenth and fifteenth legislatures, the senate president assigned such bills to the State Affairs Committee, chaired by Anchorage Republican Mitch Abood. His committee earned the name "Abood's Tomb" because whatever entered, died there. Second, complex bills often are referred to more than one committee, increasing the likelihood that action will be delayed or killed. In 1993, house Speaker Ramona Barnes referred a senate bill on electric interties to fifteen committees because the bill's title was so specific she could not easily make changes in it.

Substantive committees, of which there are nine in each house, typically hold hearings on bills in which some committee member exhibits interest. Hearings may be conducted in the intersession at locations other than Juneau. Customarily, testimony by teleconference or audioconference is permitted on bills of great public interest. The legislative committee system in Alaska encourages the transformation of bills in committee: committee members rewrite most major bills, frequently in association with interest groups and agency bureaucrats. The committee stage ends when members send bills forth with a "do pass," "no pass," or "no recommendation" label.

Both houses have rules committees, whose main activity is to calendar bills for action (second and third readings) on the floor. Until the final days of the session, uncontroversial bills move smoothly through these committees.

The Alaska house and senate are small bodies, and their rules encourage discussion of public issues. Daily orders devote a large block of time for debate on legislation. Most debates are tame affairs and do not influence outcomes, which tend to follow committee recommendations. On issues such as oil and gas taxation, offshore oil leasing, capital punishment, and recriminalization of marijuana, however, spirited debates ensue, primarily for media and public consumption.

Sponsors typically file bills in their own house and arrange for filing in the other, but only rarely do the bills travel at the same rate through committees. Usually, the house of the prime sponsor acts first. The version of the bill it produces is then introduced in the second house to facilitate resolution. Two routes are open to dissimilar senate and house bills: one house may agree to the other's version, or the two may work out their differences in a conference committee. Presiding officers select conference committees from members of the substantive committees.

Alaska's legislative process has the same amount of redundancy and veto points as that of other states. Its budget system, however, is unique.

The State Budget and the Legislative Process

From the viewpoint of lawmakers, the state budget is legislation too, but on a grander scale. Budget action drives the legislative session; when the budget is done, the legislature adjourns.

Over the decades, the budget initiative has come from different quarters. Until the oil boom years, the legislature reacted to the recommendations of the executive, making few adjustments to the operating budgets and only minor alterations to the modest capital budgets. The flush of oil revenues in the late 1970s and early 1980s geometrically increased the available revenue, far exceeding agency requirements. Legislators pursuing large capital budgets, partly to ameliorate the post-pipeline recession, aggressively sought control of the budget process. From 1979 until the middle of the Sheffield administration in 1984, the multibillion-dollar capital budget was cut up into "equal thirds." The governor, house, and senate independently drew up essentially veto-proof project lists.

The operating budget has plotted a steadier course over the years. Finance subcommittees examine the executive budget, which undergoes extensive hearings early in the session. Legislators use the hearings to scrutinize policy implementation and agency operations; commissioners and deputies appear to defend agency appropriations. After soliciting the recommendations of substantive committees, the finance committee of each house meets to set target ceilings for the two categories of the operating budget: agency budgets and "pass-through" funds to school districts and municipalities. The budget process, particularly since oil prices crashed in 1985–86, is incremental. Target ceilings established by finance committees closely compare to current expenditures for the year. The houses tend to accept finance committee numbers. A joint finance conference committee reconciles differences between house and senate budget versions. Finance conference committee members usually are selected in the course of the initial organization of the houses; to have the last word on the budget is a big bonus.

Two interesting quirks in budget policy making developed during the 1960s and 1970s. The first was a shift of power from house and senate finance committees to the budget "free conference" committee.[20] As joint committees found it increasingly difficult to reconcile different versions of the budget, conferees took greater liberties. By the early 1970s, a free conference committee was redesigning the state budget behind locked doors. A rules change in the 1970s halted the practice and limited the power of free conferences. In a second policy-making twist, one house would complete its work on the budget, then adjourn. The abdication left the other house either to accept the budget or attempt to call the absent house back into session. This maneuver is still used from time to time.

Undisciplined is the most flattering way to describe Alaska's budget politics dating from the late 1970s to the mid-1980s (see chapter 3). Political parties, legislative leaders, and the governor all exercised little fiscal restraint. As a result, they created a budget behemoth that cried out for more and more money, even as oil revenues dried up. The state operating budget ballooned from $1.1 billion in 1979 to a high of $4.1 billion in 1985. Per capita spending grew from $2,664 to $7,817 in the same period.[21]

Influences on Legislators

Myriad influences operate on the Alaska legislature, but generalizing about their overall and comparative impact is hazardous. No behavioral studies exist of legislative voting, and journalistic accounts are useful but highly impressionistic. Nevertheless, we can examine sources of influence: constituents, interest groups, political parties, fellow legislators, local governments, public-sector lobbyists, the governor, and state agencies.

Alaskans are not shy about making their feelings known to legislators. The rapport between state politicians and constituents shows in the way they welcome visitors to their home or Juneau offices. On mundane issues, legislators receive few phone calls and little mail. Controversial ones, however, send a stream of communication—letters, phone calls, personal visits, and hundreds of public opinion messages (POMS)—pouring into their offices. For any lawmaker to disregard public opinion on such issues would be foolhardy.

The interest group environment of Alaska is complex for a sparsely populated state (see chapter 10). Resource interests, including oil and gas, fisheries, minerals, and forest products, dominate the private sector. Vying for influence are transportation and communications industries, trade associations, and tourism. Lobbyists and lawyers representing interest groups have ready access to legislators, who value the information they supply.[22] Lobbyists line the halls of the capitol in Juneau, especially during budget deliberations. They frequently take part in the markup of legislation as well. For example, when Juneau senator Jim Duncan *(D)* encountered resistance to his bill on binding arbitration for teachers in 1989, he let the directors of NEA-Alaska, the state school boards association, and the association of school administrators work out their disagreements in a new version of the bill (providing a provisional right to strike for teachers), which he then quickly moved through the senate.

Political parties wield little power over lawmakers, especially when mandates issue from state or district party officials. Colleagues of the same party, however, are a different story. Typically, they rely on one another for information in their arenas of responsibility, and they often defer to each other when voting. Members of urban legislative delegations exert similar influence over one another. They meet at least weekly, often in the context of audioconferences with constituents or meetings with visitors from their districts. They may not always vote alike, but individual legislators regard their delegation as a touchstone on issues.

Alaska has a public sector nearly as large and almost as varied as its private sector. Its interests seek leverage, too. The federal government keeps the lowest profile because it requires neither money nor law from the state legislature. Local governments and school districts, on the other hand, are the most vigorous public-sector lobbyists. "Pass-throughs" make up approximately 35 to 40 percent of the state budget. Local jurisdictions believe state statutes entitle them to these monies. For instance, about 30 percent of the state budget is allocated to the state's school foundation program. Other entitlements claimed by local governments include reimbursements for pupil transportation, revenue sharing, and municipal assistance to cities and villages.

Although school districts and municipalities feel that they are the rightful heirs to the state's wealth, the legislature may fund their requests at less than 100 percent. As a result, municipal and school district officials descend on Juneau during the session. The implications of their presence are not lost on legislators, particularly ones who campaigned in favor of popular issues, such as support for schools. The Alaska legislature has been generous in funding public education. Education spending per student, which averaged seven thousand dollars in 1992, has been among the highest in the nation since the late 1970s. The state's education lobby argues, however, that the percentage of the state budget allocated to education is the lowest among American states. That is largely a result of unusually large per capita budgets in Alaska, which include expenditures such as longevity bonuses and rural power subsidies that are not found in other states' budgets.

Because roughly 60 percent of the budget pays for executive agency operations, the governor, the governor's staff, and department personnel follow the budget process carefully, attempting to sway it at every step. Each department has an information officer and special assistants who act as liaisons to the legislature. The governor has a staff of special assistants who respond to legislators' requests, a chief liaison for legislative affairs, and the Office of Management and Budget (OMB), which prepares the budget and charts its course through the legislature.

Governors vary in their methods of lobbying the legislature, but they all lobby it. Governor Sheffield pulled leaders into his office to hammer out deals; he effectively traded local district grants for Democratic support of his line-item vetoes. Governor Cowper called legislative leaders into policy "summits" to develop common targets for state operations and capital spending, but these meetings accomplished little. In the first year of his second term, Governor Hickel declined to work closely with legislators, electing instead to threaten them with sweeping, across-the-board cuts. Consequently, the legislature passed the school foundation budget relatively early in the session so it could override a veto. The act became law without the governor's signature. The governor's approach in the second half of his term was broadly to involve state elites in policy making through holding economic summits while avoiding any confrontation with agencies and interests in submitting his budget requests.

The Alaska legislature is a remarkably porous institution, presenting few barriers to those who seek to influence its behavior.

The People as Legislators

As a progressive state with a populist tradition, Alaska allows its citizens to legislate through the initiative, referendum, and recall procedures outlined in Article XI of the constitution (see chapter 6). Not all states offer their citizens so many options. Forty-two states permit referenda, twenty-three states allow initiatives, and only thirteen states offer the recall.[23] The initiative may be a call for policy, such as the 1982 plea to withdraw state funding for abortions, or it may be symbolic, such as the Tundra Rebellion of the same year.

Through referenda, citizens can endorse or reverse legislation adopted by the house and senate. Only one formal referendum has appeared on the ballot since statehood, compared to fourteen initiatives (see chapter 6). The most popular topic of referenda has been limiting legislative salaries. Attempts to recall officials through the ballot box have been even more rare, but notable. A recall petition against Governor Walter Hickel and Lt. Governor Jack Coghill in 1992 gained enough signatures to go on the ballot but seemed unlikely to succeed. Signatures were challenged, and as of 1993, the courts declined to certify the issue for a ballot proposition. (At the municipal level, however, several recalls have passed.) By his second year in office, Hickel had formed alliances with senate leaders. For example, they delayed sending him the legislature's budget so that he would have the leisure of vetoing selected appropriations and the legislature would not be in session to override the vetoes.

The constitutional framers put limits on the use of initiatives and referenda. They cannot be employed to dedicate revenues, affect appropriations, enact local legislation, or change the constitution. They also may not by used to create courts, define their jurisdiction, or prescribe their rules.[24] Furthermore, the process of placing an initiative or referendum on the ballot is cumbersome. Ten percent of the individuals who voted in the previous election, representing residents in at least two-thirds of the state's election districts, must first sign the petitions. The restraints embodied some distrust of the popular will and confidence in lawmakers on the part of the constitution's framers. Delegates to the convention also sought to consolidate dispersed territorial power in the legislature, which had always been considered "popular."

Amateurs and the Legislative Ethos

As noted earlier, few Alaska legislators list politician or lawmaker as their primary occupation, but many derive the bulk of their income from public service, and most devote the majority of their time to it. The legislature is the focal point of their lives. What explains this paradox?

Attitudes toward government and political leaders may be more hostile in Alaska than in other states. Although there is a lack of survey data, the vitriol of city taxpayer revolts and the insistence of cries to limit government size in recent years support this hypothesis. The unwieldiness of government in Alaska and individuals' reliance on monies funneled through federal, state, and local agencies create an environment of dependency that does not encourage affection for government patrons. Negative attitudes condition the behavior of legislators. They perceive that most citizens dislike the idea of career politicians deciding state policy; they want their legislators to be "of" the people in all respects.

Legislators reflect these perceptions in their behavior. They repeatedly refer major policy decisions to the public in the form of legislatively initiated "advisory" propositions on the state ballot. They invite the public to participate in committee hearings, and they sponsor statewide conferences to solicit views on Alaska's future.

Action by the House Democratic Caucus in 1989 illustrates this tendency

to defer to the public in decision making. Facing a possible $800-million de-
cline in state revenue as well as high-pitched demands to continue, and even
expand, government programs, caucus members called a series of town
meetings around the state. They asked the public to indicate what government services lawmakers could eliminate or, barring such cuts, what revenue sources they could tap. In part, the meetings were a tactic to increase
support for increased taxes, budget cuts, or both. The meetings also grew out
of a genuine desire to let the public experience the pressures and trade-offs of
balancing the state's checkbook.

COMPARISONS WITH OTHER STATES

The first Alaska legislature in 1959 confronted the task of creating a state
government. Its primary reference point was the experience of the weak territorial body. The experiences of policy-making bodies in other states concerned it less because Alaska was so different. The seventeenth Alaska legislature, meeting in 1991–92, was younger and less institutionalized than
legislatures in other states. Over the first generation of statehood, however,
the legislature has cultivated a record of potential responsiveness that compares favorably to other states. A review of legislative ethics, professionalism, and reform illustrates this point.

Legislative Ethics

Billions of dollars flowed into state coffers in the late 1970s, providing legislators with a powerful incentive for self-enrichment. The surprise, perhaps,
is that relatively little corruption tainted the legislature during the oil boom
years. The major scandal was the Hohman bribery case.

In the 1970s, George Hohman was a powerful senator representing Bethel
and western Alaska. Hohman's brother, Ron, was superintendent of the Bering Straits School District, and his sister-in-law, Jan, sat on the State Board
of Education. No budget traveled the length of the senate without Hohman's
indelible mark: large capital projects for the villages in his district as well as
increased operating funds and pass-throughs for rural Alaska as a whole.

In 1980, Hohman endeavored to change the type of aircraft used by the
state for firefighting. He authored legislation specifying planes of a Canadian manufacturer, which, it was later learned, had retained Hohman for his
influence. He sought support for his legislation in the house. After an initial
discussion with Hohman, Anchorage Democrat Russ Meekins (the leader of

the 1981 coup) went to the district attorney and offered to wear a wire for the second meeting. At that encounter, Hohman offered Meekins a substantial bribe for his support. The state filed charges against Hohman and, in 1981, convicted him. He was sentenced to three years in prison and fined twenty thousand dollars. Shortly thereafter, the senate met and expelled Hohman, an unprecedented action. (After his prison term, Hohman returned to Bethel, where voters elected him to the city council, and he later became city manager. Alaskans don't condone sleaze, but they forgive and forget transgressions.)

In 1984, the legislature enacted a new law on conflict of interest. Impeachment proceedings a year later against Governor Bill Sheffield brought to light the need for specific regulations on unethical conduct (see chapter 8). The legislature adopted an ethics act in 1986 for all state employees and public officials, with stringent conflict-of-interest provisions.

Internal and external investigations have been conducted on the dealings of other legislators. In 1983, Senator Ed Dankworth became the subject of an inquiry over the attempted sale of a pipeline camp he owned to the state. At the end of the 1988 legislative session, senate president Jan Faiks was charged with malfeasance in the use of senate leadership funds, which were parceled out to Republican members of the majority coalition and, in one case, used in a reelection bid. Also in 1988, Senator Al Adams, a Democrat from Kotzebue, was implicated in a major North Slope Borough corruption case for accepting five hundred thousand dollars in fees from developers with borough contracts. The legislature formed a committee, including members of the public, to investigate the charges against Dankworth, Faiks, and Adams. The committee concluded that the actions occurred before the ethics act was adopted, nullifying the need for further inquiry. The committee did, however, opine in Adams's case that he might have violated other statutes or federal laws. No formal action was ever taken against him, but the case fueled incentive for an ethics bill that would apply to the legislature.

During the 1990 session, the legislature tussled with ethics issues. Leaders flew up a high-priced consultant from Los Angeles who recommended a comprehensive and complex reform bill. It died in the session. The issue arose again in 1991 and 1992; finally, the legislature passed a comprehensive and stringent reform bill shortly before adjournment in 1992.[25] The legislature's resolve on ethics was tested in 1993 at the start of the eighteenth session. George Jacko, Democratic senator from Pedro Bay, had joined ten Republicans to form a Republican coalition. At the start of the session, Jacko attempted to use his position in the legislature to gain entry into the hotel room of a former female staffer. Alaska state troopers demurred to Jacko's request, and the media fed the public in a frenzy of speculation about legislative ethics. Because Jacko was the linchpin of the senate's organization, this body delayed selection of an ethics panel, mandated under 1992 legislation, until the close of the 1993 term.

In the 1980s and early 1990s, the Alaska legislature has faced several issues of ethics.[26] In all cases, they have concerned powerful members of the house and senate: Ed Dankworth (senate president), George Hohman (senate finance), Al Adams (house finance and later senate finance), down to George Jacko in 1993. There was considerable footdragging before the legislature passed ethics legislation in 1992. In general, the legislature has ducked ethics issues more often than it has confronted them.

Legislative Professionalism

A standard method of comparing legislatures is to use an index of professionalization. The index assesses each legislature's autonomy and the value citizens place on the "calling" of legislative work. The index considers, among other things, whether the legislative session is limited, whether the body meets annually, how large and independent its staff is, and the salary and benefits for legislators.

By these measures, the Alaska legislature scored highly on the scale of professionalism until 1984. Meeting in annual sessions of unlimited duration, the body regularly increased its staff and, in 1983, changed the per diem/stipend system of paying legislators with an annual salary, which, at $46,800, neared the top nationally.

The public took exception to this high degree of professionalism, however. The 1981, 1982, and 1983 sessions exceeded the norm, up to then roughly 100 days. The 1982 session dragged on for a record 165 days. It left little time to start the new fiscal year and denied school districts as well as local governments funding guarantees, on the basis of which they could hire new employees and continue old programs. The focus of discontent, however, settled on a legislature that lingered too long in Juneau. Repentant lawmakers placed a constitutional amendment on the ballot in 1984 to limit the session to 120 days; voters approved it by a three-to-two margin.

The salary increase found favor among legislators, in part because it equalized their pay. While some leaders were earning more than $60,000 a year, lawmakers who claimed no interim per diem pay made about $26,000. Failing to understand or appreciate the inequities in the existing system, citizens recognized only that lawmakers wanted the equivalent of year-round pay for part-time work. Before the issue of legislative pay raises reached the referendum stage, the legislature rescinded its action and cut salaries in half (but also restored its per diem).

Since then the legislature has declined in professionalism as measured by indices. This fact assumes that significant changes in professionalization occurred before the 1980s. Actually, both time periods saw merely superficial adjustments. The decline as measured by indices also begs the question of whether a relationship exists between the professionalization of a legislative body and its effectiveness not only in policy making but also in representing the public.

In Alaska's case, there has not been a pronounced relationship between professionalization and legislative effectiveness. No discernible differences in the quality of policy outcomes emerged at times when Alaska ranked high or low. The same applies to responsiveness. Whether legislative professionalism was high or low did not seem to be correlated to responsiveness of the legislature to the individualist and populist strains in Alaska political culture.

Legislative Reform

The legislature has undergone one major reform movement in its history, that of the "Sunshine Boys" in the mid-1970s.[27] Influenced by the national Watergate scandal, Alaska voters in 1974 elected a large Democratic majority, including several newcomers to politics. The new Democratic leaders gained control of the house of representatives and moved quickly to implement progressive reforms.

The chief target of reform was campaign spending, then unregulated. Reformers enacted disclosure laws and, for the first time in Alaska, required registration of political action committees. Reform legislation did not limit PAC control over campaigns, however. As in many states and at the federal level, the legislation permitted PACs to contribute several times to campaigns through branch offices; the impact of the legislation has been to increase PAC influence today.

Reformers enacted a "sunshine" law requiring government meetings to be open to the public. They also passed a "sunset" law calling for periodic review of boards and commissions; a negative review would lead to termination. The sunset law has had virtually no impact on Alaska government.

Through the 1980s, the legislature paid sporadic attention to reform. Progressive proposals have usually originated with the executive. For example, the Cowper administration pushed for campaign spending limits in 1988–89. Meanwhile, the legislature has consistently rejected applying the open-meetings law to its own sessions, particularly those of the ruling caucuses and finance committees. Nevertheless, opportunities for continued reform present themselves in two ways. First, Alaska, like other states, responds to national movements, such as the efforts in the early 1990s to cut legislative terms. Second, Alaska adapts national reforms to the Alaska context, as demonstrated in the three-year effort to develop ethics-reform legislation.

CONCLUSION

The Alaska legislature over the second half of the state's first generation has acted as a strong and independent body. Undisciplined by party forces, it adheres to no dogma. Instead, the legislature operates in a highly individualized manner. Each lawmaker is a free agent to make his or her own bargains with interest groups and constituents. For most of statehood, the leading coalitions have applied the normal logrolling of American state legislative practice to the basic distribution of power.

When the oil boom hit Alaska, the legislature was poorly institutionalized; the flood of oil dollars actually retarded the development of procedures and policies for an orderly management of state wealth. Lawmakers rushed to meet real and perceived needs and to build a statewide infrastructure. The legislature doled out hundreds of millions of dollars for social services and education. It constructed roads, airstrips, boat harbors, schools, and government facilities. In addition, the legislature freely contributed billions of dollars in oil revenues to the Permanent Fund. The fragmentation of economic and regional interests that dominate legislative politics has deterred the legislature from deciding the future of the fund. Increasingly, its fate is becoming intertwined with that of government in Alaska and its uncertain fiscal future.

Alaska's legislature is easily influenced by myriad forces. In one respect, that makes it appear immature in comparison to the rigid institutions of government in many states. In another respect, however, Alaska's legislature is an exemplar of responsiveness. After all, it allots time in the daily order of business personally to introduce citizens visiting the capital. It invites citizens anywhere in the state to comment on proposed legislation. It solicits comment and criticism from interest groups and individuals on all areas of public policy. In these areas of popular responsiveness, the Alaska legislature lacks peers.

Like other American legislative bodies, the Alaska legislature also serves as the butt of jokes. Alaskans like to make fun of their legislature because, as a collective decision-making body, it rarely coheres. Also, the antics of individual legislators can be humorous. Some members are notorious for napping at their desks, spouting misinformation on the issues, or engaging in spirited debate about nonissues. Senator Mitch Abood's nickname, for instance, was "Mitch Abood about Nothing," an allusion to Shakespeare's *Much Ado about Nothing*. Alaska's lawmakers, for their part, take the ribbing in the spirit in which it was intended. Instead of dividing them from the people, the jokes bring them closer. Alaskans are also remarkably tolerant of misbehavior, which explains why legislators convicted of drunken driving or assault may remain in office.

Because of the personalism of the sparsely populated political community, individual legislators reap appreciation for what they do. Communities welcome them home after the session with potlucks, parties, meetings, and accolades. Alaskans conceive of legislators as translators who return the wealth of the state to interests, regions, and, ultimately, individuals. Lawmakers acknowledge that they remain in office only so long as they meet community expectations.

Despite its institutional weaknesses, the Alaska legislature has been the most prominent player in state politics for most of the statehood period. It has spurned leadership from any single source and has been popularly responsive to a fault. Its record reflects the regionalism, individualism, conservatism, and populism of Alaska politics.

CHAPTER 8

Governor and Administration

Governor Steve Cowper stunned Alaska's citizens by announcing, midway through his third year in office, that he would not seek a second term. He broke the news to reporters on the morning of March 24, 1989, hours after the *Exxon Valdez* tanker crashed into a reef and began spewing eleven million gallons of oil into Prince William Sound. Governor Cowper's aides had scheduled his news conference in advance; at the time he announced his pending withdrawal from politics, he could not have known the full implications of the tanker wreck early that morning. Whether he would have arrived at his decision not to run again had he foreseen the furor of the next few months is a question that remains unanswered. As it happened, the events of Good Friday 1989 focused the national spotlight on Alaska's political leadership and its ability to cope with one of the world's worst environmental disasters.

Just as the media circus over the oil spill died down, another one began, this time over Cowper's successor. Seven weeks before the November 1990 election, former governor Walter Hickel entered what was shaping up to be a lackluster race between state senator Arliss Sturgulewski *(R)* and former Anchorage mayor Tony Knowles *(D)*. The Alaskan Independence Party candidates for governor and lieutenant governor bowed out, allowing Hickel and "Mr. Republican" Jack Coghill to step into their slots. The press was euphoric; the politicians sneered; senate president Tim Kelly called Hickel and Coghill "two old dogs baying at the moon." Their last-minute media blitz set them apart from the ho-hum candidates served up by the major parties. First the Hickel-Coghill team captured the public's imagination, then its votes. The Independence Party ticket won the three-way race with 39 percent of the votes, a first for an independent party in the history of the state. In December, Hickel reentered the executive mansion he had left twenty-one years earlier. He continued to grab headlines by announcing plan after plan to develop Alaska, including a "garden hose" from Alaska's streams and rivers to thirsty California.

As the 1990 race illustrates, there can be high drama to the governorship in Alaska. With the post comes the power to set the state's agenda, develop policy, and build coalitions. Most executive work, however, is mundane, consisting chiefly of implementing laws passed by the legislature. Still, because of the "strong governor" philosophy of the state constitution, Alaska's governor enjoys more discretion at this task than the governors of most other states.

THE GOVERNOR

Before Alaska achieved statehood in 1959, it had a fragmented territorial administration with dozens of agencies. Often these myriad, tangled agencies were led by weak, figurehead governors appointed by the federal government. The framers of the state's constitution envisioned a different kind of leader for their new state and made provisions for a chief executive who would not be unduly hampered by the other branches of government. Thus, the governor and lieutenant governor are the only statewide elected officials, running as a team in the state's most visible election. The governor appoints all but two of the state's fifteen commissioners[1] and can remove each without constraint. The chief executive's strong appointment authority extends to the judiciary as well as state boards and commissions. His budget leverage is significant. Not only does he initiate development of the executive budget; he also exerts sizable control over the result, through the power to strike or reduce appropriations using a line-item veto. The legislature has a difficult time overriding the governor's budget cuts because three-fourths of the body must agree to do so while meeting in joint session. As noted in chapter 7, Alaska's governor has unique power to redistrict. He may also reorganize the executive branch. The governor's potential authority extends to calling special sessions of the legislature and responding to state emergencies.

Formal powers, however, tell only part of the story. Elections clarify the political environment from which state leadership emerges. Governors' backgrounds, experiences, and personalities reveal their predispositions on issues. The nature of the chief executive's working world also conditions his behavior in office.

Electing Governors in Alaska

In two respects, gubernatorial elections are identical to those for seats in the state house and senate. Because the majority of voters (54% in 1993) identify themselves as nonpartisan, candidates cannot rely on partisan messages.

They have to craft campaign approaches aimed at the broad middle, emphasizing aspects of their lifestyle and character appealing to most voters. Second, the blanket primary system has limited the influence of party organizations in nominations. Any person can file for the Republican or Democratic nomination, and the race usually goes to the best-organized and best-funded candidate. Until 1992, everyone could vote in the party primary, and swing voting was common. For example, many Democrats appear to have crossed over in the 1982 and 1986 primaries to vote for Republican candidates perceived to be weaker than Walter Hickel, who is anathema to liberals. The large nonpartisan vote frequently tips the scales.

In three other respects, gubernatorial elections differ significantly from legislative elections. Although the outcomes of almost all gubernatorial races hinge on urban voters, candidates must campaign in each region of the state as well as in most communities. Second, friends-and-neighbors' politics bring little to bear on the race for governor. Organization, money, media, and, on some occasions, issues have the greatest impact on the outcome. Third, the governor's race attracts a larger slate of candidates than legislative contests. In the 1986 Republican primary, eight candidates, including one woman, Arliss Sturgulewski, ran. One commentator described the field as "Snow White and the Seven Dwarfs." In addition, minor party candidates and independents have competed in most general elections of the 1970s, 1980s and 1990s.

Candidates form larger, more complex organizations for gubernatorial campaigns. Typically, they include long-time friends and political mentors, party representatives, fund raisers, media consultants, pollsters, direct mail advisers, and issues analysts. Gubernatorial candidates surround themselves with more "hired guns" than legislative candidates; often they obtain political consultants and media assistance from outside the state. Candidate organizations typically locate a strong central office in Anchorage and regional offices in the remaining urban areas.

The race for governor is the costliest in the state, exceeding even U.S. Senate contests. That was not always the case. Before the 1980s, no candidate for governor had spent more than $1 million. The oil boom raised the value and price of the governorship. Total expenditures in the 1982 election surpassed $6 million. Bill Sheffield doled out more than $2 million, including more than $600,000 from his own pocket, to win. With a cost per vote of $44, the governor's race of 1982 was the most expensive in the nation.[2] Expenditures in the 1986 race totaled roughly $1 million less, partly a reflection of the economic downturn. The general election campaigns of Steve Cowper and his Republican opponent, Arliss Sturgulewski, cost about $1.4 million each; the unsuccessful gubernatorial primary race of house Speaker Joe Hayes cost $1 million. Expenses in the three-way 1990 race climbed above those in 1986.

Gubernatorial elections will not decline in cost. Increasingly, candidates for the governorship are individuals with substantial personal wealth to devote to their campaigns. In 1986, four millionaire candidates spent more than $200,000 of their own money. Ironically, the victorious Cowper was the exception, listing his only assets as a suitcase of clothes, a used pickup, and a guitar. Four years later, two of the three major candidates, Sturgulewski and Hickel, were millionaires.

Politically ambitious Alaskans without personal wealth or broad name recognition stand little chance of winning office. Money alone, however, cannot buy the governorship. In 1986, candidate Cowper spent less than his opponents in both the primary and general elections, yet he won the race by conveying honesty and integrity; he projected an image of an independent thinker, captive to no interest group. Sturgulewski's negative campaigning backfired at the polls. The late-starting Hickel-Coghill team in 1990 spent less than its rivals and won the election handily.

The same sources that fund legislative races also fuel gubernatorial campaigns. They include political parties, unions, trade associations, special interest groups, corporate political action committees, individual donations, and candidates' own contributions. The ratio is different, however. As Anchorage journalist Larry Makinson pointed out in his 1987 study, "statewide races attract a much wider array of individual and family contributors, most of whom are independent of established interest groups."[3] The governor's race attracts many out-of-state PAC dollars, especially from the oil industry. Campaign spending laws limit individual and PAC contributions to $1,000. This ceiling pushes all but the wealthiest individual contributors toward the gubernatorial campaigns and the PACs toward legislative races. There the latter can spread their influence more widely by spending $1,000 on each of several candidates. State officeholders and prospective appointees also give generously to gubernatorial candidates.

As a result of the campaign spending laws, governors tend to be less beholden to interest groups than are legislators. For example, in 1986 Cowper received a majority of his donations from individuals, in amounts lower than $1,000. His opponent, Sturgulewski, received a smaller amount from individual contributors, but interest group dollars still made up only 35 percent of her campaign funds.[4]

The campaign for governor is conducted increasingly through the media. Candidates use television and radio spots, newspaper advertisements, direct mail letters, and brochures as their chief means of reaching voters. Media advertisements can be costly, particularly in the expensive Anchorage media market. Advertising plays a key part in driving campaign costs upward.

Emphasis on media advertising has led to the ascendancy of style over substance in campaigns. In the 1986 Republican primary, Sturgulewski's most effective advertisement featured a young girl haltingly trying to pronounce her name and giving up. Then the narrator said, "Let's just call her Governor." The 1982 race was a rarity with its focus on issues: the capital-move initiative and the subsistence preference for Alaska Natives.[5]

Gubernatorial candidates actively seek elite endorsements. In 1986, former governor Hammond's endorsement of Sturgulewski may have been a factor in her primary victory. Lieutenant governor candidate Terry Miller used a previous endorsement from Hammond to win the primary for lieutenant governor. Governor Hickel is rumored to have sought the public support of Alaska's congressional delegates, who reportedly snubbed him, saying that they stand only by loyal party Republicans.

Traveling throughout the state is a big expense in the race for governor. Although candidates perform some staged door-knocking, they devote most of their energy to repeating their stump speech before collected audiences in small and large towns, raising money, and making statewide media appearances.

Profiles of Alaska's Six Governors

Six individuals have served as governor of Alaska. Their backgrounds are reflected in the issues they emphasized during their campaigns and in the records of their administrations.

Bill Egan (1958–1966, 1970–1974). The state's first and longest-serving governor, Democrat Bill Egan, was a lifelong Alaskan who kept a general store in Valdez before entering politics. He served first on the Valdez City Council and then in the territorial legislature for thirteen years. In 1955, the delegates to the constitutional convention elected him president.

In 1958, Egan ran against John Butrovich, a Fairbanksan who had served in the territorial legislature from 1945 to 1957. Few issues emerged in the race. Egan won, in part because of the Democratic landslide that year. A newspaper columnist quoted an election observer: "The unhappiest people aren't the defeated Republicans, because they have lots of company. But just think of that poor lonesome handful of Democrats who lost. They really have it rough." Egan and other Democratic leaders were viewed as more experienced than their Republican counterparts.[6] Four years later, Egan competed against Mike Stepovich, a former territorial legislator and governor. Although charges of a lackluster record on economic development cost many votes, Egan was elected to a second consecutive term, the limit under the Alaska Constitution.[7] But Egan's first term was thirty-four days short because he was sworn in after statehood was declared, in January 1959 instead of December 1958.[8] Therefore, in 1966, claiming he had served less than two full terms, Egan ran for a third. Many voters saw his action as a violation of the constitution's intent, and Egan lost.[9] After sitting out four years, Egan ran again in 1970, with a campaign emphasizing his experience. Again, he emerged the victor.

Egan administrations were moderately partisan. The governor appointed mostly Democrats. Democratic leadership in the legislature made it easier for Egan to form effective coalitions. Yet he took a pragmatic approach to governing, including in his network many Republicans. The term *Egan Democrat* referred to a nominal Democrat who was fiscally conservative and pragmatic.

The first two Egan administrations transformed territorial agencies into state government departments using federal transition grants. The administrations initiated the selection of lands, including Prudhoe Bay, from the 103.4-million-acre statehood grant. In this period, the state also established local government organizations in all urban areas under the novel borough system of government (see chapter 12).

The third Egan administration covered a period of economic and ethnic change. The 1969 oil lease sale brought a windfall of $900 million in bonuses to the state. Pent-up pressures for infrastructure development and social service spending occupied the administration. Under Egan, the state negotiated mainly to clear the way for oil development, to resolve Native land claims, and to help establish Native corporations. The third Egan administration also oversaw initial construction of the oil pipeline in 1973–74.

Many Alaskans remember Egan fondly as a moderate and practical governor. A genial manager, he was expert at making the gears of government work.

Keith Miller (1969–1970). Alaska's third governor, Keith Miller, replaced Walter Hickel when he became U.S. secretary of the interior in 1969. Before moving to Alaska, Miller owned and operated a collection agency in Seattle.

He worked for the Internal Revenue Service in Anchorage and for an oil-heating firm in Fairbanks. First elected to public office in the state house, in 1962, he ascended to secretary of state (the post is now called lieutenant governor) in 1966 and governor in 1969, a meteoric rise for a colorless politician.

Miller was a caretaker governor. He lost the opportunity to lead the state in his own right in 1970, when Egan defeated him easily.[10] Overall, his image is negative. His administration opposed land claims resolution and social service spending when money was available to address these needs. A sign of any administration's significance is recognition: few Alaskans recall that Keith Miller was the state's governor in 1969 and 1970.

Jay Hammond (1974–1982). Jay Hammond came to Alaska after World War II. He worked as a licensed guide, air taxi operator, U.S. Fish and Wildlife Service agent, and proprietor of a fishing lodge before being elected to the state house as an independent in 1958. Hammond switched to the state senate in 1967; his colleagues elected him majority leader in 1970 and senate president in 1971–72. Hammond served as mayor of the Bristol Bay Borough and became a Republican, although he deemphasized his party affiliation during his successful campaign for governor in 1974.

Hammond defeated four opponents, including former governor Hickel, in the Republican primary. He then faced Egan, who had achieved an easy primary victory. The election was extremely close; initially, the margin between Egan and Hammond was smaller than 1 percent, and Egan requested a recount. Three weeks later, after several snarls, the final tally showed Hammond the winner by 287 votes.[11] In the 1978 race, Hammond defended his record of support for balanced growth, appealing to a broad constituency of rural, Native, commercial fishing, and urban conservationist interests. He narrowly overcame his nearest rival, Walter Hickel, in the primary and again in the general election after Hickel supporters mounted a write-in campaign.[12]

The Hammond administration was the most bipartisan in the state's history. A conservative, Hammond felt uncomfortable with party labels. He selected Republicans and Democrats alike as commissioners and expected them to resolve issues through give-and-take. Hammond called his administration a microcosm of the state; critics thought it was rudderless.

Hammond governed Alaska during boom times. His administration supervised construction of the pipeline from 1974 to 1977. Then, when oil flowed from Prudhoe Bay to Valdez, it benefited from skyrocketing oil prices in the early 1980s.

The Hammond administration changed the way state revenues were spent. As a fiscal moderate, the governor watched the operating budget carefully and resisted pressures to increase government functions. Nevertheless, during his administrations, the state government workforce grew from fourteen thousand to more than seventeen thousand workers. Local government workforces, partly supported through increased state grants to cities and boroughs, grew at double this rate. Hammond acquiesced regarding the capital construction budget, ultimately leaving the legislature in charge. At its peak in 1981–82, the capital budget doubled the operating one in size. For this reason, primarily, critics called Hammond a weak governor. They gibed that, during his tenure, Alaska had sixty-three governors: Hammond himself, two powerful advisers, and every member of the legislature.

The Hammond administration originated two long-lasting conservative strategies for Alaska. The governor established in the public mind the difference between nonrenewable and renewable resources. The former, such as oil and gas resources, could fuel state government for a time but would eventually face depletion. To yield optimum value, they required conservative management. By way of reward for this stance, Hammond's administration was charged with attempting to "lock up" Alaska's land. According to Hammond, Alaska's future after oil lay with renewable resources such as fisheries, forest products, and agriculture. The Hammond administration made attempts to advance renewable resources. The most controversial was the state-assisted agricultural project in the Delta-Clearwater region, which, for a variety of economic and environmental reasons, failed to launch an agriculture industry in Alaska.

Hammond's second conservative strategy was the Permanent Fund. The idea of a Permanent Fund had been discussed previously, and several legislators, including Hugh Malone of Kenai and Oral Freeman of Ketchikan, championed it. Governor Hammond quickly adopted the concept of a state "savings account" and became its most articulate spokesman. He popularized the concept in the 1976 election, which amended the constitution to permit a dedicated fund. He supported legislation creating the dividend program in 1980. To this day, Jay Hammond remains the state's chief advocate of protecting the Permanent Fund and returning the benefits of Alaska's oil wealth directly to its citizens. After a decade out of office, Hammond endures as the state's most popular and charismatic political leader.

Bill Sheffield, (1982–1986). Bill Sheffield, like Keith Miller, was an unusual governor for a state such as Alaska. A millionaire hotelier, he staged his first serious run for public office in 1982. A colorful primary campaign that year eliminated the favored candidates in both parties: Lieutenant Governor Terry Miller *(R)* and former legislator Steve Cowper *(D)*.

Sheffield moved to Alaska in 1953, initially working as a television repairman for Sears. His life story, like that of Walter Hickel, is an Alaska version of a Horatio Alger tale. In the 1960s, he bought his first hotel in Anchorage and, over a period of ten years, added others in Anchorage, Juneau, Canada's Yukon Territory, and regional centers of rural Alaska. An active member of the Anchorage business community, he headed the state chamber of commerce and was the founding vice-chairman of Common Sense for Alaska, a strong development-oriented association of Anchorage business and political leaders. Although Sheffield participated in the Democratic party from the late 1960s on, he did not emerge a leading party figure until the late 1970s. He entered the race for the governorship in 1978 but withdrew before the primary because of his wife's ill health.

Sheffield's chief opponent in the 1982 general election was Republican Tom Fink, an Anchorage insurance agent and former Speaker of the Alaska House of Representatives. Fink took distinctive and controversial stands on issues. He advocated capital punishment and prolife initiatives; he was the only primary candidate who supported the capital move and repeal of the subsistence preference law. His positions prevailed over Terry Miller's in the primary. A third candidate figured in the general election, however. He was Dick Randolph, a former legislator and Fairbanks insurance agent who headed the Alaska Libertarian Party. Randolph drew from a similar base of support to Fink's, spoiling the race for the Republicans. The majority found Sheffield's opposition to the capital move and support for Native subsistence rights perfectly palatable. He won the 1982 race with 47 percent of the vote.

Sheffield was more partisan than Egan, and he screened his appointees carefully; few Republicans landed jobs with his administration. Believing government could and should be run like a business, Sheffield focused his early efforts on increasing government efficiency. His executive transition was a good example of successful technical changes in administration. An inexperienced politician, however, Sheffield suffered a lapse of ethical judgment early in his tenure. To repay campaign debts to himself, Sheffield hopped an oil company jet to Texas for a fundraiser at the same time the state was negotiating lease sales with oil companies. Based on this incident and others, Sheffield critics leveled charges of sleaziness at his administration.

In 1985, the *Fairbanks Daily News-Miner* raised questions about possible bid rigging and other improprieties in the state's lease of an office building in

Fairbanks. A partial owner of the building was the business manager of the local plumbers and pipefitters union, Lenny Arsenault, who had contributed large sums of money to Sheffield's campaign. A grand jury issued a report implicating the governor in violating state lease procedures; it opined that the governor had violated the public trust and that the legislature should consider impeaching him.

Leaders called the legislature into special session. It was the first time in seventy-five years that any state legislature had considered impeaching a governor. The Senate Rules Committee held hearings over a two-week period. Both the senate and the governor hired attorneys with a record of involvement in the 1974 Watergate hearings (Samuel Dash and Phillip Lecovera). Sheffield's chief of staff admitted that he had asked the Department of Administration to change bid procedures to favor the owners of the office building. The governor testified that he did not recall attending meetings at which changing the bid documents was discussed.

The senate committee, with a Republican majority, saw insufficient evidence for impeachment. The senators agreed that no "clear and convincing evidence that . . . Sheffield had committed an impeachable offense" existed. Nevertheless, they called for revisions in the state's procurement policy, and they also recommended a state ethics code and a review of grand jury proceedings. (Senators were not happy that the grand jury had dumped this case in their laps.) The episode discredited the Sheffield administration, contributing largely to his loss of the Democratic primary in 1986.

Steve Cowper (1986–1990). Steve Cowper arrived in Fairbanks in 1968 and established a law practice. He ran for the legislature six years later and achieved prominence as one of the reformist "Sunshine Boys." In 1976, he chaired the House Finance Committee. He toyed with the idea of running for Congress in 1978; later he lobbied for the state on the Alaska lands issue in Washington, D.C. Cowper used the years after his narrow defeat in the 1982 primary to serve on the Board of Trustees of the Alaska Permanent Fund and launch a mediation service in Fairbanks.

Cowper's opponent in the general election was Arliss Sturgulewski, a three-term state senator from Anchorage with a formidable background in community service.[13] The candidates differed little philosophically. Cowper, however, seized the initiative on women's issues, while subtly sending the message that Alaska's governorship should remain in the hands of a man. In the end, the voters chose Cowper's Clint Eastwood "high-plains drifter" image over Sturgulewski's good-government, League of Women Voters image. The campaign's delicate approach to issues and the absence of a major conservative candidate sent ten thousand voters (5.5% of the total) to Joe Vogler's camp. Vogler is a Fairbanks miner, acid government critic, and founder of the Alaskan Independence Party.[14]

Cowper benefited from Republican and nonpartisan votes; his administration, therefore, was only loosely partisan. He governed Alaska during an economic recession. One objective of his administration was to cushion state and local governments against revenue declines, but he made little headway with the legislature. He developed two new ventures: the Alaska Science and Technology Foundation to spur the economy through applied research and development, and several trade ventures to East Asia to promote sales of Alaska's products.

Because the *Exxon Valdez* oil spill occurred on his watch, Cowper gained points from the publicity and lost them for the state's indifferent monitoring of oil-spill contingency plans and tanker traffic. He was the first governor to question the purpose of the Permanent Fund. His education endowment plan, which would have placed earnings from the fund into an endowment dedicated to kindergarten through twelfth-grade schooling, roused the support of the education community and the opposition of many Alaskans who feared "raids" on the fund. Ultimately, Cowper's proposal died in the legislature. Very much a loner in his dealings with others, Cowper was unable to put the legislative coalition together that would establish support for the endowment.

Cowper shocked Alaskans twice, first by nullifying his campaign promises by declaring "all bets are off" shortly after taking office, and second by declining to run again. His abrupt departure left Alaskans wondering about his commitment to governing. Cowper left an indeterminate mark on the governorship.

Walter Hickel (1966–1968, 1990–). Hickel came to Alaska in 1940 with experience in construction. He developed businesses, including hotels, in Fairbanks and Anchorage and cultivated contacts that gave him a leading position in the state Republican party. He served as Republican National Committee chairman for Alaska from 1956 to 1964.

Hickel's first campaign for governor in 1966 blasted Egan for failing to develop Alaska's economy and called for new leadership. The first Hickel administration ushered in a period of radical change, at least in style. Hickel brought a partisan Republican team into office and proceeded to shake up government agencies. Two activities of his first administration deserve note.

First, Hickel fought aggressively to develop Alaska's land and resources. Interior Secretary Stewart Udall, three days after his inauguration, imposed a land freeze on Alaska until Native claims were resolved. Hickel filed suit to release the state's remaining statehood grant lands; his complaints about the federal land "lock-up" brought him national attention.

Second, the Hickel administration pushed for road improvements to transport supplies needed for development of the Prudhoe Bay oil fields. Shortly after the discovery of oil in January 1968, the governor authorized overland transport via a road hewn through the tundra, despite the fact that most shipments to the fields were by air and barge. Derisively called the "Hickel Highway," the water-filled rut enraged environmentalists.

After Richard Nixon dismissed him as interior secretary, Hickel returned to the state. In the 1970s, he formed the Yukon Pacific Corporation, whose goal, as yet unrealized, was to construct a natural gas pipeline adjacent to the oil pipeline. He became a leading force in Commonwealth North, the state's most prodevelopment business group, based in Anchorage. He remained active in politics, figuring in every gubernatorial race from 1974 to his surprise victory in 1990.

Although elected on the Alaskan Independence Party ticket, Hickel brought a partisan Republican administration into power. Its chief characteristic was allegiance to the governor's agenda. The governor and lieutenant governor delved deeper into the bureaucracy than any previous administration. They replaced not only commissioners, deputy commissioners, and directors, but even clerks in the state elections office. Millet Keller, Hickel's first administration commissioner, called for loyalty to the governor. Within weeks of assuming office, the governor fired the members of the State Board of Education and replaced them with Republicans who advocated parental choice and a voucher system. Because one appointee, a Talkeetna minister, supported the views of Louisiana lawmaker and bigot David Duke, the legislature declined to confirm him. The governor also fired the members of the boards of fish and game, replacing them with people who opposed Native subsistence rights.

Hickel's high-handed appointments upset Alaskans, who are accustomed to a balance of genders and ethnicities in the cabinet and on boards and commissions. Hickel appointed only one woman and one minority representative to his cabinet. He picked white men of advanced middle age for the remaining cabinet posts. Mike Doogan, a columnist for the *Anchorage Daily News,* referred to the Hickel cabinet as a "bunch of old white guys." Hickel sharply cut funding to the Alaska Women's Commission, the state Human

Rights Commission, and the Alaska Public Offices Commission. In the last case, he urged newspapers to investigate campaign-spending violations instead of having the state pay a watchdog government agency.

One effort of the second Hickel administration was to redirect spending priorities and arrest government growth. Hickel threatened to cut public broadcasting, social service grants, and aid to municipalities. He did not carry through completely on his warnings, but he sent a clear message: communities need to support the services they want to continue.

The activism of the second Hickel administration equaled that of the first, even though the chief executive was nearly a quarter of a century older. The bluster and confrontations that characterized Hickel's first year in office distracted attention from his agenda, which, with its emphasis on privatization and traditional social values, was much more conservative than those of previous Democratic and moderate Republican administrations.

Personalities and issues (including incumbency) figure prominently in Alaska's gubernatorial races. In addition, more than half the races have been won by less than 3 percent of the vote, which lends importance to idiosyncratic forces and personal style. The personalities and character of Alaska's statewide leaders offer a fertile field for analysis. A simple framework is one that distinguishes governors who were "managers" from those who were primarily "populizers." Alaska has had three managers and three populizers.

Governors Egan, Miller, and Sheffield were managers of the machinery of state government. They varied a great deal in personality, with Egan the common, friendly politician, Miller reclusive, and Sheffield affable but insecure. Nevertheless, each occupied himself with making the levers of the state bureaucratic machine respond to his touch. At this business, Egan succeeded most. He created the model for gubernatorial behavior in Alaska.

The other three governors, Hammond, Cowper, and Hickel, concerned themselves less with managing government than with the ideas inspiring political action. Their views were divergent, even antithetical, but each man sought to define Alaska's political future in a manner that was linked, in one way or another, to the people. We return to this theme later in a discussion of the governors' expressions of the Alaska political culture.

The Governor's World

Because of the difference in tasks and environments, the skills required to gain office have little in common with those needed to run state government. The victors in Alaska's gubernatorial races built coalitions of regions and interests during their campaigns. Once they entered the governor's office, however, they had to master two different authority systems, one roughly hierarchical, the other relatively egalitarian.

The first sixty days present the governor with the greatest opportunity to place his or her stamp on the statewide leadership. He or she may appoint roughly one thousand officials, including commissioners, deputy commissioners, and division directors; judges in the state court system; staff of the governor's office in Juneau and other urban locations; and members of 120 boards and commissions. The governor wields direct authority over these administrators. Like the chief executive of a corporation, the governor can issue orders and fire subordinates for noncompliance.

The actual reach of the governor's authority, however, is shallow. Career service rules and union dominance in state government dilute the executive's power to initiate change and alter behavior. Governor Hickel discovered that when he attempted to fire an assistant attorney general and a fisheries biologist who had criticized his policies.[15]

In dealing with legislators, statewide interest groups, local government officials, and the federal government, the governor engages in multiple bargaining exchanges. Each group stands autonomous, not fully dependent on the governor for access to resources. Although the chief executive outranks officials in all but federal agencies, he can rarely command complete adherence to his policy views.

Thus, the governor exercises formal powers over the upper echelons of the state bureaucracy and may, because of his position, exert influence in bargaining relationships. Where his formal powers end, however, he must marshal all the informal resources he possesses, chiefly the knack of persuasion. None of Alaska's governors has been especially adept in this respect, with the possible exception of Bill Egan.

THE STATE BUREAUCRACY

In theory and constitutional structure, Alaska's bureaucracy is centralized and unified, perhaps more than any other American state.[16] The fifteen executive departments all operate under the control of the governor. No commissioner has an independent power base, established through running in a statewide contest. Policy boards buffer only two commissioners: those of education and of fish and game. The governor appoints board members and can dismiss everyone whose term has not expired. Sheffield made a clean sweep in 1982, and Hickel followed suit in 1990. Both paid a political toll for their purges.

The unity of the state bureaucracy is sometimes only skin-deep, however. Appointments involve placating many autonomous groups, a process that restrains gubernatorial power. The real demands of Alaska's political environment compete with the ideals of administrative centralization and rationality.

Selecting Alaska's Administrators

Governors come into office with promises to keep or decisions already made about commissioners and key board members.[17] Governors usually fill key posts with loyalists or campaign supporters. Governor Cowper appointed Judy Brady, executive director of Commonwealth North, as commissioner of natural resources, reportedly in exchange for Walter Hickel's support of Cowper over Sturgulewski in the 1986 elections. Governor Sheffield, claiming to have promised jobs to no one on the campaign trail, nevertheless selected a key member of his steering committee, Norman Gorsuch, as attorney general. Alaska governors tend to assign value to personal and ideological compatibility and agreement on issues rather than to partisan affiliation.

It would be unrealistic for any governor to fill all the more than one thousand exempt positions with political loyalists. Many of the governor's first choices for high executive offices decline to move to Juneau. Technical requirements of the job limit the governor's discretion. For example, the head of the state law department must be someone with legal training, and the chief of military affairs must be a commissioned officer in the Alaska National Guard. Most boards specify a regional balance, and licensing boards require occupational representatives. Of greater importance are political considerations. For example, the unions must accept the labor department commissioner, and the business community must support the commissioner of commerce and economic development.

Consequently, governors use a referral process for most appointments to exempt positions as well as to boards and commissions. A special assistant in charge of appointments screens potential officeholders for qualified candidates, and then the governor's close aides conduct a political clearance. Powerful interests often have a de facto ability to blackball appointees. In this way, interest groups and, occasionally, political parties wield strong influence over the upper reaches of the bureaucracy.

Career civil servants fill the middle and lower ranks of the bureaucracy. The merit principle is enshrined in the Alaska Constitution. The majority of jobs go to qualified candidates who undergo review of credentials or examinations to establish preparedness. The state maintains a jobs list, advertises positions, and centralizes hiring under terms of the state personnel act, monitored by the Department of Administration. Alaska statutes buffer classified positions, about 80 percent of the total, from political influence. Lawmakers have placed protections, such as the "whistle-blower" bill of the 1989 legislature, on the books. It generally safeguards employees from dismissal when they disagree in public testimony with their employers.

Public-sector unions offer protections within and beyond the statutes. Alaska sustains one of the most liberal state environments for labor; nearly three-fourths of state workers belong to a union.[18] The state's Public Employee Relations Act authorizes collective bargaining and provides for third-party mediation and arbitration. All but "critical" employees possess the right to strike. Recent changes to public employee law, such as granting teachers the right to strike in 1991, have extended the protections of employee organizations.

In short, technical, geographic, and political necessities constrain the governor's selection of administrators. The Sheffield administration provides the best examples. Officials in the Department of Administration frustrated the governor's attempt to reward a campaign contributor with a lucrative office-space lease by going public with allegations of bid rigging. Sheffield was helpless either to punish or to silence them. In another instance, union opposition blocked the governor's attempt to cut state employees' salaries by 10 percent in light of falling oil revenues. Ultimately, the support of government workers for Sheffield drained away at the polls. Cowper, the "high-plains drifter," beat the millionaire hotelier handily in the next primary election.

Decentralization of Administration

State government employed about 21,200 Alaskans in 1992; only a minority, approximately 5,000, lived and worked at the state capital in Juneau, however. For the initial purpose of administration, the state was carved into six regions, a design that appeared technically rational. Eventually, geographic necessity and political pressure resulted in regional offices representing the larger departments in every town with a population greater than three thousand. These bureaus are housed in state office buildings, which serve as constant reminders of the reach of state government.

The existence of regional offices, supported by local business and community leaders, influences the execution of state policy. Regional forces least affect departments that confine their activity to administering benefits or sanctions following state and, in some cases, federal law. They include the Departments of Law, Corrections, Revenue, Administration, Health, and Social Services. Regional interests greatly sway the state's resource and construction agencies, including the Departments of Fish and Game, Environmental Conservation, Natural Resources, and Transportation and Public Facilities (DOTPF). Residents demand more roads, so lawmakers press hard for road construction projects in their areas. Residents also want control over the design and execution of new roads. For example, Fairbanks business and conservation interests stalled DOTPF plans to construct a six-lane road through the middle of town which would have disrupted thirty-one businesses and some historic sites.[19]

The High Cost of Government in Alaska

The price tag on state government is one of the most controversial topics in state politics. On a per capita basis, Alaska spends more than any other state and double the U.S. average.[20] Several factors account for the high cost of government.

First is the expense of moving people and goods to remote areas. Local companies produce few of the manufactured and consumer goods used in Alaska because of the small market and high production costs. The outlay for shipping from the contiguous states pushes prices upward. For example, Fairbanks's consumer prices exceed by 30 percent those of Seattle; Barrow's are more than 100 percent higher again than Fairbanks's. In the 1980s, state salaries topped the national norm. Studies indicate that, for the most part, the above-average salaries are attributable to the high cost of living in Alaska.

Second, economies of scale are scarce in the delivery of services in Alaska. Anchorage is the only municipality able to achieve significant economies of scale in distributing educational, social, and welfare services because it has a large population in a concentrated location. Other areas require a higher administrator-to-client ratio because people are dispersed and greater effort must be expended to reach them.

Third, the adverse climate of Alaska raises costs of administration. Public facilities, roads, vehicles, and other equipment all survive for a shorter time than in the temperate zone. The outlay for heating is much higher.

Alaska's government also provides services that are rare or nonexistent in other states. The state-operated marine ferry system, the only one of its kind in the United States, connects the waterbound cities of the Southeast to mainland Alaska, British Columbia, and Washington. The state owns the only railroad, which ties Fairbanks in the Interior to Southcentral and the Kenai Peninsula, the major population corridor. The state also owns and operates Pioneer (nursing) Homes for older Alaskans. Alaska spends a lot of money on programs such as low-cost housing and student loans, to name two, whose like is offered nowhere else in the country. Finally, the state government funds services handled by city and borough governments. State troopers provide police and emergency services outside cities. Alaska foots the entire bill for education in unorganized boroughs, and two-thirds of it in cities. State reimbursements for school construction exceed by ten times the national average.[21] Given these high costs, which are in many cases fixed, the governor must play the hand dealt and figure out how to pay for it all.

INTERBRANCH RELATIONSHIPS

The processes of funding government, regulating behavior, and umpiring outcomes display aspects of the governor's relationship with the legislature and with the courts.

Funding Government: The Executive Branch in the Budget Process

The Alaska budget involves both the executive and the legislature, with strong powers assigned to each branch. The executive develops the budget based on agency estimates formed one year before the next fiscal year, beginning on July 1. Governors typically advise agencies as to acceptable percentage increments or decrements to their budgets; since 1983, governors have asked the Office of Management and Budget to integrate and align appropriations requests from agencies. The executive budget deadline in mid-December leaves one month for public digestion and preliminary legislative analysis before the session begins.

Although legislative budget committees begin work in December and hold hearings in January and February, active budget deliberations await the state's March revenue estimates. Because the state depends on oil and gas royalties and severance taxes for 85 percent of its general revenues, the latest price of oil is critical to budget development. The oil and gas forecasting office of the Department of Revenue draws up quarterly estimates of future state revenues based on projected oil prices. Inasmuch as the March estimates are the last ones received by the legislature before the session's end, they have the greatest impact.

For six weeks, from the end of March until the second week in May, the executive branch actively participates in legislative budget deliberations. Commissioners and deputy commissioners appear at hearings to defend appropriations, the governor's legislative liaison and special assistants from the departments lobby individual legislators, and the governor stages meetings with groups of legislators (see chapter 7).

In addition to developing the executive budget and forming revenue estimates, the governor wields another significant power: the veto. Governors tend to use this prerogative sparingly; from 1959 through mid-1989, governors vetoed only 157 bills in their entirety. The legislature overrode seventeen vetoes. Before 1976, governors rarely scratched out an item in a bill or reduced an appropriation. From then until 1988, governors used line-item vetoes on fifty-three appropriations bills. The legislature brought only five of these bills back for reconsideration and overrode vetoes in three cases.[22] These numbers indicate the potential for executive control of the budget through line-item vetoes.

Governor Hammond used line-item vetoes selectively when the state budget bulged. During the tenth legislature (1977–78), he cut a deal with house finance chairman Russ Meekins and partially vetoed nineteen appropriations bills. Hammond aimed his ax at special and miscellaneous "Christmas tree" grants, under which there was a present for everyone, and capital construction projects. In response to Hammond's opposition, the "equal-thirds" system of developing the capital budget came into existence in 1979. Allocating as it did one-third of the capital budget each to the house, senate, and governor, the system was virtually veto-proof.

Governor Sheffield exercised line-item vetoes on twenty-four appropriations bills during his term. He also sought to cut or reduce special-purpose grants that legislators added to the budget to benefit special interests in their districts. The budgets swelled, and legislators counted on vetoes. Like Hammond, Sheffield executed major cuts in capital projects, paring hundreds of millions of dollars from capital grants lists. The legislature did not reconsider any of Sheffield's partial vetoes.

Through the third year of his term, Governor Cowper made only thirteen partial vetoes, but his use of the power attracted no less controversy than his predecessors'. In 1987, claiming the legislature's budget overran state revenues, he called lawmakers into a special session to remedy the deficit.[23] Before the special session began, Cowper announced his line-item vetoes to the operating budget, including cuts to popular programs such as debt reimbursement to municipalities for school construction, revenue sharing, and municipal assistance. In a public rebuke to the governor, the legislature overrode two vetoes (school debt reimbursement and senior citizen tax relief). By the next session, Cowper had learned the lesson: he exercised fewer line-item vetoes and appropriations reductions, none of which was overridden. New organizations in the senate and house, including a senate coalition more sympathetic to the governor's budget plan, supported his three vetoes in the 1989 session. The same coalition supported his 2 percent across-the-board reduction in the state operating budget in 1990.

Governor Hickel campaigned in 1990 to pare back state government spending, promising a 5 percent trim each year. When the legislature presented him with an FY 1992 budget several hundred million dollars fatter than 1991's, Hickel vetoed roughly 2 percent, still leaving a larger budget than the previous year's. His vetoes of capital appropriations did, however, approach the 5 percent figure.

A final, desperate method of governors to curb government spending is impoundment of funds. After the legislature adjourned in 1986, oil prices continued to plummet; Governor Sheffield felt forced to impound 10 percent of all agency appropriations, including those for pass-through programs, such as school funding. The Fairbanks North Star Borough mayor, assembly, and school board took the state to court, contending that fund impoundment was unconstitutional because it violated the separation of powers as well as the legislature's authority to make appropriations. The superior court upheld this position, but the legislature enacted the impoundments in its next session, rendering the issue moot before an appeal could reach the state supreme court.

The process of funding government in Alaska draws the executive and the legislature into a complex relationship. The Hammond administration acquiesced in the budget expansion of the late 1970s and early 1980s by giving the legislature primary control of the huge capital budget. Because revenues expanded faster than expenditures, the budget remained balanced. When signs of a worsening revenue situation appeared, Hammond garnered legislative support for his state spending cap, applying it primarily to the operating budget (see chapter 3).

Declining oil prices, particularly since the 1985–86 crash, and the consequent hole in state revenues have restored some discipline to the state budget process. Governors have exercised line-item vetoes and budget reductions increasingly since the mid-1980s to rein in spending. Their effective use of these powers hinges on political negotiations with legislative coalitions. The successful governors have been able to forge alliances with the leaders of both houses, as Governor Cowper did during his last year in office. The governors who failed to control the state budget did so because they alienated majorities in both houses, as Governor Sheffield did during his first year in office.

Regulating Behavior

Alaska's bureaucracy contains the same types of agencies found in other states and in the U.S. government. There are welfare agencies (e.g., health, social services, and education), security agencies (e.g., military affairs and public safety), overhead agencies (e.g., administration and revenue), and regulatory agencies (e.g., law, environmental conservation, and fish and game). Regulatory agencies engage more than the others in interbranch conflicts.

The Department of Natural Resources incorporates the Oil and Gas Division, whose mission is to advance exploration and development of mineral resources. It also encompasses the Alaska Division of Land and Water Management, whose purpose is to conserve such limited resources as gravel and to protect water rights. The Department of Fish and Game contains divisions to protect Alaska species (habitat and wildlife protection), while other divisions champion the interests of hunters and fishermen (commercial fisheries, sport fishing, and subsistence). What these agencies and their seemingly contradictory divisions share is their regulatory impact on Alaskans.

Natural conflicts between the missions of the agencies, in addition to natural conflicts between their divisions, complicate policy making. For example, the Department of Natural Resources customarily takes a permissive attitude toward seismic tests and exploratory drilling in the offshore area. On the other hand, the Department of Fish and Game, which by mission must protect fish species such as salmon, and the Department of Environmental Conservation, which implements national environmental protection laws, customarily oppose offshore drilling. Such interagency conflicts often reach the governor for resolution, but the process draws in the legislature, too.

The legislature functions as an arena for interests affected by government regulation. Oil company lobbyists not only contest higher taxes, but seek to change state leasing and permitting regulations that affect the profitability of their operations in Alaska. The Usibelli Coal Mine, the state's only producing coal mine, seeks a minimal royalty rate on extraction of coal resources and pleads for state assistance in transporting coal to market. Miners and loggers flock to Juneau to dispute the clean-water and solid-waste-disposal regulations of the Department of Environmental Conservation. Hunters and trappers desire favored species allocations and changes to regulations that restrict their area of operations. Commercial fishermen lobby for changes to limited-entry regulations, season lengths, and area and gear restrictions.

In contrast to the array of interests begging for resource development, a smaller group promotes conservation. Trustees for Alaska (Anchorage), Sierra Club Legal Defense Fund, and the Alaska Environmental Lobby Committee (representing centers in Fairbanks, Anchorage, and Juneau), strive for tighter regulations on logging and on oil, gas, and mining development. They form alliances with several national environmental and conservation organizations, now very active in Alaska. Some corporations established under the Native claims act, and Native governments, also wish to protect rural areas for Native subsistence and prevent negative development impacts.

With the exception of the "Sunshine Boys" era of the mid-1970s, the legislature has tended to yield to the strongest pressure, which in the past has originated with resource development interests. Sometimes forced into the bad guy's role, governors have vetoed legislation popular with prodevelopment lobbyists, such as a 1985 bill that would have prohibited the state from requiring that water discharged from placer mines be of higher quality than water going in. The legislature would like to have the last word through a legislative veto over administrative regulations. Such a constitutional amendment has come before the voters on three occasions and has been defeated each time.

On balance, it has been the practice for most Alaskans to support routine regulatory actions of state agencies. Legislators continue to react to controversial actions, however, through the appropriations process, performance audits, and other means of legislative oversight.

Umpiring Executive-Legislative Relations

The legislature's attempts to annul offensive regulations by passing resolutions not subject to the governor's veto have been referred to the courts repeatedly; justices have agreed with the executive that the resolutions encroach on the executive's constitutional authority. In reapportionment and redistricting cases, the courts regularly demand modification of executive action. In resource development cases, the courts have tended to interpret broadly the executive's obligation to manage resources as a public trust. In short, no consistent pattern exists of court support for the executive over the legislative branch or vice versa. In general, the courts have established a record of independence from both branches and have taken strong positions in support of the separation of powers. In chapter 9, we discuss in detail the role that courts play in adjusting relations between the executive and legislative branches.

IDEOLOGY AND CULTURE IN ALASKA STATE POLITICS

The governor is first among Alaska's opinion leaders. His pronouncements make headlines in the state's large newspapers as well as in television and radio news. Governors can extend their influence by developing unifying themes. To convey a sense of unity, they must rise above regional appeals and strike a chord reflecting broad aspects of Alaska's political culture.

Two governors left little enduring mark on the thoughts of Alaskans about government. Most Alaskans forget that Keith Miller even served. Bill Sheffield, for his part, contradicted high expectations with low acts; he was crippled by poor political judgment and unethical behavior.

Four other governors left imprints on the state's political psyche. Bill Egan was a matter-of-fact politician who thrived not on drama, but on the business of state politics. Egan put the constitution to work and established state government. He took advantage of the unifying aura of statehood to win support for his legislative agenda. Equally significant, Egan understood the importance of individualism and respected it in others. That accounted for his success with the legislature, as he observed in 1983: "Many times you're better off to go to the legislature. Don't give them the impression that you're trying to bulldoze them. Take their ideas, let them start it, let it appear to be their idea. Working this way, together with them you can get your own program through. You have to have the human touch. That's how to get it in. Think of the other guy. Recognize his importance, his obligations. We had our battles with the legislature, but never any direct confrontations."[24]

Jay Hammond also left an indelible mark on state politics. Although he barely won his first race for the governorship in 1974 and gained only a plurality of the vote in 1978, he remains the state's most popular governor with the lowest negative rating in the polls. Hammond's plea for the conservation of nonrenewable resources such as oil and gas and the enhancement of renewable resources, particularly fisheries, forest products, tourism, and agriculture, appealed to Alaskans' prudence. His emphasis on careful management regimes, though not universally admired, helped change the vocabulary of economic development in the state. In his popularization of the Permanent Fund and defense of the fund's dividend program, Hammond sponsored innovation in state politics and gave new expression to Alaska individualism. Also, more than any other governor, Hammond physically embodies the Alaska mystique: his popular image is that of the bearded, backwoods poet of strong and independent character.

The third governor to capture the imagination of Alaskans was Steve Cowper. He took an unpopular stand in favor of new taxing authority. Although he reduced the state budget to its lowest level on a per capita basis in a decade,[25] Cowper also defended the institutions of government. He brought to government a belief in duty and obligation and a moral perspective on public service. Many were shocked by Cowper's decision not to run again and by his decision to make that announcement twenty months before the end of his term, but his actions reflected his personal conviction that there is "no value to longevity in office." He said: "I thought at the end of the four-year term I would have done what I could. Your ideas, if good, will survive you. This gives a certain message that is needed today: that a person can walk away from office on his own terms. People come to think that people will stay there until their cold dead hands have to be pried off."[26] Cowper steered the state through the *Exxon Valdez* oil spill. He responded to the crisis quickly, mobilizing opinion in the state against Exxon and other big oil companies whose spill precautions were inadequate. Making the most of the media interest in the nation's worst oil spill, Cowper carried his message to a national audience. Undoubtedly, he could have exploited his new popularity at the polls; instead, he chose to stand by his resignation, delivered that fateful March morning. He acknowledged that unifying events and themes were rare: "Most times, Alaska has to be governed on a regional basis. Southeast Alaska has nothing to do with the rest of Alaska. They don't give the rest of the state a thought. Rural areas have their own realities. Traditions, cultures are enormously different. Anchorage and Fairbanks are different."[27] Cowper's personality and style represented a different facet of the stubborn individualism found in Alaska. He was a loner who had difficulty working with others. Sometimes he was very closed-minded and adamant, as in his defense of the education endowment.

Walter Hickel is the most persistent champion of resource development in Alaska. His vision of Alaska as a natural resource treasure trove critical to America's future has inspired followers inside and outside the state. He believes Alaska can forge a vital link between Asia and the United States. He has tried unrelentingly to construct a natural gas pipeline from Prudhoe Bay to tidewater at Valdez. His repeated efforts, through gubernatorial campaigns, to transform his visions into reality illustrate a strength of conviction rare among politicians. Hickel unifies the strains of Alaska's political culture more effectively than any other contemporary political leader. In 1983, he expressed his views on leading Alaska this way:

> I am tired of hearing about the potential of Alaska from the nineteenth century to the present. Potential is opportunity. Alaska is a young state; it's very much like a young child. Alaska is a child and children need guardians. Growth is the only thing that helps. . . . It is what young countries live on. Like children, young countries can't be held back; they'll stagnate; they need to be developed.
>
> Alaska is unique—its location, its climate. Alaska is so foreign to Americans. It takes a unique approach. If you think that what works in Oklahoma will work here you are wrong. . . . We have to think like a country. [28]

Through fifty years of residence in Alaska, through a lifetime of work that made him one of the state's richest men, and through political offices at the state and federal level, Hickel has learned firsthand about Alaska's brand of individualism and how it differs from that of other states. He shares the widespread notion that Alaska's independence is constantly being threatened by external forces, particularly the federal government; Hickel has been uniquely effective at transforming fed-bashing into a unifying theme in Alaska politics. He makes the moral imperative obvious: grow or die, develop the state or it will stagnate. By extending the metaphor of Alaska as "one country, one people," Hickel has attempted to play the role of a nationalist leader.

Egan, Hammond, Cowper, and Hickel have all exploited the opportunities provided by the governorship to persuade. Their distinct messages reflect divergent strains in Alaska's richly ambiguous state culture. The most integrated vision emanates from Alaska's governor in the early 1990s, Walter Hickel. He voices the conservative populism that distinguishes the citizens of the last frontier.

CONCLUSION

Alaska's governorship furnishes the state with its primary unifying force. Governors are the only state leaders for whom all citizens can vote. They manage the largest institution within the state. Governors alone possess the potential and, often, the opportunity to fuse support for a vision of Alaska's future.

In Alaska, however, centripetal forces are as powerful as centrifugal ones. Parties are weak and give little direction to development of agendas.

The media age offers channels for every view, expanding the influence of interests. Regional loyalties wax strong, dividing the electorate. Regions cut multiple swaths through the legislature and even the bureaucracy, diverse views that cannot be reconciled or resolved through the legislative process.

The power of the Alaska governorship lies in its potential to forge a consensus supporting the state's political development. The record since statehood shows that governors have played weaker parts in state politics than one might expect from their formal "strong governor" powers. The legislature is the governor's equal, especially in fiscal policy. Competition between legislative and executive branches is the norm in Alaska politics. The legislature expresses the state's individualism and regionalism to a fault. The governorship, on the other hand, has the potential to pull people together toward a common goal and has done so on several occasions: the statehood battle, the Good Friday earthquake, the creation of the Permanent Fund, and the *Exxon Valdez* oil spill, to name a few of the best-known cases.

CHAPTER 9

Courts, Judges, and Public Policy

The framers of Alaska's constitution were preoccupied with their territory's subjection by external forces. In particular, they bore strong resentment toward the territorial court system: with the exception of municipal judges, it consisted of federal officials who implemented laws not particularly responsive to Alaska conditions. The delegates to the constitutional convention aspired to a court system equal in power to the other two branches of government. To create one that embodied the values of Alaska's political culture, they followed the same logic as when they designed the executive and legislative branches. They drew up a simple, unified, centralized blueprint for a judiciary unshackled by constitutional or statutory restrictions. Reflecting the progressive tradition of state government reform, Alaska's court system has withstood the test of time. It remains an equal partner to the executive and legislative branches in the enterprise of Alaska government.

Like state courts elsewhere, Alaska's courts perform over 90 percent of the legal business in the state. They arbitrate conflicts between individual citizens, groups, businesses, political organizations, and government institutions. Generally, they apply an important brake to social change by requiring adherence to traditional norms reflected in statutes and in previous court decisions. Above all, Alaska courts are policy makers. Judicial decisions determine courses of public action and affect the behavior of citizens and organizations, including the other branches of government.

In this chapter, we begin with a nuts-and-bolts analysis of the structure and operations of Alaska's judicial system. Next we examine the distinctive aspects of this system, including its progressive method of appointing and evaluating judges. Finally, we look at the judiciary's part in the pattern of state government, its relations with the other branches, and its role as a policy maker.[1]

Unlike the governor and legislators, the people who make up the court system in Alaska are relatively unknown to the public. Few citizens recall the names of judges other than those in their community. A smaller number of Alaskans vote in judicial retention elections than in those for the legislature and governor. In terms of public apathy, Alaska's courts differ little from those of other states.

In three respects, however, Alaska's courts are unusual. First, they emerged from a historical backdrop of federal territorial justice. Second, they are progressive courts, developed during an era of nationwide court reform. Third, they confront two especially trying conditions that stretch the definitions of law and policy: resource development and use and an aboriginal population with its own legal tradition.

From Territorial to State Courts

Until the late 1800s, Alaska cases were heard in the Washington, Oregon, and California state and federal courts. With the passage of the First Organic Act in 1884, Alaska gained a court system of its own. The Organic Act extended the laws of Oregon to Alaska as applicable. It provided residents some local interpretation of the laws—a so-called local option—but no courts.

At the turn of the century, Congress enacted both civil and criminal codes for Alaska; these represented the start of the territorial justice system. The basis of the new legal system was the law of the American West, particularly that of the state of Oregon. Alaska gained a district court, and Congress divided the territory into three judicial districts. By 1909, Congress had added another judicial district. The original district lines, following the territory's transportation waterways, remain in place today.

A Unified and Centralized System of Justice

Compared to most court systems in the United States, Alaska's is highly unified. All state courts fall under the umbrella of the judiciary, financed by the legislature. Regardless of whether they serve in district courts or the state's supreme court, all judges are subject to the same rules, which are administered by the same office.[2] The Alaska court system has four tiers: the supreme court, the court of appeals, the superior court, and the district court, with its affiliated magistracies. Jurisdiction varies from court to court.

The Alaska Supreme Court is the state's highest court and, in most cases, the court of last resort. A chief justice and four justices form the court's membership. The supreme court is primarily an appellate court, hearing appeals of judgments rendered by superior courts on civil matters. It also has discretionary authority to review decisions by the court of appeals on criminal matters and quasi-criminal matters, such as juvenile delinquency cases.

The supreme court tends to enter into cases that concern significant questions of constitutional law or issues of substantial public interest. In addition, it plays a directing role with regard to all other courts. It establishes rules of practice and procedure in civil and criminal cases, as well as procedures governing the practice of law in Alaska.

The court of appeals sits on the second rung of Alaska's judicial system. It is the newest court, established by the legislature in 1980 at the request of the supreme court to reduce its workload. The three-judge panel hears appeals of judgments in criminal and certain quasi-criminal cases. It handles, for instance, juvenile delinquency cases, habeas corpus cases in which prisoners challenge the legality of their incarceration, and cases involving probation and parole decisions. Misdemeanants have the option of appealing decisions to the superior court or to the court of appeals directly.

Alaska's most important trial court is the superior court, which has original jurisdiction in all civil and criminal matters. The court hears appeals of final judgments by district courts. It retains authority over all cases involving domestic relations, juvenile delinquency, and child abuse and neglect, as well as probate, including sanity hearings, estates, guardianship, and adoptions. The superior court also hears high-interest criminal cases such as homicides, rapes, and assaults, as well as civil cases with a large dollar value. Its arm extends throughout the state; twenty-nine judges perform its work.

With the rapid expansion and turnover of the state's population during the 1980s, the superior court's felony caseload doubled from 7 percent to 13 percent of its total cases, rising from 1,230 filings in 1982 to 2,464 filings in 1988. Also indicating the social disruption of the period, domestic violence cases increased from 6 percent to 10 percent of the caseload, rising from 991 filings in 1982 to 1,823 filings in 1988 (figure 2).[3]

The busiest court in Alaska is the district court. Its criminal jurisdiction

Figure 2. Alaska Superior Courts Caseload Composition, Fiscal Year 1988.

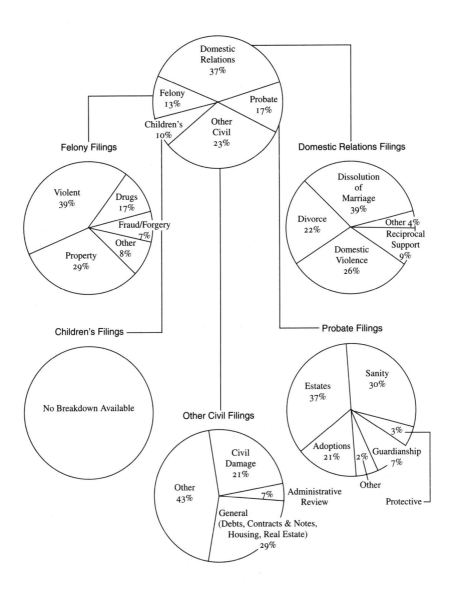

Source: Alaska Court System 1988 Annual Report

extends to all state misdemeanor violations ranging from drunk-driving infractions, shoplifting, and disorderly conduct to violations of city and borough ordinances. District court judges issue arrest and search warrants and serve as examining magistrates in arraignments. In civil matters, district court judges hear cases for recovery of property and damages up to fifty thousand dollars, well as small claims actions. District court judges also may serve as coroners, hold inquests, and record vital statistics in some parts of the state. The supreme court sets the number of district court judges within each judicial district. In 1992 there were seventeen statewide.

Magistrates hold the lowest level of judicial office. During territorial days, they were very important officials. Even today, a magistrate is often the only judicial officer in a rural area. They can issue writs of habeas corpus, marriage licenses, summonses, and search and arrest warrants. They may perform marriages, notarize documents, and serve as examining judges for preliminary examinations in criminal proceedings. In urban areas, magistrates handle routine matters, such as marriages, and ease the workload of district court judges. The presiding superior court judge appoints magistrates within each district. In 1992, Alaska had fifty district magistrates.

Problems of Bush Justice

Although a relatively high number of district magistracies exist in Alaska, most of the state's nearly two hundred Native villages lack a court official. Villages of fifty people or more are likely to have a village public safety officer (VPSO) who lives there or a state trooper who stops by periodically. Rural Alaskans miss the immediate and direct access to courts available to urban residents.[4] The dearth of courts tends to erode residents' perceptions of personal safety and social order.

A second problem villagers face is a lack of local authority to solve serious problems affecting the whole community, such as alcohol importation and abuse. Local-option laws handed down by the state legislature enable villages with self-governing powers under the state's municipal code to outlaw the use or importation of alcohol as well as to punish offenders. The laws are of shaky legality, however, and do not apply to villages without self-governing powers under state law. Many villages have adopted governments under the federal Indian Reorganization Act, and federal Indian liquor-control laws apply in some of these villages.[5]

A third and related problem is one of jurisdiction, which has two facets. First, as wards of the federal government, Alaska Natives enjoy protections under federal laws that often conflict with state laws. Federal laws strengthen Native subsistence rights and village self-determination powers. These rights conflict with state statutes on fish and game management and local government, respectively. Second, as aboriginal peoples with established practices of conflict resolution, Natives have traditionally dispensed justice in ways that conflict with local, state, and federal laws. The custom of ostracizing offending community members, for instance, does not sit well with the formal system of justice in Alaska.[6] The dilemmas of Native justice are examined in more depth in the discussion of tribal government in chapter 5.

APPOINTING AND EVALUATING JUDGES

Judges in American states attain office through either appointment or election, and most face tests at the polls sometime during their terms. Experts believe the systems used by individual states to appoint and evaluate judges affect judicial outcomes; academic studies on this relationship have proved inconclusive, however.[7]

The Missouri Plan

Alaska entered the Union at a time when judicial reformists sought to limit governors' influence over appointment of judges because of concerns about corruption. Reformists also lobbied to limit the partisanship of judges by making retention elections nonpartisan. In the 1950s, reformists preferred a judicial selection and retention system widely known as the Missouri Plan after the state in which it originated. The framers of the Alaska Constitution adopted the plan.

The mechanics of the Missouri Plan are simple. A nominating body, called the Judicial Council, screens candidates for a vacancy on the bench. It then recommends two or more people to the governor, who appoints someone from the list. The new judge sits for three years or, in the case of district court judges, for only one year, after which he or she faces the voters in a nonpartisan retention election. The interval between subsequent retention elections varies with the level of the court.

The Judicial Council

Alaska's Judicial Council is staffed full time. In most states, nominating commissions are staffed by part-time volunteers; little continuity prevails over time. The procedures Alaska's council follows for judicial selection and retention may well be more comprehensive and exhaustive than those of any other state.[8] When a vacancy arises on the supreme court bench, for example, the council sends a letter to every lawyer in the state announcing the opening and citing the minimum requirements for appointment. After the application deadline passes, the council surveys members of the Alaska Bar Association to assess the qualifications of each candidate. The council asks respondents to indicate whether they based their ratings on professional observations, personal contacts, or reputation. An independent research organization prepares a statistical analysis of all survey responses. In addition, the council analyzes a sampling of legal cases handled by applicants.

Fifteen states nationwide, including Alaska, follow the Missouri Plan. Studies of the system in other states indicate that it reduces the governor's influence over judicial appointments; it fails by and large, however, to remove politics from the selection process. Compared to other systems, the Missouri Plan does not necessarily lead to the recruitment of superior judges or to better delivery of justice.[9]

In Alaska, the Missouri Plan reduces the governor's political discretion in making judicial appointments. It increases the influence of the state's bar association and lawyers. Of the seven people who sit on the Judicial Council, three are attorneys appointed by the Alaska Bar Association and three are nonattorney members of the public appointed by the governor. The chief justice of the supreme court presides ex officio.

The Judicial Council pays close attention to bar association polls. The response rate to polls is high in the relevant area (the jurisdiction of the nominee) but low statewide, about 45 percent; thus, lawyers who take interest in the appointment and who are likely to know the applicants wield disproportionate influence. Powerful blocs include attorneys working for large law firms, attorneys employed by state government such as in the Department of Law, and the Women's Bar Association. They can give poor ratings to applicants whose interests are incompatible with theirs. A quantity of low evaluations reduces an applicant's chances to make the short list.

High-ranking applicants in bar association polls are likely to have graduated from prestigious law schools. This factor alone, however, is insufficient to measure the quality of judges selected under the Missouri Plan. Attorneys who represent the defense in criminal cases and the plaintiff in civil cases tend to vote for applicants whose records support their interests. These considerations figure strongly in retention polls as well.

Before an upcoming election, the Judicial Council solicits the opinions of members of the Alaska Bar Association as well as police and probation officers regarding those judges standing for retention. The council submits questionnaires to judges and attorneys, checks public records concerning judges' activities both on and off the bench, conducts public hearings, reviews records of proceedings, and analyzes sentencing data. A summary of survey results as well as the council's recommendations appear in a pamphlet provided to all registered voters. Candidates who receive low ratings in the bar association poll are unlikely to merit a favorable recommendation from the council. In this respect, the Missouri Plan replaces the highly visible politics of a gubernatorial selection and retention system with the more subtle politics of a system involving lawyers, criminal justice officers, and the Judicial Council. Only the final vote of the Judicial Council is open to public scrutiny.

The Commission on Judicial Conduct

The Alaska Constitution established two bodies to assist in the operation of the judiciary. The Judicial Council is the most important. In addition to screening candidates for judgeships and reviewing their performances for retention elections, it studies topics of importance to the judiciary such as plea bargaining and ethnic disparities in sentencing.

The Commission on Judicial Conduct is a larger body consisting of three judges elected by their colleagues, three lawyers appointed by the Alaska Bar Association, and three citizens appointed by the governor and confirmed by the legislature. The integrity of state court judges falls under the purview of the commission. It makes recommendations to the supreme court regarding disqualification, suspension, removal from office, retirement, and censure of judges. Only a small number of cases have come before the commission since statehood. The commission has never proposed to the state legislature that a judge be impeached. Overall, the lack of serious action on the part of the commission appears to testify to the efficacy of the selection system.[10]

Retention Elections in Alaska

At each statewide general election, Alaska voters make some retention decisions. After their first retention election, supreme court justices appear on the ballot every ten years; court of appeals judges, every eight years; superior court judges, every six years; and district court judges, every four years.

Nationally, fewer than 1 percent of judges lose retention elections. The format of the ballot question presents the voter with an uncontested candidate who is also the favored incumbent: "Do you favor or oppose the retention of Judge Smith?'' Under normal circumstances, a judge would have a hard time indeed losing a retention election.

Only three Alaska judges have gone down to defeat at the polls since statehood.[11] The first was Harry Arend, an Alaska Supreme Court justice who lost in 1964. The Alaska Bar Association, which disagreed with decisions in which Arend had participated, brought about his defeat through a well-organized campaign. No one charged Arend with incompetence as a justice.

The remaining two cases involved Anchorage district court judges, removed from the bench by voters in 1982. That year, the Judicial Council recommended that judges Joseph Brewer and Virgil Vochoska not be retained. In several previous elections, the Judicial Council's findings of incompetence had failed to garner voter support. In fact, judges had effectively run against the Judicial Council. In this election, however, the police officers' association and bar association joined forces in opposition to the judges.

The removal of only a handful of judges typically occurs with the kind of retention election Alaska uses. The elections do not present voters with a choice between candidates. If a judge is not retained, the people have little say about the replacement. Foes of a certain judge must be organized and well funded to mobilize opposition among the electorate. For example, a 1988 campaign against Alaska Supreme Court Chief Justice Jay Rabinowitz, which focused on his liberal record and hinted that he was ''soft on crime,'' shaved 10 percent off the normal retention margin of 70 percent. In the view of some observers, this campaign might have succeeded had it been better financed. Successful removals have involved law enforcement organizations, the Judicial Council, lawyers, and the state bar association, all active participants in the judicial selection process.

The justice system in Alaska strongly affects judicial behavior, in the view of professional observers, by the way in which it emphasizes peremptory challenges. A judge's collegial relationships are influenced by the frequency with which he is peremptorily challenged. Under Alaska law, prosecuting and defense attorneys may issue one peremptory challenge removing a judge from a case. The challenge must come within five days of the judge's assignment to the case. District attorneys tend to bump judges with the softest sentencing records; public defenders and defense attorneys challenge hard-line judges. Judges with extreme sentencing records preside over fewer cases, thereby increasing the workload of moderate judges who, in turn, press their extremist colleagues to alter their sentencing patterns. The overall effect of peremptory challenges is to reduce fringe sentences.

This compulsion toward the middle may, however, contradict impulses of governors and the public to move the judiciary in one direction or the other, in civil or criminal cases.

Courts in most states participate in complex relationships with executives and legislatures, and Alaska's strong, independent courts are no exception. They play two important roles with respect to the other branches. First, the courts interpret the constitutional provisions and statutes governing conduct of the executive and the legislature. Second, they arbitrate disputes between the governor and legislature. In addition to these roles, the courts place some constraints on the executive and legislative branches.

Interpreting Rules of Conduct

Two cases, both concerning appointments, demonstrate how the courts influence the conduct of the executive and legislative branches of government. The constitution gives the legislature the right to approve gubernatorial appointments of heads of major departments, a traditional legislative check on executive power. In 1976, the legislature sought to extend its confirmation authority to deputy department heads because it is they who formulate policy. The governor balked; the legislature sued. In this case, the state supreme court ruled against the legislature, supporting the governor's interpretation of the separation of powers.[12]

Seven years later, the legislature declined to confirm several of Governor Bill Sheffield's appointees. When the governor insisted that the legislature meet for this purpose in a joint session, several legislators departed. The governor dispatched state troopers to round up enough lawmakers to establish a quorum for a joint session, which then approved his appointments. Republican legislators sued the governor over what they claimed was an illegal joint session, and the court entered the dispute. The court supported the governor, opining that his actions did not violate the separation of powers.[13]

Both cases illustrate that Alaska's governors and legislators do not hesitate to call on the court system to specify roles and responsibilities of the different branches. In particular, the Alaska court system, like the federal system, has clarified the separation of powers and checks and balances described in the state constitution.

Umpiring Disputes Between Executive and Legislative

The Alaska court system also actively referees disputes between the executive and legislative branches. Two cases convey the flavor of this relationship.

In most states, the governor and lawmakers share the redistricting function. In Alaska, the framers of the constitution assigned reapportionment power to the governor and an advisory board. The board draws up a redistricting plan after each ten-year census. Legislators await each redistricting plan with understandable anxiety. Each year since 1962, legislators (and others) have petitioned the superior and supreme courts to correct perceived redistricting errors. Although the courts have not invalidated the governor's role in the redistricting process, they have thoroughly and systematically reviewed all challenges. On occasion they have mandated changes in the redistricting of the legislature.[14] In 1992, the supreme court directed Alaska Superior Court Judge Larry Weeks to redraw the lines of most districts (see chapter 7).

A second case of legislative-executive relations concerns administrative regulations. When the legislature establishes new programs and modifies existing ones, it typically affords broad latitude to administrative agencies in developing regulations consonant with its objectives. But legislators frequently complain about agency regulations that do not, in their opinion, faithfully reflect lawmakers' intent. In the 1970s and 1980s, lawmakers attempted to counteract such policy tinkering by passing resolutions that annulled regulations and were not subject to the governor's veto. The executive branch asked the courts to intervene in support of its interpretation that the legislature's annulment through resolution infringed on the governor's constitutional authority. The courts supported the executive, prompting the legislature to turn unsuccessfully to the voters in three elections for constitutional amendments authorizing "legislative vetoes" of administrative regulations.[15]

Legislative and Executive Constraints on the Courts

Despite their independence, Alaska's courts operate in an environment of constraints. The governor and legislature determine their resources and can, by extension, restrict their discretion in judicial outcomes.

In the 1960s, the state Department of Administration tried to control the court system's operating budget. The court objected, believing the attempt violated the separation of powers. The court won; now its budget is separate from that of the Department of Administration. Nevertheless, the legislature still retains oversight through the appropriations process. Although the judiciary has an excellent record in gaining support for its annual budget request, the power of legislative committees and individual lawmakers to scrutinize and reduce the court's budget limits activity.

A second constraint is the presumptive sentencing law passed by the legislature in 1978. The law responded to a study by the Judicial Council indicating that non-Caucasian offenders, particularly Native Alaskans, received longer sentences than whites. The finding pointed to unfair sentencing standards. Responding to the report as well as to national calls for sentencing reform, the legislature passed a law curbing the discretion of judges in the assignment of sentences and reducing consideration of mitigating factors. Judges now must follow formulas in developing sentences, a process that has reduced ethnic disparities.[16]

The third case concerns plea bargaining, a practice used as widely in Alaska as in other states. In the past, prosecuting attorneys frequently reduced charges against a defendant in exchange for an admission of guilt, which lowered court costs and time. Critics in the 1970s asked why a sparsely populated state such as Alaska could not handle cases without bending the rules; they pointed to the lack of overcrowding in Alaska's courts. The attorney general in 1982 proclaimed that the state would no longer bargain pleas, further constraining the court system. The proclamation has had little effect on the administration of justice, however. Prosecutors and defense attorneys now engage in "charge bargaining," which is essentially the same as plea bargaining.[17]

In short, Alaska's courts, like other branches of government, are subject to constraints on their operations. It does not appear, however, that the constraints have significantly crimped the independence or authority of the judiciary.

THE SUPREME COURT AS A STATE POLICY MAKER

All courts formulate policy through normal judicial decision making because court opinions determine courses of public action, affect behavior, and carry the force of law. The policy role of courts prompts questions about the style of judges: whether they are "activists" likely to expand the power of government through decisions based on practicality and social science more than judicial precedent, or whether they are "strict constructionists" disinclined to look beyond the letter of the law and precedent.

Whether active or passive, state courts are naturally more reactive and parochial than legislatures and executives. Courts react to specific complaints and grievances, but they cannot initiate policy. Citizens do not have access to courts unless they have a grievance or "standing to sue" because a law or its alleged violation causes them to suffer. The reliance on precedent for the large part of judicial decision making tends to localize and narrow judicial outcomes to specific circumstances.

Nevertheless, Alaska courts, particularly the supreme court, frequently compete with the governor and legislature in the policy-making arena. The following examples are drawn from four different policy areas: privacy rights, equal protection, resource management, and local governance.

The Right to Privacy

Most state constitutions omit a specific mention of privacy. In this respect, they resemble the U.S. Constitution, which only implies a right to privacy through the unreasonable search and seizures provision of the Fourth Amendment, the due process guarantees of the Fifth Amendment, and the equal protection language of the Fourteenth Amendment. Alaska voters in 1972 amended the state constitution to say: "The right of the people to privacy is recognized and shall not be infringed." The statement seemingly gave Alaskans greater protection from intrusive government acts than that available elsewhere.

In 1975, the supreme court cited the privacy right in *Ravin v. State*.[18] Irvin Ravin, an attorney, was arrested for possessing a small amount of marijuana, which he used in the privacy of his vehicle. The superior court found against Ravin, supporting the state prosecutors. The supreme court reversed the lower court's decision, declaring that the constitutional right to privacy permitted a citizen to possess a small amount of marijuana for personal use. The *Ravin* decision is an important comment on Alaska's political culture. Chief Justice Jay Rabinowitz, who wrote the decision, denoted the necessity of protecting the privacy of the home, which is "consonant with the character of life in Alaska. Our territory and now state has traditionally been the home of people who prize their individuality and who have chosen to settle or to continue living here in order to achieve a measure of control over their own lifestyles which is now virtually unattainable in many of our sister states."

The legislature has tried to circumvent the constitution and "recriminalize" marijuana possession and use. In 1990, by a ratio of five to four, Alaska voters passed an initiative in favor of making possession of marijuana a criminal offense. Alaskans for Privacy filed suit in the spring of 1991, citing the statute's incompatibility with the privacy clause of the Alaska Constitution. On the day the new law was to go into effect, it landed back in court (see chapter 6).

The court's interpretation of the right to privacy also impedes "right-to-life" legislation in Alaska. Although a vocal minority of lawmakers and citizens support an antiabortion law, it is widely believed that a woman's decision to have an abortion is a private matter, fully protected under the privacy clause of the Alaska Constitution.

These two examples perhaps best illustrate the individualist strain in Alaska's political culture. They also highlight the court's independence from the executive and legislative branches in the formation of state public policy.

Equal Protection of the Laws

Supreme courts, within the confines of the states, are the primary arbiters of the federal system and state-federal relations. The Fourteenth Amendment to the U.S. Constitution, which extends Bill of Rights protections to citizens in their relationships with state governments, obliges states to provide "equal protection of the laws" to citizens regardless of their race, creed, or national origin. The amendment amplifies the "privileges and immunities" section of Article I, which protects Americans' rights to travel and reside in any state.

Since the discovery of oil and gas at Prudhoe Bay in 1968, Alaska's state and local governments have sought to confer special benefits on Alaska citizens. Legislatures and governors have endorsed proposals that would discriminate in favor of Alaskans in hiring and in providing other benefits based on length of residence. Alaska's courts initially supported these parochial efforts but in recent years have begun to defend the Fourteenth Amendment instead.

When construction began on the trans-Alaska pipeline, union and popular interests coalesced to pressure the legislature into passing a local-hire law. Two out-of-state workers were denied jobs at Prudhoe Bay under terms of the law and sued the state labor commissioner, whose job it was to enforce it. The Alaska Supreme Court defended the state's action, ruling the law constitutional.[19] The U.S. Supreme Court, in a 1978 decision, reversed the state's high court and voided the local-hire law.[20]

Created by the legislature in 1980, the Permanent Fund dividend program doles out benefits to all Alaska citizens. The original bill provided that annual dividends would vary, increasing with length of residency. Two Anchorage attorneys, Ronald and Patricia Zobel, maintained that the residency requirements violated their right to equal protection under the law. They had lived in the state less than one year at that point. The Zobels sued the state but were unsuccessful at both superior and supreme court levels. The Alaska Supreme Court, in a three-to-two decision, ruled that durational residency was fully constitutional.[21] Justices pointed to the contributions of those who claimed long residency and had helped develop the state. The Zobels appealed the decision to the U.S. Supreme Court, which in 1982 ruled in their favor and against the concept of durational residency.[22]

Two years later, Rodney Vest, a new senior citizen of sixty-five, claimed a longevity bonus from the state, for which he was ineligible because he had lived in the state an insufficient length of time. Lawmakers established the bonus system at the outset of the oil boom to reward long-time citizens. It gave each resident over sixty-five years who had lived in the state since 1959 a monthly payment of two hundred fifty dollars. Vest's case reached the state supreme court, which supported his plea and ruled the longevity bonus program, in its current form, unconstitutional because it violated the equal protection clause.[23] Vest received a bonus, as did every other senior citizen who applied, regardless of length of residence.

The state supreme court initially did not lead the defense of new Alaska citizens. In time, however, it submitted to the authoritative interpretations issued by the U.S. Supreme Court. Since 1984, it has narrowed progressively the scope of special benefits for which long-term Alaskans alone are eligible.

Resource Management

The Alaska Constitution's special article on natural resources is unique among state constitutions. It spells out policy for resource conservation, development, and management, as well as for public access to resources. The role of state courts has been to defend public use of resources and to promote equality of use when conflicts occur between the state and federal governments.

Before statehood, the fisheries industry was controversial because it was dominated by absentee interests that employed highly efficient fish traps.

The fish traps not only competed with independent fishermen, but threatened the resource because of their unrestricted use. Alaska residents voted to ban fish traps in the 1958 statehood election, and a special provision of the constitution pledges not to extend any exclusive right or special privilege of fishery. Courts cited this provision when ruling against legislative attempts to establish a limited-entry fisheries system.[24] In 1972, the constitution was amended to limit the number of fishermen who could engage in a fishery.

The state courts have been similarly protective of the public domain. In the 1970s, legislators hatched several plans to distribute lands widely to Alaskans, responding to the popular drive for land to be used for home and recreational sites. Then, as now, less than 2 percent of the Alaska land mass was owned by individual citizens. In fact, an initiative backed by state representative Mike Beirne would have distributed land free. The state supreme court voided the initiative based on a constitutional provision that prohibited appropriation of state assets by initiative.[25]

Finally, the state courts have with some degree of uniformity applied land-use law equally to all population groups. This course has pitted state courts against federal courts, which protect Alaska Native use of traditional lands for subsistence. Federal fish and wildlife managers give high priority to subsistence use of resources by Native Alaskans. They turned over federal management authority of fish and wildlife to the state conditionally, based on recognition of that priority. The legislature passed a subsistence law in 1978 that gave rural Alaskans, including Natives, the first chance at species when they became scarce. Alaska's courts tend to rule against Alaskans, including Natives, who make special claims on use of fish and game species. For example, a Fairbanks court convicted an Athabaskan who shot a moose out of season and who claimed that the state and federal constitutions protcted his right to take it for a religious purpose, that is, a potlatch. The state supreme court, however, subsequently ruled that the religious purpose was the governing factor and found for the Indian defendant.[26] When another Native group sought to restrict public access to its salmon fishery in Chitina for reasons of private ownership and subsistence use, the state courts ruled that the public had a limited right to access.

Although the resource management area of policy making is not always as clear as these examples might suggest, the state courts have in general bolstered the resource use and public access provisions of the constitution. Over time, they have defended the notion of *public* domain. The courts have generally opposed preferential resource use by Alaska Natives on state lands. In

1989, the state supreme court struck down the state's rural subsistence preference law on the grounds that it discriminated against urban residents.[27] The high court had no hesitation in entering into this extremely complex area. Its ruling indicated that it did not hide behind precedent.

Local Governance

Alaska's constitution features perhaps the most permissive local government provisions in the United States. A trail of judicial policies supports these provisions. The supreme court has defended the right of the people to organize local governments in spite of strong pressure from corporations and adjacent municipalities. In 1974, for instance, oil companies seeking to invalidate the incorporation petition of North Slope Borough residents received an unfavorable court decision.[28]

Courts have supported the legislature's delivery of services outside boroughs and cities. Thus, they implicitly support the state's discretionary authority in the unorganized borough. When boroughs and cities have sought to expand powers, the courts have generally upheld them. In short, the courts have defended the constitution's statement that local government powers should be liberally construed.

Finally, the state supreme court has protected the continued existence of local governments by defending their taxation authority against powerful opposition. In 1978, oil companies challenged the authority of the North Slope Borough to exceed the statewide mill levy for the purpose of retiring interest on general obligation bonds. In a pivotal case on local government finance, the court upheld the borough's power to tax oil company property, without limit, in order to pay off millions of dollars in bonds sold to finance public improvements.[29]

State courts have been less tolerant of local governments that have sought to extend beyond the periphery of the state constitution and statutes, namely, those involved in the Native sovereignty movement. When the legislature tried to give social service grants directly to Native nonprofit corporations, the courts required their passage through state or local government agencies, or that traditional Native governments waive sovereign immunity from suit. State courts have steadfastly rejected the claim by villages such as Arctic Village and Venetie, which are not federal Indian reservations, that their land is Indian country in which Native governments and tribal courts rule. The supreme court took its strongest position in support of state authority and in opposition to Native sovereignty when it ruled in 1988 that the Native village of Stevens (and, by implication, virtually all Alaska Native villages) lacked status as a tribe under the state constitution and statutes.[30] This case is another example of the political activism of the Alaska high court.

In these and related cases, the state court system has established itself as a politically active and engaged policy maker. The courts have defended the position of the executive branch, the legislature, and the state of Alaska. They also have liberally construed the powers of local governments. Federal courts in Alaska and the U.S. Supreme Court have adopted different poses. They generally support Native political claims and federal prerogatives, as have federal land and resource management agencies in Alaska.

Alaska and the New Judicial Federalism

State supreme courts may broaden protection of rights under state constitutions beyond what the U.S. Supreme Court grants under the U.S. Bill of Rights. The Alaska Supreme Court has expanded such protections in three significant areas.

In civil law cases, the 1970s Alaska Supreme Court set a course different from that of other state courts and the federal branch. For example, when treating equal protection cases, the court decided to evaluate the importance of the interests affected, instead of considering whether a "suspect" category was involved. In several cases in the late 1970s and 1980s, the supreme court considered the value of long-term residence in unemployment benefits and Permanent Fund dividends.

Second, the court's *Ravin* decision in 1974 ranks as among the most liberal U.S. state court decisions based on a constitutional privacy statement. The court stood as guardian of individual liberties and expanded privacy protections beyond those afforded by federal courts.[31]

Third, for a brief window of time in the 1970s, the Alaska Supreme Court was more liberal in respecting defendants' rights than other state courts and the federal bench. Provisions under the Alaska Constitution offer stronger protections for defendants than the U.S. Constitution. The Alaska Constitution has stringent evidence requirements and procedures for search warrants and search and seizure.[32]

In the 1980s and early 1990s, the Alaska court followed the U.S. pattern more closely. This change can be attributed to more restrictive interpretations nationally on legal and constitutional issues as well as to changes in appointments to the U.S. and Alaska courts.

Alaska's Leading Justice

No one has played a more significant role in the development of Alaska law than Jay Rabinowitz, chief justice of the Alaska Supreme Court. Justice Rabinowitz is the longest-serving and most influential member of Alaska's high court. An apparent political liberal, Rabinowitz authored the court's *Ravin* decision and has supported defendants' rights and the prerogatives of Native tribal governments.

Rabinowitz came to Alaska in 1957, serving first as a law clerk in U.S. district court and then as assistant U.S. attorney for the territory of Alaska and deputy attorney general on statehood. Governor William Egan appointed him in 1960 to the superior court, where he served before assuming a seat on the state's highest court in 1965.

Lawyers may evaluate judges in terms of their craftsmanship; lay people, however, evaluate judges as liberal or conservative, because that helps place them in a zone of political expectations. Justice Rabinowitz confounds simplistic analysis, however. Rabinowitz, who has served three times as chief justice, is diligent, honest, careful, and a solid check on the court. He takes care in wading through the thicket of precedent, making his choices based on what he determines the law is, whether he agrees with it or not.[33]

CONCLUSION

Comparing the promise of the Alaska Constitution with the practice of the executive and legislative branches since statehood may be a disappointing exercise to some. Governors and legislatures have not often met Alaskans' expectations. History has written an entirely different story about Alaska's judiciary.

The outline of the contemporary state court system closely adheres to that envisioned by the framers of the state constitution. The system remains unified and centralized without local courts or courts of special jurisdiction, which are often found in other states. The Missouri Plan leads to the nonpartisan selection and retention of judges. The court system remains widely regarded as efficient in the administration of justice, with speedy trials and relatively uniform punishments.

Alaska's judiciary is a fully independent branch of government that stands above the other two branches as often as it stands as their equal or inferior. The Alaska court system, particularly its supreme court, has developed into an effective advocate of state power over private interest, of individual rights against state intrusion, and of equal protection of the laws.

Although remaining at some distance from the political process (but entering the political fray more frequently in recent years), the Alaska court system forges strong links with Alaska's political culture. Its decisions define an area of law that grants greater freedom to Alaska residents than is available to residents of other states. Also, Alaska's courts strongly champion the prerogatives of the state against the federal government. Overall, Alaska's courts foster an environment that supports frontier individualism, while making it responsive to state law.

Political Organizations

Veco International, an Anchorage-based oil support company, bundled together one-thousand-dollar checks from more than one hundred employees and directed them to pro-oil and Republican candidates in the 1984 legislative race. Word leaked to the press, and the *Anchorage Daily News* reported in full this craven attempt to influence Alaska politics. The state's campaign watchdog agency, the Alaska Public Offices Commission (APOC), audited the transactions. It found several violations of campaign funding law and fined Veco $72,666. The company sued. Although a judge eventually upheld the fine, many of Veco's candidates won their races.

This case illustrates the power of political organizations in Alaska life. Veco, like other economic interests, sought to elect candidates who would advance their objectives legislatively. Unlike most interest groups, Veco operated outside the law.

Individuals and their factions, groups, interests, and parties—collectively called political organizations—energize and direct the Alaska political process. Political organizations in many states act as a brake on government. Alaska's strong individualists are no exception, freely criticizing some government programs, protecting other programs, and zealously defending their rights against government intrusion. Although Alaska lacks an independent capitalist economy, it fosters robust groups and interests so varied and powerful that they endow politics with a rich diversity. In this chapter, we describe and analyze the nature of the Alaska political party system, media, interest groups, and lobbying.

POLITICAL PARTIES

Alaska has the weakest political party system of any state in the nation. It does not collect the different interests of the Alaska public into two or three alternative views of state public policy. This lack of party aggregation encourages interest group pluralism and conflict. A traditional way to evaluate parties is to consider their three faces: parties in the minds of the voters, parties as organizations of power, and parties as factors organizing and shaping policy from within government.[1]

Parties Outside Government

Parties have a weak image in the eyes of Alaska's electorate; only about 46 percent of voters register with any political party. Unlike the procedure in several other states, Alaska's electoral rules neither require partisan registration nor encourage partisan alignment. Citizens who register to vote can choose among the Alaskan Independence, Democratic, Republican, Green, or "other" parties, or check the "nonpartisan" box.

In addition to electoral rules, several factors appear to account for the low level of partisan registration. The majority of Alaska's adult population moved in from other states, severing many ties, including, in some cases, political ones. Also, Alaska's population is younger than the national average, and young voters are less likely to affiliate themselves with parties than are middle-aged or older voters. The political cultural traits of individualism and independence are also linked to nonpartisanship.[2] Perhaps most important, however, is the way electoral races in Alaska deemphasize partisanship. Local races are nonpartisan. Until 1992, legislative and gubernatorial races featured blanket primaries. The general elections emphasize style, character, and incumbency over partisan differences. Only the congressional and presidential contests reinforce partisan lines to the extent that they emerge in federal elections.

Parties as Organizations

Parties in most states possess some strength at the precinct level. They include strong state committees and organizations in counties and congressional districts that coordinate the flow of messages, help recruit candidates for statewide office, and play major roles in setting policy and in fund raising. In Alaska, precinct organizations are almost nonexistent. Virtually anyone can serve as precinct chairperson of a political party. Parties often face difficulty finding precinct captains at the time of the state's presidential nominating convention and the state convention.

State party organization is more effective. Both major parties sponsor state committees representing each region of the state. Alaska is one of six states that sends only one congressional representative to the U.S. House of Representatives. The state party organization is thus identical to the congressional district.

At the regional level, Alaska's political parties are organizationally weak. Alaska lacks uniform regional or territorial local government units, such as counties, found in all other states. While some regions have no organized municipality, others, such as Anchorage, Juneau, and Sitka, have highly unified municipalities.

The most common local electoral units are state house districts, each of which represented about fourteen thousand people in the early 1990s. District committees exist for most of the house seats in the state. A district secretary or chairperson is likely to arrange some activities between elections. In populous regions of the state—Anchorage, Fairbanks, Juneau, and Ketchikan—house districts may aggregate into a larger, regional unit.

Alaska parties suffer in comparison to the model of the political machine or the strong party system of states such as Indiana. They also are weaker than parties in the western states or one-party regions, such as the South. This shortcoming stems partly from the lack of incentives for loyalty to the organization. A more important factor contributing to the weak party system is a lack of party control over the nomination process.

Parties and Nominations

Until 1992, Alaska was one of three states (the others are Washington and Louisiana) with a blanket primary. Voters could cast their ballots for any candidate from any party. The ballot listed all candidates by office and did not restrict the voter's choice within the office bloc. This system was anathema to political parties: party nominees were picked by an undifferentiated voting public rather than by loyal party members.

The territorial legislature adopted the blanket primary in 1947. An article in the *Anchorage Times* during the legislative debate shows that parties wielded little more clout in the 1940s than in the 1990s:

> Inasmuch as the two parties in Alaska are different only in leadership and in their position as "in" or "out" of power, it can be argued that the blanket ballot would be appropriate here.
>
> Both parties are interested in developing Alaska. Either one would follow a program very similar to the other should it be placed in power. It has been said that the voters, during the primary election, separate into two parties for the

purpose of eliminating some candidates for public office and nominating others. The general election is a continuation of this process, only with the voters all using the same ballot with the candidates of the parties on the same list. Therefore, it is argued, there would be nothing lost by having a blanket ballot in the primary.[3]

On statehood, legislators switched to a more traditional, open primary system that presented voters with a choice between an all-Republican or an all-Democratic ballot. Strong support for further opening the nomination process grew in the 1967 legislature, which returned to the blanket primary. Ironically, then-governor Walter Hickel supported the change in electoral rules, which may have worked against him in his 1974, 1982, and 1990 primary campaigns for the governorship. Democrats and nonpartisan opponents of Hickel were able to cross over to vote for more palatable, and possibly weaker, Republican candidates.

For thirty years, party stalwarts contested the blanket primary. As the majority party in the 1960s, Democrats opposed it because they thought Republicans used it to cross over and elect the weakest Democratic candidate. In the early 1990s, Republicans obtained an edge in registration (in December 1992, there were 70,739 Republicans and 59,938 Democrats registered in Alaska). As a result, Republicans adopted a more adversarial stance toward the blanket primary than Democrats, believing that Democrats cross over and influence Republican races. At its statewide convention in March 1990, the Alaska Republican Party amended its rules with this provision: "Only registered Republicans, registered Independents, and those who state no preference of party affiliation shall be allowed to vote in the Republican primary election for Governor, Lieutenant Governor, U.S. Senator, U.S. Representative, and members of the State Legislature." The Republicans expected the Democratic party to follow suit at its convention, but it did not. They then requested the state elections office to close the Republican primary in the August 1990 election. The state declined to do so.

The Republican party filed suit against the state, asserting that the doctrine of associational rights in the *Tashjian* decision of the U.S. Supreme Court conferred on the party the prerogative to close its primary to Democrats. The state claimed that a late change in procedure would be disruptive to voters and disadvantageous to minorities, in violation of the federal Voting Rights Act of 1965. The Democratic party and the Alaska Federation of Natives filed an *amicus curiae* brief in support of the state's position. Both stressed the harm to rural Native voters that would likely ensue from a change in electoral procedures: "Any election procedure which abridges the opportunity for Native voters to enhance their political influence through bipartisan coalitions fundamentally impairs voting prerogatives protected under the 'no retrogression' provisions of the Act. Indeed, AFN suspects that the Party Rule is specifically intended to frustrate the formation of bipartisan coalitions and, in turn, to impair the influential role of legislators who represent Native voters."[4] This argument seems to be that increased partisanship in primaries would enhance partisan influence on legislative organization. Natives, who have joined coalitions led by Republicans or Democrats in the past, would have fewer options.

In 1991, Lieutenant Governor Jack Coghill, erstwhile "Mr. Republican," asked the Republicans to rescind their rule on primaries. Although the party rule was supported by the federal and state courts at this time, the state objected to the expense and disorderliness of two primary ballots—one for Republican candidates (in which Democratic, Alaskan Independence, or Green party registrants could not vote) and the second for all other candidates. At the 1992 Republican party convention, the issue was joined again and the party rule was narrowly supported. The other parties have not attempted to exercise greater control over primaries. As the result of a district court decision supporting the Republican party, the state Division of Elections printed two ballots for the 1992 primary.

The August 1992 primary election confused many voters, who could vote in the Republican primary only if they were registered as Republican, undeclared, or nonpartisan voters. The Republican primary attracted fewer voters than the other primary, which offered more choices. Nevertheless, closing the primary to Democrats initially seemed to have the desired effect in several districts. For example, Cheri Davis, a two-term Republican legislator from Ketchikan, lost a primary race to Carroll Fader, who had the support of Republican activists and the legislature's most partisan Republican, Senator Robin Taylor. Davis had angered Republican purists by joining the Democratic majority in the seventeenth legislature. In the general election, Fader lost narrowly to Democrat Bill Williams.

A clear majority of Alaska voters support the blanket primary. Most are not firmly aligned with a political party. They believe voters deserve maximum independence in balloting. Comments made during the senate debate of 1966 would not sound out of place twenty-seven years later. Senator Robert Blodgett of Teller said: "The Democratic party is a hollow shell. The Republican party is a hollow shell. How many people actually are active workers in the two parties? Darned few." Senator Robert Zeigler added, "In

Ketchikan, probably nine of every ten voters want to vote for the man, not the party."[5] Most observers believe that for either party to close itself off from unaffiliated voters would be political suicide.

As indicated in chapter 7, the parties, particularly the Republican party, have endorsed favored candidates before the primary in efforts to gain party control over nominees. Otherwise, as one Republican chairwoman said in 1985: "We don't know who they [the nominees] are, and yet we have to defend them as Republicans. Some of them seem to come from nowhere."[6] Every attempt to control nominees through preprimary endorsements, including resolutions of both Democratic and Republican state conventions, has failed, however.

Parties become more active once the primaries elect the standard bearers. In recent years, political parties have been a large source of campaign donations, especially in tightly contested races. They contribute office headquarters to candidates and also provide mailing lists, volunteer assistance, and information on polls and issues. Successful candidates are indebted less to the party organization, however, than to individual friends and neighbors, a good number of whom may not be among the party faithful. For this reason, parties cannot easily influence their candidates once they win a seat in government.

Parties in Government

Over the years, political parties have figured decreasingly in the organization and operation of the state legislature. Historically, they wielded little influence over the executive and judiciary, and the same is true today.

Political parties, primarily the Democratic party, organized the first state legislature. Democrats then held 34 of 40 seats in the house and 18 of 20 seats in the senate. At the start of the second legislature, in 1961, however, Democrats controlled only 19 seats in the house, and 13 seats in the senate. A Republican-led coalition organized the house. For well over two-fifths of the legislative sessions, no party has dominated; coalitions have organized either one or both houses (see chapter 7). Combined with the inability of any party since 1967 to control both houses as well as the governorship, this lack of organizational control testifies strongly to the absence of party control in Alaska government.

Organization of the eighteenth legislature in late 1992 appeared to alter this trend. The election of 21 Democrats, 18 Republicans, and 1 Alaskan Independence Party member to the house gave the organizational edge to Democrats. They lost it, however, when veteran Anchorage Republican Ramona

Barnes formed a Republican coalition with 23 members, including 4 Democrats and the lone Alaskan Independence Party member. The senate, divided equally between Republicans and Democrats, also was organized by a Republican coalition with one Democratic member, for an 11–9 majority. With Republicans leading both houses and a governor whose dispositions were Republican, notwithstanding his nominal membership in the Alaskan Independence Party, Alaska's state government seemed united under the Republican aegis. Because Republicans lacked firm working majorities in both houses, pundits questioned whether the organizations would hold throughout the session. The organization promised to give Republicans control over procedures and the ability to block legislation. As the session unfolded, however, tensions between the house and senate overrode those between the Republican majority and Democratic minority. One week before the end of the session, the house adjourned, attempting to force its policy preferences on the senate. This fracas indicated that partisan cues counted for little in the distribution of legislative resources.

The legislature does not elect whips from its membership to monitor the votes of Democratic or Republican officeholders. In most states and in the U.S. Congress, lawmakers frequently vote with their party on civil rights and liberties, social welfare, and environmental issues. When Alaska's parties send cues on such issues, lawmakers may act on them, but weakly.[7] Regional pressures, not political parties, influence economic development policies and state budget formation.

Some governors have relied on partisan factors in appointing people to cabinet posts and upper-level positions in state government. Governors Egan and Hickel preferred to surround themselves with members of their own party, as did Sheffield. Other governors tended to fill high-level posts, boards, and commissions with nonpartisan appointees. The governor can fill roughly one thousand such positions. State civil service rules covering over 90 percent of state government positions restrict partisanship in recruitment and dismissals. Thus, to the extent that any governor selects chief administrators based on partisan criteria, he or she is limited in the ability to affect partisan ideology.

Insofar as recruitment of judges is concerned, the judiciary is the branch least susceptible to party influences. The Missouri Plan blurs partisan and ideological factors because such a diverse array of individuals and groups participate in the selection and retention process. As we pointed out in chapter 9, the judiciary represents the interests of lawyers above the interests of political parties. Judicial retention elections focus largely on judges' sentencing records; campaigns emerge in a small percentage of cases in which judges are perceived as unusually soft or hard on criminals.

In short, Alaska's political parties are anemic, with virtually no influence over nominations to state office. As their irrelevance as electoral organizations mounts, they survive mainly to dispense funds to candidate organizations. Since the late 1980s, their patron role has pumped a little more life into them.[8] Other states have "Demipublican" coalitions or, as in the South, nonpartisan legislative coalitions. Alaska's political parties, however, have little say in government organization or policy making.

What makes Alaska parties endure despite these limitations? The heavy hand of history explains something about party survival. Entrepreneurship on the part of politically active party loyalists also contributes. A third factor is the pragmatic use of party labels as an initial device in legislative organization. Most important, however, is the rule that creates primaries for candidates of political parties. Independent candidates miss out on early exposure at the polls and the name recognition a primary campaign brings. In summary, parties play a part in Alaska politics, but it is a peripheral role, not an influential one.

ALASKA INTEREST GROUPS

Alaska's robust interest groups, in contrast to parties, effectively articulate the wants and needs of Alaskans. Their gain in mobilizing interests is surely the political parties' loss. The proliferation of interest groups in Alaska can be directly traced to the oil boom that began in the 1970s. These groups mobilize to play pressure politics and to lobby inside and outside government.

Proliferation of Interest Groups

Before the Prudhoe Bay oil-lease sale of 1969, Alaska government and politics absorbed little money and, for that reason, attracted little interest group activity. A handful of lobbyists representing business and union organizations, Native groups, and environmental coalitions put some pressure on Juneau. The intergovernmental lobby of municipalities and school districts, however, had yet to develop.

Oil wealth brought about two changes in interest group politics. First, the number of interests seeking a legislative hearing increased greatly, from approximately two hundred registered lobbying groups and individuals in 1975 to five hundred in 1985. Second, the interests themselves underwent a transformation. State agencies, local governments, universities, and school districts all hired lobbyists or government relations specialists.[9]

On a per capita basis, more registered lobbyists operate in Alaska than in any other state. The decline in state revenues after 1986 had no immediate impact on the number of interests represented at the capital. It only increased the pressure of groups on the political system.

Group Characteristics

Over the first generation of statehood, interest groups diversified into sectors: business, labor, professions, Native, and environmental. As the years passed, the nature of the sectors changed, the intergovernmental lobby's influence increased, and relationships between groups continued to evolve.

Business. Business interests in the newly admitted state of Alaska had as their primary goal natural resource extraction. Oil company representatives, miners, fish processors and canners, loggers, and pulp mill owners all had a say in political decisions.

Oil field development at Prudhoe Bay altered business interest representation in two ways. First, oil companies, because of their investment in the state and concern over the conditions likely to be imposed on development, emerged as the dominant interest. Second, the state's increased wealth created new economic opportunities while diversifying existing businesses. For example, the insurance and banking industries burgeoned in the 1970s; they, too, sent lobbyists to Juneau.

The number of trade associations expanded along with business groups. The "sunshine" reforms of the 1970s heated up the climate of regulation for several industries. Business interests united into federations, hiring lobbyists to provide political protection.[10]

Campaign expenditures by business groups in recent elections rank as follows: first, oil and mining with eight of the top fifty campaign contributors in the 1986 elections and more than $430,000 donated to candidates; second, miscellaneous business; third, construction; and fourth, finance, insurance, and real estate.[11]

Labor. Organized labor has undergone similar transitions with regard to representation. Traditional labor groups such as the Teamsters and AFL-CIO wielded great power during the construction of the trans-Alaska pipeline. In fact, Jesse Carr, business agent for the Teamsters Local 959, was widely regarded as one of the most influential figures in Alaska politics in the 1970s.[12]

Although pension-fund scandals damaged the credibility of the Teamsters, external economic events weakened it and AFL-CIO organizations more than internal ones. With the completion of the pipeline and ensuing slowdown in construction, traditional unions such as the Electrical Workers, Plumbers and Pipefitters, Marine Engineers, Operating Engineers, Laborers, and Teamsters scrambled to find even part-time jobs for their members. Their lobbyists, meanwhile, fought for local hire.

As the influence of traditional unions waned, Alaska's public employee unions expanded their membership and power. NEA-Alaska claims to speak for three thousand teachers. By the mid-1980s, it ranked alongside the most effective lobbying groups in the state. Several unions, foremost among them the Alaska Public Employees Association (APEA), have represented state and local public employees. The APEA, however, fell victim to discontent over its perceived failure to protect wages and benefits during the economic recession of the late 1980s. Its successor, the Alaska State Employees Association (ASEA), labored for two years to negotiate a new contract with state government.

Notwithstanding their widely different categories and membership, Alaska's unions cooperate electorally. Traditionally, they support incumbents and Democratic candidates, in that order, through donations and voting at the polls.

Professional Associations. In number alone, professional associations exceed labor unions. Like the unions, these associations increased their membership as Alaska grew wealthy in the late 1970s.

Health care professionals such as doctors, dentists, technicians, and health care administrators belong to their own professional associations, but these groups do not figure prominently in the electoral process. Because the professions by and large regulate themselves, their interest groups concentrate on appointments to licensing boards and on legislative reform in the area of malpractice.

Lawyers, on the other hand, participate avidly in the political practice. They are represented by the state bar association, which in Alaska plays a quasi-government role. The association certifies lawyers to practice in the state and disqualifies those found guilty of unethical conduct. Although lawyers have a powerful voice in judicial appointments and retention, they splinter along functional lines. The interests of attorneys employed by the state differ from the interests of attorneys representing law firms or the public interest. Lawyers also perform a generous portion of the lobbying that goes on in Alaska. With their desire to expand their clientele and advance their clients' interests, lawyers make especially effective lobbyists.[13]

Native Organizations. During territorial days, the needs and concerns of Alaska Natives were voiced primarily through the Alaska Native Brotherhood and Sisterhood, which represented traditional village leaders in southeast Alaska. The land claims issue of the mid-1960s transformed Native politics, however. By 1966, Native land claims associations had sprung up in every region of the state. They joined forces in the Alaska Federation of Natives a year later.

With the passage of the Alaska Native Claims Settlement Act (ANCSA) in December 1971, Native organizations underwent another conversion. The legislation established regional and village corporations to administer the millions of acres and dollars that accompanied ANCSA's passage. The corporations quickly siphoned off Native leadership talent. At the same time, the land claims associations metamorphosed into regional nonprofit corporations, which administer federal and some state social service programs to Natives. Both Native corporations and Native associations protect the interests of rural as well as urban Native Alaskans, including their access to fish and game for subsistence purposes.

Several ANCSA corporations have formed political action committees, three of which rank among the top fifty in the state in terms of contributions.[14] Influential Native leaders have also formed the Ice Bloc, a PAC of Native leaders and lobbyists, which is another major campaign donor. Although AFN does not contribute to campaigns, it lobbies heavily on legislation concerning Natives. In recent years, proponents of the Native sovereignty movement have banded together in the Alaska Native Coalition, which lobbied Congress as well as the state legislature.[15]

Environmental Groups. During state and national campaigns over use of federal public lands in Alaska, conflicts flared between resource development and environmental groups. Business organizations such as the oil and gas industry aligned themselves with the prodevelopment camp, as did the United Fishermen of Alaska, Alaska Placer Miners Association, and Alaska Loggers Association. Several prodevelopment umbrella groups formed, including the Resource Development Council, based in Anchorage, and Commonwealth North.

Three environmental and conservation groups fought the hardest to oppose development: the Trustees for Alaska, the Alaska Conservation Society, and the Alaska chapter of the Sierra Club. These and other Alaska environmental organizations cultivate strong ties with the national Sierra Club, Audubon Society, and Wilderness Society.

Prodevelopment and environmental/conservation groups formed PACs to influence campaigns. The largest and oldest conservation group was the Alaska Environmental Political Action Committee,[16] which represented some environmental and conservation groups around the state and contributed to legislative races.

Other Interest Groups. Alaskans are no less prone to participate in groups than citizens of other states. Considering Alaska's sparse population, the only surprise is the large number of organizations and the sizable membership they attract.

Most organizations are broadly "civic" and take no significant interest in state government and politics. For example, each of the larger communities features service clubs such as Rotary, Kiwanis, Elks, Eagles, Pioneers, Moose, and Soroptimists. Veterans' groups, primarily the Veterans of Foreign Wars and the American Legion, thrive in large towns.

Church groups have participated more prominently in the state's political process in the 1980s and 1990s than previously, paralleling nationwide developments. One example is the Personal Liberties Committee, an arm of the Alaska Moral Majority chapter. Church groups lobbied extensively in the campaign to recriminalize marijuana, which succeeded at the polls in 1990 (but remains stymied in the courts and in law enforcement practice). Prolife and prochoice groups actively support and oppose electoral campaigns, as do groups promoting gender issues, especially the National Organization for Women.

Certain interest groups, such as the National Rifle Association, the Alaska Sportsmen's Association, and the Alaska Outdoor Council, engage in debates over land use and planning. Issues of particular concern to them are subsistence hunting, fish and game regulations, access to streams, and restrictions on motorized vehicles.

The Intergovernmental Lobby

Federal, state, and local governments form the largest single group of employers by type in Alaska. Huge military installations house twenty thousand service personnel who, with their families, boost the number of people directly dependent on federal military payrolls to fifty thousand. The fact that one-tenth of the state's population is military or military-dependent affects electoral outcomes. The federal government employs another few thousand people to handle its land and resource management responsibilities as well as its communications and transportation operations.

Local government employees (31,300) outnumber the state government workforce of 21,200. They include municipal workers and the state's vast network of teachers, administrators, custodians, and support staff. In fact, state and local payrolls alone account directly for about 16 percent of personal income in the state, which is twice the U.S. average.

Federal, state, and local employees possess the same voting privileges as other Alaskans, although federal employees are restricted in their ability to run for office. Organizations that represent government workers are well versed in the study of influence; they make active and effective lobbyists in Juneau.

Interest group characteristics have changed substantially since statehood. The volume of interest group activity has grown as well, expanding the ways that groups apply pressure to the political process.

Pressure Politics and Lobbyists

Two kinds of pressure systems operate on Alaska's legislative and executive branches. The first is the traditional system of interest groups which, through lobbyists and group representation, attempts to influence political behavior. The second, newer kind of pressure system is the "intergovernmental lobby," composed of other government units, mostly municipalities, school districts, and institutions such as the University of Alaska. This category also contains umbrella organizations, such as the Alaska Municipal League, and separate organizations of mayors, assemblymen, finance officers, school board members, and school administrators.

The traditional pressure system works throughout the election cycle. State campaign finance law requires groups that wish to support candidates to contribute through PACs, which must be registered with the Alaska Public Offices Commission. PACs donate to the campaigns of candidates judged most likely to support the objectives of the interest group. Often groups offer campaign volunteers and office space as well as assistance with developing issue positions, polling, and canvassing. PAC activities during election campaigns doubtless pave the way for policy makers, once elected. The reform of Alaska's campaign finance and disclosure laws in 1974 enables us to trace PAC influence with some accuracy.

The traditional pressure system leans on policy makers in indirect as well as direct ways. The indirect method fits the classic definition of lobbying: a group retains a strategist who represents its needs and wants to policy makers. Alaska's well-known lobbyists include Lewis Dischner and Alex Miller, both retired. At the peak of their careers, they were considered the most influential power brokers in the halls of the capitol building.

The classic lobbyist has previous experience in government; Dischner is a former commissioner, Miller a gubernatorial aide. The lobbyist builds contacts with new bureaucrats and legislators, skillfully gaining access to officials for the purpose of transmitting information. Because Alaska's government is porous, interest groups' lobbyists have frequently helped draft legislation. For example, when Dischner represented the new North Slope Borough in the 1970s, he had an amendment added to a state budget protecting the borough's ability to raise revenue, based on a per capita mill levy applied to the high-volume oil fields located there.[17]

Approximately one dozen lobbyists represent client interest groups in the tradition of Dischner and Miller. Among the most successful are Kim Hutchison, Ashley Reed, and Sam Kito. An increasing number of law firms have joined in this type of lobbying, particularly when they employ as partners former commissioners or lawmakers. But interest groups usually attempt to express their interests directly during the state legislative session by sending their executive directors or other officers to Juneau. Depending on an organization's size, wealth, or issue, it may send grass-roots representatives to the capital as well.

Alaska's political pressure system differs little from that of other states with respect to lobbying techniques. Personal visits to policy makers are the preferred method, followed by phone calls, letters, and public opinion messages. POMs are unique to Alaska.

Groups Inside Government

The formation of the intergovernmental lobby has added a new dimension to interest group pressure in Alaska. The lobby does not directly participate in the state's electoral arena, diverging in this respect from traditional interest groups. Like these groups, however, the intergovernmental lobby retains lobbyists, sends its directors to Juneau to lobby, and in other ways attempts to influence executive and legislative outcomes. The two best examples of this type of lobby are local governments, including cities and boroughs, and school districts.

Local governments depend on state revenue sharing and municipal assistance, which provide them with valuable discretionary funds. Alaska's larger cities and boroughs all retain lobbyists, who work to ensure that the municipal "entitlements" are added to the state budget. Under the umbrella of the Alaska Municipal League, towns pass resolutions whose object is to influence legislative and executive policy. The director of this umbrella group has a permanent office and staff in Juneau. Mayors and members of city councils and borough assemblies regularly travel to the state capital during the session to meet with legislators. They are effective at pressing lawmakers for grants and funding. During the oil boom, the state legislature by and large financed local government, and local mill rates dropped. Even with the decline of oil revenues in the early 1990s, local governments can rely on a sizable contribution from the state, amounting to an average of about 20 percent of their budgets.

Alaska school districts consume over 30 percent of the state budget through the education foundation and funds for pupil transportation, on-base tuition payments, and reimbursements for school construction debt. School boards and administrations are simultaneously jealous of these funds and protective of their autonomy. For these reasons, most large school districts also retain lobbyists in Juneau. The districts join together in the Alaska Association of School Boards and Alaska Association of School Administrators. Both are headquartered in Juneau, where their executive directors and staffs keep a high profile during the legislative session. At least twice a session, school board members and superintendents representing most districts fly into Juneau to protect and seek to increase the foundation formula and argue for specific items on district agendas. Controversial issues among educators and board members include binding arbitration for teachers and the right to strike. In 1991, the education lobby secured full funding for the foundation formula and related expenses by persuading legislators to pass the funding bill well before the end of the session. In 1992, the education lobby secured the first increase in six years to the value of the instructional unit in the school foundation formula.

State government departments and boards also participate actively in the legislative budget process. Commissioners and board members testify at house and senate finance committee hearings. They also supply copious information in defense of budget appropriations. The University of Alaska statewide system employs a vice-president of government relations who is the institution's chief lobbyist and remains in Juneau throughout the legislative session. Chancellors, deans, directors, faculty, and students travel to Juneau to persuade legislators of the value of pet projects and operating and capital budget appropriations.

Alaska law does not require lobbyists who spend less than 40 percent of their time and derive only a small part of their income from lobbying to register. As a result, the state regulates the lobbying activities of private groups and nonprofit associations, but not those of local governments, school districts, and segments of the bureaucracy. Some analysts believe that governmental interests possess a lobbying advantage because they operate outside public scrutiny.

THE MEDIA

One reason the clout of Alaska's interest groups eclipses that of political parties is the media: newspapers, television, and radio. The media also exert independent influence over government and politics. Through their ability to lavish attention, criticism, and praise, some media bosses have gained the power to shape the political agenda in the state.

Remote Region Technology and Media Markets

Alaska's vast size, cold climate, and remote settlements increase the complexity and cost of media production, whether newspaper, radio, or television. The same factors also make the media more central and essential. On statehood, the electronic communication system in the state was in its infancy. The Alaska Communications System (ACS), operated by the U.S. Army, provided telephone service. Most communities lacked local exchange service; radio communications were unreliable or nonexistent. Commercial radio and television stations aired only in urban centers.

In 1969, RCA Global Communications, Inc. (Alascom), bought ACS and began improving it, developing a satellite system to relay television programs. In the mid-1970s, the legislature appropriated funds to construct earth stations for rural telephone service as well as for a satellite television project. By the end of the 1980s, the state provided telephone service to rural communities, largely through microwave dishes. The state-run Rural Alaska Television Network (RATNET) broadcast one channel of television, with network and public programs, to some 248 Alaska communities, eighteen hours a day, year-round.[18] The conservative Hickel administration looked askance at RATNET's costliness in the early 1990s, cutting its budget, as well as that of public broadcasting, sharply.

No other state has invested so many resources in providing telephone and television services to its citizens. In addition, public radio today reaches virtually every community, and, except for tiny villages with fewer than fifty residents, every community in Alaska can conduct legislative teleconferences.

Media Ownership and Control

State government plays a large role in the Alaska media, particularly in rural areas, where public programming prevails. Urban centers such as Anchorage, Fairbanks, and Juneau support privately owned media that engage in healthy competition.

Newspapers. Of the forty-four newspapers published in Alaska, the majority are weekly or monthly editions.[19] The state's seven largest papers appear on the stands daily in urban areas. The biggest newspaper in terms of circulation, with fifty thousand copies, is the *Anchorage Daily News.* Owned by the California-based McClatchy chain, the newspaper has distinguished itself with two Pulitzer Prizes, discussed below. The *Anchorage Times,* owned and published by Robert and Evangeline Atwood for nearly fifty years, once had the largest circulation, but it became the underdog in a protracted newspaper war with the *Daily News.* Veco, the same oil field support company that attempted to influence the 1984 election, purchased the *Times* in 1989 with profits from the oil spill cleanup. Even Alaska's largest city could not support two daily papers indefinitely, however; after significant losses by both papers, the *Times* ceased publication in June 1992. The third-ranking daily newspaper, with eighteen thousand copies in circulation, is the *Fairbanks Daily News-Miner,* published independently by C. W. Snedden until his death in 1989. In 1992, MediaNews Group, a Houston-based chain, purchased the paper from the Snedden estate and the employees (the *News-Miner* had one of the first employee stock ownership plans in the country, which was bought out by the new owners). Although the paper was published daily in the late 1980s, its Saturday issue was suspended in 1990; it resumed in 1993.

The other five dailies have smaller publication runs and do not publish on Saturdays or Sundays. They include the *Daily Sitka Sentinel, Juneau Empire, Ketchikan Daily News, Kodiak Daily Mirror,* and *Kenai Peninsula Clarion.* Except for the *Juneau Empire* and the *Peninsula Clarion,* which are owned by an Atlanta-based chain, the newspapers are privately owned within the community.

As a money-making proposition, a newspaper's daily "news hole" is determined by advertising volume. Only the Anchorage market is sufficiently large to produce newspapers of fifty or more pages. Consequently, most Alaska newspapers, like their small-market counterparts elsewhere in the nation, tend to carry wire-service reports of foreign affairs and domestic events, devoting staff time to reporting on local stories.

Television Stations. Live broadcasts did not reach Alaska until after the first walk on the moon in 1969. Before that, television programs, including the news, arrived several days after airing elsewhere in the nation. Satellite technology has brought simultaneous programming to Alaska and increased the timeliness of television broadcasts. Each of Alaska's large cities has competing television stations. Only in Anchorage, Fairbanks, and Juneau, however, do they report on local news.

Alaska's television stations are locally owned. In isolated rural communities, state-funded services provide the only live broadcasts. Recently, public and private cable systems have begun delivering live programming to rural areas for a fee.

Radio Stations. The most competitive medium in Alaska, as elsewhere in the United States, is radio. Sixty-eight stations operate across the state, competing for market shares in the large communities. Anchorage has twenty-one stations; Fairbanks, nine; Juneau, five; and Ketchikan, two.[20]

Local businesspeople own the majority of radio stations; chains own some of the rural ones. Few of the state's commercial radio stations devote much time to local or statewide news. An important exception is the radio call-in show, such as KFAR's "Problem Corner" in Fairbanks. Bill Walley developed this three-hour daily program in the late 1970s and hosted it through his multiple terms on the Fairbanks City Council and Borough Assembly and as city mayor. Until 1991, when Walley died of a heart attack at the age of fifty-four, the program attracted a broad listening audience and exerted a strong influence on local politics. Walley forged links with conservative taxpayer groups, who used his show as a forum to criticize local and state government programs as well as officials. Opponents of "Problem Corner" complained of "government by talk show."

Public Broadcasting. Alaska has four public television stations and sixteen full-service public radio stations. They furnish educational, public affairs, news, and entertainment programs. An arm of the state Department of Administration, the Alaska Public Broadcasting Commission, oversees the stations.[21]

In summary, for such a sparsely populated state, Alaska has an elaborate media network. Huge public resources have been allocated to connect various regions of the state to one another and the state as a whole to the contiguous forty-eight states. Nevertheless, the media outlets preferred by most Alaskans tend to be privately owned and not subject to state control.

Media Influence on Issues

Over the course of statehood, only newspapers have consistently figured in the state's political process. In general, they have done a good job of informing the public of issues and problems in state and local government. On some occasions, by focusing closely on an issue, the press has set or altered the agenda of public discussion. Six contrasting case studies illustrate the influential role of the Alaska media.[22]

Capital Move. From the late 1960s until 1982, Alaskans voted six times on whether to move the state capital from Juneau. Any description of how the issue came to a vote or the heat it generated is incomplete without mentioning the *Anchorage Times* and its crusading publisher, Robert Atwood.

Atwood moved to Alaska in the 1930s. His wealthy father-in-law purchased the *Times* for Atwood and his wife, Evangeline. A visionary who saw the opportunities in oil, fisheries, logging, and tourism well before most of his contemporaries, Atwood used the *Times* to boost development for the territory, the state of Alaska, and especially for Anchorage.[23]

In Atwood's view, the state capital could never respond to the people of the state when it was as inaccessible and as distant as Juneau. His paper put the capital-move issue on the front page as well as in editorials; in his crusading zeal, he changed many minds throughout the state (but not enough to achieve the move).

Teamsters' Pension Funds. In 1975, a team of *Anchorage Daily News* reporters led by Howard Weaver collected information on the pension fund of Teamsters Local 959, then the most powerful union in the state. The enterprise was risky because the Teamsters' boss, Jesse Carr, brooked little opposition to his rule; in addition, the paper could ill afford a long investigation into a dry hole.

After several weeks of study, the *Daily News* team uncovered evidence of mismanagement of the Teamsters' multimillion-dollar pension-fund accounts, along with fraud. Publication of these materials in the newspaper led to an administrative and legislative investigation, which changed the rules of pension-fund administration. Publication also brought a Pulitzer Prize in public affairs reporting to the *Daily-News*.

Native Claims. In the early 1960s, a series of events in rural Alaska changed the thinking of Native leaders. One leader in particular, Howard Rock, through his weekly newspaper, the *Tundra Times*, spread this new consciousness statewide. Rock was an artist who began editing and publishing the *Tundra Times* in 1960. The Alaska Committee for the Association of American Indian Affairs financed the paper modestly.

Rock opposed a proposal by the Atomic Energy Commission to construct a new harbor, with nuclear explosives, near Point Hope. Native leaders echoed his strong negative reaction, forming in response the Inupiat Paitot (People's Heritage). This conference of Inupiat Eskimo leaders became the forerunner of land claims associations (and was also where the idea of a Native newspaper was born). Rock's reaction to the Rampart Dam proposal also galvanized leaders.[24]

When the state government began claiming Native lands as part of the statehood land endowment, Rock covered the development in his newspaper. He worked closely with leaders of newly forming Native land claims associations in different areas of the state. No other journal of opinion followed so thoroughly the Native land claims movement in Alaska, propelling Native issues into the headlines of the state's largest papers.

Government Corruption. In early 1985, Stan Jones, a *Fairbanks Daily News-Miner* reporter, began investigating the state's intended lease of the Fifth Avenue Center, an office building partly owned by political supporters of Governor Bill Sheffield. The investigation suggested that the bid was rigged for this building alone, at the direction of the governor and his chief of staff.

The story in the *News-Miner* focused public attention on the question of unethical and illegal conduct by the governor and his staff. A grand jury found insufficient grounds for indictment but suggested that the executive's actions warranted an impeachment inquiry (see chapter 8). During the proceedings, the governor was unable to remember the crucial meeting that led to selection of the Fifth Avenue Center as the site. A dearth of direct corrobo-

ration of the governor's involvement, as well as a lack of political support in
the Senate Rules Committee for impeachment, frustrated the process. Nevertheless, the event discredited the governor, who lost the primary election
in the following year.

People in Peril. In the fifth case, the *Anchorage Daily News* assigned reporters to investigate social conditions in rural Native villages. The series
"People in Peril," published in 1988, documented a pervasive pattern of alcoholism, abuse, neglect, and suicide, rooted in the disorientation of rural
Alaska society to Western culture. The report elevated village social and
economic problems to the top spots on the governmental and public agendas.
It also garnered a second Pulitzer Prize for the *Anchorage Daily News*.

The Good Friday Oil Spill. The March 24, 1989, oil spill in Prince William
Sound attracted extensive coverage from the major media in the state as well
as from reporters and film crews worldwide. Alaska's three largest newspapers, however, invested the most time and resources in reporting on the
spill. Their focus influenced public perceptions of the event.

For two months, newspapers devoted at least one story daily to the oil
spill. Their angles varied. One angle was substance abuse: Captain Joseph
Hazelwood failed a breathalyzer test and had a history of alcoholism. Another angle was capitalist greed and excess: Alyeska failed to adhere to its oil
spill plan, failed to muster sufficient spill retardants in time, and failed to
protect tankers in the sound. A third angle was state and federal neglect: the
state had not enforced compliance with oil spill plans, and federal authorities
appeared reluctant to monitor Exxon's cleanup efforts carefully.

Media coverage kept the oil spill in the public eye and fostered a critical
attitude toward oil company activities in the state. The first impact of the
spill was to spawn legislative action increasing oil company taxes. The issue
of the Economic Limit Factor lingered from earlier sessions (see chapter 3).
The E L F was designed to protect marginal oil fields from the full bite of state
severance taxes. In reality, though, fields benefiting from the E L F in the late
1980s included Kuparuk and Prudhoe, which produced nearly two million
barrels of oil per day. Pressure to revise the E L F mounted after the *Exxon
Valdez* spill. Before the oil spill and ensuing debate, the legislation appeared
unlikely to pass the senate. The media, however, focused public scrutiny on
environmental security and altered perceptions of oil company activity.

These six cases highlight the role of the Alaska media in setting a public
agenda. In some instances, such as the *Valdez* oil spill, the government cor-

ruption case, and the "People in Peril" series, stimulation by the media intensifies or even alters public perceptions. Alaska's newspapers and radio and television stations may well wield much greater influence over issue formation than people realize.

CONCLUSION

Alaska is highly organized politically. It has a large number and variety of groups that are important vehicles for public participation. Political parties are secondary players among political organizations.

States that depend for their economic survival on nonrenewable resources tend to foster a pattern of group activity strongly influenced by economic factors. The economic interests dominate the political process to the exclusion of party and noneconomic interests. That may have been the case in territorial Alaska, when powerful economic interests, controlled by outsiders, determined political outcomes. It fails to apply to Alaska of the 1970s, 1980s, and 1990s, however. Statehood interposed the institutions of state government between economic interests and political outcomes. The state's political institutions have succeeded in moderating the direct influence of interests, including economic ones. On the other hand, the porous nature of political institutions has nurtured the expansion of interest group activity and conflict. This process, in turn, creates an environment hospitable to dynamic pluralism.

The frailty of political parties reflects and reinforces the regionalism, factionalism, transiency, and instability in Alaska's small-scale economy and society. These forces tend to strengthen the roles of interest groups and the media, which serve to tie the political system loosely together. The media function as unofficial but prominent political organizations in Alaska. Through publicity, they promote the interests of other organizations and pursue their own agendas. Many Alaskans look to the media for cues to cope with the frequently rapid and unpredictable changes that characterize life in Alaska.

CHAPTER II

Political Participation

If anyone deserves a prize for participating in Alaska politics, it is Walter J. Hickel. Elected governor in 1990 for the second time (after twenty-two years), Hickel is a consummate politician. He has held elective and appointive office: as governor, 1966–68, 1990–; as U.S. secretary of the interior, 1969–70; and as Republican national committeeman, 1954–64. He ran unsuccessfully for governor in five elections (three primaries and two general elections) in the 1970s and 1980s. A self-made multimillionaire, he has probably spent more than a million dollars of his own for his political races, including the $760,000 he invested in the 1990 campaign. As an officeholder, candidate, and all-around political activist, Hickel has undoubtedly written hundreds of letters and devoted thousands of hours to discussing politics and public policy.

Although there is no doubt that Walter Hickel represents the extreme in political participation, Alaskans in general are more involved in state and local politics than their counterparts in other states. Alaskans participate in politics in many of the same ways that residents of other states do: their involvement ranges from basic activities such as discussing politics and voting, through midrange activities such as letter writing, joining groups, and donating to campaigns, to the most substantial form of political involvement, typified by running for and serving in public office. But there is more to their political activism.

In this chapter, we focus on the ways in which the political participation of Alaskans, including Walter Hickel, differs from that of citizens in other parts of the country. We also explore patterns of political participation and public opinion in Alaska. To what extent are these patterns a simple reflection of growth and diversity in the state's population? In what ways are they associated with the political cultural traits of individualism and populism? Does contemporary participation mirror the passing of a once-dominant era of friends-and-neighbors' politics? Finally, after noting the diversification of Alaska's political society, we look at the forces that help hold it together.[1]

Where Alaskans live and whether their region is sparsely or densely populated have a significant effect on public opinion and political participation. Unlike the case in most American states, notable changes have occurred in both the size and the dispersion of the Alaska population since statehood in 1959. These population shifts have altered the balance of urban-rural and regional forces.

Changing Demographics

At statehood, Alaska's population totaled 226,167, a figure that had more than doubled by the 1990 census. With a current population of 550,043, Alaska ranks forty-ninth, smaller than all other states except Wyoming. Table 11 displays information on the composition of the Alaska population by sex and ethnicity from 1950 to 1990.

Traditionally, Alaska has had a high ratio of males to females. Men still outnumber women in today's population. The U.S. population in 1990 was 51.2 percent female and 48.8 percent male; in Alaska, the populace was 47.3 percent female and 52.7 percent male. These gender differences seem to have an impact on campaigning, which incorporates more macho politics than in other states, but the ratios are not likely to have more than a marginal effect on state policy making.

The largest minority group in the state is the Alaska Native population. Until the 1930s, Natives formed a majority of the state's inhabitants. The rapid growth of the non-Native population from the 1930s until the late 1970s was attributable primarily to migration related to resource development and the new role of Alaska in America's strategic defense, which brought a large number of military personnel and their dependents to Alaska. By 1950, Alaska Natives accounted for just one-quarter of the state's population. Natural increases in the Native population have exceeded those in the non-Native population, but they have not kept pace with non-Native in-migration; in 1990, only 16 percent of Alaska's population was Native. Still, Alaska continues to have the largest proportion of Native Americans of any state, and its politics and government bear the imprint of Native issues to a

Table 11: Composition of Alaska Population, by Race and Sex, 1950–90

Year		Total	White	Alaska Native	Black	Other
1950		128,643	92,808	33,863	n/a	1,972
	Female	49,171	32,418	16,315	n/a	438
	Male	79,472	60,390	17,548	n/a	1,534
1960		226,167	174,546	43,081	6,771	1,769
	Female	97,356	73,352	20,822	2,470	712
	Male	128,811	101,194	22,259	4,301	1,057
1970		300,382	237,798	50,819	8,803	2,962
	Female	137,300	107,233	34,833	3,671	1,563
	Male	163,082	130,565	25,986	5,132	1,399
1980		401,851	309,728	64,103	13,643	14,377
	Female	188,810	144,139	31,561	5,965	7,145
	Male	213,041	165,589	32,542	7,678	7,232
1990[a]		550,043	415,492	85,698	22,451	26,402

Source: Alaska Department of Education, Division of State Libraries and Archives, *Alaska Blue Book, 1989–90,* 9th ed. (Juneau, 1989), p. 268; revised and updated with 1990 census distribution of race.

[a] Distribution by sex not available.

greater extent than in any other state. Also, Alaska Natives remain a potent force in state policy making.

The members of other minority groups total 11 percent of the state population, with African Americans, Asian Americans, and Hispanic Americans composing the largest identified groups. These groups collectively are less numerous than Native Alaskans, and non-Native minority concerns are similarly less prominent in state politics.

The Alaska population is relatively young. Nearly one-quarter of the population in 1990 was between 25 and 34 years old; 17 percent was between 35 and 44 years old. Thirty-one percent of the state's population is preschool or school age, while only 4.1 percent is over 65. Alaska has the youngest voting-age population of any state. Young people tend to vote less often than middle-aged persons, a fact that depresses the rate of political participation, as does the large proportion of military personnel who lack roots in the state. In fact, the state's population is far more transient than that of other states, which means that many Alaskans are less likely to respond to state and local issues.

Nevertheless, there are incentives for establishing residency in Alaska, chief of which is receiving a Permanent Fund dividend check (see chapter 3). Candidates for office face many voters who lack a historical memory of state issues and personalities. The mobility of the state's population and its youth increase the value of the media and fresh political campaigns, while reducing the importance of friends-and-neighbors' politics.

Urban-Rural and Regional Patterns

Over 40 percent of Alaskans reside in Anchorage. The next most populous communities are Fairbanks (14 percent), Juneau (6 percent), and Ketchikan and Kodiak (both with about 3 percent). Another 15 percent of the state's population lives in and around cities and towns, such as Kenai, Homer, Seward on the Kenai Peninsula, Sitka in the Southeast, and Valdez on Prince William Sound. The remaining 20 percent of the state's population is widely dispersed in more than two hundred villages, regional centers, and roadside communities in the rural Interior, Northwest, and Southwest.

Alaska's population density is less than one person per square mile, the most sparse of any American state. Not including the Anchorage population, the population density is one person for every two square miles. This compares with an average U.S. population density of seventy persons per square mile in 1990.[2]

Anchorage's development is indicative of the larger pattern of settlement in Alaska. The state's largest city has a history of barely more than seventy years. The construction of the Alaska Railroad in the 1910s and 1920s, the building of military bases in the 1940s and 1950s, and pipeline and related development in the 1970s made Anchorage the magnet for migrants to the state. To a lesser extent, other cities such as Fairbanks, Kenai, Ketchikan, and Juneau gained population through migration. Fewer migrants located in rural areas of the state. Indeed, there is a pattern of internal migration from rural areas to Alaska cities. For example, Anchorage has the largest population of Alaska Natives—14,569 in 1990—of any community in the state.[3] Yet most villages have maintained their populations through natural increase, recirculation from the cities, and some in-migration.

Population dispersion directly affects politics because the Alaska Constitution requires decennial reapportionment of the state legislature. The state's rural representation has progressively declined over the three decades of statehood. Urban shifts have been less pronounced, with the exception of those in Anchorage and the southcentral region.

Alaska's population size and structure—its relative youth, high education, and mobility—resemble those of the mountain states of Wyoming, Idaho, Nevada, and Montana. Not including the proportionately large Native population, patterns of migration and population growth are comparable.[4] The relationship between demography and public attitudes is best illustrated in the context of public opinion.

PUBLIC OPINION

The most prevalent form of participation in politics is the discussion of issues, in which opinions are exchanged about the course of public events. Knowing the opinions of Alaskans helps explain their support for democratic institutions. It also indicates how leaders and policies fare in the minds of the public.[5]

Measuring Opinion in Alaska

Thirty years ago in Alaska, as elsewhere in the United States, such measures as straw polls, studies of barometer communities, and nonrandom surveys were used to gain a sense of popular thought. Some candidates used the results in campaign strategies and some lawmakers in decision making, but their nonscientific and unsystematic nature made them weak guides to political action. Currently, opinions are measured by scientific studies in which researchers systematically question a random sample of respondents for their views on matters of public importance. Alaskans employ the same three types of survey research used in U.S. metropolitan areas: mail surveys, phone polls, and in-person interviews.

Aides to Alaska's governor, legislators, and members of Congress conduct mail surveys, mostly unsystematically, to collect information on attitudes toward policy issues. Researchers also use them to look at the opinions of specialized populations, such as schoolteachers, village mayors, and sportsmen. Responses to mail surveys are typically low: a 30 percent rate of response is considered good. Surveyors have no control over who answers. Consequently, unless researchers offer substantial incentives, conduct multiple mailings, and enforce controls, mail surveys are largely ineffective as opinion measures on statewide issues.

The traditional method of survey research, used by the major national survey research firms such as Gallup, Roper, and the National Opinion Research Center, is in-person interviewing. Trained interviewers visit a sample of homes where they ask respondents a predetermined list of questions. Personal interviewing is done as part of ethnographic studies in Alaska, but it is rarely used to collect public opinion on issues of the day. The high cost of travel and personnel wages explain its infrequent use. Also, Alaska's large minority population makes it difficult to rely on a measure that is highly reactive; because of cultural differences in communication patterns, rural residents often respond differently to Caucasian interviewers than do urban residents.

What is known about modern public opinion in Alaska is based almost entirely on phone surveys, done by two private firms in Anchorage: Dittman Research Corporation of Alaska and Hellenthal & Associates. Both companies have developed procedures to identify a random sample of telephone numbers representing all regions of the state in proportion to population size. They call these numbers to elicit responses to public policy issues. The sample size is somewhat greater than five hundred; David Dittman claimed in 1985 that his sample could "predict within 3 percentage points the distribution of opinion on any topic in the state."[6] Phone surveys do miss non-subscribers, however, and are limited in the range and depth of topics that can be covered.

Policy Issues in Alaska Public Opinion

Public opinion research has confirmed what researchers have long maintained: Alaskans desire an independent, self-reliant existence that places them in contact with nature. Separate studies of Anchorage and Fairbanks reveal the emphasis that urban Alaskans place on the importance of the frontier spirit.[7] No study conducted among Alaska's urban residents, however, has detected a strong desire to live the rural lifestyle or, in particular, to maintain a subsistence existence. To rural residents, on the other hand, this lifestyle appears endangered and warrants protection. They cite as evidence the 1989 state supreme court decision to void the statute providing a rural subsistence preference wherever priorities must be set among competing commercial, sport, and subsistence users (see chapter 5).

Attitudes of Alaskans toward economic development are pronounced. Support for economic development waxes strong, as long as it occurs outside one's own backyard; urban and rural attitudes differ little on this score. With the single exception of polls taken immediately after the March 1989 oil spill in Prince William Sound, public opinion has regularly endorsed oil and gas development. These supportive attitudes stem from the perception that economic development will "cure" the major problems of the state. Just before the oil spill, political pollster Mark Hellenthal found that Alaskans were most concerned about "improving the economy" (17.5%) and "more jobs, local hire" (12.7%).[8] In the same survey, a statewide majority of 80 percent strongly supported resource development, with rural support only slightly lower than that in Anchorage, Fairbanks, and Valdez.

Alaskans also place a premium on environmental conservation. The 1989 Hellenthal survey revealed that 71 percent of the public favored "strong laws and regulations to protect the environment." Stronger support for environmental protection existed in rural areas (86%) than in Anchorage (67%) or Fairbanks (68%). One-third of respondents thought the quality of life in Alaska had deteriorated; a slightly higher number believed it had improved. Fifty percent expressed optimism that, within two years, the quality of life would be better. In the same vein, political scientist Richard Ender reports on the public's ability to understand trade-offs between economic development and environmental security, and its inclination to compromise on both.[9]

Polls also reveal public attitudes toward political leaders and institutions. Notwithstanding criticism of high public salaries and the state's handling of Alaska's oil wealth during the boom years, surveys reveal strong support for state benefit programs. The public's approval of state programs ranks twelve percentage points higher than its rating of the federal government. Local government attracts the strongest support.[10]

A higher percentage of Alaskans can identify their state and federal leaders than residents of most states. The institutional context in which state leaders work strongly colors public ratings of them. When he served as governor, Jay Hammond had an approval rating of around 50 percent. In 1989, however, seven years later, Hellenthal polls gave Hammond an approval rating of 70 percent. Hammond has remained prominent in the public eye in the intervening years, serving as host of a television program, as a commercial spokesman for a major telecommunications firm, and as defender of the Permanent Fund.

Regionalism and Attitudes Toward Government

Alaskans from different parts of the state agree on many issues, such as support for resource development. When considering economic development opportunities, Fairbanks and Anchorage residents tend to respond similarly, while inhabitants of Juneau and, to a lesser extent, smaller cities in Southcentral place less emphasis on government's role in promoting economic development. Improving the economy rates as a lower priority in rural than in urban areas. Rural residents point more frequently to problems with drug and alcohol abuse in the schools and to the need to balance the state budget than to improving the economy.[11]

Views on paying the price of government vary from region to region as well. The 1989 Hellenthal report found a greater likelihood of supporting increased taxes on oil companies in rural areas (65%) than in Anchorage (38%). There was greater support for reimposition of the state income tax in Juneau, whose economy depends on an adequately financed state government, than in any other place in Alaska. Residents of rural areas voiced the strongest opposition to increasing taxes on corporations, a policy that would affect corporations established under the Native claims settlement act. Regions generally united in their opposition to a sales tax.[12]

Generalizing from Alaska's public opinion studies is hazardous. On general issues, there tends to be considerable uniformity, as with the questions of resource development and environmental protection. More specific questions tend to elicit responses based on community economies and cultures. For example, southeast Alaska's economy depends greatly on government and fisheries, both of which achieve a higher priority in the pattern of southeast responses than in those from other parts of the state.

PARTICIPATION IN ELECTIONS

The second most common form of political participation, after discussing issues about government and politics, is voting. Alaskans' voting participation is strongly linked to campaign financing and technology. Other factors, such as competition and partisanship, also influence voting in Alaska.[13]

Financing and Technology of Campaigns

Alaska's campaigns for state office rank among the most expensive in the nation. For example, in the 1986 and 1988 legislative elections, races cost an average of $60,000 for a contested seat in the house and more than $100,000 for a contested seat in the senate, an average of $8 per house vote and $7 per senate vote. The 1986 gubernatorial election cost a record-setting $7.3 million. No single candidate has broken the record of Bill Sheffield, who spent more than $2 million, or nearly $44 per vote, to win the 1982 gubernatorial election. In 1990, three major candidates spent a total of $4.4 million, with the largest expenditure by losing Republican candidate Arliss Sturgulewski, at $1.8 million.

State races were not always so expensive. Even after 1959, gubernatorial races were relatively low-cost affairs in which candidates could rely on friends and neighbors for support. Alaska's population is now too large, dispersed, and mobile, however, for informal, personal campaigning by statewide candidates and even most legislative ones. Furthermore, the prevalence of statewide and regional media now provides a substitute for personal contact.

In chapters 7 and 8, we discussed campaign spending and technology in the context of gubernatorial and legislative campaigns. The source of candidates' funding varies by type of campaign, with political action committees contributing higher total dollars to gubernatorial elections but proportionately higher dollars to legislative races. Contributions from individuals are important in all campaigns, as are the candidates' donations to their own campaigns. Walter Hickel, as previously noted, spent $760,000 of his personal fortune after his late entry into the 1990 gubernatorial race. Political party donations make a difference, with the Republican party spending nearly twice the amount spent by the Alaska Democratic Party in recent elections.

Most of the funds in Alaska campaigns originate within the state; in gubernatorial races, however, and in races for the state's three-member congressional delegation, national PACs contribute large sums. The Alaska Public Offices Commission, the state's campaign-disclosure monitoring agency, collects quarterly, monthly, and weekly reports that it makes available to the news media. Many legislators resent APOC's watchdog role and keep the agency on a short budgetary leash.

Campaign technology in state elections diverges little from that in other states. Most candidates for the governorship retain expensive political consulting services and issues analysts, spend thousands for television, radio, and newspaper advertisements, and purchase buttons, balloons, bumper stickers, and other campaign paraphernalia. They spend more on travel in Alaska, for the obvious reason of distance. Door-to-door campaigning is done in local and state legislative races but rarely for gubernatorial elections. In short, urban campaigns in Alaska use similar technologies, paid for through similar sources, as campaigns in other states.

Registration and Election Rules

Approximately 80 percent of Alaska's voting-age residents are registered to vote, representing one of the highest registration rates in the nation. Registrars are available in most communities, and the registration procedure is simple: a person must have resided in the state for thirty days and must register thirty days before an election to vote in it. The form is half a page in length, asking for little more than name, address, birth date, and information on registration in other states. Registration does require an expenditure of effort, unlike the case in states that permit mail-in or on-site registration, but incentives for registration nevertheless exist. The state regards proof of voter registration as evidence toward fulfillment of state residency requirements for the purpose of collecting benefits, such as the Permanent Fund dividend, longevity bonus, or state loans.

The rules of registration do not favor partisanship. In late 1992, only 18.6 percent of registered voters identified themselves as Democrats and 22 percent as Republicans. About 5.4 percent of the voters registered under various third-party labels, with only 3 percent identifying themselves as Alaskan Independence Party followers. About 54 percent of registered voters identified themselves as nonpartisan or undeclared, due in part to the influence of the registration system, the openness of the primaries, and the absence of strong party rules in state statutes.[14] Alaska's blanket primary, as noted in chapters 8 and 10, has been the most permissive type of open primary in the United States. The plethora of choices it granted voters led to its nickname: the "free love" primary.

Alaska's political party organizations object to selecting nominees by a system that allows crossover voting by the opposition party or independent voters. As noted in the previous chapter, the Republicans at their 1990 and 1992 state conventions in Anchorage called for a return to the more restrictive primary used in Alaska before 1967. The Democrats, meeting in Nome in 1990, passed a similar resolution, indicating that they also opposed the impact that crossover voters supposedly had on the selection of party nominees. Still, by the 1992 elections, only the Republicans had closed their primary to registrants of other parties.

No systematic study has been done on the effect of crossover voting in Alaska. Competitive races draw substantial voter interest, however, and primary voting bears little resemblance to party registration figures. During the 1970s and 1980s, an average of 45 percent of registered voters participated in primary elections. There is no evidence that registered Democrats have determined outcomes in Republican primaries or vice versa. It does seem plausible that, given the high interest in competitive primary races, nonpartisan and undeclared voters play a significant "swing" role. The independent Alaska voter is the enemy of party organizations.

Voting Turnout in Alaska

Until the 1980s, the voting rate of Alaskans was lower than that of residents of the mountain states and western states generally. Turnout in presidential years fell below even the national norm until the 1980s. This relatively lower rate of electoral participation may be attributable to several factors, including the population's distance from national events, isolation, mobility, and youth.

In the 1980 election, Alaskans' electoral participation began to change significantly from that in other states (table 12). Turnout rates in the 1980s were unusual for state elections and significantly higher than the national norm for presidential elections. Because the early to mid-1980s corresponded with the oil boom years, economic factors appear to account for the change. The new, young voters in the state had stable jobs, for a few years at least, and high incomes. Of equal importance is the fact that the 1980s saw very competitive elections in Alaska, with high-stakes issues at the polls, such as moving the state capital, changing subsistence laws, and favoring resident hire. Furthermore, the same forces that drove new Alaskans to register—desire to provide proof of residence—may have steered some to the polls. Thus, as state elections attracted more voter interest, the normal drop-off in turnout from presidential to gubernatorial election years reversed. There was an unusually strong turnout for the 1982 gubernatorial election because the ballot included highly controversial measures, discussed later in this chapter.

The 1986 slump in Alaska's economy, due to a crash in world oil prices, saw a corresponding decline in voting turnout. Elections through 1992 nonetheless indicated a generally higher level of voting activity than in the previous twenty years.

The three-way presidential election in 1992 between George Bush, Bill Clinton, and Ross Perot generated the state's highest voter turnout ever in a presidential election year. Alaska ranked among the top ten states in turnout, with 64 percent of the voting-age population participating in the election. (The highest state rate was recorded by Maine, at 72%.) Nationally, the turnout rate was 54 percent, the highest in twenty years.

A major factor in Alaska's 1992 turnout, as well as the nation's, was the independent candidacy of Ross Perot, who attracted 19 percent of the national presidential vote. Perot won 27 percent of the vote in Alaska, which placed it among the top five Perot-voting states in the nation. On this measure, Maine, at 30 percent, again ranked first among the states, a reflection

Table 12: Turnout of Alaska Voting-Age Population in Presidential and Gubernatorial Election Years (In Percent)

Year	Presidential Election	Gubernatorial Election	Difference
1960	53.0		
1962		47.3	–5.7
1964	51.6		
1966		46.8	–4.8
1968	55.8		
1970		48.6	–7.2
1972	52.2		
1974		47.4	–4.5
1976	50.7		
1978		49.9	–0.8
1980	59.8		
1982		66.5	+6.7
1984	60.0		
1986		52.6	–7.4
1988	55.0		
1990		53.4	–1.6
1992	64.0		

Sources: Alaska Division of Elections reports; U.S. Bureau of the Census, *Statistical Abstract of the United States: 1990* (Washington, D.C., 1990).

of the positive relationship between the Perot vote and turnout generally. Like voters of the mountain states, who also were strongly attracted to Perot, Alaskans have a penchant for independent, conservative, third-party candidates.

Competition and Partisanship in Alaska's Elections

As noted earlier, most Alaskans identify with neither the Republican nor Democratic party; their votes seem directed more toward issues and personalities than symbols of partisanship. In this respect, Alaskans resemble westerners, who lead the nation in their "dealignment" from political party influence. Nonetheless, party organizations contest elections in Alaska as elsewhere, and support for party candidates indicates some measure of party strength and support. That support has changed over the thirty-year period of statehood.

In national elections, Alaska began its state history as a competitive two-party state; voters tended to vote more Republican than Democratic, except for the 1964 election. But in the 1970s and 1980s, Alaskans voted over-whelmingly for Republicans over Democrats in presidential elections. In 1992, Bush took 41 percent and Clinton 32 percent of the vote; these figures compare to the national split of 38 percent for Bush and 43 percent for Clinton. No Democratic presidential candidate has won Alaska's three electoral votes except Lyndon Johnson, whose 1964 national landslide extended to Alaska. The state's congressional delegation from 1980 through the early 1990s has been Republican. By 1992, Republican Ted Stevens had held his seat in the U.S. Senate for twenty-four years. Stevens was reelected by large margins through the 1980s. In the 1990 election, he faced token opposition on the Democratic ticket and was reelected by a two-to-one vote.

State legislative races are competitive in urban areas; it is a rare race that lacks candidates from both major parties. Rural legislative races are more likely to go uncontested, with several districts being virtually one-party (Democratic) areas. Urban voters tend to align themselves more with the Republican party than with the Democratic party. This trend suggests that Republican votes for legislative candidates, because of their concentration in a few urban areas, are "wasted" on a statewide basis. That Democratic candidates can be competitive in urban areas, and sometimes win more legislative seats than Republicans, is another indication of the weakness of partisan affiliation.

In gubernatorial elections, Alaska has been a competitive two-party and, at times, three-party state. In each election since 1972, the two major parties and at least one minor party have fielded candidates in intensely contested elections. Minor parties, whether Libertarian as in 1982 or the Alaskan Independence Party as in 1986, generally have been spoilers. In both cases, the minor party spoiled the gubernatorial election for the Republican party by attracting Republican votes. Democratic party candidates thus appear more likely to win elections with a plurality of the vote than Republican candidates, but that is not necessarily the case. In the 1978 gubernatorial election, Republican Jay Hammond won a 39 percent plurality against a Democrat (Chancy Croft, 20%), an independent (Tom Kelly, 12%), and a write-in Republican (Walter Hickel, 26%). A fifth candidate, Don Wright, running on the Alaskan Independence ticket, won only 2 percent of the vote.

Two organizations, both led by Fairbanksans, have made the strongest third-party bids. Dick Randolph, who founded the Libertarian party in Alaska in 1978, ran for the state house as a Libertarian in 1980 and for the governorship under the Libertarian label in 1982. In the last race, he garnered 15 percent of the vote, a strong showing for a third-party candidate and one that denied victory to the Republican candidate, Tom Fink. In 1986, Joe Vogler, founder of the Alaskan Independence Party, which has promoted secession of Alaska from the Union as well as prodevelopment policies, entered the gubernatorial race. In a surprise showing, he won ten thousand votes (5.5% of the total) despite spending virtually nothing. His strength at the polls may be traced in part to the absence of significant policy differences between the major party candidates, as well as to the protest vote normally associated with elections in Alaska.

In 1990, Vogler's Alaskan Independence Party played a prominent and controversial supporting role in the gubernatorial election by lending its ticket to Republican Walter Hickel, who entered the race just seven weeks before the election. As noted in chapter 8, A I P candidates for governor and lieutenant governor resigned to clear the way for Hickel and his running mate, Jack Coghill, who were then appointed to the ticket by the A I P state committee, chaired by Vogler.

Hickel claimed that the party wanted to give voters a "choice": both the Republican and Democratic candidates, in his view, were too closely tied to big government and not sufficiently committed to economic growth. By entering the race, Hickel not only undercut the Republican candidate, state senator Arliss Sturgulewski, but lured away her running mate, long-time state senator Coghill, who enthusiastically joined Hickel to complete the A I P team. This coup occurred just hours before the deadline for placing another name on the Republican ticket. Sturgulewski quickly recruited Anchorage businessman Jim Campbell, whom she had defeated in the Republican primary, as her running mate for lieutenant governor.

The Hickel-Coghill team won the 1990 election with a 39 percent plurality. Democrat Tony Knowles, a former Anchorage mayor, came in second at 31 percent; Sturgulewski placed third, at 26 percent. In the same election, voters decided to outlaw the possession of even a small quantity of marijuana in the privacy of one's home, an outcome that, with some qualifications by Knowles, all the candidates favored. On the yes-or-no question of recriminalization, some ten thousand more people voted no than voted for Hickel. A postelection bumper sticker commented ironically on the ambivalence of Alaska's political culture, proclaiming, "Pot got more votes than Hickel."

Another unusual feature of the 1990 general election was the presence of Green Party candidates for governor and lieutenant governor, which resulted from a successful petition drive. More surprising was that the Green candidates won over 3 percent of the total vote (6,600 out of 195,000), which qualified the Greens as an official state party in Alaska. This means, among other things, that they automatically qualify for a place on future ballots, provided they continue to win at least 3 percent of the vote. Alaska is the first state in which the Greens have attained official party status.

In the 1980s, Alaskans voted at record levels in state and federal elections, ranking among the top twenty states in voter turnout. Parties organized electoral competition, but there was considerable room for unorthodox maneuvers and third-party surges. Voters concerned themselves little with party labels, particularly in state legislative and gubernatorial elections.

CITIZEN PARTICIPATION AND POLICY-MAKING

Political participation may be a self-fulfilling activity, but it is also a primary means of influencing government outcomes. Change in democratic societies occurs as a result of the ballot box and because leaders anticipate the need for policy revision. Elections as the means of controlling policy makers, however, are uncertain affairs and do not often send clear signals. In this section, we examine the concept of controlling government through parties and coalitions, the relationship of elections to issues in the public imagination, direct democracy in the Alaska context, and the management of influence through media and money.

Divided Government

As indicated in chapter 7, throughout the state's history, Alaska's government has been divided as often as it has been unified. In fact, only during the 1960s did the same political party (the Democratic party) control both houses and the governorship most of the time. Of that period it can be said that individual voters, through alignment with political parties, potentially affected public policy in the state.

In the 1970s and 1980s, however, no instances occurred of unified executive-legislative branch control by political parties. The governor came from one party, and at least one house of the legislature was controlled by the other. Additionally, bipartisan coalitions prevailed in the sessions of the late 1970s and 1980s, making it unclear which factors influenced outcomes. Within the legislature, leadership positions were traded for regional shares in the distribution of the state's annual oil booty. Officeholders, clustered in regional coalitions, did respond to the public. The control voters exercised was retrospective, however, because there was no way to determine in advance which candidate would best further the interests of voters in each region.

Incumbency has figured less in state legislative election outcomes in Alaska than elsewhere in the nation. The rate of incumbent success in the legislature has been far lower than in the federal government, where 96 percent of incumbents were reelected to the House and 76 percent to the Senate in the 1980s. Even the 1992 elections, occurring amid widespread public disapproval of the House check-kiting scandal and government gridlock, did not break the incumbency lock on congressional seats; long-term effects are not at all clear. Further, turnover in Alaska legislative and executive politics exceeds that of most other states. Nearly 30 percent of the seats in the Alaska senate and over 40 percent of the house seats in recent election years went to challengers in open or contested elections. In the 1992 legislative elections, 50 percent of house seats and 55 percent of senate seats were won by newcomers to the legislature. Incumbency figures more prominently in rural than in urban areas, contributing to the strength of the Native rural caucus in the state legislature.

Elections and Issues

In the absence of strong party cues and party control over government branches, one might expect issues to play a significant role in Alaska politics. In most elections, that is not the case. In at least one recent election, however, the 1982 gubernatorial campaign, issues dominated.[15]

In the 1982 primary season, attention centered on the Republican primary, in which Anchorage insurance agent and experienced state legislator Tom Fink campaigned against the young lieutenant governor, Terry Miller, originally from Fairbanks. Other primary candidates adopted campaign positions not sharply delineated from those of Miller, who opposed two initiatives then emerging into public view: the attempt to move the state capital to Anchorage and the effort to end the rural subsistence preference. Fink was the upset victor in the primary, largely because moderate candidates canceled one another's influence. Also, urban Republican voters tended to favor the two initiatives Miller opposed.

In the Democratic primary, Bill Sheffield, an Anchorage hotelier, narrowly defeated former legislator and Fairbanks lawyer Steve Cowper. Both Sheffield and Cowper opposed the initiatives to move the capital and repeal the subsistence preference. A former Republican legislator who had championed the development of the Libertarian party in Alaska, Fairbanks insurance agent Dick Randolph, became the gubernatorial candidate of the Libertarians.

The 1982 general election campaign saw a three-way race among Fink, Sheffield, and Randolph. Eight propositions appeared on the ballot, but the major issues dividing candidates were the capital-move and subsistence propositions. Randolph's positions on both issues came closer to Fink's than to Sheffield's; as a Fairbanks candidate, he also drew interior support from Fink. Rural voters solidly backed Sheffield because of his support for the rural preference in subsistence; southeast Alaska voters also supported Sheffield strongly because of his opposition to the capital move.

Voters opposed both propositions: 58 percent voted against repeal of the rural subsistence preference, and 53 percent voted against the capital move. The issue positions of the candidates appeared to influence strongly the majority of the votes cast in 1982. Although Sheffield attracted only 47 percent of the popular vote, he won overwhelming majorities in the Southeast and rural regions most affected by the propositions. Randolph was a spoiler because his positions for the capital move and against subsistence resembled Fink's; also, he still claimed a residue of support within the Republican party, which divided that vote. Fink's 38 percent of the vote, combined with Randolph's 15 percent of the vote, represented a majority that favored urban and non-Native points of view. Thus, the three-way split in the vote indicates that many voters supported candidates despite their positions on the issues. Nevertheless, this election provides the clearest indication of the power that issues can wield in state electoral politics; they probably were more decisive in this case than in any other statewide election since statehood.

Initiatives, Referenda, and Recalls

The 1982 ballot was unusually crowded, with eight different measures coming before the voters for resolution. Only three were initiatives, however, and there were no referenda. The other measures consisted of three constitutional amendments, the question of calling a constitutional convention, and the capital-move proposition placed before the voters by the legislature. Although Alaska interest groups, political parties, and independent political entrepreneurs rarely shrink from drives to place issues on the ballot, neither the initiative nor the referendum has been used greatly in state elections. Recall elections have occurred sporadically in local jurisdictions but rarely at the state level. The attempt in 1991, 1992, and 1993 to recall Governor Walter Hickel and Lieutenant Governor Jack Coghill was the first of its kind.

The types of issues that come before voters as ballot propositions reflect the most controversial items of the day: access to government, such as the capital-move proposition; state–federal relations, such as local-hire initiatives; the Tundra Rebellion, which sought to assert state ownership over the vast federal domain in Alaska; recriminalization of marijuana; limitations on state spending; and tax caps on local governments. Some questions, particularly measures limiting spending, resemble those of other states. Most, however, are specific to conditions of life and governmental relations that reign in Alaska. Surprisingly, compared to other western states, Alaska has seen few "style" issues come before the voters in the form of ballot propositions. National concerns of the 1970s and 1980s, such as school prayer and AIDS, have not become subjects of statewide debate on the ballot.

The Media and Politics

Political participation in Alaska is less structured by party organizations and themes than in any other state. Issues play a role in local elections, frequently as catalysts for change in response to events such as the revenue shortfalls of 1985–86, which propelled taxpayer groups into prominence in some cities (see chapter 13). In most state elections, however, issues tend to fade into the background. Candidate image, appeal, and personality influence elections, promoting politicians as "free agents" who subscribe to no organized agenda.

The sparse population of Alaska and the general neighborliness of its small communities once fostered highly individualistic styles of political action. Before the 1970s and the development of the modern media age in Alaska, word-of-mouth advertising plus work in the state's network of community organizations usually sufficed to establish the name recognition needed to win elections. Population growth resulting largely from an inmigration created the need for vehicles to transmit images to voters who lacked local roots. This need emerged simultaneously with the development of television in Alaska. The new medium was expensive, raising the salience of money in politics.

The use of a new communications medium to reach an increasingly mobile citizenry, the creation of persuasive images that travel well in that medium, and the cultivation of financial resources to pay the bill have all affected the character and quality of Alaska political participation. They have also increased the freedom of political agents and reduced their accountability to the public. Although personal ties between politicians and Alaskans have become less vital, they have not disappeared. Alaska remains a state where citizens have no compunction about calling up or visiting lawmakers to insist on a personal interview; often they get it.

CONCLUSION

Alaskans' strong sense of independence, readiness to protest, commitment to development, and hostility toward "outsiders" shape a characteristic pattern of participation in politics. The level and quality of participation respond to Alaska's changing economic fortunes and prospects; Alaskans are receptive to the appeals of political mavericks, independents, and third parties. All these factors reflect, and contribute to, looseness and volatility in the electoral system.

Like voters elsewhere, Alaskans are more likely to mobilize in response to perceived threats to their well-being than to positive goals. Their political leaders play to and reinforce this trait. The federal government often presents the most prominent target. The state's leaders and citizens unite the most readily when they see the federal government as controlling outcomes against the popular will, as in the "lock-up" of more than one hundred million acres in federal land conservation systems or the delays in opening the coastal plain of the Arctic National Wildlife Refuge to oil development.

Sometimes Alaskans unite to conserve the environment, as they did for a time after the Prince William Sound oil spill. They also come together to support the production of oil and other natural resource wealth. When environmental and development interests conflict, majority sentiment usually favors development and the production of wealth.

Beyond these very general themes, however, simple patterns of consensus and conflict disappear. No party or interest group themes draw large numbers of Alaskans into a small number of opposing camps. The closest analogue to major-party divisions in Alaska is competition between urban and rural (often defined as Native) values. This division is irregular, however, occurring in cycles and often related to the conflict between state and federal governments, rather than to fissures between Alaska's urban and rural citizens.

Most participation in Alaska is rooted in community and regional issues. These are the concerns of everyday life, strongly affected by statewide and federal influences but not necessarily determined by external forces. Viewed from the perspective of the state as a whole, Alaska's source of energy and dynamism lies in its regions: mainly Anchorage, Fairbanks, the Southeast, and rural areas. Legislators gather as representatives of their regions, as ambassadors from different nations. They interact briefly with other lawmakers, much as though they occupied a confederation instead of a state. Any deal can be unraveled; thus, bargains must be cemented with side payments and guarantees, increasing vastly the cost of Alaska politics.

The individualism and populism that flavor Alaska politics continue into the second generation of statehood. What we have described in this and other chapters is a gradual process of dislocation of the state's prime participants, its legislative and executive leadership, from the public. The ties between leaders and citizens increasingly take the form of mediated images and exchanges of campaign contributions and votes for the delivery of public projects, favors, and funds. In Alaska's open political system, dissenters reduce their participation or they redirect their loyalties toward third parties or, more commonly, toward independent and idiosyncratic candidates regardless of party labels.

CHAPTER 12

Two Systems of Local Government

Frank Barr was a man obsessed. Like his fellow delegates at the Alaska Constitutional Convention, the Fairbanks bush pilot did not question the need for a new system of local government in Alaska. The territorial system had been limited and, in some areas, irrelevant. The new state would need a flexible type of local government that would serve the needs of rural and urban residents. What Barr objected to was the proposed name of this new unit: *borough*. "I don't particularly like the word borough; I don't like the sound of it and I think it's confusing to some people; as a matter of fact, if they don't know how to spell it, they might confuse it with another kind of burro, which is a donkey."[1] The delegates considered other labels, such as *county, canton, province,* and *division,* but after a series of votes on the matter, the title *borough* was approved, much to Barr's disappointment. "I want to be able to walk down the streets without having people throw rocks at me," he told the other delegates.

The delegates envisioned the borough as a midlevel governmental unit that would provide a framework within which city governments, school districts, and other local responsibilities could be administered. Their vision of this unit was not perfectly clear, though, and that may explain why the development of local institutions has not been consistent throughout the state. Instead, two separate systems of local government have emerged: one urban and the other rural. An integrated set of government institutions has developed in urban Alaska. Fewer than twenty-five local and regional governments serve the needs of the large majority of the state's population. Nine of these governments are boroughs, strong county-like governments with broad powers and responsibilities, and about fifteen are cities. Three boroughs have become unified home-rule municipalities merged with the cities

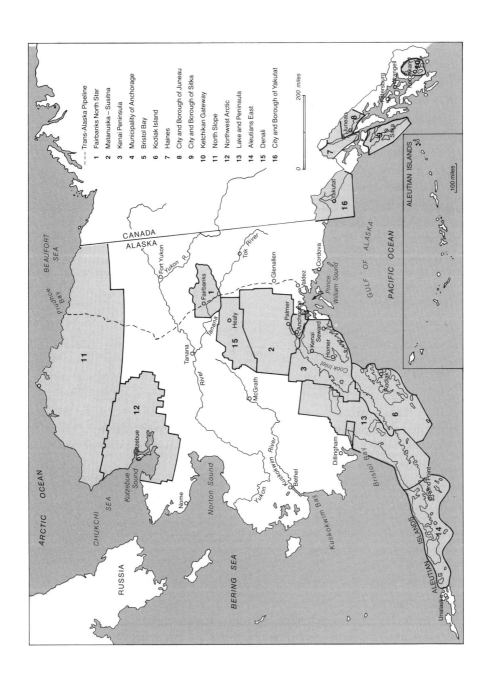

Map 4. Boroughs and Selected Cities of Alaska

within them. Broad local government powers are concentrated in these structures, which have been well supported with revenues from state and local sources.

In rural Alaska, local and regional institutions have proliferated. Several hundred such units meet the needs of Native villagers and other rural Alaskans, who make up only a small part of Alaska's population. These units include traditional Native governments, state-authorized municipalities, Native regional and local corporations and nonprofit associations, boroughs, rural school districts, and other forms of special government and quasi-government. In 1993, there were more than five hundred such organizations in rural Alaska, most of them small "city" governments and village corporations established under the Alaska Native Claims Settlement Act . Most rural organizations are weak, poorly managed, and underfinanced.

In this chapter, we focus on the environments, evolution, and current status of Alaska's two distinct systems of local government.[2]

URBAN AND RURAL SETTINGS

Defining "Urban" and "Rural"

The U.S. Bureau of the Census defines "urban" communities nationwide as those with populations of 2,500 or more; by this definition about two-thirds of Alaskans lived in urban settlements in the 1980s. In Alaska, however, factors other than population size are important in marking communities as "urban" or "rural." In this book, definitions are more flexible than those of the census bureau.

Except for Anchorage, Alaska's towns are small. The urban category includes some communities in Southcentral, Interior, and Southeast with populations under 2,500, but Alaskans perceive them as "cities." Conversely, there are several communities in western and northern Alaska, including Barrow, Kotzebue, Nome, and Bethel, whose populations exceed 2,500. But these communities are Native regional centers with strong links to village life in their areas. There are more than two hundred Native villages statewide, and they typically have only a few hundred residents each.

Under the modified definition, from 75 to 80 percent of Alaska's population is urban and the remainder rural. Urban Alaskans, although making up most of the state's population, live in local political jurisdictions that cover only about 10 to 15 percent of Alaska's total land area. Yet Alaska's urban governments collectively cover an area larger than the total area of Florida, Michigan, or New York. The immense remainder, under the jurisdiction of rural governments and quasi-governments, encompasses an area larger than the combined states of California, Nevada, Arizona, and Utah: almost five hundred thousand square miles.

Local Government and Statehood

The territory of Alaska had few organized local governments. At statehood, it contained only about forty cities and twenty special districts. Roughly half the cities were urban and predominantly non-Native; the other half were Native villages, classified as fourth-class cities, in rural regions. The special districts, for schools and public utilities, were mainly urban. Fewer than half the cities had populations of one thousand or more. Anchorage and Fairbanks, the two largest cities, accounted for more than a fifth of Alaska's total population. With nearly another third of Alaskans living in special districts and state-serviced areas around their borders, these two cities and their environs accounted for roughly 50 percent of the state's population in 1960. Except in the few populous areas, local tax bases were small or nonexistent. Federal and territorial agencies met the basic service and regulatory needs of settlements outside the larger cities.

Many Alaskans opposed creating new governments and extending existing local boundaries and tax powers. Alaska had a small population and limited prospects for economic growth. At the time of statehood, many believed that Alaska had enough government and that what it needed most was a larger economic base to support what it already had.

Most of Alaska's growth after statehood occurred in a few urban areas: along the railbelt from Fairbanks in the Interior to the Matanuska-Susitna river valleys, in the Anchorage bowl, and on the Kenai Peninsula in Southcentral. Communities in this part of Alaska, although distinguished by their spectacular natural settings, look familiar to Americans from other states. They now have most of the civic amenities and many of the problems of comparably sized cities elsewhere.

The social and physical facts about rural Alaska raise questions about the relevance of Western government institutions in the region. In most of rural Alaska, extreme environmental conditions discourage human habitation. Winters are long, dark, and extremely cold. Travel is often unreliable, difficult, and costly. Areas suitable for settlement are isolated from other communities. And the people who live in rural Alaska have distinct histories, cultures, and motivations.

Harsh physical conditions have limited population growth in most parts of rural Alaska. Today less than one-fourth of the state's residents live in this land area, which comprises more than three-fourths of Alaska. Few rural towns or villages contain more than one hundred families. Bethel, Kotze-bue, Nome, and Barrow are the exceptions, each with populations of more than three thousand. These larger Native communities have become cultur-ally heterogeneous. Between one hundred and five hundred people inhabit most rural communities; these are the homelands of Alaska's aboriginal peo-ples. Throughout rural Alaska, Natives continue to express their cultures through blood relationships that frequently connect all members of a locality and in rituals of sharing that reaffirm a sense of cultural identity. In some places, Native cultures also contribute to the movement toward Native tribal governments with powers separate and distinct from those of the state.

CONSTITUTIONAL PROVISIONS

The local government committee of the Alaska Constitutional Convention (see chapter 6) tried to follow the advice of its principal consultant, the Pub-lic Administration Service:

> Alaska's opportunity lies in boldly recognizing that units of local self-govern-ment can prove satisfactory in the long run only if such units are based on natu-ral geographic, economic, and social communities large enough to meet the service needs of the natural regions, and endowed with sufficient resources to support adequately a minimum standard and level of necessary services. Sim-ilarly, by recognizing that all local legislative authority and all local executive and administrative functions can and should be vested in one unified local government, Alaskans will be reaching at one stride a goal that local govern-ment reformers and specialists have been striving to attain in many states over a period of several generations.[3]

This model for areawide metropolitan government was the one that re-formers at the time advocated for fast-growing urban areas of the United States. Alaska's constitution writers were attracted to this efficiency-ori-ented, urban-services model for local government. They wanted to adapt the ideal concept of unified metropolitan government to Alaska's unique condi-tions. Their deliberations resulted in the concept of borough government.

The purpose of Article X of the constitution is "to provide for maximum local self-government with a minimum of local government units, and to prevent duplication of tax-levying jurisdictions."[4] The constitution's framers envisioned boroughs as intermediate levels of government provid-ing for both local self-government and performance of state functions. Cities within borough boundaries were to form "part of" boroughs. Only boroughs and cities were to possess local taxing powers. Special districts were to be "integrated" with the boroughs, but school district boards and organizations were not to be eliminated. Also, borough assemblies were to be empowered to establish service areas to provide specified services sought by the residents of the area and paid for by them through special taxes, charges, or assessments authorized by the assembly.

Organized and unorganized boroughs were to cover the entire state. The people of each area were to determine the details of borough structures, functions, and powers. In rural areas, boroughs were to be allowed to start out as "unorganized" or limited-function governments, with the state legislature acting as the borough assembly. In urban areas, they could proceed more directly toward their ideal status as broadly empowered self-governing units operating under strong home-rule charters. Two state agencies would help to implement the new local government system: a local boundary commission to rule on changes in local government boundaries and a local government agency to "advise and assist" local governments.

The authors of the article took for granted the desirability and inevitability of local government organization; they did not dwell on problematic features of their scheme. For instance, Article X calls for both self-government and state authority in local affairs. Its aim is a unified system, but it recognizes two forms of local government—boroughs and cities—and preserves separate school organizations. It visualizes different kinds of boroughs—organized and unorganized—in urban and rural areas, but it does not describe either kind. It disclaims overlapping taxing authorities, but it leaves cities with their taxing powers while granting areawide taxing powers to the boroughs that encompass them.

DEVELOPMENT OF THE URBAN SYSTEM

At statehood, cities and special districts covered all the state's urban areas, where most of the population and taxable wealth were concentrated. These areas had the resources to support new local government structures, but, except for fringe settlements outside city and school district boundaries, they already were organized, serviced, taxed, and regulated locally.

Borough Acts of 1961 and 1963

Two years of hearings and studies by the state Local Boundary Commission and the Local Affairs Agency (the "local government agency" described by

Article X) led to the Borough Act of 1961. The act required that all special districts "integrate" with organized boroughs by July 1, 1963. Local groups were expected to petition for borough formation and to request the commission's approval of the boundaries, structures, and functions they wanted for their borough governments.

Local voters were allowed to choose between an elected chairman or an appointed manager for the executive and to select first- or second-class borough status. The law required all incorporated boroughs to perform three areawide functions: education, planning and zoning, and property tax assessment and collection. Education, the most significant borough areawide power, would remain largely under the control of elected school boards, except that borough assemblies would have authority to approve school budgets.

The 1961 act reflected the constitution framers' ideas about home rule and classes of boroughs. Home-rule boroughs were to retain all powers not prohibited by state law or the boroughs' charters. Also, first-class boroughs could acquire powers in areas outside cities by assembly ordinance, while second-class boroughs required a vote of the residents of those areas. Both classes of borough needed an areawide vote to take on additional areawide powers.

The first two years after the 1961 act saw little progress in establishing boroughs. The boundary commission and local affairs agency encountered strong local resistance in urban areas targeted by the 1961 act: school district officials foresaw a loss of autonomy, city officials were skeptical of an overlapping areawide government, city residents recognized no need for a new layer of government and taxation, and people living outside cities and school districts wished to preserve their tax-free status while receiving education and other state services.

When the legislature met in January 1963, no boroughs existed with which special districts could "integrate" before the July deadline. The legislature extended the life of the special districts for another year and passed the Mandatory Borough Act of 1963, probably the most disputed legislation of the early years of statehood.[5] The act required incorporation of boroughs in eight urban areas containing public utility and school districts as of January 1, 1964. Election district lines were to serve as borough boundaries. The act gave the people in these areas the option of initiating incorporation and proposing alternative boundaries in the time remaining before the new deadline.

Under the state's threat of mandatory incorporation, the Ketchikan, Sitka, Juneau, and Kodiak areas formed "local option" boroughs in the 1963 elections. Incorporation went nowhere in the railbelt. Proposals were defeated in the Fairbanks and Anchorage areas. These two, plus the Kenai Peninsula and Matanuska-Susitna Valley areas, were mandatorily incorporated as boroughs in January 1964. Except for Juneau residents, voters in the eight areas chose the more limited second-class status rather than first-class status for their new boroughs. Voters in all areas preferred the elected chairman (later redesignated mayor) to the appointed manager form of executive.

Immediately after the legislative session, several efforts were made to repeal the law: a special legislative session, a referendum petition drive, and court suits, none of which succeeded. State courts found that the constitution not only authorized but required incorporation of boroughs; state legislators had no desire to struggle further with the borough issue.

Expansion of Borough Powers

Most of Alaska's current urban residents did not live in the state or had not yet been born during the conflicts over borough formation. Many migrants brought urban service standards and expectations with them from more developed parts of the country. In most urban areas, the controversy over the creation of boroughs faded rather quickly; newer residents were especially inclined to look to the boroughs to supply familiar urban services. (Table 13 lists the classes and structures of the state's nine urban boroughs; table 14 shows their 1991 areas and populations.) Although Alaskans now generally accept boroughs as facts of life, antigovernment sentiments still find a voice on Alaska's "urban frontiers," particularly concerning local taxes and property rights.

All first- and second-class boroughs possess planning and zoning, taxation, and education powers. Some borough residents still view planning and zoning authority as an infringement on their property rights. Every borough contains at least a few residents who insist that the rusting hulks of automobiles sitting in their yards are valuable assets (or aesthetic displays of "Alaska yard sculpture") and, in any case, are no one's business but their own. Because not all boroughs consistently implement planning and zoning authority, many "junk" collectors get to do as they please with their property, even in some residential areas. As for taxation, few citizens are likely to credit their boroughs with efficiently administering this power, which is usually viewed as intrusive. Borough residents did enjoy substantial decreases in local tax rates in the early 1980s, however, when the state transferred large chunks of oil revenues to local governments. Finally, citizens generally

Table 13: Structure of Urban Boroughs and Unified Municipalities in Alaska, 1991

Borough or Unified Municipality	Class	Executive	Assembly	Incorporation Date
Municipality of Anchorage	Unified Home rule	Mayor	11 members, by district	1964, 1975
Fairbanks North Star Borough	Second class	Mayor	11 members, at large	1964
Haines Borough	Third class	Mayor	6 members, at large	1968
City and Borough of Juneau	Unified Home rule	Mayor Manager	8 members, at large/by district	1963, 1970
Kenai Peninsula Borough	Second class	Mayor	16 members, by district	1964
Ketchikan Gateway Borough	Second class	Mayor Manager	7 members, at large	1963
Kodiak Island Borough	Second class	Mayor	7 members, at large	1963
Matanuska-Susitna Borough	Second class	Mayor Manager	7 members, by district	1964
City and Borough of Sitka	Unified Home rule	Mayor Administrator	6 members, at large	1963, 1971

Source: Alaska Department of Community and Regional Affairs.

credit effective delivery of public education programs to semiautonomous school boards and administrations, not to borough governments.

Boroughs have attracted constituencies and justified their existence primarily because they have consistently expanded their menu of urban services. In five urban areas—Fairbanks, the Kenai Peninsula, Ketchikan, Kodiak, and the Matanuska and Susitna valleys—second-class boroughs have taken on many additional areawide service functions. Some second-class boroughs have also expanded their nonareawide powers, those exercised within the borough but outside city limits.

The greatest growth in borough services has occurred in service areas. These areas have proliferated particularly in locations with urban centers surrounded by scattered settlements: Anchorage, Fairbanks, the Matanuska-Susitna region, the Kenai Peninsula, and Juneau. The most common service area functions are fire protection, water and sewer utilities, and road maintenance.

Table 14: Areas and Populations of Urban Boroughs in Alaska, 1991

Borough or Unified Municipality	Area (sq. mi.)	Population
Municipality of Anchorage	1,884	230,185
Fairbanks North Star Borough	7,361	74,031
Haines Borough	2,620	2,058
City and Borough of Juneau	3,100	28,881
Kenai Peninsula Borough	25,600	40,312
Ketchikan Gateway Borough	1,250	13,259
Kodiak Island Borough	17,783	15,679
Matanuska-Susitna Borough	20,544	38,953
City and Borough of Sitka	7,927	8,526

Source: Alaska Department of Community and Regional Affairs.

Service areas meet "good government" standards: they decentralize local decision making and administration, enhance local autonomy, and strengthen local representation in areawide government. They also Balkanize a borough, however, and can lead to duplication, waste, and disparities in service standards. Citizens and officials complain about overlapping service areas, widely varying mill rates, uneven service standards, and unequal distribution of property tax resources. The Fairbanks North Star Borough contains about one hundred service areas, for example, whose representatives constantly complain about borough administration of their areas' accounts.

The Haines Borough, at the northern terminus of the southeastern ferry system, illustrates the urban services trend in an unusual way. In 1968, the people of Haines incorporated Alaska's only third-class borough. Partly because of the area's small population (about fifteen hundred at the time) and the existence of a far-reaching city government, Haines for several years avoided state constitutional and statutory requirements to establish a borough government where independent school districts existed. Five years after the mandatory borough act and several forced incorporations elsewhere in urban Alaska, the illegal existence of Haines's independent school district could no longer be ignored. Instead of forcing Haines to incorporate as a first- or second-class borough, however, the legislature authorized a third-class "school borough," specifically to legalize Haines's special district government.

Despite their resistance to the standard forms of borough government, the people of Haines soon began following trends in other urban areas and adding regularly to the services provided through their school borough. They have created several service areas for fire protection, and they have exercised their public education authority to provide "educationally related" community facilities: a library, museum, tennis courts, cultural facilities, and a swimming pool, all built with substantial state financial assistance. The state's successor to the Local Affairs Agency, the Department of Community and Regional Affairs, considers the third-class Haines Borough "outmoded" because it lacks sufficient urban areawide powers. A former mayor of Haines, on the other hand, called it "one of the best forms of local government yet devised."[6]

Conflict and Accommodation

Expanded local property tax revenues and increased state funding of local governments and public education have supported growth in borough services. For a while during the 1980s, the distribution of billions of dollars of oil revenues to local governments helped suppress turf wars among boroughs, cities, and school districts.

The framers of the constitution's local government article anticipated conflict between boroughs and cities. They believed they could encourage greater cooperation between the two governments by giving city council members designated seats on the borough assembly. The legislature implemented this provision in 1962 by establishing a scheme for assembly apportionment and weighted voting which gave city representatives, regardless of their numbers on the assembly, a majority vote on all "areawide" matters wherever city residents made up a majority of the borough population.

This scheme led to continuous struggle between city and noncity assembly members over the application of the weighted vote and the definition of *areawide*. After clashes with the borough, the city of Juneau won a favorable court ruling based on the one-person, one-vote standard. Similar disputes occurred in most other boroughs. Finally, the legislature proposed a constitutional amendment to eliminate city representation on borough assemblies; the voters approved it in 1972.

In Juneau, Sitka, and Anchorage, dissatisfaction with duplication and conflict between borough and city governments in the early and mid-1970s led to a merger creating urban areawide "city-boroughs" or "unified home-rule municipalities." Majorities of voters inside and outside the cities approved the unification measures. In each case, the borough centered on one populous city, and city interests advocated unification most strongly. Residents of the smaller incorporated and unincorporated communities outside the city opposed unification because they feared a loss of community identity, "big city" control, and higher taxes.

As in the case of the original controversies over the establishment of boroughs, residents became accustomed to the new arrangements and especially to increased state financial aid and low local property taxes. City and noncity residents have also found that provisions for service areas, district election of assembly members, and community councils have helped to protect their neighborhood interests within the larger community.

Localism thrives in the second-class boroughs, especially in the areas of the Kenai Peninsula, Matanuska-Susitna, Fairbanks, and Kodiak, where there are several widely separated incorporated and unincorporated communities, all protective of their separate identities. In the case of the Kodiak Island Borough, for example, the majority of the population lives in the city of Kodiak, but the population of five other villages is made up predominantly of Natives with little in common with the majority non-Native fishing port that dominates the island.

Institutional battles continue on the borough–school district front. Like their counterparts in other states, Alaska school district officials want as much independent local government authority as possible, and they especially desire separate taxing and spending powers. This movement toward school independence was partially blocked in Alaska's urban areas when the legislature gave fiscal control of education programs to borough assemblies. School boards and district bureaucracies nonetheless retain much power of their own. Since their "integration" with the boroughs, they have reclaimed substantial leverage over school budgets, fiscal management, and construction programs.

School interests early on persuaded the state legislature to narrow the scope of the assemblies' budget approval authority. Borough assemblies can set only the local revenue share, which averages 25 to 30 percent of the total school budget. Assemblies are also formally barred from program and line-item review of these budgets. Of course, assemblies often influence school board decisions, school programs, and budget line items, using the leverage of their control over the local financial share. School boards counter with restrictive interpretations of the assemblies' authority and demand local money to preserve popular programs that might otherwise be jeopardized. Participants on both sides have characterized assembly–school board relationships as "institutionalized warfare" (see chapter 13). Yet the constitution framers' intent to give general borough governments a check on special school governments remains in force, despite school officials' regular calls for independence.

Borough governments in urban Alaska were born of controversy and turmoil, underwent rapid expansion during the oil boom, and are now adjusting to economic recession, increased competition for resources, and an uncertain fiscal future. Nevertheless, boroughs in most places have become commonplace local institutions valued primarily for the services they deliver at relatively low cost to their citizen-consumers. The "natural" areawide, consumer-services model of the borough envisioned by the framers of the constitution has largely been realized in urban Alaska.

DEVELOPMENT OF THE RURAL SYSTEM

Native regional corporations and Regional Education Attendance Areas (REAAS), established in the early and mid-1970s, blocked movement toward incorporation of boroughs in rural Alaska. Native corporations, established under the Alaska Native Claims Settlement Act, generally opposed regional governments with powers to tax and regulate land and resources. The REAAS, regional school districts financed 100 percent by the state, delivered the most expensive local service without local taxation.

Moreover, during the boom years of the 1970s and 1980s, officials of cities and nonprofit associations had little reason to support incorporation of boroughs in their regions. Boroughs would limit their roles and compete with them for state money. Further, with the fiscal pressures off and money flowing freely to urban and rural areas alike, state political leaders from urban areas had little concern about rural Alaskans' "free ride" (the absence of local property taxation in most of rural Alaska). Their interests in statewide "equity" had shifted from a focus on local government taxation to preoccupation with state government spending.

This situation began to change in the late 1980s with the decline of oil revenues, formation of new rural boroughs, and a revival of Native tribal government. Over the years, the forms and functions of rural governments have changed.

The Unorganized Borough, Native Governments, and Cities

Early in 1962, the people of Naknek, King Salmon, and nearby villages on the great Bristol Bay fishing grounds at Kvichak Bay petitioned the state to incorporate a borough government in their area. They were the only Alaska

communities that voluntarily sought incorporation in response to the borough act passed by the legislature the previous year. But these Bristol Bay
communities were rural and remote, and they had no special districts that
had to be integrated into boroughs. Also, their proposed borough was very
small in both area (873 square miles) and population (about one thousand
year-round residents). Theirs was not the kind of place that state officials had
envisioned for borough government.

The people of Kvichak Bay saw borough incorporation as a way to tax the
canneries in their area and to gain control of local school programs. Despite
state officials' reservations about the need for such a proposed borough and
its size, the people of these small fishing communities were the first and only
group of Alaskans to incorporate a borough voluntarily; they were determined to set a good if not pertinent example for urban Alaskans. So, with
state acquiescence, the tiny (by Alaska standards) and anomalous Bristol
Bay Borough incorporated in 1962. It remained the only borough in rural
Alaska until incorporation of the huge, 85,000-square-mile North Slope
Borough ten years later.

The constitution writers were particularly vague about unorganized boroughs. The legislature treated them as a residual category that became one
great unorganized borough in the 1961 borough act. After the forced incorporation of the eight urban boroughs in 1964, the rest of the state—87 percent of its land area—remained in the "unorganized borough." The legislature did not act as an unorganized borough assembly as authorized by the
constitution; until the creation of REAAs in 1975, no legislation was enacted
to provide regionwide public services anywhere in this gigantic, 490,000-
square-mile area.

The unorganized borough did not lack local government, however. Federally recognized Native village governments had existed for many years before statehood. Also, the territorial government had chartered fourteen city
governments in rural Alaska and, during the first decade of statehood, the
state chartered more than forty additional such governments. Most of these
"cities" were minimal forms of village government with fourth-class status,
later redesignated second class. Except for a few first-class cities, such as
Nome and some well-established towns in the Southeast, most of the Native
village and city governments of rural Alaska have extremely limited resources and functions.

One form of Native village government is federally chartered under the
Indian Reorganization Act of 1934, which Congress extended to Alaska in
1936. The IRA legislation signaled the American Indians' "new deal." The

law's purpose was to promote self-government and economic development on Indian reservations. In Alaska, where reservations were the exception, Natives could petition the secretary of the interior for IRA incorporation of their villages. They could elect councils, write village constitutions, and request the secretary's certification of their IRA governments.

Today about seventy IRA governments function in rural Alaska. Fewer than half operate in towns or villages that are also first- or second-class cities. In most IRA villages, the council is the only local government. The council selects a head, chief, or president, who manages village affairs on its behalf. Proponents of tribal government argue that IRA villages wield powers similar to those of Indian tribes on reservations elsewhere.[7] State officials and tribal government advocates dispute just how far these powers extend in the case of Alaska Native villages (see chapter 5). The conflict has grown in recent years, particularly since the early 1980s, when tribal leaders organized statewide. Many Native villages have since submitted applications for IRA tribal constitutions to the secretary of the interior, but, at the state's request, the secretary has suspended action on them until the powers of IRA governments are clarified.

Although many Natives favor IRA governments, the state objects to them primarily because of their potential "sovereignty": independent power to own and control land and resources, to avoid state taxes and assess their own, and to regulate both Native and non-Native activities in the villages. Such authority is recognized in "Indian country," generally reservations, elsewhere in the United States. The state's position is that, in Alaska, Indian country exists only in the southeast village of Metlakatla, Alaska's sole federal Indian reservation. The state maintains that, otherwise, Native village governments, like other local governments, should be subject to common standards of equal protection, representation, and accountability under state law.[8]

Another form of Native government is the "traditional village." Though less formal, it resembles the IRA council government and raises essentially the same political issues. Under doctrines of federal Indian law, traditional villages may possess inherent self-governing powers, or sovereignty, and such powers may be limited only by the federal government, not the state. The federal Bureau of Indian Affairs, which oversees Indian tribes, gives "priority" to some 195 Alaska Native organizations for funding and services. In BIA terms, *priority* means administrative recognition for specific purposes. Approximately 125 of the 195 organizations are traditional governments, while the remainder are IRA governments. About half the Native governments operate in state-chartered second-class cities. The BIA also recognizes, for specified purposes, approximately two hundred villages and regional corporations established under the Alaska Native Claims Settlement Act.

Most traditional governments lack formal structure and regular procedures for conducting business. As in the case of IRA governments, the state questions the representativeness and accountability of traditional councils.

While largely neglecting borough formation in rural areas, the state government launched a drive to incorporate what are now second-class cities during the first two decades after statehood. From 1960 to 1980, about one hundred such "cities" were incorporated throughout rural Alaska, many of them villages of only a few hundred people. In addition to the state, federal poverty programs also promoted organization in the 1960s. Still other incorporations in the 1970s responded to provisions of the Alaska Native Claims Settlement Act requiring that certain Native lands be transferred to municipalities. In 1990, Alaska had 115 second-class cities, all but a few of them in rural Alaska. Except for Bethel, with 4,400 residents, and Kotzebue, with 3,700, all had fewer than 1,000 residents. Their average population hovered around 350.

Money and skilled management are in short supply in most second-class cities, as is the case with Native IRA and traditional governments. They lack local tax bases and economic development prospects. In an increasing number of villages, second-class city governments and Native governments compete for resources and constituencies. Although they have agreed on a division of labor in some villages, one organization has had to give way to the other in many villages. Most Native villages are simply too small to accommodate two forms of local government of any kind, particularly two whose legal bases and political purposes conflict.

Approximately thirty communities in rural Alaska's unorganized borough have no local governments at all. Most lie along the state's road system in Southcentral and in the Interior, and their residents are predominantly non-Native. Many of these "settler" communities, such as Tok and Glennallen, are large enough to support second-class city governments, but they refuse to incorporate. In their determination to avoid local taxes and regulations of any kind, residents of these communities clearly express the individualistic, antigovernment strain in Alaska's political culture.

Native Associations and Corporations

The Native land claims movement and settlement act stimulated creation of "quasi-governments," including regional associations and regional and vil-

lage corporations. Alaska's quasi-governments are primarily social and economic agencies that perform political functions, such as representing constituent interests and providing public services. The regional corporations
and associations have played important roles in rural Alaska; their existence
helps to account for the absence of rural boroughs or the long delay in creating them.

The twelve Native regional associations that led the land claims movement of the 1960s accomplished their primary purpose when Congress passed the settlement act in 1971. Eleven of the twelve subsequently incorporated as regional nonprofit associations. (The twelfth, Arctic Slope Native
Association, was succeeded by the North Slope Borough.) Nine of the original associations now operate in rural Alaska, and they serve areas coinciding
with the boundaries of the regional Native corporations. The associations'
main purpose is to address socioeconomic problems of Natives. Aside from
boroughs and school districts, Native associations provide a large part of the
regional representation and public services available to villagers in rural
Alaska. The federal Indian Self-Determination and Educational Assistance
Act of 1975 decentralized the administration of Indian programs, strengthening and expanding the associations' role in education and training, health,
welfare, and other service areas.

Associations in most regions have sponsored the creation of semiautonomous health corporations and housing authorities. These organizations are chartered by the state and funded by state and federal agencies. Regional nonprofit associations thus play roles similar to borough governments
in the "unorganized" borough, which, in the 1990s, is probably far more
"organized" than the constitution writers ever envisioned.

The wealthiest and most powerful organizations in rural Alaska, apart
from federal and state governments and the oil industry, are Native regional
corporations established under the Alaska Native Claims Settlement Act.
Corporations in most regions have not significantly affected the development of local or regional government institutions. While they have watched
out for threats to their interests, such as potential borough taxes and regulation, most corporations have deferred to nonprofit and tribal leaders on matters of local organization and programs. Some corporations have not had
much economic impact within their regions, mainly because of limited economic potential in rural Alaska. Corporations invest substantially outside
their regions and, in some cases, outside the state (see chapter 5).

NANA, the regional corporation in northwest Alaska, has had exceptional economic and political involvement with the villages in its region. It

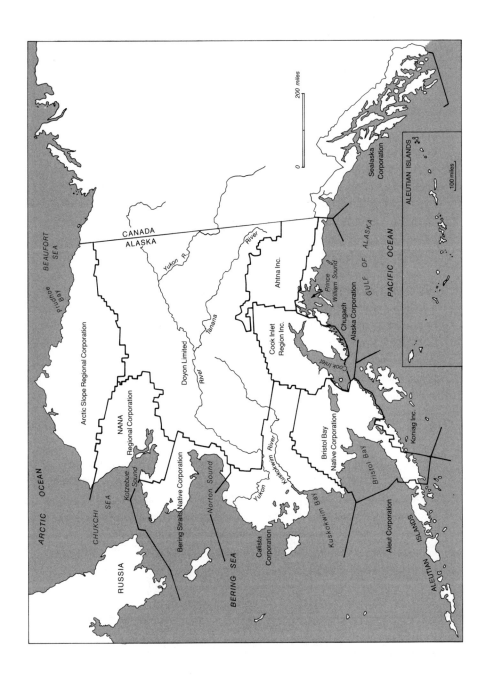

Map 5. Alaska Native Regional Corporations

has invested in local businesses, promoted development of the Red Dog zinc mine north of Kotzebue, arranged the merger of the regional corporation and the region's ten village corporations, and sponsored the 1986 borough incorporation of the region.

Few of the two hundred village corporations established under the claims settlement act are active or effective economic enterprises. Like their regional counterparts, the village corporations were chartered under state law as for-profit businesses. Each village corporation received surface rights to land and a limited amount of cash. Although money and management pose major problems for these corporations, they remain the most prominent local organizations in many villages, sometimes acting as de facto local governments.

In smaller villages, the corporation and the traditional council, IRA government, or second-class city government may have merged informally. It is not uncommon in rural Alaska for one person to wear several official hats: as a member of the city council, IRA council, village corporation, and school board, for example. In most cases, however, different people serve as members of corporation boards and government councils. There may be a division of labor based on age, education, and expertise. Conflict may arise when factional or family rivals head different organizations or when the community has a substantial non-Native minority that controls, or wants to control, city government.

Borough Governments

Within a decade after the incorporation of the Bristol Bay Borough in 1962, the Native land claims movement created the political base, and the oil discovery at Prudhoe Bay provided the primary motivation, for creation of a borough government on Alaska's North Slope. North Slope Native leaders and their advisers recognized that a borough could extend powers of taxation and regulation across the vast Arctic shelf overlying one of North America's richest petroleum provinces.

The North Slope Borough was incorporated in 1972 after its backers overcame the opposition of a vacillating state government and a determined oil industry. Within a few years of Congress's 1973 authorization to construct the trans-Alaska oil pipeline, property values in the North Slope oil fields and pipeline corridor soared to billions of dollars in what previously had been an impoverished region. Prudhoe Bay and related North Slope oil fields formed the property tax base for a borough with fewer than six thousand permanent residents. Most are Inupiat Eskimos living mainly in Barrow, the borough seat, and in eight outlying villages of several hundred residents each.

It quickly became clear that the new borough would have the highest per capita property values of any local government in the nation. The state administration proposed early in 1972 to reserve the huge tax base for taxation by the state on behalf of the residents of the unorganized borough, which was virtually all rural Alaska at the time. In the face of opposition from Native leaders statewide, the complexity of the legislation, and state officials' preoccupation with more pressing oil industry policy matters, the legislature did not act on the governor's bill. The governor chose not to force the issue.[9]

Having secured its tax base, the borough launched a huge capital construction program that brought schools, utilities, community halls, transportation and communication facilities, and a full employment economy to Barrow and surrounding villages. The borough also effectively reinforced Inupiat claims on subsistence resources, strengthened Inupiat self-government, and brought a renewed sense of the values of Inupiat culture to the people of the region.[10]

The negative side of the borough's record has, however, obscured the borough's positive accomplishments, particularly in the eyes of outside observers. By the mid-1980s, the borough's bonded debt exceeded $1 billion, and many millions had been poorly managed and wasted. It was also apparent that the borough lacked the long-term capacity to support the jobs it had created and the extensive public infrastructure it had built. Moreover, statewide public attention was focused on a scandal of major proportions: several former borough officials and consultants had been charged, indicted, or convicted of financial corruption. In 1989, a court convicted two prominent non-Native consultants, both with numerous political connections statewide, of racketeering, extortion, and fraud.[11]

As a rural Alaska local government, the North Slope Borough has been exceptional, both in the circumstances of its creation and in the scale and turbulence of its operations. For nearly a decade and a half after its incorporation, no other borough government was established in rural Alaska. Instead, the state legislature chose to create special service districts: Regional Education Attendance Areas and Coastal Resource Service Areas. Beginning in the mid-1970s, state public education programs were decentralized to twenty-three R E A As; also, as called for by the federal Coastal Zone Management Act of 1972, all the state's coastal regions were organized, though not necessarily well equipped or supported, for the planning and regulation of coastal resources.

During most of the 1970s and 1980s, the state was able to pay for the facilities and services it extended to rural areas; rural communities, for their part, generally lacked the taxable resources or incentives to establish borough governments. But the decline in state oil revenues in the late 1980s stimulated new movement toward borough formation in rural Alaska.

In several regions, local leaders began to reassess the taxable resource potential of their areas. They also wanted to preempt claims on those resources by nearby communities. Officials of established boroughs, such as Fairbanks, Kodiak, and Mat-Su, considered annexing adjacent areas for their taxable resources. This move, in turn, stimulated defensive proposals to incorporate boroughs on the part of residents of those areas. Finally, in some areas, rural leaders anticipated that the 1990 census would result in further losses of rural seats in the state legislature. Consequently, they believed it would be in their communities' interests to establish stronger forms of local control and representation through borough government.

In 1986, leaders of the NANA regional corporation initiated incorporation of the Northwest Arctic Borough. Development of the Red Dog zinc mine, located on NANA corporation lands, provided the impetus behind the incorporation. The mine is the borough's richest tax resource and a major source of employment for the region's residents, most of whom are also members of the NANA corporation. Before the borough was formed, the Local Boundary Commission approved transfer of the lands where the mine is located from the North Slope Borough to the new borough.

The following year, the Aleutians East Borough formed in the area extending from the end of the Alaska Peninsula to Akutan Island in the Aleutians. The boundaries also encompass part of the Aleut regional corporation, the Aleutian REAA, and the Aleutians East coastal resource area. In this productive fisheries region, both onshore and offshore fish processors contribute significant tax revenues to the borough.

Incorporation of the Lake and Peninsula Borough in 1989 was largely a defensive move on the part of the area's residents, who felt pressure from the surrounding Aleutians East, Kodiak Island, Kenai Peninsula, and Bristol Bay boroughs. After losing land within the Lake and Peninsula REAA to the Aleutians East Borough, and in the face of a Kodiak Island Borough petition to annex valuable salmon stream territory on the southeast shore of the Alaska Peninsula, area residents felt compelled to initiate an incorporation petition of their own. Although they lost the salmon streams to Kodiak, Lake and Peninsula residents obtained jurisdiction over important fisheries resources of their own.

The Denali Borough came about after a three-way struggle for control of an area containing Denali National Park and Mount McKinley, as well as Alaska's only producing coal mine at Healy. The Matanuska-Susitna Borough sought to annex much of the area, and residents of the town of Nenana, just north of the new borough, wanted to preempt tax and regulatory powers with their preferred "Valleys Borough" proposal. The Nenana plan would have required the new borough to obtain a two-thirds popular vote to approve local taxes or ordinances that would "circumscribe any resident's rights or liberties."

The Local Boundary Commission approved the Denali Borough petition, denying the Nenana and Mat-Su bids. Voters of four small settler communities along the Parks Highway between the Fairbanks and Mat-Su boroughs approved incorporation of the Denali Borough in late 1990. Its principal sources of revenue are a 4 percent "bed tax" on overnight accommodations for tourists and a severance tax of five cents per ton on coal produced from the Usibelli Coal Mine at Healy.

Incorporation of the City and Borough of Yakutat in 1992 most clearly raised the old issue of the appropriate size and purposes of boroughs and the question of what distinguishes a borough from a city. Located at the top of the southeast panhandle, the first-class city of Yakutat had a 1990 population of 534, a majority of whom are Tlingit Indians. About 170 people resided outside city limits but mostly within five miles of the city and on the local road system. This area could have been added to the city by annexation. (The city dissolved at the same time the borough incorporated.)

By incorporating the borough, however, the community accomplished several purposes that it could not have accomplished through a relatively simple annexation. First, it extended its juristiction over a 5,875 square mile area including fish processors and timber and private recreational properties, which nearly doubled the local tax base. (City leaders had sought several thousand miles more, but the Local Boundary Commission reduced the proposed boundaries.) In addition, the community became eligible for six hundred thousand dollars in state funds for new borough organization, a substantial increase in shared receipts from the Tongass National Forest, an entitlement to 10 percent of state lands in the area, and increases in state revenue sharing, municipal assistance, and shared fish taxes. Moreover, the new borough boundaries defend Yakutat against any future move to create a multiple-community borough in a region encompassing Yakutat.

In approving the Yakutat borough, the Local Boundary Commission made exceptions to the general rule that boroughs must include two or more

Table 15: Structures of Rural Boroughs in Alaska, 1992

Borough	Class	Executive	Assembly	Incorporation Date
Bristol Bay	Second class	Mayor Manager	5 members, at large	1962
North Slope	Home rule	Mayor	7 members, at large	1972
Aleutians East	Second class	Mayor Administrator	9 members, by district	1986
Northwest Arctic	Home rule	Mayor	11 members, by district	1987
Lake and Peninsula	Home rule	Mayor Manager	6 members, by district	1989
Denali	Home rule	Mayor	9 members, by district	1990
Yakutat	Home rule	Mayor Manager	7 members, at large	1992

Source: Alaska Department of Community and Regional Affairs.

communities and a population of at least one thousand. The commission's rationale was essentially that Yakutat was geographically isolated and it was "large enough"[12]—characteristics that describe many small communities in rural Alaska.

Tables 15 and 16 list current structural, area, and population characteristics of the seven rural boroughs. In addition to the five new borough incorporations, ten borough feasibility studies covering 80 percent of the unorganized borough were completed in the late 1980s and early 1990s. Nearly all involved competing local claims on taxable resources: the trans-Alaska pipeline, fisheries, and mines. The 1990s are likely to see further incorporations in some of the more economically promising of these areas, and issues raised in the Yakutat case—the appropriate size, purposes, and configuration of boroughs—may be played several times over.

Tribal Government Movement

The modern movement for tribal government, or Native sovereignty, in Alaska arose with the "Indian new deal" and I R A governments of the 1930s. The movement faded during the 1940s and 1950s, with World War II and the

Table 16: Areas and Populations of Rural Boroughs in Alaska, 1992

Borough	Area (sq. mi.)	Population
Bristol Bay	873	1,451
North Slope	84,983	7,813
Aleutians East	15,405	2,567
Northwest Arctic	37,296	7,081
Lake and Peninsula	25,061	1,844
Denali	12,800	1,992
Yakutat	5,875	705

Source: Alaska Department of Community and Regional Affairs.

drive toward Alaska statehood. After statehood, Native tribal interests revived as part of the land claims movement of the 1960s. Then passage of the Alaska Native Claims Settlement Act in 1971 diverted attention from the broader political and cultural dimensions of Native claims toward the narrower economic concerns of the new corporations.[13]

A decade after the claims act, the tribal movement emerged once again, this time to challenge the older Native elite who had led the campaign for a land settlement and who had assumed top posts in the regional corporations. A small cadre of younger, village-based leaders rose to advocate a distinctly Native alternative to Western-style corporations and state-chartered local governments in rural Alaska.

The tribal government movement of the 1980s and early 1990s emerged from economically undeveloped parts of the state. The most active IRA and traditional councils function mainly in about a dozen Yupik villages in the lower Yukon-Kuskokwim Delta in southwest Alaska and in several Athabaskan villages in the Interior north and west of Fairbanks. The leaders in these villages are also associated with the nonprofit associations in their regions; the Association of Village Council Presidents in the Southwest and the Tanana Chiefs Conference in the Interior. In the late 1980s, these two associations temporarily withdrew from the Alaska Federation of Natives, the preeminent statewide Native political organization. Association leaders charged that AFN, dominated by regional corporations, paid too little attention to the social, cultural, and political concerns of villages.[14]

Akiachak, a Yupik village of about 480 on the Kuskokwim River north of Bethel, is a leading tribal government village. It is the home base of the "Yupiit Nation," an association of thirteen traditional and IRA governments in the Yukon-Kuskokwim area. To pursue its aims, the Yupiit Nation obtained grant funds from the federal Administration for Native Americans under the Department of Health and Human Services; it also gained the support of the Association of Village Council Presidents. A primary goal of the Yupiit Nation is to establish a Native-controlled regional government with independent powers recognized by both state and federal governments. The state showed no sign, however, at the threshold of the 1990s, of reversing its policy of opposing independent Native governments, or "sovereignty."

In late 1992, representatives of traditional and IRA councils of 138 villages formed the Alaska Inter-Tribal Council. Its objectives were to provide a unified voice for tribal governments and to put pressure on state and local governments on jurisdictional and funding issues.

IMPACTS OF OIL REVENUES

The oil booms of the 1970s and 1980s led to expansion, opportunity, and crises for Alaska's urban and rural local governments. In many boroughs, cities, and villages, the surge of money and projects overwhelmed local management capacities. Local governments everywhere scrambled to hire professionals, managers, technicians, and laborers, but few local officials felt they kept pace with demands. Then, when state grants to local governments abruptly fell, these same local officials were forced quickly to reduce budgets, raise local tax rates, and lay off workers.

Those effects were short term. The economic slowdown also had important long-term effects. Local governments throughout the state found themselves saddled with facilities and programs more costly to maintain than they could afford without significant increases in local revenues. In Anchorage, "Project 80s" resulted in state-financed construction of a monumental performing arts center at a cost of $72 million, 70 percent over budget, as well as a sports arena, convention center, library, and major addition to the municipal museum. None of the facilities is self-supporting.

Many other communities face similar problems. A few, however, managed to save for a rainy day. The unified City and Borough of Sitka, for example, created a municipal "permanent fund," investing cash surpluses and fund balances that could legally be skimmed from the flow of state-financed projects. Local officials everywhere marveled at the freedom they had in managing (or mismanaging) state money. There was too much of it to keep track of; the legislature, in any case, did not wish to see state grants tied up in red tape.

Following the unification of cities and boroughs in the Juneau, Sitka, and

Anchorage areas between 1970 and 1975, no other major government organization changes occurred in urban Alaska. Large increases in state funding for school districts, cities, and boroughs made it possible for officials of all three units to fund most of what they wanted without competing with the other two and without making hard decisions about spending priorities. There was little incentive to be more efficient or to reform overlapping or redundant government units. The budget and turf struggles between various urban government institutions and their officials subsided.

As state revenues declined in the late 1980s, however, competition and conflict among urban government institutions intensified. Borough assemblies and school boards began to clash more regularly over school budgets; borough assemblies, city councils, and mayors fought more frequently over executive and legislative prerogatives (see chapter 13). It was not clear in the early 1990s whether the politics of scarcity might also lead to such urban institutional changes as consolidation of borough service areas or additional borough-city unifications.

The 1980s saw the rise, peak, and fall of state aid to school districts and local governments (table 17). The largest percentage increases and decreases affected municipal operating and capital grants, on which rural communities depend much more heavily than urban communities. The state expended the largest amount for school district operations; it funds 100 percent of rural REAA "foundation" programs and an average of two-thirds or more of urban school district programs. The grants have remained at relatively high levels even during the oil recession, indicating the priority that state policy makers place on public education.

Capital grants for schools consist of "bonded debt reimbursement," in which the state covers 80 to 90 percent of the local debt obligation, and "capital aid" for discretionary projects approved by the legislature. As long as the state guaranteed reimbursement of local school construction debt, school districts were eager to build. State guarantees piled up into the late 1980s before the legislature finally ended debt reimbursement in 1990. Discretionary capital project grants rose and fell with the increases and decreases in state oil revenues.

Between 1967 and 1987, real per capita spending by Alaska local governments quadrupled from $900 to $3,700 (figure 3). Spending was 30 percent below the national average in 1967 and 85 percent above it in 1987. Half the spending above the national average went for capital projects; most of the rest was for employee salaries and wages and for interest on debt. State

Table 17: State Aid to Schools and Municipalities in Alaska, 1981–90 (In Millions of Current Dollars)

	1981	1983	1985	1987	1989	1990
Aid to Alaska schools						
Foundation program	255	409	467	415	456[a]	490[a]
Bonded debt reimbursement	38	56	93	116	109	109
Other support	52	62	54	53	59	57
Capital aid	28	42	164	45	41	34
Subtotal	373	569	778	629	665	690
Aid to municipalities						
Operating grants	117	166	166	121	113	114
Capital grants	81	333	493	191	68	45
Subtotal	198	499	659	312	181	159
TOTAL	571	1068	1437	941	846	849

Sources: Institute of Social and Economic Research, "Where Have All the Billions Gone, Part II," ISER Research Summary, February 1989; Alaska Department of Administration, Division of Finance, Printouts of State Expenditures and State Capital Expenditures, May 28, 1990, and June 21, 1991.

[a]Increases are largely a result of changes in the state's accounting system rather than actual increases in funds.

Figure 3: Local Spending Per Capita, Alaska and U.S. Average (In 1988 Dollars)

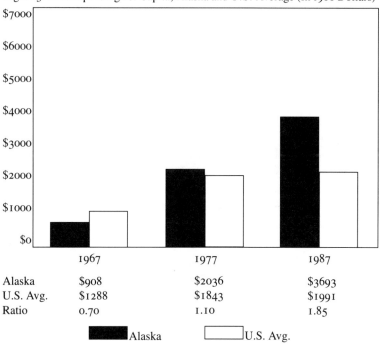

	1967	1977	1987
Alaska	$908	$2036	$3693
U.S. Avg.	$1288	$1843	$1991
Ratio	0.70	1.10	1.85

Note: U.S. averages are inflated by Alaska cost-of-living allowance.

Source: Adapted from Oliver Scott Goldsmith, Lee Gorsuch, and Linda Leask, *Facts and Fables of State Spending,* ISER Fiscal Policy Papers, no. 2 (Anchorage: Institute of Social and Economic Research, University of Alaska Anchorage, 1989), fig. 6, p. 11.

grants and rapid growth in local property tax bases supported the increase in local spending.[15]

The oil boom supported construction of public facilities, commercial buildings, and whole new residential subdivisions in communities throughout the state. This burgeoning growth fueled rapid increases in local property values, which received an additional push from inflationary pressures. Because of this growth and the increased state aid, local governments were able to increase spending and services while reducing local property taxes. Borough property values increased an incredible fivefold between 1976 and 1986, then decreased sharply with the sudden decline in state capital spending.

Local government employment also increased dramatically as a consequence of the oil boom. Local public employment more than tripled between 1970 and 1989 (table 18). During the same period, state employment doubled while federal employment remained stable, increasing by only 6 percent. The especially large increases in local employment in the 1970s are partly due to the creation of the REAAS and the transfer of rural school administration to the local level.

Alaska's local governments face difficult fiscal and economic challenges in the 1990s. Both urban and rural communities must cope with the operations and maintenance costs of expanded local programs and facilities bought with temporary surplus revenues. They are also under pressure to meet public expectations for continuing high levels of services at low local tax rates. Meanwhile, local public employees' and teachers' unions, which grew in membership and political strength during the boom years, strongly defend their shares of local budgets.

Most local governments trimmed budgets and, particularly in urban areas, raised tax rates at the end of the 1980s. In many places, these measures could be taken without significant reductions in local government employment, major increases in taxes, or serious cutbacks in essential local services. In the face of continuing declines in state oil revenues, local choices will narrow and decisions will be increasingly hard to make.

CONCLUSION

Alaska has different systems of local government for urban and rural areas. The urban system is relatively simple, with only two dozen general governmental units. The rural system is very complex, comprising more than five hundred governments and quasi-governments with specialized political and administrative functions. The small number of urban governments serve most of Alaska's population; the many rural governments serve relatively few.

The urban system developed in response to the 1950s municipal reform proposals adopted by the writers of Alaska's constitution. Despite strong local resistance to the novel concept of areawide boroughs, the legislature imposed them on urban areas with little or no long-term harm. The urban boroughs overall have fulfilled their service functions, and they are now generally accepted in their communities. In a few places, boroughs and the cities within them have merged into unified, areawide governments, a development that probably comes as close as possible to realizing the reformist visions of the authors of Article X of the constitution.

Table 18: Government Employment in Alaska, 1970–89 (In Thousands)

Year	State	Local	Federal Civilian
1970	10.4	8.1	17.1
1972	13.3	10.0	17.2
1974	14.2	11.6	18.0
1976	14.1	15.2	17.9
1978	14.3	19.8	18.1
1980	15.4	20.9	17.7
1982	18.0	23.5	17.6
1984	19.3	27.1	18.1
1986	20.2	28.6	17.8
1988	19.4	27.8	17.9
1989	20.7	28.2	18.2
Change, 1970–89	99%	248%	6%

Sources: Alaska Department of Labor, *Statistical Quarterly.*

The borough scheme led to inevitable conflicts because boroughs, cities, and school districts had overlapping and competing interests. These conflicts nearly disappeared during the few years when there was enough state money to satisfy their institutional appetites. When money became scarcer once again, the conflicts flared up, but the borough system appeared capable of accommodating and managing local conflict.

A different set of conditions characterizes rural Alaska. Its regions are much too undeveloped, vast, and unfamiliar to be accommodated by an abstract model of urban areawide government. The vague idea of "unorganized boroughs" was not of much use either, except that its lack of content may have helped to deter state policy makers from trying to reform rural Alaska governments. Consequently, an extensive array of rural organizations was left to evolve in response to changing and mostly unanticipated requirements, opportunities, and problems.

The Alaska Native Claims Settlement Act and state oil revenues promoted the proliferation of governmental and quasi-governmental institutions in rural areas. The act created at one stroke more than two hundred village corporations and a dozen new regional corporation "superpowers"; the state followed up with more than twenty regional school districts and some other service areas. This accumulation of local and regional organizations has provided multiple vehicles for meeting a variety of rural needs, and it taps the assistance programs of many federal and state agencies. It also provides these services at the cost of overextending scarce local resources.

The contrast between urban and rural governmental systems might be less significant if state government could continue to supply the resources needed to support them. Even with federal help for rural Native communities, that appears increasingly unlikely. Both systems of local government will come under pressure in the 1990s. As the competition for resources intensifies, Alaska's urban majority probably will renew its demands for "urban-rural equity," demanding that rural communities organize and tax themselves to pay their "fair share" of the costs of public education and other local services. The problem is that, beyond those regions already organized as boroughs, most rural communities lack the resources or the economic prospects necessary to meet urban definitions of statewide equity.

CHAPTER 13

Community Politics

Former Speaker of the U.S. House of Representatives Thomas P. "Tip" O'Neill was fond of saying, "All politics is local." By that he meant that all members of Congress are elected by states and communities, and to stay in office they must serve local needs. O'Neill's observation applies well to Alaska. Voters rate governors and legislators by how much "bacon" they bring home to constituents. Voters also rate local officeholders by their ability to provide maximum services at minimal costs. Local politics is the wellspring of candidates for state offices, as well as for issues that shape state events.

In this chapter, we begin by comparing local politics in urban and rural Alaska. We look at the process of getting elected to local offices and briefly characterize Alaska's local politicians. We consider how issues develop in local communities and describe some of the conflicts and tensions in local politics of the 1970s, 1980s, and early 1990s.

URBAN AND RURAL COMPARISONS

In most parts of the United States, the boundaries blur between cities, suburbs, and countryside. In Alaska, these boundaries emerge nearly as sharply as lines and dots on the map. The vast territory and sparse population of the state, and the human tendency to congregate, mean that most of Alaska's two-hundred-some communities are isolated from one another. Fewer than five miles outside any Alaska city, one enters what most Americans would consider wilderness, where small towns and villages resemble outposts on the frontier.

Urban Political Environments

Three characteristics define Alaska's urban political environments: social diversity, institutional strength, and political competition. With regard to these qualities, the political life of Alaska's cities compares to that in other states.[1]

Urban diversity begins in the economy. Government dominates the economy of all Alaska cities, yet each has a private sector existing in a symbiotic relationship with government. Without government procurements and government employees, many urban service and trade firms would be bankrupt. This dependence on government rankles many businesspeople, however. One notes an edge of hostility in urban private-public sector relations that tends to be absent in communities where the private sector drives the local economy. In elections, people pay attention to whether candidates are private- or public-sector employees. Some refuse to vote for public employees out of the belief that they might add to the size of government and raise taxes.

Caucasians dominate the populations of Alaska's cities, but each has a large Native population, usually 10 to 15 percent; a small but well-organized black community; and growing Latin and Asian populations. The cultural life of Alaska's cities is quite rich despite their small populations: a plethora of performing groups, such as orchestras, theatrical troupes, dance companies, and artists' organizations, thrives. Religious life is varied, with all major denominations represented. Social clubs, veterans' organizations, lodges, and service clubs all add to the variety of community life.

Urban political diversity springs from the economic and social conditions described above. Branches of national party organizations operate in Alaska cities. Yet partisan differences do not constitute the major source of political diversity. Where people happen to live in cities, their occupation, education, income—in short, their lifestyle—influence most strongly their inclination to participate in local politics and the direction their involvement takes.

Like cities elsewhere, Alaska cities are unable within themselves to provide all the resources for collective life, yet each has some measure of self-sufficiency. In American politics, relative differences are important, and the relative independence of Alaska's cities contrasts sharply with the rural experience.

Alaska's urban governments are comparatively strong institutions. The history of cities and school districts predates statehood. As noted in chapter 12, boroughs were at one time controversial units. Now they are accepted and established institutions. This tradition enables governments in Anchorage, Fairbanks, and Juneau to set rules and develop routines, which residents follow more often than not.

Urban governments act as arenas for political conflict in Alaska. The legislature puts on a highly visible show every year, but it neither operates year-round nor has annual elections. Decisions handed down by urban governments may be less exciting than the ones made by the state and federal government, but such decisions have an immediate effect and are highly visible. Citizens care about getting snow plowed from city streets and limiting classroom size in their children's schools.

Newspapers and radio and television stations closely monitor the operations of urban governments in Alaska. Print and broadcast reporters regularly attend meetings of city councils, borough assemblies, and school boards. They report the mundane and focus on any hint of controversy, which then makes the front pages of daily newspapers or the evening news. Coverage of the state legislature, in contrast, tends to be less comprehensive, except by Anchorage and Juneau media.

Interest groups also screen closely local government activities. Public employee unions (municipal workers, police, firefighters, teachers) use their access to officials to keep well informed. Chambers of commerce scrutinize city halls. One Alaska city, Fairbanks, has an active taxpayer group. Multiple interest groups with vested interests in local government outcomes lead to a pluralistic and intense environment.

Local governments were less close to individual citizens in the 1980s and 1990s than at statehood. Then organizations were weaker; friends-and-neighbors' politics were stronger. Although local politics remain highly personal, with individual whims and antagonisms often producing tension, the process is more like group conflict than individual conflict. For example, when the Anchorage Assembly and mayor cut the school district budget by $13 million in 1990, teachers and students packed the chamber at the next meeting and demanded restored funding. A continuing theme of urban local government is popular control. When people are agitated about issues, elected officials must respond, or fall.

Rural Political Environments

The characteristics of rural Alaska communities are virtually the opposite of those in cities. They lack diversity and depend heavily on external funding. Local governments are weak institutions with noncompetitive politics.

Rural towns and villages have simple economies, which constrict the choices of residents.[2] Most rural Natives rely on subsistence hunting, fishing, and gathering activities to some extent. The few jobs usually exist within government organizations or government-supported nonprofit corporations. Transfer payments from governments supply the cash needed for purchases in the market economy. A private for-profit sector does not exist in most places with fewer than five hundred inhabitants, or 75 percent of rural communities. Private enterprise is likely to be a small village store or fuel distributorship; often it is not locally owned.

Rural places also lack cultural diversity. Few villages and towns have an even mixture of ethnic groups. About twenty towns with Caucasian majorities dot the map of rural Alaska. Most villages, however, have Native majorities, and Caucasian residents are likely to be transients. For example, non-Native teachers staff most rural schools. They earn high salaries and often live in quarters segregated from Natives. During summer and winter vacations, teachers depart the village for homes Outside. Small villages rarely have more than one church, to which everyone in the community belongs. They usually lack social clubs, veterans' organizations, lodges, and fraternities. What organizational life there is depends largely on government and nonprofit associations.

For most rural Alaskans, this lack of diversity is a positive attribute. Small communities have no strangers. Sharing is widespread, and no one is alone. Village life follows the rhythm of the environment and adapts quickly to seasonal changes. For example, North Slope village workers and youth take "subsistence leave" from jobs and school during the spring whaling season.

No one talks much about political parties in rural places. The role of politics differs, too: it is not a separate function, distinct from jobs, school, and play. Politics form part of family and clan relationships, friendships and factions. Recalls of entire councils or boards are not unusual events in rural Alaska, when one section of a divided community conducts warfare against the other. More typically, villages operate on the basis of consensus, without much change of leadership at all.

As institutions, rural local governments, as pointed out in chapter 12, lack power and authority. Many rural places fall into the unorganized borough and have no regional government of any kind. Most towns or cities have "second-class" governments, which means that they lack the mandatory power to tax property; in most rural places, there is little real property to tax. The state limits their regulatory authority.[3] The plethora of quasi-governments made up of school districts (REAAS), nonprofit Native associations, regional and village corporations, and planning units dilute what power rural cities and towns possess. Without a pool of trained local administrators and teachers, rural governments and schools depend on outsiders, whose tenure of work in the community is limited. For example, Bethel, one of the largest rural communities in Alaska, typically retains a city manager for less than two years.[4] Under these conditions, local governments, even ones with long histories such as those in Nome and Nenana, play less prominent roles in communities and cannot easily initiate change.

Rural politics tend to be noncompetitive. Rural seats in the state legislature are frequently not contested. Rural mayors, assembly members, council members, and school board members do not regularly face competition at the polls. That is the most important factor explaining their seniority in office.

Interest groups function in larger rural places. Organizations have their headquarters in regional centers such as Barrow, Kotzebue, Nome, Dillingham, and Tok. Most have Native regional corporations, Native nonprofit associations, and R E A A districts, which perform services in villages of the region. Corporate officials, social service administrators, and schoolteachers form interest groups in the regional centers and exercise influence in the different government and quasi-government arenas. Interest groups do not compete for influence, however. In the new rural regional boroughs, therefore, regional corporations face no strong rivals for influence.[5] In R E A A districts, teachers' unions do not confront chambers of commerce or taxpayer groups seeking to limit salary and benefit increases. Such confrontations are more likely to occur in the state arena.

If politics are defined as competition over scarce resources, then little traditional political activity is found in rural areas because of the absence of organized competition. If politics are defined as competition over policies, then some political activity is reflected in the existence of opinion differences. They occur within and between families, for in many villages all are kin.

Rural governments tend to be close to the community, as one would expect given the small populations. The advantage of this closeness is that governments pinpoint quickly the problems that bother people. The disadvantage is that there is no institutional buffer to refine consensus or muffle the clash of factions.

CAMPAIGNS IN ALASKA COMMUNITIES

In Alaska, *rural* and *urban* define separate political worlds. Campaigns for local office display the differences. Municipal elections are the most frequent and numerous; every October, races for city council, borough assembly, and school board seats occur.

Urban Campaigns in Alaska

In the early years of statehood, campaigns for local office in Anchorage, Fairbanks, and Juneau were small-scale, informal affairs. Connections with established families were the ticket to entry into local politics; long-term residence in the community was a virtual prerequisite for election. These campaigns typified the small-town, friends-and-neighbors' politics throughout America. The winners were usually the best-known contestants in the community. They had the largest number of friends and neighbors, who spread word to their friends in the informal exchange of views that led to voters' decisions.

Such elections have faded into history in most Alaska cities. Over the generation since statehood, Alaska's largest communities have grown greatly in population. Residents cannot know candidates for office on a first-hand basis. In the 1950s and 1960s, newspapers were the source of news about elections. Daily newspapers covered elections in each of Alaska's seven largest cities: Anchorage, Fairbanks, Juneau, Ketchikan, Sitka, Kodiak, and Kenai. From the 1970s to the present, however, radio and especially television coverage of politics has competed with print media. Electronic media are the chief agents transforming campaigns and elections in urban areas.

Electronic media make it possible for newcomers to establish name recognition rapidly and to compete on a par with community notables. This development has had three significant effects. First, community leaders have lost their ability to preselect candidates through an informal elite screening process. Today candidates for office are mostly self-starters who develop a campaign by dint of their own efforts. This trend has individualized the local political process and brought into office more people with no connection to established sources of power in communities, a development that also breeds professional politicians and officeholders.

Second, the electronic media, operating within the environment of nonpartisan elections, have enhanced the value of organization in Alaska's largest cities. The candidate-centered campaign organization is now the chief vehicle in urban elections, as has been the case in legislative and gubernatorial races since the early 1970s.

Third, electronic media costs are high in Alaska, where the market is small and has few economies of scale. Production and airing costs for one thirty-second spot shown over a three-week period reach nearly ten thousand dollars. Such television advertisements are the most crucial expense in local elections, and they raise the ante for campaigns. Candidates rely more on campaign donations. The easiest money to raise comes from interest groups, primarily unions and business corporations; increasingly, however, ad hoc groups, including taxpayer associations, have fronted contributions for local candidates.

Local election costs have more than tripled in recent years. Mayoral races are the most expensive because the mayor holds the most powerful and most visible post in local communities. Mayors of large cities and boroughs are the sole full-time local elected officials and the only ones with patronage powers. In the 1950s and 1960s, the expenses for mayoral races in Alaska's largest city, Anchorage, rarely exceeded $30,000. The reelection campaign of Tony Knowles in 1984 cost almost ten times that amount. The state's most expensive mayoral race was the 1990 Anchorage contest between Tom Fink and Rich Mystrom, which cost $1.5 million.[6]

Borough assembly races are the next most expensive. These seats are usually contested, and average costs per race run in the neighborhood of $15,000 in Fairbanks and more than twice that amount in Anchorage. High-interest races, such as the 1989 competition between incumbent Fairbanks assemblywoman Valerie Therrien and Donna Gilbert, or the replay of that race in 1992, cost more than $40,000.[7] Therrien, a youthful attorney, raised the most liberal voice on the assembly, heading up the arts committee and supporting social services. Gilbert was a local motel manager who gained prominence as the vocal leader of the conservative and populist Interior Taxpayers Association. Her aggressive style prompted a supporter to christen her the "Tiger Lady of Fairbanks."[8] Gilbert, the low spender in the Fairbanks assembly race, won in 1989, providing a reversal of the usual big-money trend. In 1992, Therrien outspent and outpolled Gilbert, whose negative behavior on the assembly had soured community support.

Even school board races, once rarely costing more than a few thousand dollars for competition over open seats, have escalated in price. A competitive election in the state's largest cities can cost nearly $25,000. Electronic media have raised the price of access to electoral politics, increasing the influence of political action committees on the policy process.

Local elections in Alaska incorporate national themes. The Christian right has been active in Alaska communities and in hotly contested school board races. When the Fairbanks school board retained the "Impressions" language arts series in 1991 (which fundamentalists attacked for its alleged "satanic" and "occult" themes), opponents formed a local chapter of the rightist Citizens for Excellence in Education. This group sponsored a stealth candidate in the October 1991 school board election who avoided controversial stands in the campaign and defeated an incumbent "Impressions" supporter with 70 percent of the vote. In October 1992, the Christian right ran a second stealth candidate against a two-term incumbent and university professor, regarded by political insiders as unbeatable, who had supported the "Impressions" series. In this expensive campaign, in which the stealth candidate was not visibly connected to the Christian right until election eve, the incumbent won with only twenty-seven votes to spare.

Winning local elections in urban Alaska requires what is needed elsewhere, namely, cultivation of a "minimum winning coalition." Candidates ask interest groups for donations to establish name recognition. Volunteers from interest groups also assist in get-out-the-vote efforts to rouse supporters to go to the polls. Traditional grass-roots methods still figure in local elections: door-to-door campaigning, neighborhood coffee parties, community meetings, and candidate forums sponsored by interest groups. Borough assembly members look for support from public-sector unions, taxpayers' associations, media, and chambers of commerce. Both celebrity and mass endorsements remain an effective campaign tool in larger communities. Insiders watch newspapers carefully to note which candidates gain the support of community notables and which candidate has managed to attract the largest and best-balanced "signature ad," a list of individuals in the community who endorse the candidate.

Municipal elections attract low turnouts, usually about 30 percent of registered voters. Thus interest groups able to mobilize voters achieve broad influence at the polls. Anchorage represents the extreme toward which some other cities are moving: disappearance of friends-and-neighbors' politics, prominence of the media, emergence of professional politicians, and growing distance between citizens and public life generally.

Rural Campaigns in Alaska

Some rural areas have had expensive election races. For example, in the 1985 municipal election, North Slope Borough mayor Eugene Brower[9] faced Barrow village corporation leader George Ahmagoak. Both candidates visited each of the eight villages in the borough by chartered small plane. Villages then were awash with money from capital improvements projects commissioned during Brower's term.

Elections on the North Slope during oil boom years, however, were not typical rural races. Rural seats often go begging for candidates; in many towns and villages, it is hard to find anyone to run. City clerks frantically conduct a roundup to have at least one name for every seat.

Larger towns such as Bethel, Nome, and Dillingham do feature competitive races, unless incumbents are running. An incumbent is normally reelected unless there has been a falling-out among extended family and associates.

Rural areas receive television broadcasts, but small towns and villages lack private production facilities. Television news and entertainment programs carry no locally produced commercials. Most medium-size rural places publish weekly newspapers, which carry political advertisements during campaigns. The majority of villages also have a small commercial radio station that broadcasts radio spots for candidates. In few rural elections, however, do candidates exploit the advertising potential of radio or print media. Instead, they distribute flyers, hold a few campaign forums, and leave persuasive appeals to word-of-mouth advertising.

As a result, rural election campaigns are highly personalized, influenced by the likes and dislikes of extended family members, friends, and neighbors. The rural election pattern, however, has little in common with the rural and small-town elections of the past described by V. O. Key in the American South, which emphasized popularity more than family ties.[10]

Nonpartisan Elections

Alaska entered statehood under a highly progressive constitution, and state lawmakers followed the lead of many progressive western states, which banned partisan identification and balloting in local elections. The rationale for nonpartisan elections is to focus attention on issues and problems in the local context, to force an examination of candidates' stands, and to eliminate the impact of organizations, such as parties, that might taint the local process.

Neither party endorsements nor party labels accompany names on ballots. Some groups, however, including political parties, endorse candidates for election to local office. Groups that typically support a slate of candidates for borough assembly and city council are teachers' and municipal employees' unions, minority coalitions, and, more recently, taxpayers' associations. They also represent sources of campaign donations.

In the 1980s, the Republican Party of Alaska attempted to influence election outcomes in local races. In 1982, district party chairs in Fairbanks endorsed candidates for city and borough races.[11] In 1989, a year when no statewide races were held, the state Republican party gave thousand-dollar contributions to ten candidates throughout the state, but mostly in Fairbanks and Anchorage. When asked why the party involved itself in nonpartisan elections, chairman James Crawford said that legislative and gubernatorial candidates rose from borough assemblies and city councils and thus it was in the party's interest to influence selection of the candidates likely to run for state offices.[12] The Democratic Party of Alaska cried foul at this partisan intervention in local elections. Democrats, however, are strongly linked with unions, which have ample access to the local election process. In both cases, parties have some impact, but it is invisible to the average resident.

Party impact is not always clear to local politicians, either. Jane Angvik, a contender for the lieutenant governorship in the Democratic primary of 1986, remarked on her two terms as a member of the Anchorage Assembly, saying she was never sure which assembly members were Democrats and which Republicans.[13] This observation applies to local government officials. Partisan factors may influence their behavior, but there is no easy way for the public or other officials to know about it.

LOCAL POLITICIANS

Local elected officials in Alaska number fewer than two thousand. A minority come from urban areas of the state. Cities are more prone to have unified governments and, thus, fewer officials per capita than rural areas. The majority of local elected officials serve on councils from villages or towns numbering around five hundred people or as members of Regional Educational Attendance Areas or city school boards.

Whether they serve on the borough assembly, city council, or school board or as mayor, these officials form an elite cadre. To the extent that Alaska has an establishment in local politics, it is likely to be a democratic one, composed of such officials rather than scions of old families or local notables.

Local elected officials and local appointed officials forge important links in some communities, links assumed by most Alaskans to be strong. Appointed officials include not only department heads in city and borough governments, but all local government workers whose contracts are subject to approval by the municipality or school district. Nearly half are teachers and other school personnel.

Local government jobs in Alaska pay well. Salaries of schoolteachers are the highest in the nation, averaging $46,000 a year in the early 1990s. Police and firefighters, utilities workers, and planning officers earn in the range of $50,000 to $70,000. Clerks, secretaries, and school custodians make over $30,000 a year. Health benefits are liberal, as are provisions for sick and annual leave.

Because the contracts of these appointed officials are subject to approval by local governments, the assumption is that politicians share their interests and support their growth. The fastest growing sector in government employment since statehood has been the local government workforce.[14] In Anchorage and Fairbanks at the end of the 1980s, however, officials split in their attitude toward the municipal workforce. Anchorage mayor Tom Fink acted openly hostile and clashed with municipal employee unions. He sought to privatize the Anchorage Telephone Utility, a proposal that failed in the 1989 election. Although it was approved by the Anchorage Assembly for a public vote in 1991, the public turned it down again. The conservative majority on the Fairbanks North Star Borough Assembly sought unsuccessfully to eliminate 15 percent of borough positions during budget deliberations in 1990.

What differentiates local politicians from the Alaskans they represent? The first and obvious difference is gender: local politicians are far more likely to be male than female. A second difference is age: politicians are somewhat older than the average Alaskan. Politicians tend to be of the same race as the majority of residents, however.

Local politicians are somewhat better educated than the public at large, and most urban politicians have college degrees. An interesting note, given the criticism of the public sector when oil prices fell in 1986, is the proportion of local politicians who have been employed in that sector. Urban politicians are somewhat more likely to emerge from the private sector, whereas rural politicians are prone to rise from the public sector (an unsurprising trend, given the lack of private jobs in rural areas). Finally, local politicians of both urban and rural areas tend to earn higher incomes than the community average. All local politicians except big-city mayors serve as part-time officials. They usually receive stipends, and in some cases, pension contributions, for their public service, which further expands the income gap. In social characteristics, then, the politicians of urban and rural Alaska are unrepresentative of the public, except for ethnicity and race. Local politicians, especially from rural areas, communicate far better than the average resident.

Local politicians, by virtue of living in the same place as residents, tend to echo residents' values and beliefs. The nature of the issues reflects this representation. For example, the leader of a group protesting the Fairbanks school board's decision to terminate a special contract for a rural bus route said board members acted against the group's interests because they "lived in $100,000 houses and got preferred service" as politicians.[15] Class differences between voters and elected officials are noted most often during times of economic distress.

Local politicians travel to Juneau during the legislative session to meet with lawmakers and to press their requests for funding and legislation serving their communities' interests. They are represented in the capital city by advocacy groups and lobbyists, as are appointed officials.

Local government lobbying groups during the 1980s formed the most powerful coalition of forces in Juneau, at a time when the legislature made large increases in pass-through grants and revenues to local governments. They were situationally and opportunistically powerful because the state had the dollars and legislators were ready to spend in their districts. Alaska's public-sector lobby rivals any private-sector lobby, with the possible exception of oil interests.[16]

Alaska has its share of local officials who entered office with axes to grind and who play mean-spirited roles of spoilers, demagogues, and cheats. Most local officials, however, are hardworking and dedicated, and they make significant contributions in their communities. Because of the open nature of the Alaska local government system, officials spend long hours listening to public testimony, answering phone complaints, and responding to correspondence. Given the complex web of federal-state-local relations in Alaska, officials must master an impossibly broad range of issues and read volumes of information to be prepared for decisional meetings. The meetings often drag on until three or four o'clock in the morning. Inclement weather makes attending evening meetings inconvenient for several months of the year. The average local official commits twenty hours a week to government service. Considering the criticism they take from community members, regardless of their decisions, one hardly wonders why local officials, such as Anchorage assemblyman Joe Evans, complain that their work is thankless. In part for this reason, Evans announced that he would not run for reelection in 1991.

ISSUES IN ALASKA LOCAL POLITICS

Most conflict in local government arises, of course, from divergent points of view or interests. There are many ways to sort out the interests that divide competitors. The simplest classification is the best: issues of permanence in local governments concern the rationale and services of government itself, such as the amount of funding for schools, in contrast to those that appear temporary, such as demonstrations by right-to-life groups. Examples of situations producing conflict on both types of issues are given below.

The Costs and Services of Local Government

The perennial issues of local government spring from two sources. Some arise from opposition to the cost of government or government's existence and to the kinds and amounts of services provided by government. Others are produced by the tensions and conflicting interpretations of authority between and within governments. Because the construction of the Alaska local government system is unique, these issues often take on a different aspect than in other parts of the United States.

Proportionately, Alaska appears to attract a far larger collection of antigovernment activists than any other state. They want a minimal state delivering maximum dollar benefits to individuals, with no local governments to regulate and tax. The chief representative of this point of view is Fairbanksan Joe Vogler, three-time candidate for governor and chief of the Alaskan Independence Party, a lawyer and miner strongly averse to local taxation of property, which he calls theft.

A second source of conflict is the cost of government. Alaska has always nurtured critics of salaries for public officials and other government expenses, but the revenue downturn beginning in 1985 increased their number dramatically. This issue pits fiscal conservatives against public-sector unions, which defend and seek to increase wages and benefits of union members. No local government can afford to be insensitive to the cost of government, and many officials across the state have lost their offices because voters thought they were "giving away the store" to public employees. The Interior Taxpayers Association in Fairbanks has become the most virulent opponent of public-sector salary levels, effectively gaining public support for tax caps, low mill rates, and no new taxes.[17] Anchorage mayor Tom Fink has also distinguished himself as a foe of public employee unions and their wage and benefit demands.

Although candidates regularly clash over the cost of government during election campaigns, the conflict is chiefly associated with the cycle of labor negotiations. During the oil boom years, peace reigned during most labor negotiations. Expanding revenues to local governments led to annual raises and step increases. The bust produced heated and drawn-out labor negotiations. More often than not, negotiations between teachers and school districts, particularly in urban areas, went into advisory arbitration. Unusual developments fueled conflict in two areas of the state. The Copper River School District declared bankruptcy and proceeded to cut by 10 percent the salaries of its teachers, then the most highly paid in the state with an average salary of $52,000. A bankruptcy judge investigated the claims of the union and school district, finding authority for the district to cancel contracts but siding with the union's authority to represent teachers and gain recovery of lost wages.[18] The second action was taken by the Ketchikan School District, which after a one-year impasse with teachers unilaterally imposed contract terms that froze wages and eliminated longevity steps from the negotiated agreement.

State labor-relations statutes limit the right of Alaska's local government employees to strike. The public workforce is divided into classes. Workers performing essential fire, life, health, and safety functions are not permitted to strike but are covered under binding arbitration. Teachers, who make up the single largest group of local government employees, formerly had neither the right to strike nor the protection of binding arbitration. In the words of NEA-Alaska, teachers lacked "finality" in the bargaining process, and that was unfair. The 1989 state legislature changed the law, giving teachers a limited right to strike with a two-year sunset provision. In 1991, the legislature removed the sunset provision and overrode the governor's veto, making the right to strike permanent. Conflicts over teacher negotiations are likely to escalate.

Debate over the third issue of local government, the kinds and amounts of service that communities should provide, is equally intense. It centers on such matters as mass transit, staffing levels in police and fire departments, road service, and the amount of latitude in zoning codes. The strife tends to become most intense during the annual budget cycle of cities and boroughs. For example, in 1992, the Anchorage Assembly debated rent-free use of public parkland for a Native heritage theme park. Supporters wanted to educate and enlighten while attracting tourist dollars. Opponents feared the park would degenerate into a sad caricature of Native culture and also damage recreational areas and fish streams used by neighborhoods.

In both Anchorage and Fairbanks, discord has developed over community activity centers. State dollars enabled both cities to build handsome new facilities. In the case of Anchorage, "Project 80s" included the Sullivan Sports Arena, the Egan Convention Center, and an opulent performing arts center. Operation and maintenance costs of these projects are major irritants during budget deliberations. As long as these facilities require taxpayer support, they will cause dissent.

Institutional Conflicts in Local Government

In chapter 12, we noted three types of institutional relationships that often produce conflict in Alaska local government: relations between mayors and councils or assemblies, between cities and boroughs, and between school districts and borough assemblies.[19] A fourth institutional conflict concerns federal and state mandates on local governments.

Most of Alaska's small towns have council-manager forms of government. The mayor is only marginally stronger than the ordinary council member. Mayors lack independent authority to hire and fire department heads and other municipal employees. Councils appoint managers, who serve at the pleasure of the council; thus, there tends to be little structural conflict. Nevertheless, different majorities on the councils may clash with the city manager, leading to abrupt dismissals with changes in council coalitions. Managers have as little longevity in Alaska cities as they do elsewhere.

Alaska's larger cities and unified municipalities are more likely to feature strong mayor-assembly systems of local government. The mayor is elected independently of the assembly, and a municipal code provides the mayor with the authority to hire borough administrators and submit a budget. Mayors wield veto powers, including a line-item veto of appropriations, which are difficult to override, requiring two-thirds of the typical eleven-member assembly.

Relations between mayors and assemblies on occasion have erupted into shouting matches. In Anchorage, the 1987 election of a conservative mayor, Tom Fink, led to battles with the municipal assembly, particularly when the mayor sought to cut municipal expenditures radically and when he attempted to replace the upper echelon of municipal administration with his political supporters. He also fought with the assembly over negotiations with unions and control of the budget.

In Fairbanks, the election of an extremely conservative assembly, seven of whose members were endorsed and strongly supported by the Interior

Taxpayers' Association, pitched the 1989 assembly into open warfare with liberal mayor Juanita Helms. After a month of acrimonious exchanges, the mayor declined to permit departmental administrators to attend assembly meetings because of the abuse they allegedly suffered there. This action prompted the conservative assembly majority to seek to redress the balance of powers by limiting the mayor's veto power and requiring each intradepartmental transfer of funds to be approved by the assembly.[20] Like the tension between executive and legislature in the state arena, mayors and assemblies often go head-to-head because both possess strong powers and both are independently elected by the voters.

Interinstitutional conflict occurs with school districts, too. Alaska's school superintendents are appointed by school boards for fixed contractual terms. As boards change through elections, tension with superintendents may develop, often surfacing in the media. Disgruntled members of school boards sometimes go to the media with allegations of misconduct. For example, in 1981 a dissatisfied board member publicized the fact that the Bering Straits School District superintendent, Ron Hohman, had spent more than one hundred thousand dollars on an "adventure-based education" scheme that took him, several teachers, and a half-dozen students on a junket to Europe. He also used school district funds to pay for his residence in Juneau, where he spent most of the legislative session lobbying for the district.[21]

In 1984, Fairbanks board dissidents publicized information about Superintendent Bryce Stallard's alleged misuse of his automobile allowance for personal shopping and his improper handling of purchase contracts. In 1988, Copper River teachers petitioned the Professional Teaching Practices Commission, which regulates schoolteachers and administrators, to seek the revocation of Superintendent Leland Dishman's administrative credentials because he had leaked information about a teacher's misconduct, forcing the teacher to resign. In 1989, a majority of Delta-Greely board members retained their own law firm, which revealed that the superintendent had endorsed questionable accounting practices. The board fired the superintendent; meanwhile, voters recalled four board members for holding an illegal executive session to hire an attorney. In most of these cases, the school boards have split, with one faction seeking to remove the superintendent.

The Alaska Constitution dictates that cities are "parts of" boroughs in organized regions of the state. This mandate has not eliminated conflict between cities and boroughs, however. Cities retain authority to set their own property tax rates, establish sales taxes, and regulate building construction. The greatest conflict between cities and boroughs concerns regulation. On occasion, city building inspectors refuse to agree to borough requests for conditional use permits. Moreover, as municipal revenues declined, cities and boroughs competed for scarce resources from the state. In Fairbanks, when the city lost millions in state revenue-sharing funds, it reduced its functions and transferred several responsibilities, such as the operation of the Alaskaland theme park, to the borough. Further revenue shortfalls in 1992 prompted the mayor to propose transferring the fire department to the borough or turning it over to the private sector.[22]

Provision of services has constituted another angle of city-borough conflict. The unified municipalities of Anchorage, Juneau, and Sitka lack, by definition, city-borough conflict. But a degree of dissension has arisen over equity in service provisions in the geographically vast boroughs of Kenai, the Matanuska-Susitna Valley, Fairbanks, and the North Slope. Initial objections to North Slope Borough power came from distant villages such as Point Hope and Wainwright, whose residents believed they received far less from the borough than residents of Barrow.[23] City councils in Wasilla and Palmer publicized their discontent over services in a petition to secede from the Mat-Su Borough, then seeking to expand its territory by absorbing Denali National Park to the north.[24]

Borough–school district conflicts are also rooted in the legal division of authority between institutions (see chapter 12). The state constitution unifies taxation powers in boroughs, a power that is one of three mandatory areas of borough government (the other two are education and planning/zoning). State statutes assign the function of education to school districts, which are fully in charge of operating schools and providing educational programs. The borough assembly may not alter on a line-item basis the local contribution to education, which constitutes 20 to 40 percent of urban school districts' budgets.

The major conflict is fiscal. Borough assemblies are required by law to contribute to education, within a specified range, but they may not determine how the money is spent. Borough assembly members must respond to taxpayers' protests, as it is the assembly that sets the mill rate for property taxation. As the sole taxation authority, the borough government must exercise fiscal control and provide for all general government services. It cannot view the school district budget in isolation from other competing services. School districts, on the other hand, wield full authority to spend. Unlike most American school districts, however, they lack authority to assess taxes or raise the amount contributed by the borough. School districts must respond to parents, unions, and special interests that invariably seek to expand the size of the education budget to accommodate particular needs, but they can exert little control over the revenues required to support increased expenditures.[25]

Alaska's major conflict involving a borough assembly, school board, and superintendent occurred in Anchorage in 1992. The outgoing board of education in 1990 recruited as superintendent Thomas O'Rourke, from upstate New York, and sweetened his contract by allowing his dismissal only with the concurrence of a third-party arbitrator. Over the next two years, a new board majority encountered problems in its relationship with the superintendent and voted not to retain him. O'Rourke, meanwhile, had cultivated good relations with the municipal assembly, which indicated that it would provide an additional $5 million sought by the school district only if the board kept the superintendent. The board capitulated, but the anti-O'Rourke majority met in a rump session and removed its president (an O'Rourke supporter). His sister-in-law then launched a recall campaign against the four-person board majority. Over three months, the board negotiated terms of departure with O'Rourke, which cost the district $284,000. One member of the majority resigned before the recall election in mid-December. The remaining three members were recalled by a two-to-one vote. The sentiment of most Anchorage voters was one of embarrassment that the board could not reconcile its differences with the superintendent and borough assembly and focus on educational issues.

Other conflicts concern school construction and maintenance. By law, school districts determine the educational specifications for new school construction, but boroughs have the authority to raise taxes and sell bonds (if the voters agree) to pay for construction. Often the interests of the two bodies differ with respect to the need for new school buildings or for repair and renovation of existing ones. School districts maintain school buildings, but boroughs own them; borough administrations, however, sometimes feel reluctant to embark on expensive repairs of buildings they do not fully control.

State law provides for the existence of a centralized treasury in organized municipalities, leaving the borough in charge of unexpended funds, drawing interest into the borough treasury, and giving school districts little flexibility to protect against emergencies. On the other hand, as the body with taxation powers, the borough treasury must pay for lawsuits lost by school districts. Yet it cannot curb school practices or decisions that might lead to expensive litigation.

Finally, local governments operate as agencies of the state and must respond to both state and federal mandates. Regulatory requirements are unpopular because they cost money and time of local officials and because they do not originate in communities. Special education and environmental protection mandates are illustrations of this area of conflict.

Alaska school districts fall under state and federal programs of bilingual/ bicultural education, special education, and provisions for the handicapped. Regulatory language is highly complex, requiring specialized staff in school districts. To obtain state and federal funding, local "maintenance of effort" is required, and reporting requirements are rigorous. Such programs reduce the discretionary authority of school districts and expose them to risk if they comply less than fully.

When local areas fail to meet ambient air standards set by the Environmental Protection Agency, local governments must develop and gain approval of compliance plans. Winter weather conditions in Alaska compound normal vehicle-emission problems. Local governments in large cities enforce emission-control programs, which require vehicle owners to test cars and trucks at their own expense. Residents object to being penalized for conditions of the environment. Recent changes in toxic waste-disposal standards have placed an additional burden on Alaska local governments.

Revenue shortfalls have exacerbated all the intra- and interinstitutional conflicts mentioned here. For this reason, local government conflict reached a level of intensity in Alaska during the late 1980s higher than at any previous time. Alaska local government is lively because of these structural issues. It also manages conflict and defuses tension, without much interference from the state, and that is no mean accomplishment.

Ad Hoc Issues

Other conflict in Alaska local communities springs not from governments but from the people. Alaskans highly prize their independence and personal liberty, which they manifest in different lifestyles within the same community. These disparate lifestyles frequently clash, and relevant parties land in the arena of local government, which has the regulatory power to decide which lifestyle to sanction or restrict.

Control of animals, particularly dogs, emerges as an issue occasionally in all parts of Alaska. Many Alaskans believe that the wilderness environment of the state makes leashing and controlling dogs unnecessary. This attitude is compounded by the state's most famous winter sport, dog mushing, which makes the needs of raising dog teams a high priority in rural and suburban areas. Municipalities establish animal-control policies to protect public health. Policy tightness and enforcement are typically controversial.

Alcohol use and regulation are also contentious. The state regulates beverage control through a commission and listens to local government input on liquor licenses. Heated arguments are presented by urban property owners who object to a bar, liquor store, or restaurant dispensing alcohol in their neighborhood. Similar controversy arises over the location of sleep-off and detoxification centers. Also, local governments set the hours of bar openings and closings. This issue, which frequently goes on the ballot, draws the highest rates of turnout at local elections.

The liquor industry lobby in Alaska is strong and well financed. It is an active and influential player in both local and state politics. It was largely the liquor lobby that kept the Anchorage Municipal Assembly from placing an increase in the alcohol beverage tax on the ballot for voter approval. Polls showed that a liquor tax would have passed.[26]

No large Alaska city has tried to exclude all sales and uses of alcohol. Alaska Native villages and rural communities, however, have sought to prohibit importation of alcohol, the sale of alcohol, and even the use of alcohol within their boundaries. This form of substance abuse is particularly devastating to small communities, where alcohol abuse may affect each family negatively, leading to spouse and child abuse, crimes of violence against property and life, and suicide. The legislature has responded to villages' requests by enlarging the statutory power of village councils to declare the village "dry." Monitoring and enforcement of such prohibitions have been difficult and disputatious; the most controversial case is the village of Kipnuk, whose officials conducted body searches of all persons coming from planes into the village.[27]

A third conflict stems from the power of cities and boroughs to regulate land use. Planning and zoning codes usually reflect fragile compromises between those who desire unrestricted use of their own property and those whose neighborhoods and lifestyles might be adversely affected by change. Issues include the development of ski areas, mining claims, commercial businesses, and large residential complexes, and the protection of remaining wetlands and wildlife areas in cities. These conflicts are episodic events, depending as they do on the initiative of property owners who approach local governments with requests for conditional use permits or zoning variances. When the events occur, they often result in packed assembly chambers where a small number of developers, with their allies in the business community, face large numbers of neighborhood residents, enraged at the prospect of losing their lifestyle.

These examples focus on conflict, and conflict is what keeps local governments in the news. The typical sessions of local governments, however, are tame to the point of boredom. Most actions reflect incremental adjustments; few votes are divided. Consensus is easily achieved on most issues.

The fact that local governments frequently do change indicates the responsiveness of institutions and the effectiveness of the electoral process. The fiscal downturn Alaska experienced in the late 1980s drew new actors into the spotlight of local government. It weakened the power of established community forces, such as chambers of commerce and public employee unions. It gave newly formed groups, such as Fairbanks's taxpayer association, the power to transform assemblies.

CONCLUSION

Local governments were weakly developed in all parts of Alaska at statehood. The constitution proposed a novel scheme for integrating local government services. Like the state government itself, new local governments came about during the early statehood period. Increased funneling of wealth from the state to local governments helped to legitimize the latter bodies. By the same token, however, local governments became more dependent on state appropriations. Thus, for most of the 1970s and early 1980s, Juneau was the focus of local fiscal action. Comparatively little attention was paid to budget-setting and tax issues in cities and towns;[28] little conflict ensued at the local level.

The state's revenue crisis produced critical changes in this pattern of development. It increased the need of localities to press for a larger share of dwindling state resources. For the first time in nearly a decade, it forced local governments to raise taxes. Although previous reductions in local property taxes had produced a great deal of slack, the relative increases spurred strife. Occurring at a time of economic depression, when many residents lost jobs and homes, any act of raising taxes was wildly unpopular and required considerable reduction of public services. When the reductions did not take effect immediately, a typical occurrence among organizations with multiple contracts of varying durations, popular opposition formed, seeking control over local governments.

Campaigns and elections in the mid-1980s and early 1990s reflected this tension in some bitter and highly competitive urban races. Local government institutions came under attack; many officials complained about negativism, distrust, and alienation. Another view of this era, however, is more optimistic. It suggests that the struggle for power in local government demonstrates the importance of local institutions in Alaskans' lives. In some cases, committed opponents of local government have been elected to office; they have assumed the mantle of power, renewing the representativeness and vitality of institutions. Tax increases to support local services are signs of hope that Alaskans are becoming more realistic about future revenues and the need for greater self-reliance.

Conclusion

Three interrelated themes have provided the interpretative framework for this study of Alaska's government and politics: the drive of Alaskans for power, equality, and wealth. These themes express the culture of ideas and values Alaskans have developed in response to their remote, isolated, northern environment. They explain many of the policy choices Alaskans have made as they have encountered the vagaries of resource constraints and opportunities in the twentieth century. In this chapter, we conclude the analysis by summarizing dimensions of each theme. We also examine prospects for the future of government and politics in Alaska.

SELF-GOVERNMENT: THE DRIVE FOR POWER

Independence and individualism are outstanding characteristics of Alaskans and the Alaska political process. Much of the story of Alaska government is a retelling of this theme as individuals and groups established themselves in conditions of frontier isolation and sought to protect themselves against severe environmental forces.

Alaska's people came to the Great Land in pursuit of its resources. Natives migrated first, a fact that entitles them to special status under American law. Unlike their counterparts in the contiguous forty-eight states, Alaska Natives live in or near places inhabited by their ancestors thousands of years ago.

Alaska's history and development in the nineteenth and twentieth centuries feature transients and settlers. Some came to exploit Alaska resources and departed; others fell in love with the land and established enterprises, homes, and families. There were colorful personalities. Some were saints, such as E. L. "Bob" Bartlett, Alaska's visionary delegate to Congress from 1944 until his death in 1968. Others were sinners, such as "Soapy" Smith, the bandit of Skagway, or E. T. Barnette, the crooked riverboat captain-turned-banker who founded Fairbanks. Most embodied a combination of virtue and vice conducive to survival in the harsh environment of the northern frontier. Alaskans revere, for instance, the memory of Judge James Wickersham, a man of dubious morals as far as women and whiskey were concerned, but who devoted much of his life to the furthering of his beloved territory. The attitudes of Alaskans toward such figures reflect the individualism of the state's political culture.

The struggle for statehood is part of the distant past in most American states, but it is a living memory in Alaska. It also represented a rare period of unity in Alaska's history. A confluence of forces, perhaps never to be recreated, achieved what many thought impossible at the time. Statehood advocates forged a coalition of those who sought instant development of Alaska resources, those who opposed federal government intervention, those who demanded local rule, and those who wanted to improve living conditions. The statehood movement fortuitously coincided with the end of one movement for progressive reform in state and local government and the beginning of another. The Alaska Constitution resulted.

A localized constitution promised Alaskans the ability to control their environment. Framers paid serious attention to the mechanics of government: how to ensure that institutions of government could respond to people's needs through their elected representatives. In practical terms, the state constitution, as implemented by the legislature and governor, expanded geometrically the powers of government in Alaska.

American states rarely see the dynamic tension between the executive and the legislative branches which has distinguished Alaska government in the 1980s and 1990s. To witness this competition for power, alongside a court system that is the acknowledged equal of both branches, is exceptional. Although the power of government in Alaska has expanded, it has adhered strongly to the checks-and-balances model developed by the framers of the U.S. Constitution. Nevertheless, balance within Alaska government is attributable less to institutional ethics than to popular control.

State and local governments have empowered Alaskans and given them a voice to express their needs and influence to affect outcomes. The political system of Alaska incorporates not only groups but individuals who seek to influence the distribution of power. During the territorial era, a relatively small number of groups joined in the political process. On statehood and with population growth and economic development, many new interests developed. They stimulated the formation of groups such as the Alaska Native claims associations of the 1960s. By the early 1990s, one could safely say that all relevant interests were represented in the Alaska political process.

The panoply of interests in Alaska might prompt an observer to complain of hyperpluralism. What distinguishes Alaska is the ability of any group, even any individual, to voice its views. The institutions of government encourage expression in countless ways. Moreover, bureaucratic agencies and branches of governments often attempt to respond to opinions, down to the individual level.

The relatively high degree of organized power in Alaska government stimulates conflict with individuals who see increased government influence coming at the expense of individual and group liberties. This perception fuels support for the populist distribution policies of Alaska government, chief among which is the Permanent Fund dividend program. This perception also is one of several factors explaining the reluctance of citizens to increase state and local taxation as Prudhoe Bay oil revenues decline. Today Alaska ranks among the top five states in terms of per capita income. Conversely, Alaskans bear a ridiculously low tax burden compared to residents of the other forty-nine states and the District of Columbia.

Alaska has evolved from a backward territory with a weak government to a wealthy state with a powerful system of state and local government. The power and independence of Alaska state government are constrained in three major ways. First is federal ownership and control. Alaska's relationship with the federal government contributes tension to state politics because the federal government owns 60 percent of Alaska's land and determines access to these areas. The federal government also controls commercial access to Alaska, which is one of only two noncontiguous states. Second, the federal government is trustee of Alaska Natives and their lands in a "special relationship" that curbs state sovereignty and policy. Third, Alaska's reliance on oil ties the state to a highly volatile global oil market, which severely constrains economic policy making.

Nevertheless, after one generation of statehood, the governmental institutions of power at the state level are well established. Structural ambiguities—particularly in the relationship among the state and the federal governments and Alaska Natives—promise to continue dynamic tension in Alaska self-government. Political and ideological tensions among Alaskans concerning their expectations for government services and for a certain quality of life, and the limits faced by government in fulfilling those expectations, also guarantee continuing conflict.

DEPENDENCE: THE QUEST FOR EQUALITY

Alaska epitomizes the drama of core-peripheral relations found in most nations and exacerbated in northern states. Alaska was the last American region colonized by Westerners and is today as remote and isolated as Hawaii. Its economic and political dependence caused frustration for transients and settlers and fired passions in the statehood movement.

The Alaska statehood act, in the opinion of the new state's political leaders, brought Alaska to an equal footing with the other American states. The story of statehood, however, is replete with examples of differential or unequal treatment. Until the 1970s oil boom, Alaska was economically dependent on the federal government. Oil wealth changed the locus of economic dependence to the unstable global oil market. Depletion of Prudhoe Bay reserves and limited prospects for filling the consequent economic gap make the economic future uncertain but decidedly dependent.

Although Alaska's land grant from the federal government was generous, use of the land was restricted by federal policy—first, by the prior need to resolve Native claims, then by the imposition of the federal monuments act, and currently by the conservationist strictures of the Alaska National Interest Lands Conservation Act.

Alaska's oil resources are treated differently than those of other states in the oil patch. North Slope oil cannot be exported to closer, energy-hungry nations in East Asia, which would increase the state's revenue from oil. Alaska's exports and imports must be transported on American ships, which increases their cost. This treatment of Alaska's commerce is discriminatory and has stimulated countless nativistic movements, from the Tundra Rebellion in 1982, through the campaigns of the Alaskan Independence Party in 1986 and 1990, to the fed-bashing rhetoric of Governor Walter Hickel's administration.

These real and perceived constraints on use of the Alaska environment make new residents as well as old-time settlers feel that their American citizenship is second-class. The isolation and remoteness from other states builds up the perception of neglect and discrimination. It also increases conflict inside Alaska between Natives and non-Natives, because of the special status of Alaska Natives under the federal Constitution.

The short period of wealth during the oil boom years brought Alaska to a par with the other states. Then state actions, particularly through the Permanent Fund dividend program and the abolition of the state income tax, increased calls from other states for federal taxation of Alaska's share of the oil wealth. Attempts by Alaska political leaders to provide special benefits to Alaska's residents through durational residency and local-hire legislation repeatedly were struck down by federal courts.

Alaskans' quest for equality on their terms, like their drive for full powers of self-government, faces continuing challenges by the federal government and coalitions of the other states. Alaskans' dependence on federal spending, programs, and controls aggravates these traditionally strained relationships.

SUSTAINABLE ECONOMIC DEVELOPMENT:
THE PURSUIT OF WEALTH

In territorial days, Alaskans were not affluent. Some had "struck it rich" in one or another of the big strikes of that era, but most non-Natives had comfortable, not wealthy, lifestyles. Although Native poverty was a reality, it had not yet become a public issue. In the 1990s, after half a decade or more of recession, Alaska remains one of America's richest states, because of its oil wealth.

Chance and fortune have ruled Alaska's economic development. Alaska's natural resource export economy reacts abruptly to unpredictable resource discoveries and fluctuations in world commodity prices. Workers surge in and out of the state, real estate markets boom and crash, and expectations rise and fall. Except for the uncertainties of natural resources, Alaska's economy remains mostly underdeveloped outside Anchorage. There is limited in-state processing of natural resources; service industries are unevenly developed and, in many places, nonexistent; subsistence hunting, fishing, and gathering are still vital parts of the rural economy.

The most stable components of the economy have been commercial fisheries and the federal government, whose civilian and military expenditures in Alaska match the state government's annual budget totals. Yet even these relatively stable industries lead to disturbance. The fishing industry is highly seasonal and has a large nonresident component. Many federal workers and virtually all military personnel live in the state only temporarily.

Government plays an unusually large role in the economy and society of Alaska, and many residents see state government as both a major benefactor and a threat. Like all state governments, Alaska's government taxes, regulates, and spends. Unlike the case in other states, however, Alaska's government also owns a substantial share of the state's land and resources. Especially since the oil boom began, state government has depended heavily on revenues derived from selling and leasing those resources.

Alaskans are acutely aware of the scope of their state government and the resources it owns and controls. They view the state as the lead agency for economic development and their primary source of benefits. Consequently, in the oil era, Alaska became an extreme example of a "rent-seeking" state: a place where entrepreneurial energies flow largely toward extracting wealth, favors, and privileges from government rather than toward creating and capturing wealth in the private market.

During the peak years of spending, groups of all kinds converged on the state capital demanding even larger shares of the oil revenue windfall. Ironically, the oil industry, the greatest force for change in Alaska since statehood, raised the loudest voice in favor of moderation. It sought to dampen public demands for increasing state government spending, which, as North Slope oil production began to decline, might be sustained through higher taxes on the oil industry. As in the other states, private citizens and groups seek opportunities to create wealth and urge government to reduce its taxation and regulation burden so private enterprise may flourish.

Government has always been the dominant institution in Alaska. In territorial days, federal officials determined the basic rules governing Alaska's settlement and development. After statehood, federal and state institutions divided control over Alaska's land, resources, and people. The oil era raised the stakes, intensified the action, and shifted more emphasis to state government.

A main concern is about the state government's long-term capacity to deliver the benefits that Alaskans demand. A fragmented state government, extremely responsive to disparate regional, local, and other special interests, may be incapable of the coherent and responsible action needed to secure Alaska's future as an economy and a society. Given state government's role as the balance wheel of Alaska's economy, the concern extends beyond abstract values of "good government." Can state government accommodate social diversity, economic volatility, and intergovernmental complexity to become an effective instrument for pursuing the shared, long-term interests of Alaska's people?

The record is a disturbing one. The oil boom decades brought boundless opportunities and high risk. State policy makers responded to unrelenting pressures to spend huge amounts of oil revenues without public rationale, planning, or controls. With the advice and consent of the people, they also created the Permanent Fund, an impressive accomplishment under the circumstances. Yet, in the early 1990s, earnings from the fund still were not earmarked for any long-term public purpose. They were claimed strictly for the private use of any individual who could declare Alaska residency, regardless of need and regardless of commitment to remain in the state.

Conflicts within state government are not limited to quarrels between executive and legislative institutions, where differences are expected. Many other points of contention arise between the state's roles as political sovereign, resource proprietor, and trustee of wealth. For one, dividend payments have absorbed the earnings of the Permanent Fund, the state's most reliable source of recurring revenues. Through limited-entry permits, the state has also privatized more than $1 billion in fisheries values.

In managing its resources, the state has struggled continuously with the problems of balancing its interests as an owner-developer with its responsibilities as a taxing and regulatory authority. Oil is the only resource that has returned more revenues to the state treasury than the state government has spent on managing it for public and private use. Reconciling these often conflicting roles and responsibilities is one of the major challenges confronting Alaska's government in the next generation of statehood.

THE CAPABILITY OF ALASKA'S POLITICAL SYSTEM

The fundamental weakness in Alaska's governmental system results not from institutional flaws, but from the state's economic and social marginality and its comparative economic and social disadvantages as a noncontiguous state on the continent's northern periphery. This marginal status, together with relentless change, is a true constant in the Alaska experience. The precarious, high-cost economy of the state offers big gains offset by high risks. Since statehood, there have been more winners than losers in Alaska's casino economy, mainly due to the big strike at Prudhoe Bay. Yet, because of economic uncertainty and volatility, many Alaskans make only tentative commitments to remain in the state and participate in its political development. No matter how long they have resided in the state, numerous non-Native Alaskans, perhaps a majority, habitually refer to communities in other states as "home." High rates of transiency register the decisions of many tentative Alaskans to return home or seek other frontiers.

If the ability to overcome these deficiencies and deal with the state's future challenges is to be found anywhere, it is in the character of the people of Alaska and the ideas they bring to bear on their political problems. Despite their unsteadiness, Alaskans' greatest strength is their capacity to learn from and adapt to the most protean environment of any American state. Alaskans are nothing if not a resourceful and resilient mix of peoples.

Along with their economic ambitions and tentative commitments, Alaska's transients often bring a vigorous mobility and a youthfully naive sense of adventure to Alaska's political culture, continually renewing the store of social energy. Settlers have helped balance transiency with civic pride, a sense of dedication to place, and a commitment to building community institutions for the long term. At the indigenous roots of the political culture are the Native peoples, whose rich, diverse heritages, intimately connected to the natural environment, stretch back for hundreds of generations.

Although their aspirations and expectations vary greatly, Alaskans share, and even thrive on, the experience of coping with rapid change and facing uncertain futures. Alaskans are unusually adept at creating and adapting ideologies, as well as at using them to interpret and respond to the challenges of their changing northern world. Their ideologies include myths made up of varying combinations of facts and fantasy. Alaskans typically are optimists, and their experience tells them to expect significant changes in their lives. As a result, their myths almost always contain large shares of fantasy, particularly about their economic prospects.

A large fantasy quotient can be both a weakness and a strength: a weakness because it can lead to foolish, inappropriate action; a strength because it can sustain spirit and energy through adversity. Governor Hickel's vision of the "owner state" is not likely to be the kind of positive myth that helps ensure Alaska's future and the well-being of its citizens. Such myths are more likely to be grounded in the enduring characteristics of Alaska's mix of peoples than in the evanescent natural resource economy. At best, the economy, whatever its leading component, is not an end but a means to realizing one's vision of the worthwhile life.

The most characteristic and persistent components of Alaska's ideologies have been values of individualism, self-reliance, and independence, with all their contradictory undertones of dependence, interdependence, and community. These are classic American frontier values that drive people apart as well as bring them together. For better or worse, these values continue to shape American ideas and experiences; nowhere do they do so with greater impact, or with more disquieting tensions, than on America's last frontier.

Reading about Alaska

Reference Works

The primary reference work on Alaska is the *Alaska Blue Book* (Juneau: Alaska State Library), compiled and published biennially by the Division of State Libraries and Archives in the Alaska Department of Education. Other general reference works include the *Dictionary of Alaska Place Names* (Washington, D.C.: U.S. Government Printing Office), the annual *Milepost* (Anchorage: Alaska Northwest Publishing Co.) (the best Alaska road guide), the *Alaska Almanac* (Anchorage: Alaska Northwest Publishing Co.), and the *Alaska Local Government Encyclopedia* (Juneau: Alaska Department of Community and Regional Affairs).

Histories

The best general history of Alaska is *Alaska: A History of the Forty-ninth State,* 2d ed., by Claus-M. Naske and Herman E. Slotnick (Norman: University of Oklahoma Press, 1987). This survey has an excellent bibliographic essay on the sources of Alaska's history, pp. 321–335, on which our account of historical sources is based. Another general history is William Hunt's *Alaska,* published in The States and the Nation Series (New York: W. W. Norton, 1976).

Specific studies abound on Native precontact history, the colonial era, territorial history, and statehood. Most relevant to understanding the state's political development are Jeannette Paddock Nichols's *Alaska: A Short His-*

tory of Its Administration (Cleveland, Ohio: Arthur H. Clark, 1924), Alfred H. Brooks's *Blazing Alaska's Trails* (Fairbanks: University of Alaska Press, 1973), Clarence Andrews's *The Story of Alaska* (Caldwell, Id.: Caxton Printers, 1938), Ernest Gruening's *The State of Alaska* (New York: Random House, 1954), Howard Kushner's *Conflict on the Northwest Coast: American-Russian Rivalry in the Pacific Northwest, 1790–1867* (Westport, Conn.: Greenwood Press, 1975), Morgan Sherwood's *Exploration of Alaska, 1865–1900* (New Haven: Yale University Press, 1965), and Ted Hinckley's *The Americanization of Alaska, 1867–1897* (Palo Alto, Calif.: Pacific Books, 1973).

Useful specialized studies on political change and development include Orlando W. Miller's *The Frontier in Alaska and the Matanuska Colony* (New Haven: Yale University Press, 1975), William Wilson's *Railroad in the Clouds: The Alaska Railroad in the Age of Steam, 1914–1945* (Boulder, Colo.: Pruett, 1977), and Claus-M. Naske's *A History of Alaska Statehood* (Lanham, Md.: University Press of America, 1985). Several studies have been done on the public policy aspects of natural resource products, such as Richard Cooley's *Politics and Conservation: The Decline of the Alaska Salmon* (New York: Harper and Row, 1963).

General Government and Politics

The first book published on Alaska government under statehood was Ronald C. Cease and Jerome R. Saroff's *The Metropolitan Experience in Alaska: A Study of Borough Government* (New York: Praeger, 1968). Thomas A. Morehouse and Victor Fischer looked at this topic in 1971 in *Borough Government in Alaska* (Fairbanks: Institute of Social, Economic and Government Research, University of Alaska). In 1984, the University Press of America (Lanham, Md.) published Thomas Morehouse, Gerald McBeath, and Linda Leask's comprehensive volume, *Alaska's Urban and Rural Governments*.

Interpretive studies of Alaska politics and society, such as George Rogers's *The Future of Alaska: Economic Consequences of Statehood* (Baltimore: Johns Hopkins University Press, 1962), add insight to understanding. Systematic studies of state politics and government did not commence until the 1980s, when eleven of the state's political scientists and one historian authored chapters in Gerald A. McBeath and Thomas A. Morehouse, eds., *Alaska State Government and Politics* (Fairbanks: University of Alaska Press, 1987). General and specialized papers on issues of Alaska state and local government are presented annually to four academic confer-

ences: the Western Political Science Conference and Western Regional Social Science Conference and meetings of the Western Regional Science Association and the American Political Science Association. The largest regular conference on Alaska politics and society occurs as part of the annual
science conference of the Alaska Division, American Association for the
Advancement of Science. Sometimes these papers are collected for publication, as with the twentieth science conference proceedings, edited by George
Rogers in *Change in Alaska: People, Petroleum, and Politics* (Seattle: University of Washington Press, 1970).

A host of studies has been published on policy areas. In Native politics,
the Federal Field Committee for Development Planning in Alaska, designed
to help the state recover from the 1964 earthquake, also aided in the settlement of Native land claims by publishing *Alaska Natives and the Land*
(Washington, D.C.: U.S. Government Printing Office, 1968), which demonstrated continued Native dependence on the land. Gerald A. McBeath and
Thomas A. Morehouse wrote *The Dynamics of Alaska Native Self-Government* (Lanham, Md.: University Press of America, 1980), which put the
Alaska Native Claims Settlement Act into the context of Native self-determination movements. David Case's *Alaska Natives and American Laws*
(Fairbanks: University of Alaska Press, 1984) provides a comprehensive and
detailed history and analysis of the legal status of Alaska Native institutions
in the context of federal Indian law. Native political and economic development problems are explored in Theodore Lane, ed., *Developing America's
Northern Frontier* (Lanham, Md.: University Press of America, 1987). Tom
Kizzia, in *The Wake of the Unseen Object: Among the Native Cultures of
Bush Alaska* (New York: Henry Holt, 1991), provides a contemporary view
of life in Alaska Native communities.

Uses of Alaska resources have been the focus of many studies. Richard
Cooley set the terms of the debate in his 1966 study, *Alaska: A Challenge in
Conservation* (Madison: University of Wisconsin Press). Mary Clay Berry
focused on the critical events launching Alaska's era of big oil in *The Alaska
Pipeline: The Politics of Oil and Native Land Claims* (Bloomington: Indiana
University Press, 1975). Robert Weeden stated the conservation position
strongly in *Alaska: Promises to Keep* (Boston: Houghton Mifflin, 1978).
Thomas A. Morehouse edited a balanced volume entitled *Alaska Resources
Development: Issues of the 1980s* (Boulder, Colo.: Westview Press, 1984).
This work continued an established pattern of review of resource controver-
sies, including Gordon Harrison's *Alaska Public Policy: Current Problems
and Issues* (Fairbanks: Institute of Social, Economic and Government Re-

search, University of Alaska, 1971, 1973); David T. Kresge, Thomas A. Morehouse, and George W. Rogers's *Issues in Alaska Development* (Seattle: University of Washington Press, 1977); and Arlon Tussing, Thomas A. Morehouse, and James D. Babb, eds., *Alaska Fisheries Policy* (Fairbanks: Institute of Social, Economic and Government Research, University of Alaska, 1972).

Personalities

Alaska political personalities are often individuals in some drama who warrant biographical accounts. Robert Hanrahan and Peter Gruenstein included several vignettes in their 1977 *Lost Frontier: The Marketing of Alaska* (New York: W. W. Norton), including chapters on Jay Hammond, Jesse Carr, and Robert Atwood. Evangeline Atwood and Robert DeArmond compiled information on Alaska's governors and other personalities in *Who's Who in Alaskan Politics* (Portland, Ore.: Binford and Mort, 1977). Claus-M. Naske has written a biography of the last territorial delegate and first U.S. senator, *Edward Lewis (Bob) Bartlett of Alaska: A Life in Politics* (Fairbanks: University of Alaska Press, 1979) and a forthcoming biography on Ernest Gruening, territorial governor and U.S. senator. Some general-interest biographies add information on Alaska's region, such as W. Leslie Yaw's *Sixty Years in Sitka* (Sitka, Alaska: Sheldon Jackson College Press, 1985).

Travels and Narratives

The romance and adventure associated with Alaska have made it the setting for numerous fictionalized accounts. Three bestsellers in the 1970s and 1980s were set in Alaska. Most popular was James Michener's *Alaska* (New York: Random House, 1988), which followed a Native family over the period of Alaska's history from precontact times. Joe McGinniss's *Going to Extremes* (New York: Alfred A. Knopf, 1980) pictures the obsession Alaskans have with the state while emphasizing its danger and excitement. John McPhee's *Coming into the Country* (New York: Farrar, Straus and Giroux, 1977) is a sensitive portrayal of different regional cultures in the state.

A dozen other romances and nonfiction narratives were published in the 1980s which use Alaska as a setting for the adversity that the novel's hero or heroine overcomes. A good example is *Libby: The Alaskan Diaries and Letters of Libby Beaman, 1879–1880, as Presented by Her Granddaughter Betty John* (Boston: Houghton Mifflin, 1987).

GOVERNMENT DOCUMENTS

The state government is the repository of much information about Alaska's political institutions and development.

The Constitution

The *Alaska Constitutional Convention Proceedings* (Juneau: Alaska Legislative Council, 1965) are the authoritative source of information on the construction of the state constitution. There are three fine studies of the state document. Victor Fischer's *Alaska's Constitutional Convention* (Fairbanks: University of Alaska Press, 1975) describes the process of framing the constitution, from both an analytical and a personal perspective (Fischer was a delegate). Gerald E. Bowkett's *Reaching for a Star: The Final Campaign for Alaska Statehood* (Fairbanks and Seattle: Epicenter Press, 1989) is a journalistic account of the statehood movement, focusing on the constitutional convention. Gordon S. Harrison's *Alaska's Constitution: A Citizen's Guide* (Anchorage: Institute of Social and Economic Research, University of Alaska, 1986) is an analysis of each provision of the constitution in terms of the objectives of the framers and principles of good government.

The Legislature

The Alaska legislature operates under uniform rules of procedure. Both the senate and the house maintain daily sessional journals. Standing committees of each house are less likely to maintain committee journals, but hearing reports and analyses are an important source of information on the legislature.

The Legislative Affairs Agency operates the Division of Public Services, which makes available generic information on legislative processes and procedures, such as "Legislative Process in Alaska" and "Uniform Rules, Alaska State Legislature." Specialized information on policy proposals and examinations of legislative history depend on the interest of individual legislators. The Legislative Research Agency is a nonpartisan agency supplying information to members of the legislature. Services include short-term issue analysis, solicitation and evaluation of contract bids, monitoring of contractual research, evaluation of state programs, historical research, tracking implementation of statutes, and analysis of federal legislation and regulations affecting Alaska. The House Research Agency was merged with the senate's

Advisory Council in the 1990 legislative session to form the Legislative Research Agency. Nearly 350 specialized reports were issued in the 1970s and 1980s.

Critical studies of the legislature are few (beyond newspaper coverage during the session, which tends to be focused and critical). One example is Richard Fineberg's *Chaos in the Capital: The Budget System in Crisis* (Anchorage: Alaska Public Interest Research Group, 1982), a critique of the capital budget process during the oil boom years. The League of Women Voters published a useful summary pamphlet on the state legislature in 1978.

Executive

Two excellent reference sources describe administrative activity and organization in Alaska. *A Handbook on Alaska State Government* is published annually by the Legislative Affairs Agency. *Alaska Report of Performance* is an annual compilation of agency activities and accomplishments, published by the Alaska Office of Management and Budget (OMB) (in the governor's office). Activities of Alaska's public corporations are described in *Alaska's Public Corporations,* a report to the Legislative Budget and Audit Committee (1982). This committee routinely prepares reports on administrative agencies and policies affecting government operations, such as *A Special Report on the Sunset Process in Alaska* (1982).

OMB maintains detailed information on the history of budget development and expenditures in Alaska. It also issues policy reports. The press department of the governor's office maintains a file of the governor's addresses to the legislature and to the public.

Academic studies of the governorship are relatively few. Gerald McBeath's article "Alaska's Gubernatorial Transition," in Thad Beyle, ed., *Gubernatorial Transitions: The 1982 Elections* (Durham, N.C.: Duke University Press, 1985) is one source comparing the Alaska executive to other state executives.

Judiciary

The "Alaska Rules of Court Procedure," published in the *Alaska Blue Book,* provide information on the history of the judicial system in territorial days. This subject has been studied by Claus-M. Naske, who has written several academic papers on the subject and one lengthy article entitled "The Shaky Beginnings of Alaska's Judicial System," *Western Legal History* 1 (Summer/Fall 1988): 163–210. William R. Hunt captured the color of territorial law enforcement in his *Distant Justice*. Decisions of the Alaska courts are maintained by the administrative director of the state court system, who serves the chief justice of the supreme court. The administrative director also recommends policies for improving the judicial system. The Alaska Judicial Council, operating independently of the state court system, conducts studies for the improvement of the administration of justice. These studies provide a helpful overview of problems in the state's judicial system. The Alaska court system prepares annual reports on caseload composition.

DATA SOURCES

Not all the information about Alaska government and politics is published in book or article form. Indeed, many essential pieces of information are available from nontraditional sources.

Research Centers

The state has one research institution that specializes in economic and governmental studies: the Institute of Social and Economic Research (ISER) of the University of Alaska Anchorage. This unit performs contractual research for private and public agencies, and its staff engages in scholarly research. ISER's publications are an important source of information on state policy issues. They include the *Alaska Review of Social and Economic Conditions*, ISER Occasional Papers, and the 1989–92 series (by Oliver Scott Goldsmith and others) on the Alaska fiscal gap and related fiscal policy issues.

Social science departments of the senior university campuses, also engage in research on the state's development. University anthropology faculty have compiled many useful studies and reports on the adaptation of Alaska's Native population. The history and political science departments of the University of Alaska Fairbanks have issued reports on the Alaska statehood experience, state government processes, and state–local and state–federal relations. University faculty in academic departments of the three university campuses (Anchorage, Fairbanks, and Southeast) are the chief source of the journal literature on Alaska, published in such places as *Western Political Quarterly, Publius: The Journal of Federalism, Pacific Historical Review, Journal of American History, Journal of the West, Polar Record, Arctic, Alaska Journal, Alaska Review, Pacific Northwest Quarterly, Western Historical Quarterly,* and *Growth and Change*.

Socioeconomic and Impact Data

The Legislative Finance Division publishes annual reports on operating budgets by agency. The Department of Revenue makes an annual Alaska financial report. This department prepares the quarterly revenue estimates on the basis of which state projections are made. The Department of Community and Regional Affairs, through its local government assistance division, reports annually on municipal property assessments and equalized full-value determinations in *Alaska Taxable*. The Permanent Fund Corporation prepares monthly as well as annual reports on the management of fund assets and the distribution of oil revenues in the state.

A wealth of data is available through the requirements of the federal government for environmental impact analyses. Two large changes in land use, construction of the trans-Alaska pipeline, authorized in 1973, and passage of the Alaska National Interest Lands Conservation Act of 1980, resulted in shelves of environmental statements and studies produced by federal, state, and local government bodies; Native groups; and private industry.

Finally, areas particularly affected by economic development have established community impact centers. In Fairbanks, an Impact Information Center was set up in the mid-1970s: its director, Mim Dixon, published *What Happened to Fairbanks: The Effects of the Trans-Alaska Oil Pipeline on the Community of Fairbanks, Alaska* (Boulder, Colo.: Westview Press, 1978). This center has continued, under borough auspices, as the Community Research Center, and publishes sophisticated quarterly reports on socioeconomic impacts in the Interior. The Urban Observatory performed a similar function in Anchorage in the late 1970s.

Public Opinion

Alaska has two public opinion polling firms: Dittman Research and Hellenthal & Associates. Both carry out contract polling for political candidates and for state government agencies. Some of the polls, such as Hellenthal's "Alaska Public Opinion Research Survey" (April 1985), are available for interested readers.

University researchers have done a considerable amount of polling. Perhaps the major survey researcher in the UA system is Jack Kruse, whose surveys now cover most regions of the state and are reported regularly by ISER. The senior campus at Anchorage once supported an Urban Observatory, under whose auspices some polls were conducted by Richard Ender. Examples of this work include "Citizen's Attitudes toward Anchorage Local Government and Issues of Public Policy: A Collection of Reports" (1976) and "The Opinions of the Anchorage Citizen on Local Public Policy Issues" (1977). One published attempt to interpret polling data on Anchorage was Lee Cuba's *Identity and Community on the Alaska Frontier* (Philadelphia: Temple University Press, 1987).

Campaigns and Elections

Since 1974, campaign spending in elections has been regulated by the Alaska Public Offices Commission (APOC). Statutes place limits on the amount that can be spent on different races and require full disclosure. APOC receives campaign spending reports and monitors election spending. It is the chief repository of information on the role of money in Alaska politics.

Reporters from the state's largest media study APOC's records before elections. The single most useful compilation of election data was made by former *Anchorage Daily News* reporter Larry Makinson. *Daily News* editors authorized his plan to computerize Alaska's campaign contribution records on the 1984 elections, which he published in 1985. Makinson's 1986 election work was more extensive and is presented in *Open Secrets* (Anchorage: Rosebud Publishing, 1987) the best analysis of campaign spending and electoral outcomes for any American state.

The state Division of Elections prints voter registration lists and descriptions of election results by precinct from each primary and general election. Political scientists have analyzed these data in two publications: Thomas A. Morehouse and Gordon S. Harrison's *An Electoral Profile of Alaska: Interparty Competition between 1958 and 1972* (Fairbanks: Institute of Social, Economic and Government Research, 1973), an evaluation of voting trends from 1958 to 1973, and Morehouse's "Alaska's Elections," in *Alaska State Government and Politics,* an extension of the analysis through 1984.

News

Alaska's forty-four newspapers are another rich resource. The *Anchorage Daily News* and the *Fairbanks Daily News-Miner,* the state's two largest daily papers, probably are the easiest to use. Local news coverage is comprehensive in both, and each sends reporters to Juneau during the winter to cover the legislative session.

Until 1980, none of the state's newspapers had an index of issues. Now each of the major papers is indexed annually, and some indexing is available for early years. Daily and weekly newspapers from across the state are microfilmed, and copies are retained in the Rasmuson Library at the University of Alaska Fairbanks and other state libraries.

OTHER SOURCES

Some public policy issues and governmental operations in Alaska are treated in master's and doctoral dissertations. These dissertations, if written in the state university system, are available through the manuscripts division of the U A F's Rasmuson Library. College students' papers, which may be available through some departments, colleges, and schools, are often useful sources of information.

Alaska politics are unusually open, and Alaska politicians are very accessible. Much can be learned from observing local public meetings and watching the legislative process. Campaigns focus attention on government and public issues and provide maximum opportunities to analyze candidates' responses—and the roles of political organizations and government institutions. Unlike many states, where politics are invisible or clouded, Alaska has governments that are highly visible. Popular involvement is encouraged, and the state provides numerous opportunities for this.

Notes

INTRODUCTION

1 "Governor Will Sue Feds," *Fairbanks Daily News-Miner,* January 15, 1992, p. 1.
2 Ibid.

CHAPTER I

1 Hudson Stuck, *10,000 Miles with a Dog Sled* (New York: Charles Scribner's Sons, 1915) pp. ix–x.
2 *The Alaska Almanac: Facts about Alaska,* 15th ed. (Bothell, Wash.: Alaska Northwest Books, 1991), p. 171.
3 Ibid., p. 29.
4 Robert J. Wolfe and Robert J. Walker, "Subsistence Economies in Alaska: Productivity, Geography, and Development Impacts," *Arctic Anthropology* 24, no. 2 (1987): 59.
5 Alyeska Pipeline Service Co., Fairbanks.
6 *Alaska Almanac,* p. 168.
7 "Woman Held after Trek Try," *Fairbanks Daily News-Miner,* January 3, 1989, p. 2.
8 See chapter 5; see also David S. Case, *Alaska Natives and American Laws* (Fairbanks: University of Alaska Press, 1984).
9 Daniel J. Elazar, *American Federalism: A View from the States* (New York: Thomas Y. Crowell, 1966), pp. 85–86.
10 Ibid., p. 86.
11 Ibid., p. 90.
12 Ibid., pp. 92–93.
13 "In Brief," *Polar Record,* 24, no. 150 (1988): 257.
14 Wallace M. Olson, *The Tlingit: An Introduction to Their Culture and History,* 2nd ed. (Auke Bay, Alaska: Heritage Research, 1991), pp. 27, 31.

CHAPTER 2

1 William H. Wilson, "Alaska's Past, Alaska's Future," *Alaska Review*, 4, no. 1 (1970): 2.

2 Claus-M. Naske and Herman Slotnick, *Alaska: A History of the Forty-ninth State*, 2d ed. (Norman: University of Oklahoma Press, 1987), p. 9.

3 Ibid., pp. 9–10.

4 See, for example, Philip Drucker, *Indians of the Northwest Coast* (Garden City, N.Y.: Natural History Press, 1963); James Van Stone, *Athapaskan Adaptations* (Chicago: Aldine, 1974); Margaret Lantis, ed., *Ethnohistory in Southwestern Alaska and the Southern Yukon: Method and Content* (Lexington: University of Kentucky Press, 1970); Don E. Drummond, *The Eskimos and Aleuts* (London: Thames and Hudson, 1977); Hans-Georg Bandi, *Eskimo Prehistory*, trans. Ann E. Keep (College, Alaska: University of Alaska Press, 1969); William C. Sturtevant, ed., *Handbook of North American Indians*, vol. 5, *Arctic*, ed. David Dumas (Washington, D.C.: Smithsonian Institution, 1984).

5 Ernest S. Burch, Jr., "From Skeptic to Believer: The Making of an Oral Historian," *Alaska History* 6, (Spring 1991): 12–13.

6 Naske and Slotnick, *Alaska*, pp. 24–25.

7 Ibid., p. 27.

8 Cornelia Goodhue, *Journey into the Fog* (Garden City, N.Y.: Doubleday, Duran, 1944), p. 147.

9 Naske and Slotnick, *Alaska*, pp. 29–30.

10 Hector Chevigny, *Lord of Alaska: Baranof and the Russian Adventure* (Portland, Ore.: Binford and Mort, 1951), p. 25.

11 Ibid., p. 18.

12 Ibid., p. 44.

13 Ibid., p. 50.

14 Ibid.

15 Margaret Lantis, "The Aleut Social System, 1750 to 1810, from Early Historical Sources," in Lantis, *Ethnohistory in Southwestern Alaska*, p. 179.

16 Naske and Slotnick, *Alaska*, pp. 55–56.

17 Ibid., p. 31.

18 P. A. Tikhmenev, *A History of the Russian American Company*, trans. and ed. Richard Pierce and Alton Donnelly (Seattle: University of Washington Press, 1978), pp. 54–56.

19 Chevigny, *Lord of Alaska*, pp. 86–87.

20 Ibid., p. 229.

21 Naske and Slotnick, *Alaska*, p. 43.

22 Chevigny, *Lord of Alaska*, p. 291.

23 John S. Galbraith, *The Hudson's Bay Company as an Imperial Factor* (Berkeley: University of California Press, 1957), p. 139.

24 Naske and Slotnick, *Alaska,* pp. 51–57.

25 Ibid., p. 59.

26 Ronald J. Jensen, *The Alaska Purchase and Russian-American Relations* (Seattle: University of Washington Press, 1975), pp. 63–66.

27 Naske and Slotnick, *Alaska,* p. 65.

28 Ernest Gruening, *The State of Alaska,* 2d ed. (New York: Random House, 1968), p. 35.

29 Chevigny, *Lord of Alaska,* p. 196.

30 Naske and Slotnick, *Alaska,* pp. 68–69.

31 Ted C. Hinckley, *The Americanization of Alaska, 1867–1897* (Palo Alto, Cali.: Pacific Books, 1973), pp. 153–156.

32 Harriet S. Pullen, *Soapy Smith, Bandit of Skagway: How He Lived; How He Died* (Seattle: Sourdough Press), pp. 12–15.

33 William R. Hunt, *North of 53 Degrees: The Wild Days of the Alaska-Yukon Mining Frontier* (New York: Macmillan, 1974), p. 42.

34 Ibid., pp. 124–128. See also Terrence Cole, *Nome: City of the Golden Beaches* (Anchorage: Alaska Geographic Society, 1984).

35 Naske and Slotnick, *Alaska,* pp. 86–87.

36 Evangeline Atwood, *Frontier Politics: Alaska's James Wickersham* (Portland, Ore.: Binford and Mort, 1979), p. 210.

37 Ibid., p. 69.

38 Ibid., pp. 31–34.

39 See Richard A. Cooley, *Politics and Conservation: The Decline of the Alaska Salmon* (New York: Harper and Row, 1963), pp. 35, 37.

40 Naske and Slotnick, *Alaska,* pp. 101–105.

41 Orlando W. Miller, *The Frontier in Alaska and the Matanuska Colony* (New Haven: Yale University Press, 1975), pp. 69–72.

42 See William H. Wilson, *Railroad in the Clouds: The Alaska Railroad in the Age of Steam, 1914–1945* (Boulder, Colo.: Pruett, 1977).

43 Quoted in Naske and Slotnick, *Alaska,* p. 108.

44 See Wilson, "Alaska's Past, Alaska's Future."

45 Terrence Cole, "The History of a History," *Pacific Northwest Quarterly* 77 (October 1986): 138.

46 Naske and Slotnick, *Alaska,* p. 122.

47 Brian Garfield, *The Thousand Mile War: World War II in Alaska and the Aleutians* (Toronto: Bantam Books, 1982), p. ii.

48 Naske and Slotnick, *Alaska,* p. 131.

49 Ibid., pp. 145–147.

50 Ibid., pp. 149–151.

51 Claus-M. Naske, *An Interpretive History of Alaskan Statehood* (Anchorage: Alaska Northwest Publishing Co., 1973), p. 146.

52 Ernest Gruening, *The Battle for Alaska Statehood* (College, Alaska: University of Alaska Press, 1967), p. 102.

CHAPTER 3

1 "Back to the Boom Days," *Anchorage Times,* May 26, 1989, p. B4. The *Times,* which was purchased by the oil field service company Veco, Inc., shortly after the spill, ceased publication in June 1992.

2 See Arlon R. Tussing, "Alaska's Petroleum-Based Economy," in Thomas A. Morehouse, ed., *Alaska Resources Development: Issues of the 1980s* (Boulder, Colo.: Westview Press, 1984), pp. 51–52.

3 See Mary Clay Berry, *The Alaska Pipeline: The Politics of Oil and Native Land Claims* (Bloomington: Indiana University Press, 1975.)

4 See chapter 11; see also Richard L. Ender, "Public Opinion and Political Attitudes in Alaska," in Gerald A. McBeath and Thomas A. Morehouse, eds., *Alaska State Government and Politics* (Fairbanks: University of Alaska Press, 1987), pp. 196–201.

5 It was the first in a series of annual payments from the Alaska Permanent Fund, created by the state with dedicated portions of its petroleum revenues. The Permanent Fund is discussed in detail later in this chapter.

6 See chapter 7; see also Clive S. Thomas, "Interest Groups and Lobbying in Alaska," in McBeath and Morehouse, *Alaska State Government and Politics,* pp. 161–183.

7 Eric G. Sutcliffe, Unalaska and Anchorage, July 8, 1983.

8 John Kruse, "Urban Impacts of Oil Development—The Fairbanks Experience," *Alaska Review of Business and Economic Conditions* 13 (December 1976): 16.

9 Robert R. Richards, "A Leading Economist's View of the 'Horrible Mess' in Juneau," *Anchorage Times,* April 8, 1984, p. B11.

10 Oliver Scott Goldsmith, *The Alaska Fiscal Gap,* ISER Fiscal Policy Papers, no. 1 (Anchorage: Institute of Social and Economic Research, University of Alaska Anchorage, 1989), p. 1.

11 Oliver Scott Goldsmith, *Alaska's Dependence on State Spending,* ISER Fiscal Policy Papers, no. 5 (Anchorage: Institute of Social and Economic Research, University of Alaska Anchorage, 1990), pp. 3–8.

12 See Tussing, "Alaska's Petroleum-Based Economy"; and Thomas A. More-

house, "Resource Development and Alaska Wealth Management," chap. 7 in Morehouse, *Alaska Resources Development*.

13 Ibid.; see also Oliver Scott Goldsmith, Matthew Berman, and Linda Leask, *Alaska's Potential Tax Revenues*, ISER Fiscal Policy Papers, no. 3 (Anchorage: Institute of Social and Economic Research, University of Alaska Anchorage, 1990), pp. 12–15.

14 See Gordon S. Harrison, *The Years of Big Spending in Alaska: How Good Is the Record?* ISER Occasional Papers, no. 20 (Anchorage: Institute of Social and Economic Research, University of Alaska Anchorage, 1989).

15 See Richard A. Fineberg, *Chaos in the Capital: The Budget System in Crisis* (Anchorage: Alaska Public Interest Research Group, 1982).

16 Robert W. Rafuse, Jr., *Representative Expenditures: Addressing the Neglected Dimension of Fiscal Capacity*, Information Report M-174 (Washington, D.C.: Advisory Commission on Intergovernmental Relations, 1990), p. viii. In essence, the "representative expenditures" method facilitates comparisons of states' spending levels, taking into account their differences in population, service responsibilities, and labor costs.

17 Stephen F. Johnson, "The Alaska Legislature," in McBeath and Morehouse, *Alaska State Government and Politics*, pp. 253–254.

18 Alaska Permanent Fund Corporation, *1990 Annual Report* (Juneau, 1991).

19 *U.S. News and World Report*, August 13, 1990, pp. 49–50.

20 Quoted in "Hammond Pushes Spending Plan," *Anchorage Daily News*, October 29, 1982, p. B3.

21 See Oliver Scott Goldsmith, "Sustainable Spending Levels from Alaska State Revenue," *Alaska Review of Social and Economic Conditions* 20 (February 1983): 15–20; Goldsmith, "Alaska Fiscal Gap," p. 11.

22 Alaska Growth Policy Council, *1981 Report to the Governor* (Juneau, 1981); Governor's Council on Economic Policy, *Final Reports* (1982); Alaska Permanent Fund Corporation, *The Trustee Papers* (Juneau: Alaska Permanent Fund Corporation Board of Trustees, 1982).

23 Among the few formal statements of the spenders' position is Commonwealth North, Resource Income Committee, *Alaska's Golden Opportunity: Resource Revenues and State Spending* (Anchorage, 1980); and more recently, Commonwealth North, Permanent Fund Committee, *Using the Permanent Fund as a Positive Counter-Cyclical Force in the Alaska Economy* (Anchorage, 1988).

24 Alaska Permanent Fund Corporation, *1990 Annual Report*, p. 6.

25 Quoted in "Miller Says He Wants Spending Limit, Investment Strategy," *Anchorage Daily News*, July 26, 1982, p. 1.

26 For an account of Alaska oil tax policy changes, see Charles L. Logsdon, "Alaska's Relationship with the Major Oil Companies" (Paper presented at the Energy Issues for the 1990s Conference, jointly sponsored by the University of Alaska Anchorage and the Organization of Petroleum Exporting Countries, Anchorage, July 23–24, 1992).

27 State of Alaska, Division of Policy, Office of the Governor, "The ELF: A Policy Perspective," April 1988 (Photocopy).

28 State of Alaska, "The ELF," p. 13.

29 David Hulen and Steve Rinehart, "Oil, Labor Spend Most on Races," *Anchorage Daily News,* November 1, 1992, p. A1; David Postman, "Lobbyists Best at Effective Use of Donations," *Anchorage Daily News,* November 7, 1992, p. B1.

30 Goldsmith et al., *Alaska's Potential Tax Revenues,* p. 12. The public or government share of oil-production values in the United States, however, is significantly less than the share taken by other major oil-producing nations. Our colleague Matthew Berman provided this and related information on the oil economy.

31 One university-based petroleum accountant estimated that between 1969 and 1987, the industry's after-tax profits totaled 44 percent of the returns, while the state of Alaska's receipts were 30 percent and the federal government's were 26 percent (Edward B. Deakin, "Oil Industry Profitability in Alaska, 1969 through 1987" [prepared for the Department of Revenue, State of Alaska, March 15, 1989], p. ii [Photocopy]). These estimates are extremely difficult to derive or confirm, however. They are affected by, among other things, the timing of revenue collection, assumptions about rates of return on investments, and what is included in or excluded from the base "returns."

32 Advisory Commission on Intergovernmental Relations, *1988 State Fiscal Capacity and Effort,* Information Report M-170 (Washington, D.C., 1990), pp. 33–34, 54–55, 61. ACIR explains that the Representative Tax System and Representative Revenue System "define fiscal capacity as the relative per capita amounts of revenue states would raise if they used 'representative' tax and revenue systems," which "consist of national average tax rates applied to all commonly used tax or revenue bases." With these measures, "states' capacities vary solely because of differing tax base levels" (p. 12).

33 Goldsmith, "Alaska Fiscal Gap," p. 11.

CHAPTER 4

1 Quoted in the *Anchorage Times,* November 20, 1971.

2 Alaska Statehood Commission, *More Perfect Union: A Plan for Action,* Final Report (Anchorage, 1983), p. 1.

3 Ibid., p. 2.

4 See chapter 2. See also William H. Wilson, "Alaska's Past, Alaska's Future," *Alaska Review* 4, no. 1 (1970): 1–11; and Claus-M. Naske and Herman E. Slotnick, *Alaska: A History of the Forty-ninth State,* 2d ed. (Norman: University of Oklahoma Press, 1987), chaps. 4–6.

5 George W. Rogers, *The Future of Alaska: Economic Consequences of Statehood* (Baltimore: Johns Hopkins University Press, 1962), pp. 80–92.

6 The Trans-Alaska Pipeline Authorization Act of 1973 and the Export Administration Act of 1979 prohibit the export of North Slope oil. The Merchant Marine Act of 1920 prohibits registration of foreign-built ships as vessels of the United States and bars foreign-registered ships from carrying passengers, vehicles, and cargo except U.S. mail between U.S. ports. See Arlon Tussing, *Alaska's Economy and the Merchant Marine Act of 1920* (Anchorage: Alaska Statehood Commission, 1982); and Naske and Slotnick, *Alaska,* p. 97.

7 Increasing political support exists for phasing out the longevity bonus because of its high and growing costs. (Persons over age sixty-five are a relatively small minority in this youthful state.) The bonus is paid from general funds, while dividends are paid from the earnings of the Alaska Permanent Fund.

8 This power of Congress is also derived from the U.S. Constitution's commerce clause, in this case as it refers to the regulation of commerce with "Indian Tribes" (Article I, Section 8).

9 The classic statement of mistreatment and neglect is Ernest Gruening, *The State of Alaska* (New York: Random House, 1954). See also Claus-M. Naske, *An Interpretive History of Alaskan Statehood* (Anchorage: Alaska Northwest Publishing Co., 1973); and Naske, "Alaska's Long and Sometimes Painful Relationship with the Lower Forty-Eight," in David H. Stratton and George A. Frykman, eds., *The Changing Pacific Northwest* (Pullman: Washington State University Press, 1988), pp. 57–75.

10 *Fairbanks Daily News-Miner,* November 11, 1981, p. 1.

11 Matthew Berman and Karen Pyle Foster, *Poverty among Alaska Natives,* ISER Research Summary, no. 31 (Anchorage: Institute of Social and Economic Research, University of Alaska Anchorage, 1986).

12 *The Alaska Almanac: Facts about Alaska,* 15th ed. (Bothell, Wash.: Alaska Northwest Books, 1991), p. 2.

13 Mary Clay Berry, *The Alaska Pipeline: The Politics of Oil and Native Land Claims* (Bloomington: Indiana University Press, 1975), pp. 254–278.

14 *Fairbanks Daily News-Miner,* December 4, 1985, p. 4.

15 See Wilson, "Alaska's Past, Alaska's Future."

16 See Gruening, *State of Alaska.*

17 Jan Juran and Daniel Raff, "Theodore F. Stevens: Republican Senator from Alaska," in the Ralph Nader Congress Project, *Citizens Look at Congress* (Washington, D.C.: Grossman Publishers, 1972), p. 16.

18 Communications with John W. Katz, director of state–federal relations, state of Alaska, Washington, D.C., October 29, 1986, and November 15, 1988; Alaska governor's Washington, D.C., office, "Transition Report," August 1990 (Photocopy).

CHAPTER 5

1 See, for example, Francis Jennings, *The Invasion of America: Indians, Colonialism, and the Cant of Conquest* (Chapel Hill: University of North Carolina Press, 1975); and Alvin M. Josephy, Jr., *The Patriot Chiefs: A Chronicle of American Indian Resistance* (New York: Penguin Books, 1976).

2 Charles F. Wilkinson, *American Indians, Time, and the Law* (New Haven: Yale University Press, 1987), p. 24; for application of the Marshall trilogy to Alaska, see Eric Smith and Mary Kancewick, "The Tribal Status of Alaska Natives," *University of Colorado Law Review* 61, no. 3 (1990): 474–476; and Thomas R. Berger, *Village Journey: The Report of the Alaska Native Review Commission* (New York: Hill and Wang, 1985), pp. 121–124.

3 Francis Paul Prucha, *The Indians in American Society: From the Revolutionary War to the Present* (Berkeley: University of California Press, 1985), pp. 14–16.

4 See John Ehle, *Trail of Tears: The Rise and Fall of the Cherokee Nation* (New York: Anchor Books, 1989).

5 Dee Brown, *Bury My Heart at Wounded Knee* (New York: Washington Square Press, 1981).

6 Emma R. Gross, *Contemporary Federal Policy toward American Indians* (New York: Greenwood Press, 1989), p. 20; for the Dawes Act, see Brian W. Dippie, *The Vanishing American: White Attitudes and U.S. Indian Policy* (Middletown, Conn.: Wesleyan University Press, 1982), pp. 161–176.

7 Dippie, *Vanishing American,* pp. 297–321.

8 Ibid., pp. 318–319; Wilkinson, *American Indians,* p. 68.

9 Gross, *Contemporary Federal Policy,* pp. 21–23.

10 Ibid., pp. 22–23; Prucha, *Indians in American Society,* pp. 80–103.

11 Wilkinson, *American Indians,* p. 121.

12 David S. Case, *Alaska Natives and American Laws* (Fairbanks: University of Alaska Press, 1984); Robert E. Price, *Legal Status of Alaska Natives* (Anchorage: Alaska Statehood Commission, 1982); Smith and Kancewick, "Tribal Status of Alaska Natives"; and Berger, *Village Journey.*

13 State of Alaska, *Report of the Governor's Task Force on Federal-State-Tribal Relations*, submitted to Governor Bill Sheffield (Juneau, 1986), pp. 57–67, 84–86; Case, *Alaska Natives and American Laws;* Price, *Legal Status of Alaska Natives;* Smith and Kancewick, "Tribal Status of Alaska Natives."

14 State of Alaska, *Report of the Governor's Task Force,* pp.145–147; Case, *Alaska Natives and American Laws,* pp. 472–473.

15 Felix S. Cohen, *Handbook of Federal Indian Law* (Charlottesville, Va.: Michie Bobbs-Merrill, 1982), pp. 765–767.

16 Case, *Alaska Natives and American Laws,* pp. 457–458; State of Alaska, *Report of the Governor's Task Force,* pp. 121–137.

17 Robert E. Price, *The Great Father in Alaska: The Case of the Tlingit and Haida Salmon Fishery* (Douglas, Alaska: First Street Press, 1990), pp. 78–83.

18 See Prucha, *Indians in American Society,* pp. 28–54.

19 Price, *Great Father in Alaska,* pp. 23–42; State of Alaska, *Report of the Governor's Task Force,* pp. 74–76.

20 Case, *Alaska Natives and American Laws,* p. 10; State of Alaska, *Report of the Governor's Task Force,* pp. 71–121.

21 Case, *Alaska Natives and American Laws,* pp. 208–210; Diamond Jenness, *Eskimo Administration: I. Alaska,* Technical Paper no. 10 (Montreal: Arctic Institute of North America, 1962), pp. 35–37.

22 George W. Rogers, *The Future of Alaska: Economic Consequences of Statehood* (Baltimore: Johns Hopkins University Press, 1962), p. 61.

23 Jenness, *Eskimo Administration,* pp. 19–20.

24 Smith and Kancewick, "Tribal Status of Alaska Natives," p. 506; State of Alaska, *Report of the Governor's Task Force,* p.15.

25 Case, *Alaska Natives and American Laws,* pp. 83–111.

26 Claus-M. Naske and Herman E. Slotnick, *Alaska: A History of the Forty-ninth State,* 2d ed. (Norman: University of Oklahoma Press, 1987), p. 191; State of Alaska, *Report of the Governor's Task Force,* pp. 118–119.

27 Case, *Alaska Natives and American Laws,* pp. 10–12, 99–107.

28 Ernest Gruening, *The State of Alaska* (New York: Random House, 1954), p. 381.

29 Case, *Alaska Natives and American Laws,* pp. 65–68.

30 Gerald A. McBeath and Thomas A. Morehouse, *The Dynamics of Alaska Native Self-Government* (Lanham, Md.: University Press of America, 1980), pp. 39–56.

31 Mary Clay Berry, *The Alaska Pipeline: The Politics of Oil and Native Land Claims* (Bloomington: Indiana University Press, 1975).

32 Steve Colt, "Financial Performance of Native Regional Corporations," *Alaska Review of Social and Economic Conditions* 28 (December 1991): 13–14; Bob Ortega, "Ice Fishing," *Washington Monthly* 20 (July–August 1988): 3, 10–14.

33 Colt, "Financial Performance," pp. 3, 11.

34 Ibid., p. 20.

35 Estimate derived from Colt, "Financial Performance." For the entire 1974–90 period, the range of ANCSA direct payments and cumulative dividends per capita was $2,000 to $12,500. All the figures cited are in 1990 dollars and account for inflation.

36 John Kruse, "Changes in the Well-Being of Alaska Natives since ANCSA," *Alaska Review of Social and Economic Conditions* 21 (November 1984): 1–12.

37 Thomas A. Morehouse, *Rebuilding the Political Economies of Alaska Native Villages,* ISER Occasional Papers, no. 21 (Anchorage: Institute of Social and Economic Research, University of Alaska Anchorage, 1989), pp. 9–12.

38 Alaska Federation of Natives, *The AFN Report on the Status of Alaska Natives: A Call for Action* (Anchorage, 1989).

39 U.S. Senate, *Alaska Native Claims Settlement Act,* Senate Report No. 92-581, 92d Cong., 1st sess., Committee of Conference, December 14, 1971, p. 37.

40 Tom Kizzia, "Kenai Is Law's First Test," *Anchorage Daily News,* June 24, 1992, p. A1.

41 Wilkinson, *American Indians,* p. 103.

CHAPTER 6

1 Gerald E. Bowkett, *Reaching for a Star: The Final Campaign for Alaska Statehood* (Fairbanks and Seattle: Epicenter Press, 1989), p. 93.

2 Quoted in ibid., p. 93.

3 See Advisory Commission on Intergovernmental Relations, *The Question of State Government Capability,* Commission Report A-98 (Washington, D.C., 1985), p. 40; Deil S. Wright, "The Origins, Emergence, and Maturity of Federalism and Intergovernmental Relations: Two Centuries of Territory and Power," in Jack Rabin, W. Bartley Hildreth, and Gerald J. Miller, eds., *Handbook of Public Administration* (New York: Marcel Dekker, 1989), p. 353.

4 Advisory Commission on Intergovernmental Relations, *State Government Capability,* p. 40.

5 Quoted in ibid., p. 39.

6 Ibid., p. 41.

7 Victor Fischer, *Alaska's Constitutional Convention* (Fairbanks: University of Alaska Press, 1975), p. 9. See also Gordon S. Harrison, *Alaska's Constitution: A Citizen's Guide,* 2d ed. (Anchorage: Institute of Social and Economic Research, University of Alaska Anchorage, 1986), pp. 6–8.

8 Fischer, *Alaska's Constitutional Convention,* p. 10. For a detailed account of the

national politics of the statehood issue, see Claus-M. Naske, *An Interpretative History of Alaskan Statehood* (Anchorage: Alaska Northwest Publishing Co., 1973).

9 Quoted in Victor Fischer, "Alaska's Constitution," chap. 2 in Gerald A. McBeath and Thomas A. Morehouse, eds., *Alaska State Government and Politics* (Fairbanks: University of Alaska Press, 1987), p. 29.

10 Fischer, *Alaska's Constitutional Convention*, pp. 23, 269–275.

11 John E. Bebout, "Alaska's Constitution," unpublished manuscript, March 8, 1956, pp. 5–6; Fischer, *Alaska's Constitutional Convention*, pp. 40–42, 49.

12 Quoted in Bowkett, *Reaching for a Star*, p. 24.

13 Fischer, "Alaska's Constitution," p. 31; see also Fischer, *Alaska's Constitutional Convention*, pp. 171–172, 186.

14 For a detailed background on constitutional articles, see Fischer, *Alaska's Constitutional Convention*, pp. 67–146; and Harrison, *Alaska's Constitution*, pp. 9–116.

15 Bebout, "Alaska's Constitution," p. 9.

16 Bowkett, *Reaching for a Star*, pp. 39–41.

17 Public Administration Service, *Constitutional Studies*, vol. 3 (Prepared on behalf of the Alaska Statehood Committee for the Alaska Constitutional Convention, November 1955, Mimeographed), pp. 60–61.

18 Bowkett, *Reaching for a Star*, p. 61.

19 See George Rogers, *Alaska in Transition: The Southeast Region* (Baltimore: Johns Hopkins University Press, 1960), pp. 6–15; and George Rogers, *The Future of Alaska: Economic Consequences of Statehood* (Baltimore: Johns Hopkins University Press, 1962), pp. 177–179.

20 Bowkett, *Reaching for a Star*, p. 74.

21 Ibid., p. 75.

22 Stephen Langdon, "Commercial Fisheries: Implications for Western Alaska Development," chap. 1 in Theodore Lane, ed., *Developing North America's Northern Frontier* (Lanham, Md.: University Press of America, 1987), pp. 16–17; Alaska Commercial Fisheries Entry Commission, *Changes in the Distribution of Alaska's Commercial Fisheries Entry Permits, 1975–1988*, CFEC Report no. 89–3 (Juneau, 1989), pp. 23–25.

23 See Advisory Commission on Intergovernmental Relations, *State Government Capability*, p. 40.

24 Fischer, *Alaska's Constitutional Convention*, p. 74.

25 *Ravin v. State of Alaska*, 537 P.2d 494 (1975).

26 Bowkett, *Reaching for a Star*, p. 58.

27 Harrison, *Alaska's Constitution*, pp. 108–109.

28 Bowkett, *Reaching for a Star*, p. 42.

29 Ibid., p. 43.

30 Fischer, *Alaska's Constitutional Convention,* pp. 152–155.

31 Advisory Commission on Intergovernmental Relations, *State Government Capability,* p. 42.

32 Ibid., p. 44.

1 In 1900, President Theodore Roosevelt created three judicial districts in Alaska. The first district was in Juneau (Southeast), the second in Nome (Northwest), and the third in Eagle, Fairbanks, Valdez, and Anchorage. An additional, fourth, district was created in 1909 with headquarters in Fairbanks. See Claus-M. Naske and Herman E. Slotnick, *Alaska: A History of the Forty-ninth State* (Norman: University of Oklahoma Press, 1987), p. 294.

2 Victor Fischer, *Alaska's Constitutional Convention* (Fairbanks: University of Alaska Press, 1975), pp. 95–96.

3 George Frost, "Election Districts Rejected," *Anchorage Daily News,* May 12, 1992, p. 1.

4 "Judge Extends Filing Deadline for Legislative Candidates," Associated Press, June 1, 1992; see also Ralph Thomas, "Primary Election Delayed," *Anchorage Daily News,* June 6, 1992, p. 1.

5 See Gerald McBeath, "Alaska," in Leroy Hardy, Alan Heslop, and George Blair, eds., *Redistricting in the 1980s* (Claremont, Calif.: Rose Institute of State and Local Government, Claremont McKenna College, 1992).

6 *The Alaska Almanac: Facts about Alaska,* 15th ed. (Bothell, Wash.: Alaska Northwest Books, 1991), p. 21.

7 See Alan Ehrenhalt, *The United States of Ambition: Politicians, Power, and the Pursuit of Office* (New York: Times Books, 1991).

8 Alaska first adopted a blanket primary in 1947, during territorial days. In 1959, it was replaced by a single-ballot open primary. The legislature, with bipartisan support and the endorsement of Governor Hickel, returned to the blanket primary in 1967. See Alaska State Legislature, Legislative Research Agency, "Alaska's Blanket Primary," by Gordon S. Harrison (Juneau, May 23, 1990).

9 Randolph was an established vote-getter but controversial because of his association with the Libertarian party. He changed from Republican to Libertarian while in the legislature and then ran as a Libertarian candidate for governor in 1982, spoiling the race for Republican candidate Tom Fink.

10 Larry Makinson, *Open Secrets* (Anchorage: Rosebud Publishing, 1987), p. 8.

11 Representatives must be at least twenty-one years old and senators must be at least twenty-five at the time they assume office.

12 As of the 1980 census, Alaska had the highest percentage of high school graduates in the nation and the second highest percentage of college graduates. The high level of education is related to demographic, economic, and political factors. Alaska has a young population, and educational opportunities have been greater for younger people than for senior citizens. Second, government and service trades dominate Alaska's workforce, occupations that require greater educational preparation than industrial jobs, of which Alaska has few. Third, the state provides incentives for young people to complete high school and attend college, including the nation's most generous student loan program. Until recently, the program included a "forgiveness clause" that erased up to 50 percent of the debt if the students returned to Alaska to live for five years after graduation. The clause fell victim to hard times, however, in the late 1980s.

13 Nicholas Henry, *Governing at the Grassroots: State and Local Politics,* 3d ed. (Englewood Cliffs, N.J.: Prentice-Hall, 1987), p. 146.

14 Alaska State Legislature, Legislative Research Agency, "Turnover in Each Alaska Legislature since Statehood" (Juneau, April 20, 1990).

15 Thomas R. Dye, *Politics in States and Communities,* 6th ed. (Englewood Cliffs, N.J.: Prentice Hall, 1988), p. 155.

16 "Pettyjohn Defends G O P Coalition Ban," *Anchorage Daily News,* October 20, 1983, p. B3.

17 Makinson, *Open Secrets,* p. 112.

18 Eric Redman, *The Dance of Legislation* (New York: Simon and Schuster, 1973).

19 Alaska State Legislature, Legislative Affairs Agency, "Legislative Process in Alaska" (Juneau, 1984).

20 Richard Fineberg, *Chaos in the Capital: The Budget System in Crisis* (Anchorage: Alaska Public Interest Research Group, 1982), p. 27.

21 Office of the Governor, Division of Policy, "State Spending: Why Alaska Spends More" (Juneau, November 1989), p. 2.

22 Clive S. Thomas, "Interest Groups and Lobbying in Alaska," in Gerald A. McBeath and Thomas A. Morehouse, eds., *Alaska State Government and Politics* (Fairbanks: University of Alaska Press, 1987), p. 171.

23 Henry, *Governing at the Grassroots,* pp. 53–55; see also Advisory Commission on Intergovernmental Relations, *The Question of State Government Capability,* Commission Report A-98 (Washington, D.C., 1985), pp. 273–281.

24 Gordon S. Harrison, *A Citizen's Guide to the Constitution of the State of Alaska* (Anchorage: Institute of Social and Economic Research, University of Alaska Anchorage, 1986), pp. 98–104.

25 *Anchorage Daily News,* June 27, 1992, p. 1.

26 See Gordon S. Harrison, *The Years of Big Spending in Alaska: How Good Is the Record?* ISER Occasional Papers, no. 20 (Anchorage: Institute of Social and Economic Research, University of Alaska Anchorage, 1989), pp. 11–12.

27 See Stephen F. Johnson, "The Alaska Legislature," chap. 10 in McBeath and Morehouse, *Alaska State Government and Politics.*

CHAPTER 8

1 The two exceptions are the commissioner of education, appointed by the Board of Education subject to the governor's approval, and the commissioner of the Department of Fish and Game, appointed by the governor from a list of qualified persons nominated by the fish and game boards.

2 Gerald A. McBeath, "Alaska's Gubernatorial Transition," in Thad L. Beyle, ed., *Gubernatorial Transitions: The 1982 Elections* (Durham, N.C.: Duke University Press, 1985), pp. 12–13, 72.

3 Larry Makinson, *Open Secrets* (Anchorage: Rosebud Publishing, 1987), p. 18.

4 Ibid., pp. 88–91.

5 See chapter 11; see also Thomas A. Morehouse, "Alaska's Elections," in Gerald A. McBeath and Thomas A. Morehouse, eds., *Alaska State Government and Politics* (Fairbanks: University of Alaska Press, 1987), pp. 133–140; McBeath, "Alaska's Gubernatorial Transition," pp. 69–71.

6 Bob Kederick, "All around Alaska," *Anchorage Times,* November 29, 1958, p. 4.

7 "Republican Candidates Assail Democratic Performances," *Juneau Empire,* September 8, 1962, p. 1.

8 Ward Sims, "Grasse May Help Decide the Winner," *Anchorage Times,* November 7, 1966, p. 1.

9 "The Third Term Issue Was the Fatal Factor," *Anchorage Times,* November 11, 1966, p. 4.

10 "Egan Is Governor," *Juneau Empire,* November 4, 1970, p. 1.

11 "Hammond Tops Election Recount," *Fairbanks Daily News-Miner,* November 29, 1974, p. 1.

12 "Hammond Wins Easily," *Fairbanks Daily News-Miner,* November 8, 1978, p. 1.

13 Makinson, *Open Secrets,* p. 90.

14 Ibid., p. 75; see also chapter 4.

15 "Hickel's First Year: It's Been a Circus," *Anchorage Daily News,* January 5, 1992, p. A1.

16 For details on the Alaska bureaucracy, see Gordon S. Harrison's informative chapter, "Alaska's Administrative System," in McBeath and Morehouse, *Alaska State Government and Politics,* pp. 289–317.

17 Boards are of roughly four types: boards heading departments (Board of Educa-

tion, Regents of the University of Alaska); regulatory boards such as the Board of Fisheries, Board of Game, and Alaska Public Utilities Commission; public corporations such as the Alaska Power Authority, Permanent Fund Corporation, and Alaska Railroad Commission; and symbolic or promotional boards such as the Women's Commission. See Harrison, "Alaska's Administrative System," pp. 296–298, for analysis of boards and commissions.

18 Harrison, "Alaska's Administrative System," p. 312. The percentage of unionized state employees is nearly as high as in the strong labor states of Connecticut, New York, and Massachusetts.

19 *Fairbanks Daily News-Miner,* August 23, 1989, p. B1.

20 Advisory Commission on Intergovernmental Relations, *Significant Features of Fiscal Federalism,* 1982–83 ed. (Washington, D.C., 1984), p. 128, cited in Harrison, "Alaska's Administrative System," p. 317. Alaska had 820 state/local employees per 10,000, compared to a national average of 468. See also Oliver Scott Goldsmith, *Alaska's Future Tax Revenues,* ISER Fiscal Policy Papers, no. 3 (Anchorage: Institute of Social and Economic Research, University of Alaska Anchorage, 1990).

21 "State Spending to Hit Ten-Year Low—Cowper," *Fairbanks Daily News-Miner,* August 11, 1989, p. 7.

22 Alaska State Legislature, House of Representatives Research Agency, "History of Vetoes since Statehood" (Juneau, April 9, 1984); Alaska Legislative Affairs Agency, records of sessions, 1984–89.

23 Ten special sessions of the legislature have been called since statehood. The governor has called nine, but only three have dealt with reductions in state spending.

24 Personal interview, February 13, 1983.

25 Cowper cited a figure of $4,281 per resident for fiscal year 1990 (*Fairbanks Daily News-Miner,* August 11, 1989, p. 1). Common Sense for Alaska immediately challenged this figure, pointing out in a letter to the editor that appropriations and numbers of state employees were higher than Cowper reported (*Fairbanks Daily News-Miner,* August 23, 1989, p. 4).

26 Personal interview, November 20, 1989.

27 Ibid.

28 Personal interview, February 16, 1983.

CHAPTER 9

1 For a general introduction to the Alaska court system, see Andrea R. C. Helms, "Courts in Alaska," in Gerald A. McBeath and Thomas A. Morehouse, eds., *Alaska State Government and Politics* (Fairbanks: University of Alaska Press, 1987), pp. 319–334.

2 See Alaska Department of Education, Division of State Libraries and Archives, *Alaska Blue Book, 1989–90*, 9th ed. (Juneau, 1989), pp. 143–164, for descriptions of Alaska's courts, judges' biographies, and caseload statistics.

3 *Alaska Blue Book, 1983*, 6th ed., pp. 138–139; *Alaska Blue Book, 1989–90*, 9th ed., pp. 158–159.

4 See Stephen Conn, "Rural Legal Process and Development in the North," chap. 10 in Theodore Lane, ed., *Developing America's Northern Frontier* (Lanham, Md.: University Press of America, 1987), pp. 199–229.

5 David S. Case, *Alaska Natives and American Laws* (Fairbanks: University of Alaska Press, 1984), p. 460.

6 Conn, "Rural Legal Process," p. 205; see also Arthur Hippler and Stephen Conn, *Northern Eskimo Law Ways and Their Relationship to Contemporary Problems of "Bush Justice,"* ISEGR Occasional Papers, no. 10 (Fairbanks: Institute of Social, Economic, and Government Research, University of Alaska, Fairbanks, 1973); and Case's discussion of criminal and civil jurisdiction in "Indian Country," in *Alaska Natives and American Laws*, pp. 450–461.

7 See Richard A. Watson and Randall G. Downing, *The Politics of the Bench and Bar: Judicial Selection under the Missouri Nonpartisan Court Plan* (New York: John Wiley, 1969), chap. 6.

8 Francis Bremson, Executive Director of the Judicial Council, in report of House Research Agency, Request 85-042, November 26, 1984.

9 Advisory Commission on Intergovernmental Relations, *The Question of State Government Capability,* Commission Report A-98 (Washington, D.C., 1985), p. 191.

10 Helms, "Courts in Alaska," p. 329.

11 Ibid., pp. 328–329. Retention elections alone are not an adequate test of judicial quality. Judges who do poorly on polls may resign before the election. For example, in 1990, twenty-two judges were scheduled for retention elections, but only fifteen made it to the ballot. Of the other seven judges, at least two had been negatively evaluated and might have gone down to defeat in the election had they not resigned. Personal interview with Jim Cotton, Executive Director, Alaska Judicial Council, July 29, 1990.

12 *Bradner v. Hammond,* 553 P.2d 1 (1976), in Gordon S. Harrison, *Alaska's Constitution: A Citizen's Guide,* 2d ed. (Anchorage: Institute of Social and Economic Research, University of Alaska Anchorage, 1986), p. 47.

13 "Leaders Say Session Will End by June 23," *Anchorage Daily News,* June 11, 1983, p. 1. See also Harrison, *Alaska's Constitution*, pp. 42–93.

14 See Harrison, *Alaska's Constitution,* pp. 60–61.

15 The Alaska Supreme Court held, in *State v. ALIVE Voluntary* (606 P.2d 769; 1980), that the legislature must use bills, not joint resolutions, to annul administrative regulations and that such bills are subject to the governor's veto. See Harrison, *Alaska's Constitution,* p. 32.

16 Alaska Judicial Council, "Alaska's Plea Bargaining Ban Re-evaluated" (Juneau, January 1991), pp. 128–129.

17 Ibid.

18 *Ravin v. State,* Alaska, 537 P.2d 494 (1975).

19 *Hicklin v. Orbeck,* Alaska, 565 P.2d 159, 165 (1977).

20 *Hicklin v. Orbeck,* 437 U.S. 518, 57 L. Ed. 2d 397, 98 S. Ct. 2482 (1978 AK).

21 *Zobel v. Williams,* Alaska, 619 P.2d 448 (1980).

22 *Zobel v. Williams,* U.S. 102 S. Ct. 2309, 72 L. Ed. 2d 672 (1982).

23 *Vest v. Schafer,* Alaska, 757 P.2d 558 (1988).

24 *Bozanich v. Reetz,* 297 F. Supp. 300 (1969).

25 Alaska Constitution, Article XI, Section 7. The case was *Thomas v. Baily,* Alaska, 595 P.2d 1 (1979). See Harrison, *Alaska's Constitution,* pp. 103–104.

26 *Frank v. State,* Alaska, 604 P.2d 1068 (1978). See Harrison, *Alaska's Constitution,* pp. 12–13.

27 *McDowell v. Collingsworth,* Alaska, 784 P.2d 1 (1989); see also chapter 5.

28 *Mobil Oil Company v. Local Boundary Commission*; see Thomas A. Morehouse and Linda Leask, "Alaska's North Slope Borough: Oil, Money, and Eskimo Self-Government," *Polar Record* 20, 124 (1980): 22–23.

29 *Sohio Petroleum v. State of Alaska;* see Morehouse and Leask, "Alaska's North Slope Borough," pp. 22–23.

30 *Native Village of Stevens v. Alaska Planning and Management,* 757 P.2d 32 (1988). Federal courts, on the other hand, have generally supported the tribal status of certain villages. See *Native Village of Noatak v. Hoffman,* 896 F. 2d 1157 (9th Cir. 1990).

31 See John Kincaid, "State Court Protection of Individual Rights under State Constitutions: The New Judicial Federalism," *Journal of State Government* 61 (September/October 1988): 163–169.

32 Personal interview with Mark Regan, Alaska Legal Services, Juneau, July 24, 1991.

33 Personal interview with Judge Andrew J. Kleinfeld, Ninth Circuit Court of Appeals, October 13, 1991.

CHAPTER 10

1 Frank Sorauf, *Party Politics in America,* 5th ed. (Boston: Little, Brown, 1984), p. 40.

2 For a different view of party in the electorate, see Carl Shepro, "Alaska's Political Parties," in Gerald A. McBeath and Thomas A. Morehouse, eds., *Alaska State Government and Politics* (Fairbanks: University of Alaska Press, 1987), p. 152.

3 "It's up to the Voters," *Anchorage Times,* October 7, 1946, p. 2.

4 Quoted in Alaska State Legislature, Legislative Research Agency, "Alaska's Blanket Primary and the *Tashjian* Decision," by Gordon Harrison, Research Request 90.080 (Juneau, January 15, 1991), p. 11.

5 "Senate Smothers Open Primaries Again, but Backs Transportation Commission," *Anchorage Times,* March 28, 1966, p. 1.

6 Comments of District 20 Republican chairwoman Judy Reece, at Taft Seminar for Teachers, University of Alaska Fairbanks, June 21, 1985.

7 See Shepro, "Alaska's Political Parties," p. 154.

8 Larry Makinson, *Open Secrets* (Anchorage: Rosebud Publishing, 1987), p. 26.

9 See Clive S. Thomas, "Interest Groups and Lobbying in Alaska," in McBeath and Morehouse, *Alaska State Government,* pp. 161–185, for an overview of interest group activity; and annual Alaska Public Offices Commission reports that identify contract lobbyists, their clients, and fees.

10 Thomas, "Interest Groups," p. 167.

11 Makinson, *Open Secrets,* pp. 16–18.

12 Robert Hanrahan and Peter Gruenstein, *Lost Frontier: The Marketing of Alaska* (New York: Random House, 1979), pp. 135–147.

13 Makinson, *Open Secrets,* p. 24.

14 Ibid., pp. 18, 23.

15 See Thomas A. Morehouse, *The Alaska Native Claims Settlement Act, 1991, and Tribal Governance,* ISER Occasional Papers, no. 19 (Anchorage: Institute of Social and Economic Research, University of Alaska Anchorage, 1988).

16 Ibid., pp. 23, 30.

17 Gerald A. McBeath, *North Slope Borough Government and Policymaking* (Anchorage: Institute of Social and Economic Research, University of Alaska, 1981), pp. 101–103. After representing the borough for a dozen years, Dischner was indicted on charges of accepting kickbacks on construction projects. A string of North Slope Borough corruption trials resulted in convictions for Dischner and high-ranking borough officials. See Gunnar Knapp and Thomas A. Morehouse, "Alaska's North Slope Borough Revisited," *Polar Record* 27, no. 163 (1991): 307–308.

18 Alaska Department of Education, Division of State Libraries and Archives, *Alaska Blue Book, 1989–90,* 9th ed. (Juneau, 1989), p. 318.

19 Ibid., pp. 321–323.

20 Ibid., pp. 327–328.

21 Ibid., p. 319.

22 See Richard A. Fineberg, "The Press and Alaska Politics," in McBeath and Morehouse, *Alaska State Government*, pp. 213–231, for a review of the media in Alaska.

23 Hanrahan and Gruenstein, *Lost Frontier*, p. 187.

24 Gerald A. McBeath and Thomas A. Morehouse, *The Dynamics of Alaska Native Self-Government* (Lanham, Md.: University Press of America, 1980), p. 17.

CHAPTER 11

1 For further discussion of Alaska elections and public opinion, see Thomas A. Morehouse, "Alaska's Elections," chap. 5, and Richard L. Ender, "Public Opinion and Political Attitudes in Alaska," chap. 8, in Gerald A. McBeath and Thomas A. Morehouse, eds., *Alaska State Government and Politics* (Fairbanks: University of Alaska Press, 1987).

2 Alaska Department of Labor, *Alaska Population Overview, 1990 Census and Estimate* (Juneau, 1991), p. 9.

3 Ibid., p. 42.

4 See Thomas A. Morehouse, *Alaska's Elections, 1958–1984,"* ISER Occasional Papers, no. 17 (Anchorage: Institute of Social and Economic Research, University of Alaska Anchorage, 1985), pp. 2–4.

5 See Ender, "Public Opinion and Political Attitudes."

6 Remarks made at the Taft Seminar for Teachers, University of Alaska Fairbanks, June 1985.

7 Lee J. Cuba, "Reorientations of Self: Residential Identification in Anchorage, Alaska," unpublished paper, 1982; John Kruse, "Urban Impacts of Oil Development—The Fairbanks Experience," *Alaska Review of Business and Economic Conditions* 13 (December 1976); 1–18; Mim Dixon, *What Happened to Fairbanks: The Effects of the Trans-Alaska Oil Pipeline on the Community of Fairbanks, Alaska* (Boulder, Colo.: Westview Press, 1978).

8 Hellenthal & Associates, Inc., "Areas of Alaska among All Adults by Political and General Demographics, Behaviors and Perceptions," unpublished report of survey conducted December 19 through March 21, 1989 (Photocopy).

9 Ender, "Public Opinion and Political Attitudes," pp. 197–198.

10 Ibid., p. 202.

11 Hellenthal & Associates, "Areas of Alaska," pp. 5–7.

12 Ibid., p. 11.

13 See Morehouse, *Alaska's Elections*.

14 Carl E. Shepro, "Alaska's Political Parties," in McBeath and Morehouse, *Alaska State Government and Politics,* pp. 146–152.

15 See Morehouse, *Alaska's Elections,* pp. 133–140.

CHAPTER 12

1 Alaska Legislative Council, *Alaska Constitutional Convention Proceedings* (Juneau, March 1965), p. 2618.

2 This chapter is based in part on our earlier comprehensive study of local government in Alaska: Thomas A. Morehouse, Gerald A. McBeath, and Linda Leask, *Alaska's Urban and Rural Governments* (Lanham, Md.: University Press of America, 1984).

3 Public Administration Service, *Constitutional Studies,* vol. 3, prepared on behalf of the Alaska Statehood Committee for the Alaska Constitutional Convention, November 1955 (Mimeographed), p. 60.

4 Alaska Constitution, Article X, Section 1.

5 Ronald C. Cease and Jerome R. Saroff, eds., *The Metropolitan Experiment in Alaska* (New York: Frederick R. Praeger, 1968), pp. 20–27, 83–134.

6 Morehouse, McBeath, and Leask, *Alaska's Urban and Rural Governments,* p. 67.

7 See David S. Case, *Alaska Natives and American Laws* (Fairbanks: University of Alaska Press, 1984), chap. 10.

8 State of Alaska, Office of the Governor, "Native Policy Statement" (Juneau, October 1988) (Photocopy).

9 Richard W. Garnett, *Equalization of Local Government Revenues in Alaska,* ISEGR Occasional Paper, no. 9 (Fairbanks: Institute of Social, Economic, and Government Research, University of Alaska, 1973).

10 Gerald A. McBeath, *North Slope Borough Government and Policymaking,* (Anchorage: Institute of Social and Economic Research, University of Alaska, 1981); see also Thomas A. Morehouse and Linda Leask, "Alaska's North Slope Borough: Oil, Money, and Eskimo Self-Government," *Polar Record* 20, no. 124 (1980): 19–29; Morehouse, McBeath, and Leask, *Alaska's Urban and Rural Governments,* chap. 9; and Gunnar Knapp and Thomas A. Morehouse, "Alaska's North Slope Borough Revisited," *Polar Record* 27, no. 163 (1991): 303–312.

11 Don Hunter, "Dischner, Mathisen Guilty in Slope Case," *Anchorage Daily News,* May 23, 1989, p. 1.

12 Alaska Local Boundary Commission, "Statement of Decision in the Matter of the

Petition to Dissolve the City of Yakutat and Incorporate the City and Borough of Yakutat,'' April 13, 1992, pp. 10–11.

13 See Case, *Alaska Natives and American Laws,* chaps. 1 and 10.

14 Thomas A. Morehouse, "Sovereignty, Tribal Government, and the Alaska Native Claims Settlement Act Amendments of 1987," *Polar Record,* 25, no. 154 (1989): 203.

15 Oliver Scott Goldsmith, Lee Gorsuch, and Linda Leask, *Facts and Fables of State Spending,* ISER Fiscal Policy Papers, no. 2 (Anchorage: Institute of Social and Economic Research, University of Alaska Anchorage, 1989), pp. 10–11.

CHAPTER 13

1 Thomas A. Morehouse, Gerald A. McBeath, and Linda Leask, *Alaska's Urban and Rural Governments* (Lanham, Md.: University Press of America, 1984), p. 233.

2 See George Rogers, "The Nature of Rural Economic Development in Alaska," in Peter Cornwall and Gerald McBeath, eds., *Alaska's Rural Development* (Boulder, Colo.: Westview Press, 1982), p. 10.

3 Morehouse, McBeath, and Leask, *Alaska's Urban and Rural Governments,* p. 132. See also Alaska Department of Education, Division of State Libraries and Archives, *Alaska Blue Book, 1989–90,* 9th ed. (Juneau, 1989), pp. 188–189.

4 Interview with Bethel city manager, January 19, 1989.

5 See description of the relationship between the Arctic Slope Regional Corporation and the North Slope Borough in Gerald A. McBeath, *North Slope Borough Government and Policymaking* (Anchorage: Institute of Social and Economic Research, University of Alaska, 1981).

6 Alaska Public Offices Commission, 1990 Municipal Elections.

7 "Election Spending Surpasses '87 Tally," *Fairbanks Daily News-Miner,* November 1, 1989, p. B1.

8 Ibid., p. A4.

9 Caught up in the North Slope Borough financial scandal, Brower was charged with receiving bribes and giving kickbacks to campaign contributors. In a deal with the prosecution, he was convicted of tax evasion in 1990.

10 V. O. Key, *American Political Parties* (New York: Van Nostrand, 1956), pp. 135–137.

11 *Fairbanks Daily News-Miner,* September 10, 1982, p. B1.

12 *Anchorage Daily News,* October 8, 1989, p. 8.

13 Presentation to Taft Seminar for Teachers, University of Alaska Fairbanks, June 20, 1985.

14 Morehouse, McBeath, and Leask, *Alaska's Urban and Rural Governments,* p. 86. See chapter 12 for information on government growth in Alaska.

15 Personal observation, regular meeting of the Fairbanks North Star Borough Board of Education, August 30, 1986.

16 For contrasting views on the public-sector lobbies, see Clive Thomas, "Interest Groups and Lobbying in Alaska," in Gerald A. McBeath and Thomas A. Morehouse, eds., *Alaska State Government and Politics* (Fairbanks: University of Alaska Press, 1987), p. 177; and Morehouse, McBeath, and Leask, *Alaska's Urban and Rural Government,* p. 112.

17 From 1987 to 1989, voters turned down sales taxes at the city and borough level on five separate occasions.

18 *Anchorage Daily News,* September 12, 1988, p. 13.

19 See Morehouse, McBeath, and Leask, *Alaska's Urban and Rural Governments,* pp. 56–60, for a similar discussion of conflict and accommodation.

20 "Helms, Assembly at Boiling Point," *Fairbanks Daily News-Miner,* January 5–6, 1989, p. 1.

21 Hohman's brother, George, was then a powerful state senator from Bethel (he was later convicted of bribery); Ron's spouse, Jan, was president of the State Board of Education. This situation was the closest Alaska has come in recent years to producing a dynasty fit for the soaps.

22 *Fairbanks Daily News-Miner,* June 15, 1992, p. A1.

23 McBeath, *North Slope Borough Government,* p. 47.

24 *Anchorage Daily News,* December 13, 1989, p. 11.

25 Fiscal conflicts between assemblies and school districts prompted some Anchorage Assembly members to seek amendments of the state constitution, severing ties of the two bodies (*Anchorage Daily News,* August 28, 1989).

26 *Anchorage Daily News,* July 31, 1991, p. 1.

27 *Tundra Drums,* July 8, 1989, p. 1.

28 Morehouse, McBeath, and Leask, *Alaska's Urban and Rural Governments,* pp. 235–236.

Index